Theatres of the Body

Lynn Matluck Brooks

THEATRES OF THE BODY

Dance and Discourse in Antebellum Philadelphia

TEMPLE UNIVERSITY PRESS
Philadelphia • Rome • Tokyo

TEMPLE UNIVERSITY PRESS
Philadelphia, Pennsylvania 19122
tupress.temple.edu

Copyright © 2025 by Temple University—Of The Commonwealth System
  of Higher Education
All rights reserved
Published 2025

Library of Congress Cataloging-in-Publication Data

Names: Brooks, Lynn Matluck, author.
Title: Theatres of the body : dance and discourse in antebellum
  Philadelphia / Lynn Matluck Brooks.
Other titles: Dance and discourse in antebellum Philadelphia
Description: Philadelphia : Temple University Press, 2025. | Includes
  bibliographical references and index. | Summary: "This book presents an
  expansive study of Philadelphia's significant contributions to early
  U.S. dance in the nineteenth century, revealing dance as a force
  grappling with candescent issues in the nation's political, social, and
  intellectual unfolding"— Provided by publisher.
Identifiers: LCCN 2025003084 (print) | LCCN 2025003085 (ebook) | ISBN
  9781439923030 (cloth) | ISBN 9781439923047 (paperback) | ISBN
  9781439923054 (pdf)
Subjects: LCSH: Dance—Pennsylvania—Philadelphia—History—19th century. |
  Theater—Pennsylvania—Philadelphia—History—19th century. | Body image
  in the performing arts—Pennsylvania—Philadelphia. |
  Ballet—Pennsylvania—Philadelphia—History—19th century. | Blackface
  minstrel shows—Pennsylvania—Philadelphia—History—19th century. |
  Philadelphia (Pa.)—Social life and customs—19th century. |
  Philadelphia (Pa.)—Social conditions—19th century.
Classification: LCC GV1624.5.P45 B76 2025 (print) | LCC GV1624.5.P45
  (ebook) | DDC 792.809748/11—dc23/eng/20250403
LC record available at https://lccn.loc.gov/2025003084
LC ebook record available at https://lccn.loc.gov/2025003085

The manufacturer's authorized representative in the EU for product safety is
Temple University Rome, Via di San Sebastianello, 16, 00187 Rome RM, Italy
(https://rome.temple.edu/).
tempress@temple.edu

9 8 7 6 5 4 3 2 1

To George Dorris, my first editor, beloved mentor, and lifelong friend.

Contents

Acknowledgments ix

1. Introduction: Dancing, Bodies, and Philadelphia History 1
2. Tumultuous Pleasures: Graphic Lessons in Dancing from the 1820s 24
3. The 1830s: Politics Performed 60
4. Dancing "Philadelphia in Slices": The 1840s 99
5. Order and Entropy: Science, Stage, and Society, 1850–1860 142
6. Conclusions: Dance as Discourse in Antebellum Philadelphia 182

Notes 209
Bibliography 247
Index 277

Acknowledgments

This book could not have been written without the gracious support of the staffs at the Free Library of Philadelphia, the Historical Society of Pennsylvania, and the Library Company of Philadelphia, for which I am sincerely grateful. I also extend my gratitude to the Andrew W. Mellon Foundation, which granted me a summer research fellowship in Philadelphia at the Historical Society and Library Company that deepened my immersion in the rich holdings of these institutions. Franklin & Marshall College awarded Hackman Summer Research Fellowships to students who generously assisted me with data collection; I thank Emily Hawk, Jael Lewis, Maria Meriwether, and Amanda de Santos for their energetic contributions to this work. Finally, family (Christopher and Ethan Brooks, and Marjorie Virgili) and friends (Genevieve Oswald above and beyond all others) sustained me as I brought this research and this book to fruition. Endless thanks to you all!

Theatres of the Body

1

Introduction

Dancing, Bodies, and Philadelphia History

Bodying Forth on the Philadelphia Stage

In autumn 1832 in the City of Brotherly Love, Thomas Dartmouth Rice debuted a semi-improvised act in his first Philadelphia season, at the Walnut Street Theatre, as his blackface character "Jim Crow" (Figure 1.1). Dancing raucously onto the stage with a sack over his raggedly clad shoulder, Rice—a white, working-class New Yorker masked in burnt cork—sang, "O Ladies and Gentlemen, I'd have for you to know / That I've got a little darky here that jumps Jim Crow." Out of the sack sprang four-year-old Joseph Jefferson III, latest entrant into the Philadelphia-based Jefferson theatrical dynasty. Joe, dressed and blackened as Jim Crow miniature, sang and danced in perfect synchrony with Rice.[1] The act drew "roars of laughter" from the crowd, furthering Rice's meteoric rise as "lion" of the popular theater in Philadelphia and beyond.[2] Although not the first American performer to "black up" or "delineate" African Americans, Rice, as the wily, ragged, offensive, prescient, protean "Jim Crow," became the most famous solo blackface artist of the time. Young Jefferson accompanied Rice in only a few performances, but Rice/Jim Crow went on to years of success on city, national, and international stages—a prototype of what became blackface minstrelsy.

As Rice danced onto the Walnut Street stage in 1832, the Chestnut Street Theatre—Philadelphia's "Old Drury"—presented the Ravels, a French family

Figure 1.1. "Mr. T. Rice as the Original Jim Crow," Edward W. Clay. *(Library Company of Philadelphia, Rice [P.9369])*

Figure 1.2. "L'incomparable Ravel." *(Jerome Robbins Dance Division. New York Public Library Digital Collections, Public Domain. Accessed June 19, 2024. https://digitalcollections.nypl.org/items/2396b730-fcd9-0132-4955-58d385a7b928)*

of acrobat-dancers (Figure 1.2), in their first major season in the city. Among their extensive repertoire was the pantomime-ballet *Jocko, the Brazilian Ape*, while they, or the Walnut's own company, also showed the "serio-comic romance," *Cherry and Fair Star*. Since *Jocko* appeared on U.S. stages as early as 1825, viewers could compare performances. American theater professional and historian Charles Durang, contemporary of the Ravels and Rice, described Gabriel Ravel's performance of the acrobatic Ape as "so unique, so natural and so astonishing in every respect as to place it among the wonders of the stage."[3] *Cherry and Fair Star* Durang knew firsthand; he staged its "grand fairy ballet" as early as 1825. The ballet combined "Eastern" flavor with romantic spectacle, giving a female lead opportunity to perform the role of Cherry (the "male" protagonist) in travesty.[4]

Two theaters in Philadelphia, in the young United States, simultaneously presenting these two hit acts, apparently so different. Rice claimed that his Jim Crow character was based on dress, speech, and movement of Black workers he observed in his theatrical travels, starting with his home territory—New York City's rougher wards and stages—and traversing the Western frontier circuit. The "Jump Jim Crow" song and dance varied endlessly to encompass topical commentary and movement innovations, sweeping the nation's theaters and making Rice an international star. Crowned "prince of darkies" for "his wonderful imitative talent of the plantation negro,"[5] Rice developed this "talent" into full-scale "Ethiopian operas" featuring Jim Crow–based characters. He held nearly annual seasons in Philadelphia for the next two decades, as blackface troupes flooded major and minor theaters everywhere. Such "Ethiopian" minstrelsy, performed in blackface by (mostly) white men, claiming to "delineate" the bodies and behaviors of African-descended people in the United States, was lauded by some as *the* truly American contribution to world culture.[6]

Like Rice, the Ravels presented lengthy Philadelphia seasons nearly annually in this period. Their repertoire, including "pantomime ballets" like *Jocko*, was advertised to Americans, and appreciated, as European imports "from the old world."[7] That Philadelphians might see the same works as Parisians or Londoners, danced by French-trained artists, sold tickets. Their 1832 debut season, according to Philadelphia theater manager William Wood, "established a popularity" for the Ravels "undiminished to this hour" (1855), owing to their "admirable discipline" and "rare capabilities."[8] As European dance artists swept U.S. stages, American performers took on the refinements of that "old world," exquisitely represented in the balletic bodies they observed.

Making sense of such simultaneous stage productions in antebellum Philadelphia motivates this book. Fundamental to this research has been documentation of the wide range of works, performers, and techniques that appeared in antebellum Philadelphia (1820 to 1860). I concentrate, in documentation and analysis, on two dance-focused genres emerging in the late 1820s and early 1830s that came to dominate the city's and the nation's stages: ballet and blackface minstrelsy. Beyond the data of that dancing lie deeper questions informing this book: What motivated creation and presentation of these works? Why did these two distinct forms emerge at this moment, on Philadelphia and other U.S. stages? What contexts, what information, did audiences and creators bring to their interpretations of these stage dances? Did these acts represent broader trends in the nation's cultural, intellectual, and political life?

Theatrical forms, including dance, that drew audiences to theaters in antebellum Philadelphia were indeed shaped by and responsive to the period's cultural discourses, those "common threads or contours of conversation that signal particular patterns in the spread or dissemination of information."[9] In this book, I make these connections through the discourses of visual art, political developments, print culture, and the ranked classifications proclaimed through scientific research. Other areas of discourse—religion, education, music, immigration, economics, and more—while not directly organizing this book's themes, arise in discussion, pointing to "the ability of theatrical and performative stagecraft to foster habits of mind, to transform spectators' reading of the world offstage."[10]

This book moves by decade through forty years of danced history to explore emergences, change, and persistence among these discourses in the antebellum period. These interpenetrating discourses appear with varying degrees of emphasis throughout the entire book: no age nor decade starts or stops at one moment, nor are cultural manifestations bounded by borders of city, state, or nation. Such demarcations, however, are useful for conceptualizing the movement of (and in) history. Thus, there is blurring at decades' edges and Philadelphia's borders, responding to the continuity and expansiveness of developments through the period. Each decade is linked with a discursive focus, while the complexities of culture also invite other concerns to appear throughout this investigation.

In Chapter 2, addressing the 1820s, *visual art* is the cultural discourse shaping investigation of the decade's dancing. In this great age of printmaking and distribution, dance imagery came to life in works by European and American artists. Philadelphia cartoonist E. W. Clay's work organizes this chapter, covering social and theatrical dancing across social classes.

Chapter 3, investigating the 1830s, looks at ballet and blackface works through a *political* lens. Philadelphians engaged energetically with national questions of citizenship, slave- and free-state designation, and the franchise, which pointed attention to which bodies counted as fully human. On city stages, local performers emerged, some claiming through their bodies access to European art forms, as others created blackface works, homegrown and enduring through much of the century.

The 1840s, studied in Chapter 4, are viewed through the burgeoning *print culture* of the age. Affordable newspapers, magazines for particular publics, treatises for specialists and autodidacts, and popular fiction appeared in Philadelphia, providing documentation of dancing on city stages, as well as recording bodily understandings—in everyday life and enlivened in dance—that underlay responses of dance commentators and practitioners.

In Chapter 5, the *classificatory drive* of the age organizes understandings and practices of dance in the 1850s. Scientific categorization and systemization saturated public discourses of the human body—its capacities, intelligence, morality, and dangers. The city's entertainment offerings and built environment reflected such divides. How classifications both hardened and crumbled in the crucible of Philadelphia's aesthetic, social, and political pressures reveals the complexity of dancing to the edge of civil war.

Chapter 6 draws together findings of previous chapters, focusing on the nature of movement techniques, sources, and dissemination that shaped the two dance genres—ballet and blackface minstrelsy—investigated here, deepening understanding of dance as a discourse of its own, participating in the unfolding of antebellum culture and history.

Why Philadelphia?

Established by William Penn as capital of a Quaker colony intended to represent principles of religious freedom, rational order, and democracy, Philadelphia was a fitting location for articulating the nation's philosophical foundations—a position the city served before, during, and after the War of Independence. At the State House (Independence Hall), three founding documents of the new nation were debated and signed in final form: the Declaration of Independence (adopted July 4, 1776); the Articles of Confederation (ratified Mar. 1, 1781); and the United States Constitution (signed Sept. 17, 1787). Philadelphia shone as "the Athens of America" for its architecture, educational institutions, and dedication to arts and sciences.[11] Its docks bustled with sailors, travelers, and merchants exchanging goods, news, music, and ideas among people of different ethnicities and classes.[12] As the nation's capital through much of the Revolutionary War and from 1790 to 1800, Philadelphia was also capital of Pennsylvania until 1799. Although New York surpassed it in growth and commerce in the 1820s, Philadelphia remained a beacon of liberal political vision for independence fighters throughout the Americas and Europe.

However, the political philosophies undergirding the new nation, articulated in Philadelphia, were immediately under challenge. The ideal of human equality debated at the State House and published in the Declaration of Independence remained a cherished guidepost for many politicians, citizens, and oppressed people but was abrogated by the nation's Constitution: in calculating legislative representation, each human being enslaved was counted as three-fifths of a free person. This denial of human value kept the slave states in the new nation but betrayed Black people, outraged many white people, and haunted the Constitution's framers and the nation.[13] The emerging nation's philosophical-legal writings forged a republic of letters, shaped by classically educated literati arguing their points through print, but the nation's early unfolding moved from heady philosophy to the feet treading the nation's soil.[14] The human body, from feet to head, from outer appearance to inner qualities, was increasingly at stake.

About 18 percent of those bodies at the Constitution's writing were enslaved. In 1818, the political flashpoint of slavery flamed anew as Missouri applied for statehood, sparking debate between those seeking slave-state status and those insisting Missouri be free. In 1820, the Missouri Compromise extended the Mason-Dixon Line from Pennsylvania's southern border westward, a marker between slave and free states in the expanding national geography, placing Pennsylvania and its south-lying port city, Philadelphia, at a point of enflamed encounter. That year marks the start of this book's investigation.

Beyond the Constitution's "three-fifths" clause, voting rights were determined by states. These too came to depend on the perceived natures of bodies, strikingly evident through such factors as gender and race, making the body the turning point in citizenship and enfranchisement debates. Ballet and blackface minstrelsy would highlight just such bodily differences.

With independence, Philadelphia went about shaping its distinct communities and institutions—banks, courts, hospitals, churches, benevolent societies, schools, museums, and theaters. Visitors remarked on the city's order and prosperity,[15] which attracted a rich mix of immigrants to established communities. Among those communities was "the largest urban concentration of free Blacks of any place where slavery had been established in the English-speaking" Western world.[16] By 1820, Philadelphia's free Black population numbered over twelve thousand, a visible though slim minority of whom were financially comfortable, while most Black city dwellers struggled at low-wage labor. Pressures from outside and within the city's African American community were intense for free Black people to conform to standards of propriety and moral behavior,[17] as race became a volatile civic and national issue.

Race was a pivotal matter in Philadelphia, where Quakers formalized opposition to slavery in 1775, founding the Pennsylvania Abolition Society (PAS). In 1780, Pennsylvania passed one of the nation's first abolition acts—a gradual one—after which its enslaved population diminished sharply.[18] Black Philadelphians were national leaders among African Americans; they birthed the country's independent African church movement, founding St. Thomas Episcopal (1792) and Bethel African Methodist Episcopal (1794) churches—centers of religious, social, educational, and political activity. As the first state north of the Mason-Dixon line, Pennsylvania received, and many of its citizens Black and white aided, enslaved people fleeing Southern bondage. Pennsylvania citizens widely, though not uniformly, refused cooperation with federal fugitive-slave mandates promulgated in 1793 and 1850. But as news reached Philadelphia from Black-led uprisings—the Haitian Revolution (1791–1804), Gabriel Prosser's aborted rebellion (Virginia, 1800), Denmark

Vesey's planned revolt (South Carolina, 1822), Nat Turner's insurrection (Virginia, 1831), and others—even some liberal-minded white residents feared violence would overtake their city. Yet the violence perpetrated in the City of Brotherly Love was overwhelmingly by white against Black people, or white Protestants against the Irish.[19]

Thus, despite—or exacerbated by—Quaker and abolitionist stances, race prejudice came to saturate Philadelphia.[20] Black bodies and behavior were subjects of ranking and ridicule as the City of Brotherly Love birthed American racial cartooning that viciously caricatured African Americans as attempting to strut their way to respectability. Such minstrelsy on the page foreshadowed and prepared viewers for stage versions of African American characters that, through blackface acts, soon dominated popular U.S. amusements. Language—in political commentary, literature, science writing, dramatic texts, personal journals, and elsewhere—reflected prejudices and fears addressed in this volume, exemplifying the categorizations and assumptions such writings promulgated and perpetuated.

Observers visiting the new nation took note. In his 1835 *Democracy in America*, Alexis de Tocqueville recorded that, in the new American republic, "the prejudice which repels the negroes seems to increase in proportion as they are emancipated, and inequality is sanctioned by the manners whilst it is effaced from the laws of the country."[21] In 1841, an English visitor observed that "the prejudice against colour prevailing" in Philadelphia was "much stronger than in the slave States"; it was "the metropolis of this odious prejudice," for "there is probably no city in the known world, where dislike, amounting to hatred of the coloured population, prevails more than in the city of brotherly love!"[22] Even former U.S. President John Quincy Adams of Massachusetts lamented, in 1838, Philadelphia's role in suppressing antislavery debate and action.[23] Just a few years earlier, "Jim Crow" Rice had swept Philadelphia (and other) stages with his blackface act, dancing and singing his ludicrous "delineation" of supposed African American appearance and behavior.

Politically vibrant and volatile, Philadelphia saw women stepping up in this period to make political appearances on civic and national stages—a daring move connected to the plight of African Americans. Philadelphia's determined abolitionist women, largely from the Quaker and educated free Black communities, formed the Philadelphia Female AntiSlavery Society (PFASS) in 1833.[24] At this same moment, women became dominant on theatrical stages as ballet dancers, participating in women's efforts to access personal and professional opportunity. PFASS women too contributed creative expressions in prose, poetry, songs, and artwork publicizing antislavery views; they understood the position of women in the United States as akin to that of the nation's enslaved Black people, whose conditions they had studied closely. Karen Sánchez-Eppler points to "the crossing of feminist and abolitionist rhetoric," resulting in the two groups forming "an alliance with the body of the other," wherein each one found "the [bodily] prison of the other . . . liberating."[25] Both political and theatrical stages would create spaces for women's liberatory action.

Philadelphians had been observing and commenting on bodies long before U.S. independence, an interest manifested in city theaters. Despite Quaker-led opposition to amusements like the stage and ballroom, theatrical performances appeared in the city by the 1760s, when the Southwark Theatre opened, just outside the city limits, thus evading Philadelphia's antitheater regulations.[26] The Southwark hosted mostly English plays and players, although once the new nation was declared, the troupe renamed itself the Old American Company (OAC) and hired the United States' first enduring native-born performer, John Durang, who debuted in 1785, dancing a hornpipe. Dance would be Durang's strong suit throughout his multifaceted career.

Battles over the morality of theater and dancing persisted through the early American period. The Pennsylvania legislature bore down on the OAC, forcing its move to New York City soon after Durang joined them. The company gained legal right to perform openly in Philadelphia in 1789, with support of the city's "Dramatic Association," whose membership included many prominent citizens.[27] The theater's audience varied in class and race, drawing to its benches all shades of Philadelphia's population, a version of the city's "commons."[28] Until the Southwark's closing in 1817, its spectators might include widely respected African American sailmaker and abolitionist James Forten. In May 1792, the OAC brought to Philadelphia the accomplished French acrobatic and dance troupe of Alexander Placide, a taste of French artistry that gave U.S. spectators an early appreciation of ballet, pantomime, and elegant acrobatics.[29] It also gave the self-taught Durang occasion to observe and attempt emerging balletic style. Observation, imitation, and occasional lessons with touring European dancers would be a consistent mode of training for U.S.-born dance aspirants.

By the mid-1790s, the "old" players faced competition from Philadelphia's imported company at the nation's best-equipped new playhouse, the Chestnut Street Theatre. Among the Chestnut Street's specialists was English pantomime artist William Francis, while the theater's orchestra was filled with French émigrés, many fleeing their country's revolution.[30] The company, with Francis and, eventually, Durang, presented pantomimes in the English harlequinade style, melodramas, and ballets. Francis and Durang also taught social dance, supporting the select society aspiring to the Philadelphia Dancing Assembly, established to bring elite Philadelphians sociality approaching the elegance of Bath or London. These aspirations and class distinctions, despite denunciations by American critics and ridicule by European visitors, persisted among local and national elites, white and Black. Watching and presenting elegantly trained bodies in ordered motion at theaters and in ballrooms mattered to many Philadelphians, as did their display of themselves in those settings.

The Body as Subject

The stage was set for the simultaneous emergence, in the late 1820s, of the imported art of European ballet and the U.S.-grown corked-up acts that coalesced into blackface minstrelsy. Each performance type brought attention to human bodies—their appearance, capacities, and expressive malleability. Philadelphia would serve as a creative platform for blackface performers like T. D. Rice, dancer Frank Brower, and manager Sam Sanford. At the same time, the city became home to more American ballet dancers than was any other city in the nation. Philadelphians became ballet masters, choreographers, and authors of dance manuals, contributing to the drive for American cultural achievement. Theaters, circuses, summer gardens, museum halls, concert venues, saloons with stages, and neighborhood sites hosted performances, including ballet and blackface dancing. How did viewers understand these dancing bodies?

As the *body itself* became a determining factor in assessing who deserved full U.S. citizenship, scientists undergirded political debate through rankings of bodies by perceived shape, size, sex, color, intelligence, and moral capacities. All races and national groupings came under scrutiny, but the primary comparative concerns were differences among bodies understood as "white" or "Black." Gender too concerned scientists, engaging contests for control over women's health, social status, education, employment, and rights. Entertainment and sociality reflected these fault lines: some Americans staked claims to expressive forms they regarded as reflecting U.S. concerns and cultures; others sought to flaunt their mastery of European arts. In all cases—political, intellectual, and aesthetic—the body was at the center of observation and controversy. Karen Sánchez-Eppler notes, "The extent to which the condition of the human body designates identity is a question of American culture and consciousness as well as politics," the answers to which "can be sought not only in political speeches but also in a variety of more ostensibly aesthetic forms."[31] Responses to the legal formulations shaping the young nation were corporealized in the dancing out of movement, characters, and themes, reflecting back to viewers issues that assailed them in political debates, on the streets, at work, and through text and graphic publications.

In recent decades, the body has emerged as a vital theme for historical study as scholars turn attention beyond earlier historiographic focuses on political, technological, and economic change.[32] Elisabeth Grosz notes that "the discursive practices of the natural sciences"—vibrant in the period under study—have "colonized" understanding of the body as a "brute, . . . unchangeable, inert" material susceptible to manipulation by scientists and doctors.[33] American scientists aligned their research and findings with political positions regarding African-descended people, women, and human rankings across the globe as empires fell, swelled, or shifted. Tony Ballantyne and Antoinette Burton point out that, across time and place, bodies "have been a subject of concern, scrutiny, anxiety, and surveillance" as power holders demonstrated "how crucial" the body's "management was believed to be for social order and political stability."[34] The body was candescently at stake in nineteenth-century America—from the elite to the enslaved, from the pious to the performer.

Literary scholar Susan Crane defines performances as "heightened and deliberately communicative behaviors, public displays that use visual as well as rhetorical resources."[35] This "immensely compelling act at the intersection of agency and prescription, innovation and memory, self and social group," includes dress: "The body is costumed, and clothing, not skin, is the frontier of the self." Yet in the antebellum United States, skin certainly defined self, group, and social rank, impinging not just on the "frontier of the self," but also on frontier lands entering the new nation as "slave" or "free."[36] Skin defined an entire theatrical genre: blackface minstrelsy. The body beneath that skin mattered too. Brenda Dixon Gottschild, studying *The Black Dancing Body*, creates "a geography of the body itself,"[37] "Mapping the Territories" of bodies through specifics of "Feet," "Butt," and "Skin/Hair"—features investigated by antebellum scientists, artists, writers, and performers. Thomas DeFrantz identifies the different values these body parts express as manifestations of "body power," transmitting "dual transcripts of 'public' and 'private' meaning."[38] That power marks the dancing of the period and place under study in *Theatres of the Body*.

The body played a role in the drive toward distinguishing a distinctly U.S. public culture, felt from the republic's first days, heating up as social and political divisions increased in subsequent decades.[39] This aspiration appeared in calls for "American" arts, literature, and learning that would awaken Europeans' notice of the new nation's place on the world stage. Philadelphia, famed for its beauty, rational design, and prosperity, attracted artists' attention, including city residents William and Thomas Birch, William L. Breton, Robert Douglass Jr., David Kennedy, Charles Willson Peale and his children, and Moses Williams.[40] They depicted cityscapes and, significant to this volume, city people. Cartoons—politically or socially motivated—were widely circulated, many in illustrated magazines achieving popularity in the period.[41] Lithographic and other engraving techniques were supplemented in the mid-nineteenth century by the daguerreotype. These fed the information-hungry U.S. public, offering to those who could create, circulate, purchase, or view such items a selection of visual images and imaginaries of their own environment and of worlds otherwise out of immediate reach in science, geography, sociality, and history. Such prints reveal how artists of the day, and those who viewed their art, visually understood human beings of various types—different ages, sexes, complexions, ethnicities, cultures. Colorfully illustrated accounts included text describing people in exotically "othered" lands, along with graphics of their appearances—complexion, build, costume, and movement, often dancing.[42] Visual imagery was understood as a tool for mental cultivation, social instruction, and moral persuasion; at least as powerful were such visual impressions when viewed in live motion on city stages.

The age of the ballet lithograph blossomed: U.S. audiences could ogle European stars who never crossed the ocean, creating a kind of ballerina pin-up culture.[43] Prints typically idealized a ballerina's lightness, depicted her revealing or exotic costume, highlighted her facial beauty, and presented her figure as either voluptuous or modest, as the artist intended viewers to see her. Artists contributing to the visual record of dancers on American stages in this period included E. W. Clay of Philadelphia and Nathaniel Currier of New York, creating affordable, appealing, reproducible images for public purchase. Dancers immortalized in Clay's and Currier's prints appeared on Philadelphia stages, from Mme. Hutin in the 1820s to Lola Montez in the 1850s. Other visual depictions, some featuring dance, were far less flattering. Cartooning and "othering" came together in "cuts and placards" mocking African Americans, which New England minister Hosea Easton well understood as visual training in corporeal abhorrence.[44] Clay depicted not only social and theatrical scenes but also the racial mockery that Easton, an African American, excoriated. Gary Nash notes that the popularity of such prints "led to a new commercial art form—graphic racial caricatures produced to adorn the walls of the city's genteel white citizens"[45]—a décor choice shared by lower-class sites like bars and taverns, Easton reported. These images disseminated the pervasive insult feeding the intellectual climate of the age, nurtured by race science and economic-geographic expansion, and motivating white performers to imitate Black people in staged "delineations," a term suggesting a drawing, sketch, or cartoon. Stage animated page.

The Body of Science

The United States in this period saw the ascent of science as a decisive methodology for understanding human beings. Biology, anatomy, ethnology, phrenology, and related sciences (as these fields were then understood) treated bodies as determinant of intellectual capacity, moral behavior, social status, and political empowerment. This turn proved dramatic for populations fighting for rights and recognition—a drama depicted with many shadings on U.S. stages.

Continuing the eighteenth-century drive of Western science toward collecting and classifying flora and fauna, early nineteenth-century investigators increasingly turned attention to the human being. Earlier European naturalists—Carl Linnaeus, Comte de Buffon (Georges-Louis Leclerc), Johann Friedrich Blumenbach, and others—had sought answers to questions of human geographic, linguistic, social, and physical diversity, and of borders between species and varieties. These matters gained urgency as conquest, colonization, and commerce revealed the range of ways human beings looked and lived. U.S. naturalists had immediate access to the three races occupying their own continent, reflected in the influential *Notes on the State of Virginia* (Philadelphia, 1788) by philosopher, founding father, slaveholder, and naturalist Thomas Jefferson. Squirming under his tormented outrage at slavery, Jefferson denounced the institution in which he participated, praying for "a total emancipation" "under the auspices of heaven" (p. 174), while also asserting the impossibility of absorbing "the blacks into the state" (p. 147). Jefferson's objections to such inclusion were "political" as well as "physical and moral" in the "real distinctions" he saw between white and Black people—the "colour" of their skin, blood, and bile, their hair, "kidnie" excretions, "pulmonary apparatus," emotional depth, sexuality, and intelligence (pp. 147–49). Jefferson wondered that, "though for a century and a half we have had under our eyes the races of black and of red men, they have never yet been viewed by us"—American intellectuals—"as subjects of natural history" (p. 153). That soon changed: by the antebellum age, under pressure from abolitionism and its opponents, Western men of science made "a shift away from geography to the body as the locus of identity and difference."[46] Study and classification of human bodies became identified, even abroad, as a field of notable U.S. contribution. Philadelphia-educated thinkers were at the vanguard,[47] many trained at the University of Pennsylvania (Penn), the first colonial-era university to formalize a medical school and faculty. Its unique physician training made Philadelphia "the medical metropolis of our continent," drawing students from all states.[48]

Eminent Quaker physician and abolitionist Benjamin Rush (1746–1813), professor of medicine at Penn, investigated the nature of the human mind, predating the systemized model of the brain expounded by phrenologists Franz Joseph Gall and Johann Spurzheim.[49] Rush also suggested that skin color in Africans was "derived from the Leprosy"—identifying dark skin with disease.[50] Among Rush's students at Penn was North Carolinian Charles Caldwell, a contributor to the field called "ethnology" or "anthropology."[51] Caldwell's phrenological research convinced him that Africans were meant for servitude and differed more greatly from Caucasians than did dogs from wolves.[52] The claims of phrenologists, the relationships between enslavers and enslaved, and perceptions of Black people as links to lower animals would become themes of the blackface stage. Phrenology, which itself became a form of entertainment, would also be spoofed on the minstrel stage, but it was grasped by serious researchers as evidence for the "qualities of mind" and "physical powers" of no less a cultural icon than Viennese ballerina Fanny Elssler.[53]

Southerner and Penn graduate Samuel Henry Dickson, a physician and public intellectual, wrote of Africans and other non-European people as "brutal," "savage,"[54] and "retrograded,"[55] their enslavement resulting from their innate, eternal status as a people "conquered, subject, in servitude." Dickson deplored cruelty toward the enslaved but blamed what he saw as outrageous demands of Northern abolitionists for retarding amelioration of Southern slavery's ills. Blackface stage acts featuring "Southern Darkies in Plantation Sports" and "Uncle Tom at Home; or, Southern Life as it Really Is" would enliven this claim for Northern audiences.

Scientific research was not Dickson's forte; others supplied his evidence. Among these was Samuel George Morton, "of whom," Dickson wrote, "American science is justly proud" for "his profound, extensive, and cautious researches."[56] Morton attended Quaker schools, Penn's medical school, and the University of Edinburgh. In *Crania Americana* (1839), Morton used his measurement of cranial specimens from the world over to put to rest questions of racial differences, rankings, and origins. To *Crania Americana*, Morton appended an essay by Scottish phrenologist George Combe, "Phrenological Remarks on the Relation between the Natural Talents and Dispositions of Nations, and the Developments of their Brains," which considered different peoples' "freedom from foreign yoke" (p. 282): phrenologically legible qualities resulted in some people's subjugation of others, some groups' choice of "extermination in preference to subjection," and others being "subdued" by more dominant people with superior "aggregate development of brain." Thus were political dominance and social hierarchy justified by perceived biological factors shaping the world order. The *Charleston Medical Journal* praised Morton as the South's "benefactor" in scientifically grounding the enslavement of Africans.[57] Spectators unfamiliar with slavery could observe its caricatured theatricalization in blackface entertainments where the supposed foibles, capacities, tricks, and contentment of those in bondage were danced across the stage, alongside slicked-up characters delineating free Black dandies attempting, laughably, to assume behaviors and privileges of respectable white society.

Morton's scientific charge was taken up by Penn-educated Josiah Clark Nott, of South Carolina, who dedicated his *Types of Mankind* (1854) to Morton.[58] Nott was among the few U.S. scientists to read ("skim," he noted in a letter) Charles Darwin's *The Origin of Species* (1859), which he encountered while touring Europe, declaring flatly of the work's author that "the man is clearly crazy.'"[59] *Origin* reached the United States in 1860, as the nation and its physician-ethnologists were occupied with the imminent Civil War; repercussions of Darwin's work would be felt after that national cataclysm.

Some scientists contested the polygenist, racialist claims of the "American school" of ethnologists. Penn-educated physician and cranium collector Richard Harlan and clergyman Cortlandt Van Rensselaer, editor of Philadelphia's *Presbyterian Magazine*, energetically opposed polygenism. Black intellectuals joined the fray,[60] including Jacob Oson, Hosea Easton, Robert Benjamin Lewis, James Pennington, Martin Delany, James McCune Smith, and Frederick Douglass. African Americans were denied access to U.S. universities and scientific resources that fed ethnological arguments, and their publications were excluded from broad avenues of circulation, making each such response a challenging step. Black print networks shared these responses among African Americans and supporters in Philadelphia and elsewhere.[61]

American ethnologists marched onward, hardening racial classifications and rankings. Samuel Cartwright, another Penn-educated Southerner, published "Unity of the Human Race Disproved by the Hebrew Bible" (1858), attempting to equate the serpent who beguiled Eve and Adam with a black man-like creature.[62] As discussed later, blackface performer T. D. Rice subverted Cartwright's view by making the devil the only "white" figure in one of Rice's most-performed blackface plays, *Bone Squash Diavolo*. That show might have been enjoyed by Philadelphia farmer-lawyer Sidney George Fisher (1809–1871), a regular at city theaters. In 1860, as the nation careened toward civil war, Fisher tied law and politics to race science: "Slavery does not rest on the Constitution or laws as a basis," he wrote, "but they on it. It is not the creature, but the director of our policy. It is a permanent, commanding fact in our country."[63] After belaboring his pen to support racialist policies, Fisher lightened his days with social dancing, theater attendance, and diary-keeping.

While the prevalence of racial types on early U.S. stages reflected dominant concerns of intellectuals investigating humankind, these thinkers also turned attention to gender. As Cynthia Russett has noted, "Of all the permutations of physical differentiation sex is, together with color, the most evident," making "race and gender . . . two of the great themes of nineteenth-century science"[64]—and of nineteenth-century theatrical dancing. Ethnologists and phrenologists noted that men's crania were typically larger than women's, surely evidence, they claimed, of men's intellectual superiority. But it was the field of obstetrics that placed women squarely in scientists' sights, though ethnologists and obstetricians shared common intellectual ground and membership in prominent Philadelphia institutions like the American Philosophical Society and the Academy of Natural Sciences.[65]

University of Pennsylvania–connected doctors were at the forefront, investigating diseases and treatment of women and leading the charge to edge women out of the centuries-old female field of midwifery. Penn-educated Quaker physician Thomas C. James was the first professor assigned to a chair of obstetrics. His successor, William P. Dewees, was hailed as another pioneering Penn professor (and graduate) in the late eighteenth century, when, as a colleague later reminisced, "The Practice of Midwifery was . . . almost exclusively in the hands of ignorant females," whose blunders could "be relieved only by the well-directed efforts of the scientific"—male—"Accoucheur."[66] Demanding recognition as a medical science, obstetrics suppressed entrenched practices, since even as recently as the turn into the nineteenth century, bemoaned Penn professor Hugh Hodge, "the mass, even of intelligent and well informed females, would entrust themselves and their progeny during the agonizing and dangerous process of parturition to the most aged, and often the most imbecile of their sex—a practice still common" in 1835. No women were then admitted to medical schools, so obstetricians must be male. A decade later, Hodge conceded that "parturition is a natural process," but birthing had become dangerous for "modern, refined woman" owing to the effects of "civilized" as opposed to "savage life,"[67] making obstetrics "essential to the comfort, the happiness, the health and lives of females and their infants."

And what could be more primary than that pairing—"females and their infants"? As Dewees noted, woman's "particular organization, and her temperament, are made subservient to the important part she is destined to perform: upon her devolves . . . all the contingencies" of motherhood.[68] This demanding role for the continuity of humanity—the obligation of "republican motherhood," as some scholars term it—was understood as a strain on women since, Dewees added, "one of the most striking differences between the male and female, is the inferiority of her stature. Her whole osseous fabric is more delicate," while "the bones of her cranium are thinner, smaller, and more pliant"—a bow to phrenology—"and the space destined to be filled with the brain, is smaller." Woman was dominated—pushed and pulled—by her uterus, which Dewees found an organ of suspicious unruliness. Dr. Charles Meigs, also trained at Penn, agreed that the subject of the uterus was challenging, remarking indignantly to his all-male class at Jefferson Medical College, "Who wants to know, or ought to know that the ladies have abdomens and wombs but us doctors? When I was young a woman had no legs even"—legs would much occupy ballet commentary—"but only feet, and possibly ankles."[69] How, then, to tolerate the exposed flesh (ankles, legs, and more), powerful performances, and complicated lives of female stage dancers, who overcame these supposed innate physical disadvantages in their public and private endeavors?

Meigs, an admirer of Morton, memorialized the esteemed craniologist for the Philadelphia Academy of Natural Sciences, where he highlighted Morton's "observation of his [the human being's] real physical attributes" to resolve "many dark questions both in history and chronology, as well as in morals and faith."[70] Medicine and morality were inextricable and only men, professionally trained, could effectively exercise both. Ballerinas who broke free of such constraints deserved condemnation for moral and maternal failings. Despite his dark views of women's physiology and, as a contemporary commentator remarked, "the low estimate which Dr. Meigs places upon their [women's] intellectual nature" in his book *Females and their Diseases*, that text served the obstetrics course at the first dedicated medical school for women, established in 1850 in Philadelphia;[71] there were then no texts written from a woman's perspective.

Women pushed against men's encroachment on what women understood to be their own ground—their medical and social treatment—just as performers like Elssler directed their own stage careers and personal lives. The medical outrage against women was a repeated motif in Elizabeth Cady Stanton's *History of Woman Suffrage*.[72] When Ann Preston, first woman dean of Philadelphia's Female Medical College, addressed the school's graduates in 1858, she urged students to ignore the naysayers denying women's capacity as physicians: "Your business is, not to war with words, but 'to make good' your position 'upon the bodies' of your patients by deeds of healing." Preston's professorship at FMC was preceded by her taking the stage for public lectures to women outside the college, where she enlightened her public—woman to woman—on female hygiene and anatomy. Those female listeners also could and did observe living models of that anatomy, considerably exposed and in virtuosic motion, at city theaters.

Dancers, Bodies, and Meaning on Philadelphia Stages

The focus on the body in antebellum American arts, letters, and science sheds light on the body-centered entertainments that Philadelphians enjoyed, particularly theatrical dancing, dominated by the emerging forms of ballet and blackface minstrelsy.

By the early nineteenth century, European theater dance increasingly featured female performers in the stage dance that came to be known as ballet.[73] Ballerinas fulfilled Romantic notions of ethereal feminine purity, of allure veiled in mystic spirituality, of flesh made air. They rose on their pointes, played sprites and fairies, and loved and died exotically, in costumes of transparent tulle or brilliant spangles highlighting their bodily forms. As their careers propelled them beyond woman's ascribed place in the home and into the public spotlight, some dancers took control of their own itineraries and finances. Some male commentators remarked indignantly on the sums that European stars like Mme. Celeste and Elssler carried away from American tours; a few women even went on to significant managerial careers.[74] The dominant culture of respectability—demanding a social and gender hierarchy with proper women safely in the home sphere, protected by fathers or husbands—was threatened by such female artists, as gracious and modest as some attempted to appear in public.[75] One such case was America's fallen angel, ballerina Augusta Maywood, as later discussion reveals.

Theater attendees had much opportunity to see women performing in ballets and balletic interludes. While early theatrical troupes in the United States were dominated by English performers, by the late 1820s, continental Europeans were dancing over the ocean, bringing French tastes in choreography and presentation to Americans. Works reflected European tastes for exotica, melodrama, and technical wizardry. The Ravel troupe featured such works in their seasons touring the United States, while other European stars forged paths that crossed from balletic to dramatic roles—paths that inspired some young American dancers.

The public nature of theatrical work drew commentary on ballerinas' bodies. Some viewers understood such bodies as expressions of breathtaking beauty and elevated sentiment, others as shameless enticements. Margaret

Fuller and Ralph Waldo Emerson, watching Elssler in Boston, found her dancing to be not only "poetry" but even "religion."[76] Another writer expressed the opposite view, declaring indignantly that ballet "relies for its effects upon the public display of the naked limbs of women," and asking his reader if he "would willingly see your own wife, or your own sister, capering before the crowded benches of the opera-house, her limbs covered with . . . lace fig-leaves"—a biblical warning no literate reader would miss—"reaching half-way to the knee, standing on one toe," while the other pointed "up at the ventilator in the roof"?[77] Such exposure of a woman's body and the physical virtuosity it bespoke deserved condemnation, publication of which surely boosted ticket sales European ballerinas might be dismissed as products of lax, old-world societies, but to the shock of some commentators, American dancers took up the costumes, techniques, and choreographies of their transatlantic sisters, much as the women's movement shared goals and strategies on both continents.[78]

American-born ballet performers, rarely achieving the accolades of their European counterparts, learned from them, polishing their performances, expanding repertoires, and laying groundwork for American stagings. Such steps challenged prevailing scientific views: while U.S. obstetricians typically viewed dancing as a healthy and appropriate private exercise for girls and young women, they cautioned against its too-vigorous pursuit.[79] Overexertion in any exercise—with dancing often singled out—might lead to menstrual or pregnancy complications, disease, even death, an argument that some ballet scenarios, like *Giselle*, could be seen to affirm. Yet as the rise of ballet in the United States brought female bodies increasingly into visibility, professionals like Mme. Celeste and her sister-artists not only showed their expressive, vigorous bodies in costumes and attitudes that flouted accepted standards of modesty,[80] but they further transgressed by engaging in highly public careers, as did women who took to political stages or to medicine.

These very transgressions contributed to the appeal of the theatrical stage as a place where female performers, and the mixed-sex audiences watching them, might try out possibilities. African American performers, on the other hand, had almost no opportunities in the antebellum age in major U.S. theaters, as opposed to less formal sites like markets, saloons, and dance halls. A brief list of exceptions include New York's short-lived African (Grove) Theatre (c. 1816–1824); the remarkable, brief career of Juba/William Henry Lane, as a performer with otherwise all-white blackface troupes; and a possible other truly Black minstrel troupe.[81] None of these performed in Philadelphia, although one of the African Theatre's stars, Shakespearean actor James Hewlett, did so briefly (Jan. 1826).[82] With Hewlett on the stage was

Philadelphia's remarkable Black composer-musician Francis Johnson, whose participation, with his all-Black band, in elite white society balls, militia parades, and even theaters, informs later chapters.

If Philadelphians had vanishingly few opportunities to see Black performers on main stages in this era, there was no shortage of blackface players "delineating" African Americans. T. D. Rice performed his corked-up trickster-songster-dancer Jim Crow in original "Ethiopian operas" over several decades in city theaters. By the mid-1840s, blackface entertainment was dominated by large troupes—white and male. Reductionist characterizations of racial and ethnic types ascribed to Black people a childlike love and gift for music, dance, dress-up, and humor, as well as a "genius for contentment"—a perfect combination for vigorously embodied minstrel "delineations."[83] An 1832 version of "The Original Jim Crow" lyrics forefronts the character's intimate connection to dance: "For I'm of a dancing family, / An I'd radder dance dan pray, / For ob de two professions, / De dancing's de best pay"[84]— also a sly commentary on the rewards of religion. Rice's lyrics showed his grasp of both class distinctions manifested in dance and of regional styles, as he aimed his satire at high-class entertainments like opera-ballet: "Lord bless de lubly creature, I teach dem how to dance, And show dem de new step, just arrived from France," pointing not only to the latest French social dances, but also to the novelty of Parisian ballet sweeping U.S. stages. Yet far from the exotica and fairylands of the ballet, Rice sourced his understandings of the poor, working-class, and oppressed people of the young nation, fitting them into containers—songs, plays, and operas—shaped largely by U.S. and British musical theater.

The versatile and enduring blackface stage embraced all performance arts—acting, dancing, singing, instrumental music, comedy, burlesque, and improvisation, morphing into variety and vaudeville, and overlapping with clowning and circus antics. Targeting Black people for mockery with caricatured language, costume, and movement, the antebellum minstrel stage also swallowed up and regurgitated high-class entertainments like opera, ballet, and instrumental music, prized by elite audiences. Watching burlesques of such toney performances, shown in blackface, working-class spectators filling minstrel audiences could laugh at those both below and above them in the social scale, some of whom, at times, laughed along.

Dances styled as "African" were not the only "exotic" movement works seen on Philadelphia and other U.S. stages. At leading theaters, dancing attributed to different types of people was well represented in interludes performed between the longer works in a full evening's bill, showing off dances associated with different nationalities—the British hornpipe, the Spanish *bolero*, the Polish *cracovienne*. Short ballet excerpts—various *pas seul, pas de deux*, or *pas de trois* choreographies—were also presented in interludes. Many full-length ballets featured themes, with versions of dances, drawn from settings considered "exotic." Dances also appeared within plays and farces, perhaps depicting a festive ballroom scene, a foreign location's supposed customs, or interpolated at the slightest excuse for a performer to show off a specialty.

Pantomimes and harlequinades, standard components of English (and European) theater, were related to ballet and blackface acts in style, subject, movement, and musicality.⁸⁵ The expressive, virtuosic movement in such works led to frequent conflation of pantomime with ballet, as in *The Caliph of Bagdad, Nathalie,* and *L'Amour d'Quatre*.⁸⁶ Harlequinades were English versions of Italian *commedia dell'arte* themes and characters, often played as family Christmas entertainments.⁸⁷ Melodrama, widely popular by the early nineteenth century, drew on literary trends toward sentimentality, moral clarity, and cliff-hanging drama, with consistent musical underpinning for rhythmic movement and emotional support. It drew audiences throughout Europe and the United States, often to the chagrin of managers and actors who considered melodrama a low-class bastard of the stage, distracting audiences from serious drama. Among the works designated at times as melodramas were *The Falls of Clyde; Jocko, the Brazilian Ape*; and *The Willow Copse*,⁸⁸ works also advertised sometimes as "pantomimes" or "ballets," indicating overlap among categories for movement-based works.

Popular in this period were the English comic opera, Italian grand opera, and French romantic opera, circulating to the United States with their associated dance forms. Like theatrical formats just discussed, opera joined drama with music and movement. American elites embraced opera, with its European courtly associations and high production costs.⁸⁹ Ballet frequently contributed to these works, as in *Cinderella, or the Fairy and the Glass Slipper; Gustavus 3rd, or, The Masked Ball; La Bayadere, or, the Maid of Cashmere*; and *The Bohemian Girl*.⁹⁰ Unsurprisingly, blackface entertainers grasped the opportunity to mock elite snobbism through burlesques of the upper class's beloved operas; T. D. Rice pioneered the "Ethiopian" opera with works like *Bone Squash Diavolo* and *Otello*; other blackface troupes soon followed. Palmo's Ethiopian Opera Company played *Shin De-heel-a!* (Cinderella), with characters named mockingly for European ballet stars. A commentator writing in 1855 sniffed that theatergoers were "fortunate if they get to bed without being wearied and disgusted with some crude burlesque on a popular opera, served up with vulgar caricatures of the style and manner" of that genre.⁹¹

Social Dance

Dancing graced private and public assemblies for elite society and its aspirants, despite Philadelphia Quakers' (and others') disapproval. Social dances also erupted, beyond the careful containment of respectable assemblies, at city saloons and working-class "dance halls." Such rowdy physicality, often mixed with drinking and brawling, resulted in police reports detailing places, people, and circumstances, though revealing little about the dancing itself. Much more can be discerned about the city's higher-class dance participants, served by a choice of dancing masters listed in city directories and advertising classes and balls in newspapers. Some dance teachers also had stage careers, connecting theatrical and social-dance domains. Instruction by such masters was available to ladies and gents, adults and children. If the latter wished to see dancing perfected by youngsters of their own age, they could watch La Petite Gertrude, La Petite Taglioni, and the entire troupe of Danseuses Viennoises among the many child professionals, like Joe Jefferson, performing impressive renditions of short ballets and popular dances on city stages.

Through the antebellum period, interest in the "national dances" that enlivened stage performances—the "Spanish Dance," "Caledonians," polkas, mazurkas, lilts, and so on—also fed social-dance choreographies. As detailed later, notated ballroom versions of such dances reveal use of French ballet steps in social-dance vocabulary. While these dances are recorded at balls and in manuals for the city's white middle and upper classes, newspaper reports suggest that Black residents may have also found occasions for such social dancing.

As blackface performance moved toward mainstage acceptance, ballrooms catering to white socialites and aspirants embraced "Ethiopian Cotillions," with "Figures Arranged to the Most Popular African [minstrel] Airs."[92] Among the figures for such cotillions were those named for blackface acts: "Miss Lucy Long," "Boatman's Dance," "Lucy Neale," "Dan Tucker Jig," "Old Zip Coon," and "Dandy Jim." These tunes take us back to the opening of this chapter, where T. D. Rice danced his Jim Crow creation onto Philadelphia's stages, setting up a caricature and putting in motion a dance craze that would endure beyond the antebellum period.

Philadelphia was a vibrant center of early U.S. dance culture; the acts noted earlier were a slice of the rich dance world enlivening antebellum stages and ballrooms. Despite—or as a relief from—the formality, modesty, and propriety of the Quaker City, residents could enjoy dancing in styles from acrobatics to ballet, from breakdowns to boleros. This dancing is spotlighted chronologically in each chapter of this book, placed in the context of laws, learning, arts, activism, debates, and disturbances that shaped and troubled the young nation as its politicians, reformers, educators, scientists, and artists promulgated theories and representations that touched any and every body in the land.

2

Tumultuous Pleasures

Graphic Lessons in Dancing from the 1820s

The author of "An Essay on Dancing, in A Series of Letters to a Lady" astutely and disparagingly remarked, "The ballroom is actually a kind of theatre, turning everyone into a performer, like a 'rope-dancer'"—an act of daring virtuosity, drawing expectant eyes to the dancer.[1] The writer found dancing no "innocent" form of "animal gratification," for it exhausted "the lady," distracting her from home and charitable duties, so that those indulging in "the tumultuous pleasures of the dance" must "never expect the solace of an approving and well-informed conscience." Such warnings infused antidance literature for generations; the crucible of early United States formation made dancing's bodily display particularly provocative. Thus, as techniques for affordable production and distribution of graphic arts developed in the early nineteenth century, dance became a subject of interest and income for American artists.[2] Focusing on E. W. Clay's work, this chapter explores *graphic depictions as revealing dancing—and attitudes toward dancing*—in the antebellum period.

At the start of the 1820s, Americans could look back on a decade that had wrested U.S. seamen from attacks by the Barbary states and furthered independence from England through victory in the War of 1812. But as the nation asserted independence from foreign impingement, it drew lines of separation, including the 1820 Missouri Compromise, within its own borders. As Michael Harris notes, discourses of race, gender, ethnicity, and other differences "are discourses of power" that "ultimately rely on the visual in the sense that the visible body must be used by those in power to represent nonvisual realities that differentiate insiders from outsiders."[3] Differences must "not only be known but visible," making graphic depiction of bodies—differing bodies—significant. In the United States, hierarchy mattered.

E. W. Clay offered such a hierarchical depiction in *Lessons in Dancing, Exemplified by Sketches from Real Life in the City of Philadelphia* (1828).[4] That same year, a Philadelphia magazine "Devoted to General Literature and the Fine Arts" praised "fashionable" amusements, specifying dancing as "favourable to the mind" and the body, as "it conveys sprightliness to it, quickening the ideas, and calling into employment its resources: . . . its tendency is always to benevolence."[5] Dance had its advocates, even in moralistic Philadelphia. Seven of Clay's eight elegantly drawn plates focus on social dancing at various levels of class, and one on theatrical dancing. Two Philadelphia cartoonists had preceded Clay in social depiction: William Thackara and David Claypoole Johnston. Historian Gary Nash credits Johnston, from a leading Philadelphia Quaker family, as founder of U.S. racial cartooning with his lampoons of Black Masons.[6] Thackara's "A New mode of Perfuming & Preserving Clothes from Moths" (1819) burlesqued Black social aspiration, depicting two white dandies and two ludicrously overdressed African American gents; a monkey on a window ledge at the back of the scene postures, tellingly, identically with one of the Black men. Text for this image in Thackara's sketchbook reads, "The Black gentry aping their masters, dress quite as extravagantly, and frequently wear their clothes, long before they are cast off. They not only ape the dress of their masters, but also their cant terms, being well versed in the fashionable vocabulary."[7] Repetition of "ape/aping" and inclusion of the monkey figure make clear the artist's association of Black people with simian primates.

Neither Thackara nor Johnston depicted race, behavior, and the body as consistently as did Clay. This chapter, organized according to his *Lessons in Dancing* series, investigates Clay's depictions of the body's motion, presentation, and meanings not, primarily, for hints at dance reconstruction, nor for the prints' aesthetic qualities, nor to identify Clay's dance-viewing prejudices. Rather, as each image in *Lessons* sets the dancing pair on a circle of floorboards, without background, each draws our attention to the bodies, costumes, movement, and character of the dancing pair, which I read to discern how these images document and contextualize the dancing and body-understandings of the period in which Clay worked.[8]

Among the Elite

The first three etchings in Clay's series (the City Dancing Assembly, a "fancy" ball, and a dancing master's "cotillon") depict high-society social dancing.

City Assembly, Balancez

Balanced atop the pyramid of Philadelphia society was a class of wealthy, often elite power brokers whose connections to business, banking, and property allowed them fluid circulation in national and international society.[9] Some descended from Pennsylvania's founding Quaker families, supplemented by later, mostly British, arrivals. Commercial and political connections to the U.S. South created friction between Quaker austerity and egalitarianism on one hand and, on the other, the gentility of European aristocracy, favored by the Southern oligarchy and by some wealthy Northerners. Tensions erupted over elite social gatherings like the City Dancing Assembly, founded in 1749, which garnered early complaints regarding its antidemocratic exclusivity. Thus, Clay's title for his opening image (Figure 2.1) was well chosen: "City Assembly, Balancez." The balancing act sustained itself through and beyond the nineteenth century, as the Dancing Assembly waxed, waned, and endured. In the 1820s, the assembly often met at Masonic Hall, near the city's commercial and political district. Many merchants and professionals would have been both Masons and assembly members, linking social and business activities.

Figure 2.1. "City Assembly, Balancez," Edward W. Clay, *Lessons in Dancing* (1828). *(Courtesy Rosenbach Museum & Library A 8281)*

Clay's image shows an elegant gentleman in early nineteenth-century high fashion (tailcoat, high-collared shirt, fitted breeches, stockings, and dancing slippers) cutting a step with a lady who matches the daring of her off-the-shoulder bodice with a revealing lift of her skirts to ankle height, as her lightly clad feet skim the floor and her bejeweled neck's lengthened verticality holds in place her coiffure, bows, and dangling earrings. Both dancers appear gloved so that hand-to-hand touch would avoid skin contact. What steps might Clay have caught this pair dancing? According to English feminist Fanny Wright, reporting on her U.S. tour, French fashions in clothing and dance had overtaken English styles, leading to the popularity of quadrilles over country dances.[10] Clay's depiction supports Wright's remark that the young ladies of the republic "dance with much lightness, grace, and gayheartedness," although, Wright observed, their beaux were less accomplished.

In 1817, respected Philadelphia dancing master Victor Guillou forwarded the taste for French dancing in his translation of a dancing manual by Jean-Henri Gourdoux-Daux, ensuring that the *haut ton* of his adopted city had a guide beyond lessons in Guillou's academy.[11] In addition to the text's claims for dance's antiquity "amongst all the people of the earth" (Hebrews, Greeks, and "Savages"), the author extolled dancing's advantages for health and beauty, as it "enhances, embellishes, and perfects the work of nature."[12] The text describes steps and balletic movements such as *rond de jambe, grand* and *petit battement, changement, assemble, jeté, sissonne, echappé, temps levé, coupé, chassé, glissade,* and *temps de courante*. Like most dancing manuals for elite or aspiring consumers, the text offered the foundations of balletic technique, which informed both social and stage dancing. Clay's lady demonstrates Guillou's description of proper bearing: she "holds [her] robe, slightly, between the thumb and forefinger, observing to keep it at arms length" (p. 12), while showing how "the head must be carried high, and the parties reciprocally look at each other" (p. 14). The cotillon dance is much discussed in the work, with attention to deportment and "civility" (pp. 92–93) beyond the ballroom.

Although *Elements* discusses musical rhythms and styles of playing "cottilion" tunes (pp. 26–28, 74–76), it offers no music. Fortunately for Philadelphia's ball-goers, an expert musician, composer, and bandleader could supply that. Likely born on the culturally dynamic island Martinique, the mixed-race Francis Johnson arrived in Philadelphia around 1809 and became the center of musical life, crossing between white and Black circles, social and theatrical music, and military and dance worlds.[13] A trumpet virtuoso with impressive skills in several other instruments, Johnson became a highly regarded music teacher in the city and an early and widely published American composer. In addition to his engagement as bandleader with his all-Black band and composer of marches for Philadelphia's elite white militia units, Johnson played for the city's best dancing masters and assemblies, contributing dance compositions that show familiarity with theatrical hits. In fact, he and his band appeared in the theater in Joseph Cowell's *The Cataract of the Ganges* (autumn 1824), participating in a "novel and grand" procession through cascades of water. For the Chestnut Street Theatre's drama *The Avenger of Sicily* (Dec. 1830), Johnson and band were "engaged to head the Moorish and Ethiopian procession" in one scene.[14]

Philadelphia merchant, politician, and abolitionist Samuel Breck recalled a ball at the home of the elite Rush family, where Johnson was a favorite: "This 'black' musician is a man of taste, and even science in his vocation."[15] Breck noted "the talent he has of turning every lively tune in the new operas to his purpose by adapting to it a Quadrille or Cotillion of his own composing which he introduces at the parties in Philadelphia." Johnson arranged that each dance tune "gets engraved and circulated thro' the Union," making him "the author of all novelty in dancing." A master of European musical form, Johnson may also have employed richer rhythmic invention, complex structures, and opportunities for musicians' improvisation, distinguishing his music from that of other American bands, and making Johnson an audience favorite. That edge led to his invitation to lead the band at the fashionable New York summer resorts of Saratoga Springs and Ballston Spa, starting in the early 1820s and continuing for two decades. The novelty of his tunes may have encouraged Johnson to "call" some of his dances to ensure that attendees could follow his inventions, requiring that he be fully familiar with proper social-dance technique.

Johnson and band were not the only Black presence at white society's dancing assemblies: these elite gatherings included elegant dinners organized, prepared, and served by African American caterers, who dominated this field. As the "epicenter" of both U.S. cuisine and the catering business, Philadelphia's culinary leadership was maintained by Black "public waiters" like Robert Bogle and Peter Augustin, some of whom had arrived in the city from the West Indies with refugees from the Haitian Revolution. These fastidious businessmen became arbiters of both white cuisine and Black refinement.[16]

Fancy Ball, Turn Partner

Clay's second image of upper-class social dancing depicts a "fancy dress" (masquerade) ball (Figure 2.2). Condemned by religious and political authorities, disguise and costuming had been outlawed briefly in 1808, perhaps for

Figure 2.2. "Fancy Ball, Turn Partner," Edward W. Clay, *Lessons in Dancing* (1828). *(Courtesy Rosenbach Museum & Library A 8281)*

their associations with misrule and suggestions of theatricality, out of step with American morals.[17] In living memory was the notorious Philadelphia pageant the "Meschianza" (May 1778) during the War of Independence, which engaged the city's elites in British-sympathizing revelry, fancy dress, and dancing—much denounced by American patriots and Quakers. Yet masquerade balls did not disappear with the British departure; in the 1820s, the City Dancing Assembly held several such events, drawing both praise and condemnation. The *National Gazette* boasted of the assembly's well-attended "Fancy Ball" in 1828, when three hundred "ladies and gentlemen" attended in "elegant and various costume" as "a great concourse" in the street thronged "to see the dresses."[18] The ballroom glittered brighter "than any of the kind which has ever been witnessed here, or perhaps, in any part of the United States." The author assured readers that costumes included no silly clowns or pretend noblemen, for "taste and decorum marked the great diversity of imitative attire." The dancing "was as spirited as usual," but sufficiently refined for this elite gathering.

Another author, signing himself "A Representative of Thousands," took an opposite view of that "Fancy Ball." In a pamphlet of "Reflections," the writer decried the "state of depravity" that the masquerade ball revealed in Philadelphia's "first citizens."[19] Instead of using their wealth and position to serve the needy and "oppressed," these ball-goers "plung[ed] deep into a vortex of dissipation," which no "rational beings, as republicans, as Americans" could countenance. This author saw the costumes differently from the *National Gazette* reporter, condemning the "'*merry andrews*'" (clowns and mountebanks) attending the ball at exorbitant ticket prices to "caper nimbly to the lascivious pleasing, . . . to strut about a ball-room for an hour or two, in the character of a nobleman," addressed as "'My Lord'"—in republican America! Worse yet, the costumed ladies followed suit: "Has modesty lost her blush?" In summary, Representative claimed, "The *Fancy Ball* has been a source of unparalleled aggravation to the poor, and cannot but arouse them to a deeper sense of their own poverty, wretchedness and misery."

Clay's image hardly suggests to the modern viewer extravagance or sexual excess, but it does depict the gentleman dressed in Renaissance-style nobleman's costume, with tightly fitted hose exposing his legs beneath a short doublet and his crown-like cap bearing a tall feather. The lady appears in elegantly adapted peasant dress, a pretty apron, and a neat straw hat, her red-stockinged ankles exposed beneath her skirt's attractive trim. The dancers' gloved hands touch palm to palm, the partners gazing upon each other as they turn about in place. Such costumes' cost, multiplied by the hundreds in attendance at the ball, according to "Representative of Thousands," could feed, clothe, and shelter crowds of the city's poor, perhaps some of those very souls gazing in wonder from the street at the guests' arrival. The distraction of such amusements from the duties of democratic citizenship highlighted class tensions, religious fissures, and economic woes that resulted in election of populist president Andrew Jackson in 1828.[20] A French term—the *soirée dansante*—used then in reference to such elegant balls, highlighted these tensions, as American culture struggled to meet or to shun European standards.

Bonaffon's Cotillion Parties, Valtz

Documentation of the City Dancing Assembly and the cotillions featured in the Gourdoux-Daux/Guillou text point to Clay's third image (Figure 2.3), "Bonaffon's Cotillion Parties, Valtz." Guillou, in step with the Dancing

Figure 2.3. "Bonaffon's Cotillion Parties, Valtz," Edward W. Clay, *Lessons in Dancing* (1828). *(Courtesy Rosenbach Museum & Library A 8281)*

Assembly, also employed Johnson to play for his students and balls.[21] Among Guillou's competitors was the dancing master named by Clay, Anthony Bonnafon, variously spelled, listed in Philadelphia's city directories through the 1820s.[22] Other dancing masters documented in the period are Mr. B. August, C. Ignace Frazier, Francis C. Labbé (another employer of Johnson and band), F. D. Mallet, and H. Whale, whose father was a dancing master, and who as a child performed ballet solos and hornpipes as "the infant Vestris" in city theaters.[23] Several names in this group point to the draw of Philadelphia for French-speaking refugees fleeing France or Haiti, as was the case with Guillou.[24] These masters were spurned by the most morally fastidious of Philadelphia society, as befell Labbé, who in January 1822 offered a benefit ball for rebuilding of "the 'Orphan Assylum' recently, calamitously, destroyed by fire."[25] The asylum board published a declination of the "truly benevolent offer" since "many of the Members of the Society are conscientiously opposed to amusements of this kind." Other citizens flocked to them.

The "cotillion party" Clay depicted highlights the importance in the city's social whirl of dancing masters' balls, along with those of the Dancing

Assembly and dances for special occasions like George Washington's birthday. The term "cotillion" could refer to both a kind of dance and a formal dance party. In Clay's image, the dancers whirl round in a waltz, a dance that had initially shocked European upper classes, as it soon did Americans, for its dangers on the dance floor; the close embrace, hands touching the partner's body, interlacing of legs, face-to-face proximity, and the dizziness stimulated by spinning might cause a lady to lose bodily (and moral) control.[26] Clay's image captures the intimacy and challenge of the waltz, along with the lift and swirl of the lady's costume as the dancers spin.

Doctors of this period found dancing an apt exercise for girls—provided it not exceed an "exertion" that could threaten their delicate frames and interfere with reproductive health.[27] Clearly, such advice to aspiring and elite ladies ignored the fact that most women in the United States worked (many in enslaved, hard labor) and were in no position to protect their delicate innards, yet they somehow managed not only to dance, but to reproduce. Still, this perceived delicacy made women unfit for professional and political engagement, according to physicians issuing such claims. Charles Caldwell, for example, noted the "exceedingly different" brain form and size between men and women.[28] Men's "strength of development lies in the forehead, the seat of real intellect," and in women, "in the upper and posterior portions of the head, which are the seat of moral sentiment." Thus, "man surpasses in intellectual capacity and strength; woman, in tenderness, purity, benevolence, and goodness." Yet even upper-class American ladies' purity and moral goodness did not forbid many from whirling unchastely through the waltz. Surely, Mr. Bonnafon's careful management would ensure that nothing untoward occurred at his balls.

The handwritten annotations on one set of the *Lessons in Dancing* suggest that the swirling couple in this "Valtz" were the "son & daughter" of the "Spanish Minister Tacon," introducing into the ballroom another European element, with the French dancing masters and German-derived "waltz." Don Francisco Tacon was Minister Plenipotentiary from Spain to the United States, serving until 1835.[29] The Spanish-speaking population of Philadelphia, although small in this period, highlights the interests shared among the city's political, commercial, and cultural elites and those of both Spain and Spanish America. The sensitive balance-of-power strategies and negotiations that involved the United States, Spain, and the latter's American colonies, then emerging from imperial control to independence, make the dangers of the waltz a fitting symbol of Spanish-U.S. involvement.

At the "Theatre": Chesnut Street Theatre, Pas de Deux

Approaching the halfway point of Clay's *Lessons in Dancing*, we reach the rich terrain of the theater, whose stars Clay later portrayed in prints apart from this series. This one theatrical print in *Lessons* captures pivotal points about 1820s U.S. stage dance and the discourses it touched, while making evident connections between stage and social dancing. The male dancer's costume in "Chesnut Street Theatre" (Figure 2.4) resembles that of the gent in the "Fancy Ball" etching. The elite ballroom dancers whom Clay depicted would have filled the theaters' box seats to observe these fashionable European professionals. For the purposes of this history, "Chesnut Street Theatre, Pas de deux" stands in for a broad discussion of Philadelphia's ballet stage in the 1820s, assuming greater weight in this chapter than in Clay's *Lessons*.

Figure 2.4. "Chesnut Street Theatre, Pas de deux," Edward W. Clay, *Lessons in Dancing* (1828). *(Courtesy Rosenbach Museum & Library A 8281)*

The handwritten annotation on one copy of this image identifies the dancers as "Monsieur & Madame Hutin," but since Mme. Francisque Hutin was not dancing with anyone identified as her husband at her U.S. debut (she later did marry M. Labasse, a French dancer performing in the United States), it is likely that she was depicted here with one of her regular dance partners at this time—Joseph Barbiere (Barberre) or M. Achille (Soulier, a surname absent in his publicity), who brought his dancer-wife on the tour.[30] The appearance of these French artists marked a change in dancing on U.S. stages, earlier dominated by English performers whose dancing was stylistically distinct enough to mark the French dancers' appearances as opening a new era. What had Philadelphia audiences seen on their stages before Hutin and partner appeared?

The English School

Dancing was regularly featured in theatrical interludes to entertain audiences during pauses between the "main piece" (a full-length play) and the "after piece" (a farce or light dramatic work), both of which might also include music and dance. While most actors could participate in a dance scene, performers who specialized in the art would typically dance in such interludes and featured numbers. An example of a play with a few dances was *Isabelle: Or, Woman's Life*, which had dancing by a "band of Savoyards" in act I and a "wreath dance," called a "ballet," described in a prompt book from the period as a theatricalized country dance.[31] Performers like Englishman William Francis and Irishman James Byrne had helped establish in Philadelphia traditional forms such as hornpipes and harlequinades, training John Durang and his children, among others.[32] Hornpipes, reels, and lilts continued as interludes into the nineteenth century, along with French-titled choices (*pas seul, pas de deux, divertissement*, etc.), indicating performers' familiarity with evolving European stage dance before French ballet professionals swept U.S. theaters.[33] The Durang family were among these American performers, with such English professionals as Mr. Parker and family and Mr. and Mrs. Conway as lead dancers.

Parker, born in England and married to a dancer from Boston, was a skilled equestrian, harlequin, and dancer in the British pantomime tradition.[34] He directed ballets and pantomimes at New York's Park Theatre and at Philadelphia's Walnut Street, where he often featured his daughters, Jane and Sarah (aged four and five in 1824, when they did a "nosegay dance" to honor General Lafayette's visit).[35] After the successes of the French dancers on U.S. stages, Parker settled in New York as a respected social-dance teacher. This path was followed by Mr. and Mrs. Conway, described by Charles Durang as "simply English dancers, of good style, but not French opera dancers. . . . They only danced a few nights, and were not attractive."[36] Several newspaper mentions of the Conways—perhaps puffs issued by the theater—praised their "grace and agility," which earned them "continuous applause." The Conways attempted some exoticism in their interludes with a "celebrated Spanish Bollerno with Castanetts," but once Hutin and colleagues appeared, the shortcomings of the previous dance personnel became evident, for these dancers could not hold "equal rank with these expert performers from Paris."

Nonetheless, the long-standing popularity of French dancers on London stages would have brought French theatrical dance regularly before the English public. Surely, English dance professionals observed touring artists, perhaps studying privately with them, and worked toward new technical and aesthetic standards. Charles Durang found the English dancer Mrs. Rowbotham, who toured the United States, "extremely graceful in pantomime action," performing "with distinction."[37] She could take on roles in works by French dancers when they appeared in Philadelphia in 1831, and featured herself in interludes such as a "Grand Pas Seul." American dancers too sought the new French techniques, exemplified by the Hathwell sisters Matilda, Henrietta, and Louisa, the latter two born in Philadelphia once their British family moved there; in the 1820s, they appeared in works advertised as "ballets," such as *Little Red Riding Hood, Love Among the Roses*, and *Jannet's Birth Day*.[38]

Though Edmund Conway fell short when compared to the French dancers, he authored a text, *Le Maître de Danse, Or, The Art of Dancing Cotillons*—astutely leading the title with its French version. Like Guillou's earlier manual, but less detailed, Conway's booklet describes balletic and ballroom techniques: the five positions of the feet and steps (as Conway listed them, *assemblé, sissonne, jetté, changes, chassé, balancez, ballotté, glissé, pas de basque, brizé, and pas bourré*) as well as patterns for couples in "cotillons," some bearing names with theatrical references, like "Le Barbiere de Seville" and "Cinderella." These were probably named for tunes from these popular operas, not for movement references to characters or plot.

Among the most enduring ballets the "English" dancers brought to U.S. stages was a work introduced in Chapter 1, *Cherry and Fair Star*, an excerpt of which reportedly appeared in Philadelphia in December 1822, soon after its April 1822 debut at Covent Garden.[39] The full ballet—sometimes called a "fairy spectacle," "melodramatic spectacle," "serio-comic romance," or "opera"—was given in February 1825 at the Chestnut Street Theatre, choreography by Charles Durang, featuring English and American dancers

Mrs. Wallack (as Fair Star) and the Hathwell and Parker children (as fairies). The libretto, freely varied over the decades, tells of a supposed brother-sister pair (Cherry and Fair Star, respectively), banished as infants from their royal home, Cyprus, to an enchanted island, and ignorant of their royal lineage. Raised by a kind islander, they later return to Cyprus in a complicated plot involving fairy magic and the honest, humane, and comic "slave" Topack, who helps save the now teenaged children from his conniving master. Magical and monstrous scenes engaged the genius of stage engineers and created opportunities for dances, combats, and miraculous rescues. All ends in the marriage of Cherry to his cousin—for so Fair Star proves to be—and their crowning as heirs to the Cypriot throne.

The plot touches issues at the forefront of U.S. concerns: the perceived exoticism of the Middle East, of particular interest after the early nineteenth-century contests with the Barbary states; the humanity of "slave" Topack; and the opportunity to observe women in action, including in the travesty role, Cherry. I have found no reference to Topack as a blackface character, but it is possible that interpretations included that depiction, as blackface characters stretch far into English and American theater history.[40] Topack not only showed up his master's inhumanity as a slave owner and evil conniver, but his behavior also depicted the enslaved as kindly and benevolent, despite their circumstances—reassuring to the mostly white audience. Travesty dancing—women dancing male roles in male dress, or men playing women—also had a long history in Europe, transgressing gender and moral norms as it offered opportunities for exploring alternative modes of expression and spectating. In Philadelphia's 1825 season, Cherry was played by Mrs. Darley, wife of English comedian John Darley. The dancing was primarily assigned to the fairies, but a soldiers' dance in act II, scene 2, a "pas de deux" between Cherry and Fair Star, and the wedding-coronation concluding the show involved large-scale choreographed celebration. The most challenging dance scene was the "Grove of Illusion" in act II.

Durang, who never saw the work produced in England, would have learned the ballet's details from English dancers with whom he worked, staging and choreographing it as his resources permitted, attempting to re-create the visual appeal of the original production.[41] Durang's trial-and-error efforts resulted in a rich description of producing the magical effects of the Grove of Illusion, in which "the numerous fairies" in the scene "were [to be] quadrupled."[42] This required "a bower in the centre of the stage, lined with mirror plates . . . variously placed, to reflect the real dancing fairies on the stage, and those suspended from the *borders* or moving about in the foliage." Durang "had daily taught some thirty children to form groups in various figures—to kneel and attitudinize at certain points on the stage, where these looking-glasses were fixed, to secure the reflection of the *sprites* in magnified numbers. . . . At the night rehearsal the scene was set as designed by the artist," Mr. H. Warren, yet "not a fairy was reflected to the eye of a single spectator. Neither *real* nor *pasteboard* fairy could be properly reflected. Here was a dilemma in optics"—a science much investigated at the time. Consultation with "opticians" proved ineffectual, portending "a supposed deathblow to a principal scene." But, with concerted creativity, "the fatal failure was, in a measure, obviated. The scene, happily, without the mirror adjuncts, was very beautiful," and later, "the glasses were so arranged as eventually to impart some novel effects as originally intended," while Durang continued experimenting with "poses and arabesque grouping of the *corps de ballet*." Stagecraft and staging evolved as U.S. artists learned new techniques from Europe. Beyond the Grove, other dramatic effects were brilliantly achieved, including a tree bursting into bloom, burning forests, and artificial waters on which a ship appeared to sail. "The scenery, effects, and acting of 'Cherry and Fair Star' were," Durang boasted, "taken as a combination of excellence, in this kind of theatrical exhibition, never surpassed on our stage," a marker of U.S. accomplishment. Manager Francis Wemyss agreed, singling out the show's "looking-glass bower and innumerable reflected representations of dancing cupids" in this visually splendid production, "attracting crowded houses."[43]

The dancing in *Cherry and Fair Star* would, according to Guillou's and Conway's texts, include familiar balletic vocabulary in complex arrangements—the "attitudinizing" and "arabesques" comprising individual dance postures and expressive, elegant group arrangements—as Durang mentioned.[44] But even the fine English and American dancers Mrs. Wallack and the Parkers, prepared by the fastidious Charles Durang, could not touch the French dancers, whose superior training gave them a finesse, fluidity, and virtuosity immediately recognized by U.S. audiences.

The French School

Part of a decades-long migration of French music and dance artists to the "New World," French stage performers forwarded Americans' grasp of refinement and elegance in stage dancing. Hutin first appeared in Philadelphia at the Chestnut Street Theatre in July 1827, after her U.S. debut with Achille in New York.[45] She advertised herself as trained at the Paris Opera, although reportedly she had recently danced at the Théâtre Royal Italien and/or the Gaîeté. She had good reason to highlight such training, for the U.S. public kept abreast of French ballet through reports from Europe; the Hutin-Achille partnership helped usher that art onto U.S. stages.[46] It caught on; but first, Hutin had to face the moral codes she offended. Philadelphia merchant J. Fisher Leaming wrote to his wife in April 1827, during a business trip to New York, that he went to see the French dancers, promised as "great attractions."[47] Yet he was "rather disgusted" by their performance, for "their clothes did not pretend to come below the knee. And when they made any great flourishes, they had no petticoats. Of course, they wear tight silk pants." New Yorkers too were scandalized at this early exposure to "the modern French school of dancing."[48] While "an anxious look of curiosity and expectation dwelt on every face" in the crowded house, "when the graceful *danseuse* came bounding like a startled fawn upon the stage, her light and scanty drapery floating in air, and her symmetrical proportions liberally displayed by the force of a bewildering *pirouette*, the cheeks of the greater portion of the audience were crimsoned with shame, and every lady in the lower tier of boxes immediately left the house. But," this chronicler noted wryly, "time works wondrous changes, and though for a while Turkish trowsers [sic] were adopted by the lady, they were finally discarded, and the common ballet-dresses, indecent though they be, were gradually endured, and are now looked upon as a matter of course." Despite the costume shock, that author recognized Hutin as "a skillful, graceful and daring dancer," much appreciated "by the admirers of her peculiar school of art." Philadelphia's literary ladies, in a magazine aimed at that market, were urged to support Hutin's and Achille's "attractive dancing" and assured of the suitability of her costume owing to the "slight alterations in dress" that the ballerina had undertaken.[49]

The costume scandal was grasped by New York's religious press, excoriating the theater's "*public exposure of a naked female*, rendered more shameless by a pretended but ineffectual concealment of her person and more dangerous by the fascinations of graceful gesture and attitude and the charm of music."[50] What better press could an artist wish for?—although some moralists called for prosecuting Hutin and her presenters for treason. Yet, within a month, the French artists had reportedly "danced down all opposition" and their "scientific displays" of dancing proved profitable.[51] When Clay caught them in buttoned-up Philadelphia, the lady had again donned those "petticoat trousers."

The claims for these dancers' art as "scientific" connects to the hierarchical quest of European American culture at the time. French ballet's syllabus, academic rigor, and molding of the body were seen by commentators as evidence of that school's modernity. The schematic, ranked order that Clay's depictions suggest in *Lessons in Dancing* relates to the Western pursuit of the ancient conception of the "great chain of being," with new methods and evidence sustained by the Linnaean classification system and furthered by more recent investigations of phrenologists, physiologists, and ethnologists.[52] The body-centered expressivity of dance allowed performers to highlight, exaggerate, or refute such qualities with appealing verve and virtuosity. The perception that ballet dancers achieved a pinnacle of human movement expression was supported by claims of their "scientific" mastery of motion, appealing to educated, forward-thinking, socially aspiring Americans.[53]

Theatrical dance technique of the time drew on the opera-ballet tradition as well as the spectacular movement and staging of the French boulevard theaters.[54] The passage of dancers, choreographers, and teachers between French and Italian academies (and beyond) created an international pool of evolving movement and choreographic material. Dancers like Hutin and Achille had academic training and stage experience, even if they were not among the stars of European theaters. The techniques they performed can be gleaned from ballet masters' texts, particularly those of Italian master Carlo Blasis, French teacher Michel Saint Léon, and the Frenchified Englishman E. A. Theleur. Their descriptions of classroom training show the transition from eighteenth-century baroque dance technique to the romantic aesthetic emerging in the early nineteenth century. Steps that professional ballet dancers would have mastered include the *temps de courant, coupé, attitude, grand rond-de-jambe, temps de chaconne, fouetté ballotté*, and *grand fouetté*, among others, embellished with *dégagé* or *développée* movements, changes of weight, direction, facing, and level. Their rising to the toe-tip in soft slippers required virtuosic balance and strength, with elegant coordination of the upper body and arms. Clay's print shows Hutin on a high half-pointe, perhaps matched by Achille, although his front-facing position makes this less evident. Both dancers show the upward vertical pull of ballet technique: lengthened legs, pointed toes, torsos elegantly upright, neck and head balancing easily on the spine. Hutin's arms are in a slightly relaxed reach *a la seconde*, while Achille's right arm is akimbo and the left rises and gestures side-upward. The dancers appear calm and coordinated, demonstrating the mastery that so impressed commentators.

Others of the French school soon arrived. Charles Durang rapturously described Charles and Caroline Ronzi Vestris in Philadelphia (Jan. 1829): "The novelty of the style of the dancers, and their graceful elegance, conquered fastidiousness. A Vestris mania resulted, pervading all orders of society, filling the theatre nightly. The dancing of these artistes without the dramatic accessories of the ballet"—pure, plotless dance—"as simply illustrated in a pas de deux was in itself a Terpsichorean drama—a 'dramatized' theme of enchanting steps and attitudes—exhibiting the 'poetry of motion' as an intellectuality [sic] of polished art."⁵⁵ Durang applied technical knowledge to his assessment: "Monsieur Vestris was of a tall and rather attenuated figure. He had great elasticity, vigor and power of artistic execution. . . . No effort was visible, but all was grace. Madame Vestris was a bijou [jewel] of natural loveliness, and, in dancing, the infinite counterpart of her husband. Her figure was rather short, yet she was the image of grace," offering "the charms of the Venus de Medicis," pointedly linking the Vestris' presentation with high-art classical sculpture. The *National Gazette*, which initially predicted the ballet costumes would cause the Vestris to fail, was won over, reporting that Mme. Ronzi Vestris "excited lively admiration by her dancing. This *artiste*, in grace and lightness of movement, far excels any of her predecessors on the American stage."⁵⁶ The *Daily Chronicle*'s "Colley Cibber" too was charmed by their pas de deux: "A repetition was called for, and insisted on till it was given—a most unreasonable imposition, no doubt, after severe exertion of near *ten* minutes." Both Durang and Cibber stressed the elegance and approbation of the fashionable audience, further embedding ballet in upper-class taste.

National Dances

Like the English performers before them, French dancers regularly performed interlude numbers—the Ronzi Vestris' pas de deux is an example. Often, interlude titles suggested versions of national dances, staples of nineteenth-century ballet repertoire inserted into longer ballets to mark a location's exoticism, bringing visual luster to the dancing with distinctive costumes and props. Examples from the French dancers' repertoires included a "Pas de Trois Peruvian" by Hutin and Achille (July 23, 1827); the Ronzi Vestris' "National Neopolitan Dance, called Tarantella" and a "Spanish Cachucha with Castinetts" (Jan. 15–17, 1829); and Constance and Celeste Kepler in a "Greek Romaika" (Sept. 29, 1829).⁵⁷ The "Peruvian" interlude may have been excerpted from the ballet *La Belle Peruvienne*, which Marvin McAllister describes as an "Indio-European" ballet designed to demonstrate the superiority of European over "savage" culture by showing how French dance refined a raw American native (a *belle sauvage*).⁵⁸ The ballet was presented in New York in March 1822 by Claude Labasse and M. Tatin, supported by U.S. dancers, including Philadelphians Julia (Catharine Juliet) and Charlotte Durang. When Hutin and Achille arrived in 1827, they joined Labasse, elevating his ballets to new levels of appeal.

English dancers too performed national dances in interludes: siblings Harriet and Henry Wells appeared in Philadelphia in 1827, offering English and Scottish works along with interludes titled "Turkish Pas de Deux"

(Oct. 10, 1827; Mar. 5, 1829), a "Mahometan Dance" (Oct. 11, 1827), and a "Grand Moorish Pas de Deux" (Jan. 1, 1829),[59] perhaps all the same dance. Europeans' curiosity about what they understood to be national dances was rooted in earlier ages of exploration, conquest, and colonization.[60] Dancing embodied spectators' curiosities about the distinctions, strangeness, and allure of different kinds of people, particularly when such dances were ordered and adjusted by European artists to meet theatrical tastes. As ethnologists in the late eighteenth and early nineteenth centuries highlighted and ranked what they perceived as varieties of human body and mind, theatrical dancing too grappled with those varieties: borders between stage and science, entertainment and education, were permeable.

Jocko *and* La Perouse

The ballet-pantomime *Jocko, or, the Brazilian Ape*, which debuted in Philadelphia in autumn 1825, brought that permeability to the fore, engaging themes of concern in Euro-American politics, science, and society. Its Philadelphia premiere, at the circus (Walnut Street), featured English clown James Kirby in the lead role, the Ape; his interpretation, wrote Durang, "has not been excelled in agility, action, or any of the peculiar and imitative attributes of this extraordinary animal, who seemingly possesses all the sense of humanity, except only the power of speech."[61] But Jocko spoke eloquently with his body. Kirby made a specialty of ape roles, having performed superbly as the chimpanzee in the 1801 pantomime-ballet *La Perouse; or, The Desolate Island*, by John Fawcett; it played in Philadelphia in 1822 and 1823.[62]

La Perouse featured several racial types, including South Sea island natives, an African servant, the French explorer Jean-François de Galaup, comte de La Pérouse, and his family. In the play, based on a melodrama by August von Kotzebue, the chimp saves the Frenchman and his family from the wrath of the island's natives, thus endowing the animal with a humanity the islanders are depicted as lacking. La Pérouse did not, in fact, unite with his wife during his Pacific journey, from which he and his crew never returned. But the fictional version of his story, like *Jocko*'s, fed Western audiences' curiosities and misconceptions and allowed dramatists to explore, with spectacular effects, dress, and movement, questions of race and humanity percolating through Euro-U.S. culture. Were apes and monkeys, in fact, branches of the human family? Were non-Europeans distinct species of humanity? Were human types ranked, rising from the mire of animal darkness to the light of what Western scientists saw as their own endowments? These concerns infused theatrical representations—as in the case of *La Perouse* and *Jocko*.[63]

Jocko, in various manifestations, would dance across Philadelphia's stages through the antebellum period and beyond. At the Paris premiere of Frédéric-Auguste Blache's ballet-pantomime (1825), the great dancer-acrobat Charles Mazurier played the Ape, setting a standard of dramatic finesse and visible virtuosity in the role.[64] The work's success led to versions by ballet notables Jules Perrot, Jean-Antoine Petipa, and Filippo Taglioni. The 1825 *Jocko* highlights the Ape's wit and sympathetic role in saving a European child, first from a shipwreck and later from a giant snake. Ape and child play imitative games, mirroring each other's movements, as they reach across their species' differences to find common sympathies, even humanity. Jane Goodall suggests that, in this work, "Jocko has replaced Adam as the missing link, which is no longer located in the metaphysical space between the divine and animal kingdoms," but "in the natural world, between animal and man."[65] The work's long popularity resulted, in part, from its engagement of theological-biological debates, reported in popular and scientific presses. An interesting note is the representation of Don Fernandez, the Portuguese planter-merchant and father of the rescued child, as an amateur scientist with a cabinet of curiosities and library of natural history (act I, sc. III), explaining his interest in Jocko. As noted earlier, scientists of the age, many with Philadelphia connections, were deeply engaged in creating biological taxonomies that would justify the racial rankings evident in the United States and beyond. *Jocko* also involved the pretty enslaved girl Cora, loved by Dominic, son of the plantation overseer who refuses to acknowledge their love owing to their caste and racial differences. Filling out the libretto are happy, loyal slave-characters who, after contentedly working the plantation's rice fields, are depicted in carefree song and dance, enlivening the ballet with "exotic" flavor.

Versions of the libretto feature not only Jocko's thrilling, expressive acrobatics, pantomime, and dancing but scenes identified as "ballets." One is a "Pas de Trois Brazilian" and another a "Pas de Six—La Chica," supported by the full ballet troupe carrying tambourines. The *pas de trois*, if alluding to truly "Brazilian" elements, might have blended African-sourced rhythms and European melodies, which came to characterize the music of that region.[66] In dance, this might translate to balletic vocabulary adapted to driving rhythms, with more varied use of lower torso and arms. Versions of *la chica* were danced throughout the Caribbean and South America, perhaps originating with Angolan or Congolese Africans enslaved in these areas. Europeans and Euro-Americans saw *la chica*, a couple dance, as passionately lascivious, emphasizing hip movements with the arms winding around the torso, as the male dancer enticed the female into tantalizing approaches and retreats. Its marked rhythmic accompaniment might be reflected in the libretto's reference to tambourines.

Though popular in Europe, *Jocko* became an enduring hit in the United States owing to its visceral expressions of emotion, mortal danger, and urgent questions troubling the young nation. Its balletic-acrobatic-spectacular realization highlighted the bodies delineated on the stage—child, slave, woman, ape—figures that different leaders in the scientific and political communities were attempting variously to grapple with, define, demote, understand, and control. Interest in medicine and ethnology in Philadelphia was a public matter accessible in the Academy of Natural Sciences museum and meeting reports,[67] and in newspaper articles on current "natural philosophy" findings. Peale's Museum offered visitors fine portraiture, archeological displays, biological oddities, and other intermixtures of art and science demonstrating the era's classificatory orders.

For U.S. viewers, setting *Jocko* in Brazil might have taken the edge off the work's racial representations—Europeans, natives, Africans, and a most humane ape. That location for the play also allowed for exciting dance rhythms and the presence of the giant snake, exotic flora, and the ape (although in fact no apes are native to South America). By the late 1850s, Jocko—a humpbacked blackface clown speaking stereotypical dialect—meshed with the enslaved Black as "the ape-negro" servant of hero Philip Lancey in a staging of Sylvanus Cobb's Revolutionary War story, *The Pioneer Patriot; Or, the Maid of the War-Path*.[68] In the play, the loyal, jovial Jocko closes the show reassuringly, dancing gaily to celebrate the U.S. victory over England and Lancey's marriage to the "maid." European American values would, this closing scene suggests, not only succeed, but gain the support of all nature's perceived ranks.

More (and More) French Ballet

Philadelphians had other opportunities to view the high art of ballet by French (and Italian) dancers later in the decade. Along with interlude dances, ballets appeared in operas: *The Barber of Seville* (1816, music by Gioachino Rossini), *The Caliph of Bagdad* (1800, music by François-Adrien Boieldieu), and *Nina, ou la folle par amour* (adapted as a ballet in 1813, choreography by Louis Milon, music by Louis-Luc Loiseau de Persius).[69] How true to their original conceptions these presentations were cannot be determined, given the paucity of available description and the interpretive flexibility in this period, but many dancers in these works were well-schooled and knew these ballets from European engagements. For example, Arnaud Léon, who led the "Grand Parisian Ballet Dancers" in their U.S. tour (1828–1829), trained at the Paris Opera under ballet master André-Jean-Jacques Deshayes and danced leading roles at the Opera for years, as well as working with Charles Didelot in

Russia.[70] He and wife Virginia Corby Léon had danced with Italian master Carlo Blasis. Others in the troupe—principals Bertrand Benoni and Estelle Bernardin, perhaps also trained at the Paris Opera—had much experience on continental stages. While Durang assessed the troupe's greatest strengths as "what the French call the *demi-caractére* and the comic," rather than "serious" ballets, he considered their work "well done," the corps "eminently talented," and Benoni's technique "astonishing."[71]

Before leaving Clay's ballet print, standing in for so much theatrical dancing of the period, I note an enduring classic of the ballet stage, appearing in January 1829: *La Fille mal gardée*, created in 1789 by ballet master Jean Dauberval of Bordeaux, staged at the Walnut Street Theatre as *La Mariage, or Love Protected by Folly*, by Léon and a troupe of French dancers arriving in New York in April 1828.[72] As early as 1794, the Chestnut Street had presented the ballet, titled *The Fruitless Precaution*, staged by William Francis, who had likely seen London performances of *La Fille mal gardée*. Philadelphia stages were graced by versions of Europe's best-known ballets.

Quakers, Tailors, and Sailors

The images after "Chesnut Street Theatre, Pas de deux" return to Clay's social-dance focus, as in the set's first three prints. The theater image appropriately connects upper to lower classes of social dancers, just as theaters themselves brought different social strata together in distinct seating areas to enjoy the same entertainments. Each print discussed here highlights a particular sphere of lower-class conviviality familiar to Philadelphians: the countryside, the shop, and the dock.

Union Hall, Jersey, Country Dance

The couple in this Jersey "country dance" are depicted in Quaker garb; the handwritten annotation on one set of the *Lessons* identifies the figures as "Friends, Quakers," judging the figures by dress (Figure 2.5). Clay, however, leaves it to the viewer to draw this conclusion, labeling the print only by place name and dance type. Where "Union Hall" was located is unclear, although the current town of Union, New Jersey, was once a heavily farmed area.[73] Or, Clay might have set his scene in a small-town gathering place, a "union hall." While the Quakers are much associated with Pennsylvania and Philadelphia, they also settled rural New Jersey, in easy reach of the Quaker City's markets, docks, and other "Friends," as the Quakers were known. Who the figures depicted by Clay were is unknown, but his intention to show them

Figure 2.5. "Union Hall, Jersey, Country Dance," Edward W. Clay, *Lessons in Dancing* (1828). *(Courtesy Rosenbach Museum & Library A 8281)*

as Quakers suggests sly social commentary, for the Society of Friends excoriated amusements like dancing and stage entertainments as "productive of a kind of frivolous levity, and of thoughtlessness with regard to the important duties of life."[74] Clay may have placed these figures in a rural setting because many Philadelphia Quakers had already "relaxed" their behaviors and dress in order to "rank among society."[75]

Clay's depiction mixes the levity excited by the dance with the modesty typical of Friends. The lady, executing an exuberant jump that carries her off the floor, folds her arms chastely across her torso, while her garb, from bonnet to shawl to sleeves, covers her thoroughly. The skirt, however, yields to the swirling rise of her elevation, exposing her ankles. The gent is more abandoned, smiling eagerly at his partner, flinging his arms invitingly open, and lifting a knee high in what might be a jig step, as "jigs were the common dances of the commonality," unlike the fancy "contre dances" of higher society.[76] The man's angular position contrasts with Clay's depiction of upper-class dancing in the "Fancy Ball" and "City Assembly" images' long lines and elegant positions, although these ballroom dancers, too, along with the

"Valtz" etching, reveal the sexual attraction stimulated by dancing. Clay highlights the Jersey dancers' ungainliness: compared with other contemporary paintings of common folk dancing—John Lewis Krimmel's "Merrymaking at a Wayside Inn" (c. 1811–1813) or "Country Frolic and Dance" (1819)[77]—Clay's figures seem awkward, angular, and expressive (she of embarrassed modesty struggling against the joy of movement, he of bold exuberance and sexual display). Jigging was, by the time of Clay's work, a well-known form of vernacular dance "passed down . . . from older to younger, informally, intuitively," bypassing the need for dancing masters.[78] Jigs, drawn from Celtic and English cultures, were also associated with African American dance and, thus, with lower classes.

Taylor's Alley, Jig

It is, thus, no surprise that the jig defined the urban workman in "Taylor's Alley, Jig" (Figure 2.6) in *Lessons in Dancing*. Clay's class-related commentary

Figure 2.6. "Taylor's Alley, Jig," Edward W. Clay, *Lessons in Dancing* (1828). *(Courtesy Rosenbach Museum & Library A 8281)*

is evident in the exaggerated clothing of the tailor and his partner—the lady's overly broad shoulder-line and too-many ribbons, the gent's enormous stovepipe hat and goofy facial expression. Unlike the modestly dressed "Quakers" in the previous print, this tailor and his lady spiff up their showy garb (befitting a tailor) for leisure hours of sociable dancing. The street "Taylor's alley" appeared in a February 1820 newspaper report that "a whole company, consisting of not less than thirty-five persons, were taken from a ballroom in Taylor's alley on Monday night, and conveyed to the watch house," probably for disturbing the peace with their raucous party.[79] No further details appear in the report and the location of a street bearing that name is unclear; Clay was likely pointing to the artisan neighborhoods where both Black and white workers lived and labored, rubbing shoulders on the streets and frequenting the same taverns.[80] Many such warrens of alleys were located near the waterfront, along the city's eastern edge.

Among the many shades of working-class allegiance and behavior, neighborhood taverns or unlicensed tippling cellars often drew locals, sometimes in interracial groups, for relaxation. These sites—reviled as "disgusting" and "bawdy" by moralists[81]—hosted drinking, camaraderie, cockfighting, gambling, brawling, music, social dancing, and flirtation. Many, but not all, women shunned such sites. Amid the taverns, grog shops, and tippling cellars, gangs too flourished, often young white men organized into volunteer fire companies, which, in this period, competed with one another not only to be first at a fire scene but also to control territory and claim the recognition that many in the working class asserted, loudly, had been usurped by political and economic elites.[82] Toward the end of the 1820s, an influx of Irish immigrants brought increased working-class pressure to the city, along with cultural practices from Ireland, including fresh infusions of dances like the jig. In the Jacksonian age, the energies and demands of working-class white men collided with efforts by cultural elites to educate, tame, and rank the U.S. population by political rights and social privilege. Black workers and leaders were striving for jobs, security, and rights as the Irish moved into neighborhoods and work settings that African Americans occupied. Interracial sociality, including in "dance halls" or "dance houses," continued as racial tensions heightened. In 1829, an anti-Black riot followed a demonstrative African American church service that some white neighbors found "above all restraint" and "intolerable."[83] That riot opened two decades of racial and ethnic violence in the City of Brotherly Love; Clay would deal with Black sociality separately, to be discussed.

Clay's scene in "Taylor's Alley" appears one of peaceful, happy conviviality: the gent, dressed in grays and browns, has his back to the viewer, allowing the colorful, flamboyant, front-facing lady to dominate the picture. Is her dress simply displaying her love of finery, her pleasure in dressing up after a day or week of work? Or is her showy outfit advertising her "career of pleasure"?[84] "Disorderly women"—prostitutes—frequented saloons, dance halls, public parks, marketplaces, and the theater to lure men into sin. Some such women announced their profession through their clothing: loud, revealing dress and the absence of a bonnet could signal a woman's "public" status. Dancers were assumed by some fastidious citizens to be prostitutes; at the least, they were connected to licentious public display of their bodies. The "Taylor's Alley" lady is, however, extravagantly bonneted and her arms and chest are adequately covered. We can assume she is, then, enjoying her best dress at a festive dance, where managing her enormous hat limits her to modest sideward swaying. The tailor, if such the gent is, appears freer in movement, like his country neighbor in the prior print, his arms akimbo, knees slightly bent, and pants revealing feet and ankles as he bobs from toe to toe.

Shippen Street, Double Shuffle

Clay's third image of working-class social dance (Figure 2.7) in *Lessons* takes us to the long Delaware River waterfront that defined much of Philadelphia's

Figure 2.7. "Shippen Street, Double Shuffle," Edward W. Clay, *Lessons in Dancing* (1828). *(Courtesy Rosenbach Museum & Library A 8281)*

antebellum life. Shippen Street (now Bainbridge) ran from the port westward in the busy Southwark area, not officially part of the city until 1854 and thus beyond civic regulation and constabulary. Shippen and environs had once been home to respectable merchants and businesses, but by Clay's time it was a rowdy warren of alleys with taverns, brothels, and gambling dens, easily accessed by mariners. The port area allowed seepage of different peoples and classes in and out of the city, and employed workers in trades and labor from bars to brothels, merchant exchanges to marketplaces, sailmakers to boatbuilders, officers to sailors.

It appears in Clay's etching to be one of the latter—a jolly tar—cutting capers with his lady in a hornpipe, a dance often associated with sailors in the British Isles and beyond; it was popular also with stage performers and in social dancing.[85] Theatrical versions might feature some balletic vocabulary, but the popular nature of the hornpipe Clay depicted here likely included steps like "cut the buckle," "pigeon wing," "whirligig," "grasshopper," and shuffles, including the "double shuffle down," related to the step Clay's sailor is performing. This sailor's clothing is much like that in which John Durang depicted himself in his memoir, written in the early 1820s: a cap with a blue hatband, a short blue jacket open in front, loose-fitting white pants to the ankles, and black dancing slippers; both figures also carry a cane, useful in miming a sailor's actions during the dance movement. The young woman with Clay's sailor appears in her work dress, simply colored to match her apron, which she modestly holds down against her skirt. She smiles lightly, gazing at her fellow as she flicks her feet in a movement less ankle-exposing than the Quaker lady's jump in "Union Hall."

Steps like the "double shuffle" were noticed by observers of lower-class dancing, including Charles Dickens in his evocation of Black dancer Juba (William Henry Lane) at a bar in New York's notorious Five Points district.[86] Shuffles, described as Africanist by Brenda Dixon Gottschild, were part of Black dancing of the time and were adopted by blackface minstrels claiming to "delineate" African American behavior and dancing. That a sailor's dance would embrace such movement exchanges across ethnicities, races, and classes makes sense, given sailors' roles in transmitting cultural material across seas and populations, and the dock's function as a place where intermixtures of voices, music, movement, views, and news occurred. Charles Durang made clear his disdain for the low cultural level of steps like the "heel and toe double-shuffle," practiced by blackface dancers on city stages. But theaters need audiences; seeing their own dances and steps on city main stages would draw popular audiences to performances of blackface dancers in coming decades, but at the time of Clay's print, blackface minstrelsy had not yet gelled. It was on the way, and Clay played a role in its emergence.

Black and Blackface

Clay's final print in *Lessons in Dancing* crosses from the interracial world of the waterfront to African American society. It points not only to Black social dance but, more so, to theatricalized "delineations" of African Americans, the prelude to blackface minstrelsy. Like the many avenues opened by investigation of the "Chesnut Street Theatre" print, this one image—"African Fancy Ball, Pat Juba" (Figure 2.8)—requires extended discussion.

African Fancy Ball, Pat Juba

"African Fancy Ball," like the other images in *Lessons*, shows a male-female couple. While the upper-class dancing depicted in *Lessons* places the gent on the left side of the image, the placement changes starting with the "Chesnut St. Theatre" print, where the gent is on the right; this continues through the popular dance images, including "African Fancy Ball." Unlike the other images, this last print shows the figures back-to-back, a placement Clay would repeat later in a more exaggerated print of African Americans.[87] The clothing

Figure 2.8. "African Fancy Ball, Pat Juba," Edward W. Clay, *Lessons in Dancing* (1828). *(Courtesy Rosenbach Museum & Library A 8281)*

in this image is black and white, with red touches in the lady's hat and skirt and the gent's jacket. He appears to wear yellow, perhaps kid, gloves. The figures' facial skin tones are clear: both African American, he is depicted as nearly black, while she is a lighter brown. Because of his dark facial coloration, the man's features are not discernible, but the lady's head is shown in profile to the left, revealing protruding lips and sloping forehead—features ethnologists and craniologists considered characteristic of Africans.[88] The gent's dress—fitted tailcoat, high-collared shirt, gloves, tight breeches, stockings, and dancing slippers—is much like that of the male figure in the "City Assembly" print, but exaggerated, the coat curving around his broad back and buttocks, with chokingly high collar and frilly shirt. The man's fingers are splayed—"jazz hands" in today's terms. The lady's figure is broader than others in this series: she seems stuffed into her fancy, bowed dress, with her wide back showing her necklaces and shoulders somewhat like that of the slim Mme. Hutin in the "Chesnut St. Theatre" print. The lady's high-feathered cap in "Pat Juba" brings to mind the gents' feathered hats in the "Chesnut St." and "Fancy Ball" prints. Since a "fancy ball" was understood to mean a masquerade party, Clay might be suggesting, with the title "African Fancy Ball," that these figures are, in fact, dressed up like "real" ladies and gentlemen, a status he depicts them failing to achieve, whatever they wear. Another commentator of the period also disparaged the "dressy blacks and dandy coloured beaux and belles," with their "aspirings and little vanities," calling themselves "gentlemen and ladies"; he condescendingly advised that abandoning their "overweening fondness for display and vainglory" would make them "more useful to themselves and others," while sustaining "the benevolent feelings which induced their emancipation" in Pennsylvania.[89]

In Clay's image, the "African" dancers are overdressed, showy, their body mechanics awry. They fail in their verticality: Clay depicts their feet not quite managing to elevate off the ground, and the man's knees are bent, as are his wide-spread elbows, betraying his lower-class movement status. These perceptibly outlandish displays might be regarded as knowing mockeries by the Black performers of white behavior, dress, and pretension—a means of coping and reversal among both enslaved and free African Americans in this period,[90] but Clay's opus of prints about Black people suggests that the mockery here was all his.

Some scholars discussing this print exempt it from overt racial satire, since other Clay images, drawn soon after this set, are so overtly vicious.[91] In Nancy Davison's extensive study of Clay and his work, she sees this print as "a prelude" to Clay's later, full-blown satires on both Black and white social pretension; I suggest it reveals his ongoing choice to mock lower-class and, especially, Black behavior, for he indulged in overt satire in *Lessons in Dancing* only in the lower-class images. Titling the piece "African Fancy Ball, Pat Juba" illuminates his view of these dancers, not only depicted as masquerading in a character not their own but inevitably bound to a movement world associated with servitude. "Patting juba" referred to African-based percussive practices by enslaved African Americans; it could involve tapping the feet on the floor, clapping hands, snapping fingers, and slapping or patting shoulders, knees, and hips to create complex dance rhythms, even without drums (often outlawed on plantations), engaging the entire body in motion.[92] Surely no genteel couple of any race in the United States at this time would have practiced such dancing at a ball, but Clay highlights this ascribed faux pas in labeling his portrayal.

The first part of the title for this print is identical to that of an article published in 1828 about just such an "African Fancy Ball" in Philadelphia, reportedly held in February 1828.[93] The outrage and mockery expressed by some members of the city's white population at the formality of a genteel Black ball, and the malicious delight of writers describing white hoodlums' attack on arriving ball guests, brought this gathering to the attention of readers in the Quaker City and beyond. It drew responses from the Black press, including *Freedom's Journal*, the nation's first African American newspaper, widely read in Philadelphia. The event had apparently gathered the city's leading Black residents, dancing to the music of Francis Johnson in a hall decorated with liberation motifs. This grand gathering was beyond toleration for some poor whites as well as powerholders, which led to physical attacks on the guests and verbal attacks in newspapers. As Marvin McAllister points out, efforts by African Americans to claim "refinement" as an option for Black, rather than only for white, bodies deeply disturbed advocates of racial hierarchy as well as those who feared competition for jobs and resources.[94] Angry responses from African American commentators, protesting treatment of this gathering by white brawlers and reporters, hint that elite Black balls were not rare in some antebellum U.S. cities, although Black people in Philadelphia kept their refined sociality well protected from white eyes, hindering its detection now by historians. The mocking reports in the white press of Black people "emulating" their betters, of the company's longing for "amalgamation" (miscegenation), and of noted Black community leaders appearing in silly masquerade garb infuriated African American respondents, but the humor that white writers unreeled was spread across much-reproduced and imitated graphic depictions, by Clay and others, of ludicrous, failed Black aspiration, often set in elite contexts like the ballroom.

Later in 1828, Clay unleashed fuller racial satire in his ongoing series *Life in Philadelphia*, likely inspired by social parodies he saw in London, particularly cartoonists Isaac and George Cruikshank's *Life in London* illustrations (1821).[95] While Clay mocked white social pretension as well as Black, he focused more of the *Life in Philadelphia* prints—and in greater detail—on the latter. This series depicts aspiring "Black" Philadelphians shopping, making social calls, courting, singing, strutting the streets, speaking outlandish dialect, and dancing. The dance images are known by the titles, "How you like de Waltz, Mr. Lorenzo?," "Shall I hab de honour to dance de next quadrille . . . ?," and "Back to Back." This last print calls on the "African Fancy Ball, Pat Juba" image, detailing the dancers' facial features, further exaggerating their clothing, and giving the dancers' movements more spread, angularity, and proximity to the other partner. "Back to Back" includes a line of absurd dialogue, which the gent appears to speak to his lady over his shoulder: "I reckon I've cotched de figure now!"—as if he is watching and copying ("aping") someone's steps. In "How you like de Waltz," Clay not only puffs up the characters' hair, hat, dress, and lips, but also makes their movements grotesque with exaggerated inward or outward leg rotation, misshapen feet, and absurd facial expressions. The question about liking the waltz is the lady's, to which Mr. Lorenzo responds, "'Pon de honour ob a gentleman I tink it vastly indelicate—Only fit for de common people!!" In the third dance-related *Life in Philadelphia* print, the question, "Shall I hab de honour to dance de next quadrille wid you, Miss Minta?" is asked by the bowing, hat-doffing gent, while the broad, dark, and neckless lady responds, "Tank you, Mr. Cato—wid much pleasure, only I'm engaged for de nine next set!" Again, both are over-coiffed, overdressed, so dark and awkward physically that Clay may have been alluding to masquerading ape figures, drawing on public awareness of scientists' hominid rankings. Clay's cartoon "A Dead Cut" will be discussed in the subsequent chapter, drawing closer connections to blackface minstrelsy.

Among Clay's later and pointedly political images were two published in 1839, "An Amalgamation Waltz" and "An Amalgamation Polka," in a series of anti-abolition cartoons highlighting the horrors of miscegenation that Clay and others claimed abolition would precipitate.[96] The cartoons were enhanced with text and portraits of political, intellectual, and social leaders whom Clay saw as pushing the nation toward racial mixing. The "Waltz" and "Polka" images in the series show interracial dancing, flirtation, and physical affection among elegantly dressed ladies and gents in well-appointed ballrooms. Clay's objective was purely political, as no such interracial ballroom encounters occurred in the United States, but his pointed association of dancing with elegant sociality shows his views of the body's expressivity and dangerous allures. While Clay's later cartoons increased in virulence after the 1820s, he prepared the public for blackface minstrelsy's exploitation of Black figures and behaviors with these early graphics.

Early Black[face] Performance

The explosion of blackface performance is widely credited to the "sensational" stardom of T. D. Rice as Jim Crow, an act he debuted in 1828 on the western U.S. tour circuit, but Philadelphia—like other towns and cities—had seen blackface performances well before. English dramas of the late seventeenth century had included "Black" characters, played by white actors in blackface. Many such works portrayed these figures sympathetically, if condescendingly, sometimes in plots with antislavery sentiments. The most widely performed African character in the early United States was Shakespeare's Othello, played in shades of makeup and interpretation from the Moorish Arabic to the Black African.[97] Thomas Southerne's late seventeenth-century dramatic adaptation of Aphra Behn's novel *Oroonoko* featured an admirable African protagonist, and in Colman and Arnold's *Inkle and Yarico* (1787), the title's noble-native maiden was variously depicted as Black or Native American. Such dramas appeared on U.S. stages along with plays that included features ascribed to Black dialect and behavior that became stereotypes of the minstrel stage—the slave as lazy, thieving, tricky, and entertaining in song and dance. As Dale Cockrell notes, stage representations made clear that "to be black was to be, at best, comic and happy, perhaps musical, and at worst, unfortunate."[98]

Homegrown American contributions to "Black" stage characterization appeared by the late eighteenth century. In the signal year 1776, Philadelphian John Leacock wrote the play *The Fall of British Tyranny*, in which Major Cudjo, an escaped "slave" leading a pro-British Black regiment during the War for Independence, assures "Lord Kidnapper" in dialect that he and his men would shoot dead his master and other rebels.[99] The British promise to free enslaved people who joined their cause appealed to some Black Americans, while others, like Philadelphia's business leader James Forten, fought against the British. Philadelphia artisan John Murdock, who survived the devastating 1793 yellow fever outbreak owing, in part, to tireless efforts of the city's Black community in ministering to the sick, wrote the antislavery play *The Triumphs of Love; or, Happy Reconciliations*, produced in 1795, with its sympathetic, dialect-speaking "slave"-character, Sambo.[100] In 1798, Murdock authored *The Politicians, or A State of Things*, in which free Black characters Cato, Caesar, and Pompey comment, in dialect, on current events. Harlequinades, popular in England and America, featured the black-masked servant Harlequin, who was specifically connected to "Negro" delineation in John Durang's 1789 Philadelphia performance of *Robinson Crusoe; or, Harlequin Friday*. That work was transformed a year later into *Robinson Crusoe; or, the Genius of Columbia*, involving characters in "savage," "Indian," and "Negro" dances.

The African Theatre

One group of performers, not based in Philadelphia, offered audiences plays featuring actual African Americans, not corked-up white players. New York's African Grove Theatre, also called the African Theatre, presented a range of familiar and new plays and other acts, primarily from standard theatrical repertoire.[101] This remarkable endeavor, from about 1821 to 1827, was led by William Brown, who garnered broad cosmopolitan experience through service as a ship's steward. This he applied to his theatrical offerings, presenting the usual mixture, for the time, of serious and light, longer and shorter, dramatic, musical, and danced entertainments to audiences including but not limited to African Americans. The performers were nearly all Black men and women, with two stars—Ira Aldridge and James Hewlett, the latter having served, like Brown, as a ship's steward. Records of the African Grove's bills include several plays with African characters: *Othello*; Fawcett's pantomime-play *Obi, or Three-Finger'd Jack*; and Brown's original *Drama of King Shotaway*. While most of these works had Brown's Black actors "whiting up" to play characters assumed to be Caucasian, *Obi* and *King Shotaway* featured powerful Caribbean Black protagonists. Even in comic works like Moncrieff's *Tom and Jerry, or, Life in London*, the African Grove highlighted Black themes, inserting into that play a tragic love story, "Life at the Slave Market." Hewlett, like most actors of the day, sang and danced; he wrote, choreographed, and performed the ballet-pantomime *Asama* (Oct. 1821), an "Indian" romance featuring a noble "*belle sauvage*." Hewlett also created *Balililon* (June 1823), billed as a ballet, with scenes of combat and an "Indian War Dance."[102] As Brown's theatrical endeavor in New York closed, one of the African Theatre's stars headed to Pennsylvania.

In January 1826, Hewlett performed in Philadelphia at 62 1/2 S. Fourth Street, which appears to have been a frequent entertainment site for African Americans. A report on the February 1828 "African Fancy Ball," discussed earlier, placed that event at "the Assembly Room in Fourth St.," perhaps the same location Hewlett used. His "Grand Entertainments," with scenes from *Othello, Richard III, Hamlet*, and *King Lear*, may have included supporting actors, unnamed in sources; proudly announced was Francis Johnson's all-Black band in appropriate musical support.[103] In gratitude to the band,

Hewlett appeared in a benefit performance for Johnson. No dancing is mentioned, although it is unlikely that an actor of the period would put across a song without lively physicality. Hewlett appears to have performed the following year in York and Lancaster, Pennsylvania, which suggests he may have played more towns along the westward route from Philadelphia. While the African Grove's other known star, Ira Aldridge, made his career primarily in England after 1824, Hewlett remained in the United States and appears to have inspired an English visitor to adopt and mock Black character.

Trip to and through America

English comedian Charles Mathews was famed for one-man shows demanding lightning-quick changes from one figure to another as he played all characters in a skit. This he accomplished through costume elements, vocal and dialect shifts, and movement choices, but probably without time for blacking up in racial depictions.[104] On his 1823 to 1824 U.S. tour, he visited New York's African Grove, observing James Hewlett, who included Mathews among the actors whose styles Hewlett acknowledged in his performances. In one of Mathews's shows, he performed his burlesque of Hewlett playing *Hamlet*. Hewlett responded with a witty, if deeply offended, letter published in New York's *National Advocate*, shaming Mathews for having "lampooned... a brother actor," particularly for that "brother's" complexion, a choice "so unworthy" of Mathews's "genius and humanity."

Undeterred, and delighted by his discovery of "Negro" caricature and other "American" types, Mathews toured to Philadelphia in March 1823,[105] where audiences packed the Chestnut Street Theatre for his imitations of famous actors, perhaps including Hewlett's version of *Hamlet*. In his tightly woven character studies, which Philadelphians found hilarious, he debuted bits of what became his popular show, *Trip to America*, with the fat, fiddling, dancing, grinning "slave" character, Agamemnon, in the skit "All Well at Natchitoches," singing the "real Negro melody," "Opossum up a Gum Tree."[106] This jolly "slave" became the centerpiece of illustrations in Mathews's book, *The London Mathews*, published in Philadelphia. He closely observed other African American figures—preachers, coach drivers, ladies promenading—writing from Philadelphia to a friend, "I shall be rich in black fun"[107]—"fun" that would shape his gestating *Trip to America*. Goodall links this work—in which Mathews also depicted Yankees, immigrants, U.S. social aspirants, and the elite—to the ranked classificatory schemes of Western ethnologists: Mathews's act offered a theatrical parallel to Clay's *Lessons in Dancing*. In *Trip to America*, Mathews transformed the specimens of humanity he encountered into English stage vocabulary, "processing cultural strangeness through his own body, and thereby rendering it digestible" to English audiences.[108] The processing of strangeness, grappling with what were seen as radical differences in humankind, was of urgent political concern to U.S. audiences too, making both Mathews's dramatizations and Clay's cartoons of "Blackness" widely appealing to American audiences.

Philadelphians had their own contenders as blackface pioneers. Charles Durang credits precedence in such depictions to the city's Louis Mestayer, "the father of Ethiopian characters," who played "Sambo, the negro servant" in the play *Modern Honor* at Vauxhall summer theater in July 1823. Durang embraced Sambo as an American worthy of representing the new nation: "We would humbly propound the question, why should not the American character and its subjects become the basis of stage representation, and thus erect the superstructure of an American drama harmonizing with our institutions?"[109] Along with Yankees, frontiersmen, and other "American" types, Sambo-and-slavery was seen to deserve a place among the nation's "institutions." Shortly after Mathews's Philadelphia successes, another entrant into the business of "Ethiopian" delineation appeared: in June 1827, William Kelly of the Walnut Street Theatre sang and, surely, animated the blackface song "Coal Black Rose." The widely published sheet music was sometimes illustrated with figures drawn from Clay's "Pat Juba" and "Shall I hab de honour." The song composed by Philadelphia's John Clemens (according to Durang), was adopted by blackface player George Washington Dixon, but some Philadelphia historians tout their city's precedence in the song's performance: "The air of this piece became immensely popular. It was sung in parlors, hummed in offices, whistled in the streets, and performed by bands. No single piece of music had ever been so treated."[110] Rice's "Jump Jim Crow" dance-song would soon surpass it.

Beyond Clay: Black People Depicted in Art

Beyond Clay, Thackara, and Johnston, other artists, less intent on mockery, also depicted Black figures and dance in this period. While living in Philadelphia, John Lewis Krimmel observed life and leisure in and around the area and often included African American figures in his works. "Merrymaking at a Wayside Inn" (c. 1811–1813) and "Country Frolic and Dance/Barroom Dancing" (1819) show Black fiddlers playing for white dancers in relaxed (not elite) public settings, indicating the pervasive role of Black musicians in white sociality at all class levels. Several of Krimmel's works include Black peddlers, servants, and folks in the streets, offering a glimpse of everyday interraciality as the artist saw it. The painting "Black People's Prayer Meeting," sometimes attributed to Russian tourist-artist Pavel Svinin,[111] depicts exuberant, dancelike spiritual expression that some white observers found so unnerving in African American Christian worship. Drawing on his Long Island (New York) home, William Sidney Mount also depicted everyday Black life, including scenes of music and dance, which Mount, as a fiddler, knew well.

A known Philadelphia artist of the 1820s was Black: Moses Williams was an expert "cutter of profiles" during and after his servitude under Charles Willson Peale at Peale's Museum.[112] There, Williams mastered use of the "physiognotrace"—a device, understood to create an exact copy of the sitter's profile, that required the operator's judgment, skill, and interpretation. While Williams's silhouette-cutting did not include depictions of full-bodied displays like dancing, his own life crossed into the performative, as Peale sent him into the street costumed as an "Indian" to disseminate handbills of museum displays. As Williams was employed in constructing the hierarchical displays of the museum, he was treated as a feature of that very schema, both in Peale's reference to him as "my Molatto Man Moses," and in Williams's display as a figure of racial otherness.

What "lessons in dancing" could Clay's images teach? What might he mean by the work's subtitle, "Attitude Is Everything"? The series might be seen as explicating the social hierarchy in the United States, all elements of which were embroiled in shaping the nation's political, economic, and intellectual spheres. During the 1820s, the United States moved toward a social bifurcation visible on both the social-dance floor and the stage: European elegance—the dancing assembly and ballet—on one hand, and on the other popular social dances and blackface entertainment claimed as distinct "American" cultural contributions. Clay's taxonomic *Lessons in Dancing* and the broader cultural manifestations they touch upon reveal artists' and viewers' stakes in the ways that people—in bodies of different complexions, behaviors, sexes, and ethnicities—moved and expressed themselves.

Clay's depictions hint at such differences. Transgressing social spheres, women like Mme. Hutin took center stage in ballets displaying their powerful physical and expressive capacities, often in service of "exotic" plots featuring peoples and creatures of wild imagination. Black actors attempted to establish a permanent theatrical role for themselves, while white performers usurped what they claimed as Black language, movement, and music for their own blackface songs and dances. Here, Clay's *Lessons* reveal *attitudes* about presenting, seeing, and judging bodies in motion, in danced expression—a source of pleasure for Americans of many spheres. Elite white social dancers looked to Europe (England, France) for models, while other Americans found bodily delight in dancing that represented their own perceived histories, experiences, environment, concerns, and aspirations. All were delineated in *Lessons*, which contributed to creating "a shared national visual language"[113] of social and racial types, bodily expression, and political hierarchy, interlacing the "pleasures" of the time and its "tumult."

3

The 1830s

Politics Performed

Two operas performed in Philadelphia in the 1830s exemplify the engagement of theatrical dance with political issues. *La Bayadere; Or, the Maid of Cashmere* was presented in 1834 by French ballerina Mme. Celeste at the Chestnut Street Theatre; the work inspired U.S-born ballerinas to take the stage. *Bone Squash Diavolo*, playing a year later at the Walnut Street Theatre, was created by, and starred, U.S. performer T. D. Rice; it was taken up by other blackface players, while Rice continued performing and altering the work as definitions of who did and did not belong to or in the United States were enacted in theaters and beyond. Struggles over representation, citizenship, and voting rights fed themes and readings on the nation's stages.[1] This chapter illuminates *intersections of politics with aesthetic, social, and scientific concerns*, shaping the meanings performers and viewers invested in these operas and related works. As Grey Gundaker notes, "The 1830s were a pivotal decade when polarities between North and South became firmly entrenched," forecasting the divisive rift of civil war.[2] Women were demanding, and playing, ever larger roles in that and other social contests. As the human body became a central factor in determining human status, citizenship, and political power, dance served as a potent register of expression and interpretation.

Humanity and Citizenship

On the cusp of the 1830s, a publication by a Black author contributed to white anxieties of racial rebellion in the United States: David Walker's *Appeal in Four Articles, With a Preamble to the Colored Citizens of the World* (1829) spread across the nation, despite bans and suppression. Walker, born in 1786 in North Carolina, settled in the early 1820s in Philadelphia, where he met and admired Richard Allen, bishop of Mother Bethel A.M.E. Church.[3] Philadelphia's proximity to the South made it a first stop for many fugitives from enslavement and a hunting ground for those seeking to recapture them. Thus, Walker relocated northward, to Boston, where he wrote his *Appeal*, a forceful denunciation of the treatment of African-descended people in America. Walker excoriated and refuted claims, based on bodily features and supposed concomitant moral capacities, that "colored citizens" were less than human, assuring readers that "we are *men*, notwithstanding our *improminent noses* and *woolly heads*." Unlike white people, Black people had not enslaved and beaten others, prevented anyone "from learning to read the Word of God," nor lied about others "by holding them up to the world as a tribe of TALKING APES."

Two years after Walker's *Appeal* was published, Nat Turner's 1831 insurrection in Pennsylvania's neighbor state Virginia further enflamed white anxieties.[4] Would violent rebellion by African Americans, aided by white abolitionists, be unleashed in Pennsylvania, with its sensitive borderline position and liberal reputation? Calls surged to suppress African American agency and citizenship, including voting rights. A Philadelphia magazine demanded expulsion of "a class of persons who are neither freemen nor slaves," for "the mark set on them by Nature"—their complexions, their bodies—"precludes their enjoyment, in this country, of the privileges of the former; and the laws of the land do not allow them to be reduced to the latter," leaving them "degraded, profligate, vicious, turbulent and discontent."[5] Minstrelsy on page and stage animated such claims.

Pennsylvania's constitution was initially among the most liberal of any state, guaranteeing suffrage to all taxpaying free men, twenty-one years of age or older, with a year's (later, two years') state residence.[6] In the early nineteenth century, while no law forbade free African American men in Philadelphia to vote, the racial explosivity that overwhelmed the city with deadly anti-Black riots, peaking in the 1830s, deterred men "of Colour" from attempting to do so.[7] Given the city's large free Black population—over 14,500 people by 1830—the power of this minority, if permitted to vote, was undeniable. But that permission was inconceivable to those who feared Pennsylvania was already overrun by fugitives from slavery and others unprepared for useful employment, let alone responsible citizenship.[8]

Philadelphia's Black leaders were, nonetheless, politically active, organizing the nation's First Annual Convention of People of Colour in 1831, focusing on education, proposals for African colonization, race consciousness, and abolition. Philadelphia was the site of four subsequent "coloured" conventions that decade and a center of Black associations addressing educational, moral reform, and political issues.⁹ These conventions were dominated by men, but in 1835, Philadelphia's African American activists formed the American Moral Reform Society, welcoming white participants and women.¹⁰ On the other hand, the American Anti-Slavery Society (AASS), formed in Philadelphia in 1833 as an immediatist, interracial abolition group, excluded women. In response, the interracial Philadelphia Female Anti-Slavery Society formed, a proving ground for women, Black and white, to gain experience as organizers and public figures.¹¹ These skills prepared them for the women's suffrage movement and eventually led some to stages as public lecturers. Women's literary groups also offered women of both races opportunities to read, lead, and enact members' writings, a contribution to women's performance opportunities that ballet dancers would greatly expand.¹²

In 1837, during a financial panic that enflamed social anxieties (and tilted theaters toward bankruptcy), state legislation homed in on voting rights. A statewide convention, aimed at wide-ranging changes to Pennsylvania's constitution, debated an amendment for restricting the franchise to *white men* only. Speaking in favor, Bucks County delegate E. T. McDowell invoked science, warning that, as the constitution stood, taxpaying free Black men could not be legally denied the vote as, he conceded, "they were human beings and not *baboons* as some contended";¹³ Jocko could not vote, but unless specifically forbidden, African Americans could, an outcome McDowell feared. To combat the disenfranchisement proposal, abolitionists documented African Americans in Pennsylvania as overwhelmingly hardworking, taxpaying, self-sustaining, temperate, and no drain on resources.¹⁴ Given prohibitions and prejudices faced by that population, such outcomes were a noteworthy argument for African American civic engagement. The debate plodded and raged from spring 1837 to January 1838, when the amendment narrowly passed the legislature. Narrowly again, Pennsylvania voters confirmed it, formally stripping Black Pennsylvanians of the franchise.

Philadelphia's abolitionists fought on. In May 1838, facing difficulties in finding sites to host their gatherings, several abolitionist societies together built and opened their own meeting place, Pennsylvania Hall, dedicated to "Virtue, Liberty, and Independence."¹⁵ On Sixth Street between Arch and Race, near Independence Hall, it housed meetings of the AASS and the PFASS in its three-day existence. But during the Anti-Slavery Convention of American Women, opened on May 16, 1838, riotous crowds claiming "moral repulsion" at the mixing of Black men and white women among conference attendees set the hall aflame, burning it to the ground. Undaunted by terror and tragedy, the women abolitionists held the 1839 national convention in the City of Brotherly Love, although finding a site to host them proved nearly impossible. The mayor, fearing a repeat of violence, urged the ladies to avoid evening meetings, refrain from interacting with Black men, and hasten the proceedings to a close. Quaker feminist and PFASS leader Lucretia Mott, later a guiding light for women's rights, responded that no evening meetings were planned since, "to the shame of Philadelphia," the only site willing to rent to the women was an unroofed riding school, precluding nighttime lighting. She further noted, "We had never made a parade, as charged upon us, of walking with colored people, and should do as we had done before—walk with them as occasion offered," for "it was a principle with us, which we could not yield, to make no distinction on account of color."[16] The women forming this association called upon prominent Black Philadelphian James McCrummell to inform them about organizational functioning; leading Black men of the city were well versed in concerted action. Like that of African Americans at this time, Mott wrote, women's status was "the exact definition of political slavery": they paid taxes, were subject to law, but had no power to affect legislation through voting or political engagement. Mott perceived that, like African-descended people, women were restricted by false understandings of their bodies: "Man assumes, that the present is the original state designed for woman, that the existing differences" in cultural, social, and legal status "are not arbitrary nor the result of accident, but grounded in nature"—in the body. To present and see those bodies as strong, expressive, independent agents dancing across U.S. stages was itself a political statement.

Science and Others: The Politics of Measurement

Philadelphia physicians in this period substantiated Mott's view regarding readings of women's bodies. Addressing female "diseases"—a term then often associated with women's physical processes—Dr. Dewees remarked on "the moral and physical distinctions" between the sexes.[17] Women's delicate frames and organs were subject to the "evils" of the birthing process, her very reason for being. From bones to muscles, blood to lymph, woman was liable to "greater tenuity [sic] and susceptibility" both physically and morally. Her uterus—"an animal confined within another animal"—collaborated with the brain to stimulate "hysteria." Given such complications, Dewees's colleague, Dr. Hodge, asserted that only men, medically trained in the emerging field of obstetrics, could respond effectively to the "moments of sudden alarm and danger" that parturition entailed.[18] Male practitioners were "cautious, prudent, circumspect, yet bold, self-possessed, energetic," capable of "sound judgment" and "decided action." In contrast, the "ignorant females" who had served for millennia as midwives, before elevation of obstetrics to a medical discipline, only "created difficulties" and must be swept away to protect women and their offspring. Yet, female health could be bolstered by regular exercise, including "dancing moderately."[19] A popular lady's *Pocket-Book* offered similar advice: the young woman who, "in the pursuit of folly or of dissipation, exhausts the energies of her constitution," would surely "be doomed to be a childless wife, or be cursed with a short-lived, deformed and puny race of offspring, the hapless victims of a mother's folly."[20] Rather, in service to her future maternal role, a girl should engage in "running races, trundling a hoop, skipping with a rope," and dancing, in well-aired spaces and unrestrictive clothing, under family supervision, without extreme exertion.

Dr. Caldwell found that women's mental capacities fit them to serve as "mothers [who] must be the teachers" in their family's own "school of morals"—a role a woman would find "a source of the purest and most elevated enjoyment," if she were "spotless in her morals, refined in her taste, graceful in her manners, and pious in her sentiments."[21] Such qualities, Caldwell asserted, provided "the inglorious caste" of males "the thrill of admiration, and the glow of delight." That inglorious caste was, just then, thrilling to the allure of stage dancers like Mlle./Mme. Celeste, a woman whose motherhood, discussed later, was condemned by some as beneath exemplary. Caldwell's text also supported his conviction of the superiority of the "Caucasian" race over others, symbolized by the perfection depicted in classical Greek statuary like the lofty-browed Apollo Belvedere, hallmark of male beauty.[22] In contrast, Caldwell posed the example of an allegedly flat-headed Carib chieftain about whom claims of "remarkable talent" had circulated. Caldwell countered that the Caribs were "now nearly, if not quite, extinct" (he declined explaining why) and thus were unavailable for study by trained men of science. Nonetheless, Caldwell condemned the Caribs for "ferocity, savagism, and revolting brutality": judging "the size and shape of their heads" phrenologically, "their intellect was extremely limited," comparable to "the inferior animals." Lacking all "morality," their "faculties" of "Secretiveness, Covetiveness, and other animal propensities" were outsize. Caldwell believed that, compared to men of his racial type, the Caribs belonged to the realm of "the inferior animals."

Caldwell's work—perhaps, his attention in *Phrenology Vindicated* to Indigenous Americans—inspired renowned ethnologist and Philadelphia physician Samuel George Morton, who assembled a collection of nearly a thousand human skulls ("the American Golgotha") from the world over.[23] In *Crania Americana* (1839), Morton acknowledged Caldwell's work and influence,[24] but the scale of Morton's collecting, measuring, analysis, and theorization far exceeded Caldwell's. *Crania Americana* compared skulls of "various aboriginal nations of North and South America," prefaced by an "essay on the varieties of the human species." Subdued in statements that might undermine biblical claims of human unity, Morton nonetheless provided the basis for a full-fledged polygenist creation theory. His "groupings" of humans by "similarity of physical and moral character, and language" (p. 4) instructed readers in interpreting bodies and behaviors they viewed in their streets and saw essentialized, exoticized, and elevated on their stages.

The aesthetic base of Morton's categorization is evident in his language for each race.[25] Caucasians Morton described having "fair skin," "hair fine," the skull "full and elevated," and "distinguished" by "the highest intellectual endowments." His language for the Native "American Race" included descriptors like "lank hair," "deficient beard," "brow low," "averse to cultivation, and slow in acquiring knowledge; restless, revengeful," recalling Caldwell on the Caribs. In the "Ethiopian Race," Morton saw "lips thick," "black, woolly hair," "forehead low," "jaws projecting," in "disposition," "joyous, flexible, and indolent; while the many nations which compose this race present a singular diversity of intellectual character, of which the far extreme is the lowest grade of humanity" (p. 6). Such descriptors became markers of race in caricatures on blackface stages, animated by costume, makeup, tone, and movement qualities. Some African peoples, Morton asserted, were "the nearest approximation to the lower animals" (p. 90), intermediary between humans and primates. These views shaped U.S. public culture; Scottish visitor Thomas Hamilton remarked in 1833 that, in his U.S. travels, he would frequently "hear it gravely maintained by men of education and intelligence, that the Negroes were an inferior race, a link as it were between man and the brutes."[26]

Body-focused sciences stimulated popular interest in observing bodies as well as opportunities for showmanship. Aiming at popular audiences, phrenologists advertised their affordable, entertaining demonstrations of head-reading, with lectures and sales of charts and texts.[27] Today, phrenology is closely associated with race-science theories, but in its heyday many liberal thinkers supported it, including African American spokesmen Martin Delany and Frederick Douglass. Professionals claimed that an individual's deficiencies, identified through cranial examination, could be ameliorated under a trained phrenologist's guidance, forwarding Americans' drive for self-improvement. Even as the scientific community moved past phrenology, it remained of popular interest, supporting public interpretations of racial and gender-based distinctions.[28]

The omnipresence of "bumpologists," as popular head-readers were disdainfully called, was one cause of phrenology's waning status among serious scientists. Public exhibitions proved a source of income for some, and of satire for cartoonists like David Claypoole Johnston.[29] Among the popularizers were brothers Orson and Lorenzo Fowler, the "phrenological Fowlers."[30] Committed to a belief in phrenology's potential for social improvement, their views were liberal, antislavery, and profeminist, as well as entrepreneurial and popularizing. Their museum and head-reading salon in New York were thronged, and they opened a Philadelphia branch. To support the enterprise, the Fowlers recruited sister Charlotte; Lorenzo's wife, Lydia (the second woman in the United States to receive a medical degree); and half-sister Almira, studying at Philadelphia's Female Medical College. Orson Fowler lectured on topics like "Phrenology and Matrimony," "Maternity" (a lecture "to Women"), and "Temperance," also offering his personal "Examination of Heads."[31] The Fowlers published the *American Phrenological Journal* in Philadelphia from 1838 to 1842. An article in a later issue assured readers that "the coloured man has more natural talent than is generally ascribed to him; and which culture will soon develop,"[32] perhaps stimulating phrenological engagement among African Americans, who entered a crowded field of experts, personal advisors, and entertainers. In June 1831, "Mr. Lewis George Wells, a gentleman of colour," announced "a course of lectures at Baltimore on Phrenology." The editor added, "In his *carte de invitation*, he includes 'ladies and gentlemen of colour, and others.' By the 'others,' we presume he means the whites"[33]—a notable inversion of Black people "othering" whites. Wells, "a colored clergyman of the Methodist Episcopal Church," lectured in Philadelphia in August. Later, "Mr. Lively, a colored gentleman from the south," offered phrenology lectures in a "tour through the country for improving his race." As Britt Rusert has detailed, African Americans, as well as women, understood phrenology "as a radically inclusive and 'democratic' science," allowing for self-education and self-improvement.[34]

Perhaps following the Fowlers' lead in drawing women from their family into the phrenological fold, other women independently advertised head-reading expertise, including the notice that "Mrs. Hamilton will lecture this evening, at the Assembly Building, on Phrenology. A converted Seminole Indian will be present."[35] Did her lecture include exposition of phrenological views of different racial groups, exemplified by the Seminole representative? Madame Young of Gaskill Street notified the public that she would, "by her universally acknowledged skill in Phrenology, Physiology and Philology, inform those who will investigate her talents of their leading transactions of the Past, Present and the Future as if she had known them from birth."

Phrenology bled into magic, its theatricalization serving a performative sphere of body-related experience, exploration, and experimentation.

In these ways, the "classifiable differences" among races and between sexes infused public awareness as abolitionism, disenfranchisement, immigration, territorial expansion, industrial and economic pressures, and the nascent women's rights movement roiled U.S. political waters, still attempting to settle into some national form and flow since independence from Britain. As Carolyn Sorisio notes, "Wittingly or not, scientists were fleshing out the implications of Revolutionary rhetoric and contributing to the invention of a biologically determined subject whose corporeality contradicted any claim to the Declaration of Independence's higher law of equality by means of creation."[36] Such differences (and resistance to them) became the stuff of bodily staging, of dance, and of understandings audiences brought to performances. These factors played out on Philadelphia stages in two works of the 1830s: *La Bayadere*, on the ballet stage, both reveals and challenges perceptions of women's bodies (racial issues also arise), while the blackface "opera" *Bone Squash Diavolo* addresses stagings of African American bodies.

La Bayadere, Madame Celeste, and Challenges to Womanhood

In December 1834, French dancer Mme. Celeste performed the opera-ballet *La Bayadere; Or, the Maid of Cashmere* in Philadelphia (Figure 3.1).[37] She first appeared in the city in 1828 and returned the following year, primarily dancing balletic interludes, for which she was well prepared in her Paris Opera studies under ballet master Georges Maze. Celeste appeared annually from 1834 to 1842 and again in the early 1850s. U.S. theater manager Noah Ludlow recalled the young Celeste, "beautiful as a *houri*, and as lithe and graceful as a fawn," while Charles Durang appreciated her "most expressive French face of a Grecian model, complexion of olive hue, lighted and shaded at will by vivid flashing black eyes, a Juno brow, and a mouth and chin of a Venus contour."[38] Her classical figure and face elevated Celeste to the corporeal realms of the ancient Greeks, yet the exoticism that Ludlow and Durang noted in her appearance well-suited her roles; exotic others were a staple of Celeste's repertoire. Starting as a ballet dancer, Celeste soon proved her worth in the related form of melodrama, a step up in theatrical status from ballet.[39] Notices for her Philadelphia debut in "The Grand Operatic Ballet Dance from *The Maid of Cashmere*, called La Bayadere" announced she had performed it for weeks at both Drury Lane and Covent Garden. Since no other cast members are listed,

Figure 3.1. "Celeste [fac. sig.] as the Maid of Cashmere." *(Jerome Robbins Dance Division, New York Public Library Digital Collections, Public Domain. Accessed June 19, 2024. https://digitalcollections.nypl.org/items/dd3071c0-0dfe-0133-97a8-58d385a7b928)*

she may have danced selected solos from the larger work. The first full-length performance in Philadelphia (Nov. 1836) featured Celeste as the lead (Zelica), supported by a company with dancers Mlle. Arraline (Brooks) and Monsieur and Madame Checkini, all from London theaters where Celeste had recently performed.[40]

Le Dieu et la Bayadère (libretto by Eugene Scribe, based on Goethe, music Daniel Auber) debuted in Paris in 1830, choreographed by Filippo Taglioni for his remarkable daughter Marie. Its complex staging drew on opera, ballet, pantomime, and melodrama, requiring a multiply skilled ballerina.[41] In the libretto, a temple dancer of India, Zelica (or Zoloe), loves "The Unknown" (Brahma in mortal's disguise), but is coveted by the city's "Grand Judge"—a story somewhat related to the later ballet *La Bayadère* (1877, choreography Marius Petipa). Another important dancing role in *The Maid of Cashmere* is temple dancer Fatima (or Fatme), to whom The Unknown pays court to test Zelica's love, for only by finding pure, unselfish love could he return to divine status—man's salvation lies in woman's purity, much as scientists like Caldwell assured their readers. The resulting "danced duel" (the "Trial Dance") by the female leads was the ballet's high point and most-often extracted excerpt, a show of courage and physical power that took the work thrillingly beyond typical gender norms. Durang judged Celeste's production of this "great operatic ballet" as "beautiful," "elegant," "effective," and "charming."[42] The print of Celeste as Zelica highlights both her allure and her modesty as she folds her arms protectively over her exotically clad breasts and turns her bejeweled head alluringly aslant.[43] With her fine ballet training and expressive pantomime, Celeste set the U.S. standard for the work in one of her interpretations "never . . . equaled by any person attempting them."[44] And many did attempt this role: the ballet became a mainstay of the U.S. stage that aspiring ballet dancers sought to tackle.

Celeste's dramatic genius was her forte, but reviewers also praised her "brilliant" dancing.[45] Noah Ludlow saw her dance style as "French," initially "rather repulsive to the staid ladies who had not been in the habit of seeing females kick up their heels quite so high in their dancing"; but, "the daughters have got bravely over this fastidiousness of their mammas."[46] Might Celeste's displays of female expressivity and strength have inspired women in the audience to appreciate their own potential beyond the sphere prescribed by social and scientific expectations?[47] The accommodation of "the daughters" to Celeste's displays suggests this possibility. With her renowned stamina and powerful performances, her elevation may have been notable, for Ludlow added that Celeste "literally bounded into the hearts of her audience." Durang recalled that, in her earliest U.S. appearances with a French dance troupe, the "self-complacent" audience response "gradually rose to the point of enthusiasm on beholding their *pirouettes* and *entrachats*. The very lithesome and graceful motions, by neat and pretty steps, combined with a decent voluptuousness and abandon in classic attitudes, served to enchant, even to the loss of all sense of propriety. These dancers were brilliant artistes."[48] The moral threat of ballet dancing and the women presenting it was evident even to some who, like Ludlow and Durang, appreciated and benefited from it. Just that mixture of classicism and edgy sensuality enticed viewers to the ballet stage.

After her 1827 and 1828 appearances, Celeste returned to France for further training, then toured the United States in 1834. During her absence, the fine French acrobatic and ballet troupe, the Ravels, filled U.S. stages with meticulously rehearsed, elegantly performed works, including the ballets *Cocombo; or, the Embassy to Smyrna* (1832, 1834); *Monsieur Molinet; or, a Night's Adventures* (1832, 1833); *Godensky; or, The Skaters of Wilna* (1832, 1833); *La Fete Champetre* (1833); *The Bouquet d'Amour* (1833); and *The Death of Abel* (1833).[49] Such works would appear throughout their years performing in Philadelphia, although few became mainstays of the broader ballet repertoire. Still, the Ravels were well connected to mainstream balletic developments: *Monsieur Molinet*, for example (later called *Vol-au-Vent*), was based on Jean-Baptiste Blache's 1817 pantomime-ballet *Le Moulin d'André ou les Meuniers*, and *Godensky* on Jean Coralli's 1827 *La Neige*.[50] Charles Durang was so moved by *The Death of Abel* that he described it in his *History* as "most impressively given in striking pantomime attitudes by the signal of one stroke on the drum or chords by the band. Gabriel Ravel, as Cain killing his brother with a club, displayed as fine a piece of acting as I ever saw," supported by gripping visual elements: "The costume of the first dwellers of the earth, the contour of his figure, the extraordinary makeup of his countenance, which gave out the first demoniac expression of man on earth . . . are beyond the most descriptive pen to portray."[51] Durang esteemed this "corps of pantomimists, rope dancers and gymnasts" as "the most extraordinary and universally enduring popular novelty that ever came to this country from the old world." The capacity to cross oceans, performance genres, and roles also characterized Celeste's career.

In 1834, after study time in Paris, Celeste's polish was noted in her steps, postures, and aerial feats, "*a la Académie Royale* . . . placing her among the first artistes of that renowned school" in both national dances like "The Greek Romaika" and Russian mazurka, and in her ballet virtuosity, exemplified by her "pirouette of thirty revolutions."[52] Soon, she "introduced her celebrated *Lavoltas* and *Corantos*, and announced that she would execute 'a grand treble pirouette of forty revolutions! being twenty more than was ever performed by any other person in this country'"; having witnessed the feat, Durang observed, "With all due deference to Celeste, we think truth would be better satisfied by saying twenty revolutions, *more or less*. But," he added, "it is well understood that all playbills are allowed, in courtesy, to exaggerate." Still, Celeste was a virtuoso who excelled at French ballet on pointe, national dances, melodramatic acting, and combats.

Aside from dancing the lead in *La Bayadere*, Celeste played another role in the work's U.S. debut—director. That experience prepared her for a position few women achieved in this period, that of theater manager, which she later held at London's Adelphi Theatre.[53] Her expressive dancing and capacity for directorial control took Celeste far beyond expected women's roles, proving her notable skills but also subjecting her to unflattering scrutiny, including accusations that her interpretations were less "proper," "pure," "graceful," or "angelic" than was the case with a rival as Zelica, the lovely Mme. Augusta Fuchs.[54] The huge sums Celeste reportedly earned in America struck some reviewers as unladylike, even shameful, while others defended her "ample possession of those generous good qualities which characterize the unassuming modest and respectable female in private life."[55]

Celeste's private life was aired in U.S. print sources. While Zelica's dancing in *La Bayadere* might be understood to express the purity of ideal female love, Celeste herself was but a ballet dancer. Professional dancers' self-exposure and gaining their livings through their bodies brought them, in moralists' views, close to prostitution.[56] That Celeste turned good profits made such associations more condemnable. Her early marriage to Baltimorean Henry Elliott was subject to gossip; her youth, his grasping exploitation of her talents and wasting her earnings through gambling, her nursing him in his ill health but leaving him before his death and letting their daughter be raised by an American family while she pursued her career abroad—these aspects of her personal life were publicly criticized.[57] A fanciful cartoon, *Celeste-al Cabinet*, shows Celeste with arms, shoulders, and lower legs bared, dancing before President Andrew Jackson and his cabinet.[58] As depicted in the graphic and text, her beauty distracts Jackson from official duties, while "her rapid movements, her quick changes, her gracefull [*sic*] transitions," in the words the cartoonist gave Vice President Martin Van Buren, exemplified his shifty political behavior, associating Celeste with deceit and sexual allure.

As her melodramatic capacities expanded, Celeste often played multiple roles in each work, sometimes in travesty that both offended gender norms and offered titillation to some viewers. In these roles, her costuming allowed fuller exposure of legs and arms, assumption of male attributes and weapons, and display of dramatic virtuosity, physical strength, and creative vision (Figure 3.2). Durang felt that Celeste "had some idea of modesty left to guide her in her sex's appropriate sphere,"[59] but images depicting her contest his

Figure 3.2. "Madame Celeste as the wild Arab boy" in *The French Spy*. *(Jerome Robbins Dance Division, New York Public Library Digital Collections, Public Domain. Accessed June 19, 2024. https://digitalcollections.nypl.org/items/510d47e2-0d51-a3d9-e040 -e00a18064a99)*

claim that "she generally wore the old sailor 'petticoat trowsers,' half pantaloons and half petticoats," for no such costume obscures her shapely legs in these published (likely exaggerated) images. Yet her powerful acting and fine dancing spoke their own story of talent and application, while women of less capacity were of stage interest only for the flesh they revealed, appearing as provocateurs rather than artists.

When Celeste returned to the United States in 1851, Durang found her still remarkable, youthful, and unmatched in virtuosity: "Her flashing dark eyes and her arch locks spoke out her thoughts without the aid of language."[60] Durang, bred in the theater, understood Celeste differently than did other commentators, troubled by her propriety-defying choices. Yet even these cavilers saw her genius: "We have always admired the talent displayed by Celeste in some of her pantomime performances, but are not disposed to approve her style of dancing, and much less the costume in which she exhibits" beyond the limits of "female dignity and delicacy." Thus was "this light heeled" dancing "perverted" by Celeste and "the whole host of opera dancers who leave their clothing behind the scenes," making it a "degrading exhibition, offensive alike to good taste and good morals."[61] A later installment in that newspaper argued that recent exhibitions of European stage dancing were designed explicitly "to expose the person; and, aided by the dress, they do it as effectually as if the performer were naked." Worse, these movements "are intended to express ideas," crediting ballet as more than just a "light heeled" amusement. The *Public Ledger* article insisted that ballet's "ideas" "tend to influence licenticus passions": as this writer grasped, ideas resulted in emotion that propelled action. Indeed, "any woman who . . . should express such ideas" revealed herself "as not only without virtue in heart, but as without respect for virtue in appearance." The inner and outer woman were tarnished, her womanhood a failure. Among Celeste's much-repeated and applauded vehicles for such "studied indecency"—or, as others insisted, virtuosity that revealed the "force and intensity of her expressive pantomimic action"[62]—were *The French Spy*, *The Wizard Skiff*, *The Wept of Wish-ton-Wish*, and *Miami, or the Green Bushes*. Celeste's choice of exotic and travesty parts, her capacity for nonstop exertion through long engagements with multiple roles in each work, and her "marvelous exhibitions of daring ambition and successful achievement"[63] made clear to observers that this woman's body, mind, and talent defied the delicate, subservient female modeled by the respectable Jacksonian or Victorian woman.

Along with Celeste's gender-challenging roles, the works mentioned here raise issues of race and culture. *Bayadere* was set in a Western-romanticized India, a site for orientalized indulgence in sensual mysticism that flavored much ballet of the period.⁶⁴ In John Thomas Haines's "military drama" *The French Spy*, one of the three roles Celeste performed was that of the "Wild Arab Boy," a disguise for the character of a mute French girl (also played by Celeste) spying on the Arab foe as she follows her beloved, a French army colonel, to the Siege of Constantina.⁶⁵ In this role of disguise and transgression—which allowed Celeste to fight and wrestle with "gigantic Algerian warriors," to flirt with the daughter of an officer, and to perform a fierce "Arab dance"—she was often depicted, sometimes carrying weapons or even with a mustache (see Figure 3.2). Haines's *The Wizard Skiff; Or, the Tongueless Pirate Boy* engaged another ethnicity perceived in this context as "exotic"—the Greeks, who, in ancient times, were models of Western perfection, but whose moral "degeneration," lamented Morton, was sadly evident in "modern Greece."⁶⁶ As Cedric Dover notes, in the nineteenth century, "the zephyrs" of culture and morality "were blowing northwards," as Greece was regarded as sunk in oriental exoticism. Still, the Greek struggle for independence from the Ottoman Empire stirred sympathy in Western Europe and the United States, making a Greek theme attractive to audiences. *Wizard Skiff* also had Celeste in multiple roles—Alexa, the Greek Girl whose tongue was cut out in her infancy; Alexis, the same character disguised as pirate-captain of a skiff carrying her to Russian-Muslim enemies; and Agata, identified as a "Gypsy." In this "popular Grand Nautical Melo-Dramatic Romance,"⁶⁷ Celeste's gender-crossing and transgressive acts included climbing ropes, courting and rescuing another female character, and dancing the Greek Romaika, associated with pirates.

The prevalence of "Eastern" themes and people in these works reflects Europeans' fascination with "the swarthy descendants of the Arabs and Carthaginians,"⁶⁸ regarded in the West as "rapturously sensual, unabashedly suggestive," their physical and moral qualities "preserved through numberless generations" from antiquity. Morton ascribed mixed qualities to "Arabs" and "Moors": despite shaded versions of Caucasian physicality, they were "ferocious and repugnant," "hospitable" but "duplicitous," and "conspicuous for a fertile imagination" and for "music, poetry and romance."⁶⁹ The "Hindoos," in the "Indostanic Family" of the Caucasian race, were "mild, sober and industrious," but blinded by "a fantastic religion." Though sometimes "timid," they could commit "gang-robberies, incendiarism, and analogous crimes." Picking and choosing, heightening and dramatizing these qualities, widely understood by Western theatergoers, playwrights of the Euro-American stage attempted to appeal to audiences of the time with works featuring daring behaviors, sexual transgression, revealing costumes, lively dancing, and appealing music, while reinforcing conceptions about racial types and rankings that served sociopolitical objectives.

White Americans had their own "others" at home: Native Americans—the subjects of Morton's *Crania Americana*. The political fate of the "Indians" was essentially determined by this time, as their independence and territorial claims were trampled by broken treaties, forced removals, and deadly contests with Euro-U.S. settlers. Yet sympathy for their independence, courage, and ties to native soil was also romantically widespread in white culture, and "Indians," "chiefs," and their "squaws" were found on Philadelphia stages, dancing and enacting their rituals before antebellum theatergoers.[70] Celeste stepped into this sphere of "exotica": in "the Indian drama," or "American Traditionary Drama," *The Indian Girl, or, The Wept of Wish-ton-Wish*, she played both the young Puritan, Hope Gough, and the Indian girl, Narramattah.[71] A dramatization by William Bayle Bernard of James Fenimore Cooper's novel, this "burletta" was set on the then-remote western Connecticut frontier, where Puritan settlers conflicted with "Mohegan" natives. In the story, a Puritan girl is carried off during an Indian raid and wed to Chief Conanchet, with whom she falls in love and bears a daughter. He is killed by a traitorous tribesman, despite his wife's defense, and Narramattah/Hope returns to her Puritan village to die brokenhearted. The play, which premiered in 1831 at London's Adelphi Theatre, depicted interracial and cultural conflict with more sympathy to Native Americans than did Morton, who considered them "averse to cultivation, and slow in acquiring knowledge; restless, revengeful."[72] He claimed the Native Americans' incapacity for "servitude" forced the European settlers to forego enslaving them in favor of "the more pliant Negro" who "bore his heavy burthen with comparative ease." Later, Celeste debuted another "Indian" melodrama: in William Buckstone's *The Green Bushes*,[73] she played Miami, "the huntress of the Mississippi," a character who carried and effectively used a rifle. This was a woman who took her fate into her own hands—apparently an inspiration to others.

Inspired by Celeste: American Ballerinas Take the Stage

Celeste's independence and virtuosity inspired two of the young United States' early homegrown ballerinas, Augusta Maywood and Mary Ann Lee (Figures 3.3 and 3.4). Turning to one of Celeste's star vehicles, *La Bayadere*—called *The Maid of Cashmere* in their joint debut season (Dec. 1837–Jan. 1838) at the Chestnut Street Theatre—they appeared as Zoloe (Maywood) and Fatima (Lee).[74]

Maywood, aged twelve, and Lee, thirteen, had studied for the preceding year or two with Philadelphia dancing master P. H. Hazard, their tuition

Figure 3.3. "La petite Augusta, aged 12 years, in the character of Zoloe, in the Bayadere," Edward W. Clay (1838). *(Jerome Robbins Dance Division, New York Public Library Digital Collections, Public Domain. Accessed June 19, 2024. https://digitalcollections.nypl.org/items/05fe3de0-dd5d-0132-f092-58d385a7b928)*

paid by theater manager Robert Maywood of Philadelphia. Augusta was his adopted daughter, while Mary Ann came from a poor Philadelphia family of lower-rank circus players and had already been on the stage to support her widowed mother. Thus, both girls grew up around theaters, surely a factor compensating for their brief formal ballet training. Each girl's dancing in

Figure 3.4. "Miss Lee as Fatima in the Maid of Cashmere." *(Courtesy of Winterthur Museum, Garden, and Library, Maxine Waldron collection of paper dolls, games, and paper toys, Box 15, Folder 5)*

their opera-ballet debut earned accolades from Philadelphia commentators, proud of this double balletic emergence in their city, rather than before the "commercial citizens" of New York.[75] Beyond the intercity rivalry, the dancers' appearance together stimulated competitive claques supporting each, as ballerina rivalries have through history. Both young heroines were lauded by press and public as proof that Americans could master the European art of ballet.

La Bayadere's plot led to a real-life "duel" between the aspirants: in Zelica and Fatima's "trial *pas de deux*," Lee "acquired *pari passu* applause with the principal object, La Petite Augusta," resulting in "the partizanship . . . between the two young ladies."[76] Lee's admirers crowned her "'Our Mary Anne,' an endearing old song appellation, that was really chanted like a popular national air through the community," as the two parties engaged in a "spirited rivalry." Durang noted that both were trained by Hazard and "had observed and adopted the style of Celeste. Both were endowed with natural abilities for agility and grace. . . . Of course the manager's daughter had all the influence on her side." This pitting of the managerial (Maywood) against the working class (Lee) reflected broader social tensions as industrial unrest mounted in Philadelphia and elsewhere, leading to the formation of trade unions and to strikes.[77] While the Maywoods had resided and worked in Philadelphia for years, Augusta was born in New York; Mary Ann was entirely local, familiar on popular stages where her father, Charles Lee, had performed.[78] Maywood, having granted a benefit to his daughter, was accused of favoritism, and the public demanded he do the same for Mary Ann. He did.

Given the joint debut and ensuing rivalry, the girls were much compared: Durang remarked, "Augusta had more precision, more of the mind and the science of the artiste; but 'Our Mary Anne' had a pleasing expression—a smile that fascinated." Theater manager Wemyss noted, "Their success was but a just tribute to merit; and, if La Petite Augusta felt any jealous pang to mar her triumph, the injudicious conduct of her own parents toward 'our Mary Anne' . . . was the sole cause"—the failure of manager Maywood to give Lee a benefit until the public demanded it. Wemyss added, "As a foil" to Augusta's "own excellence, Miss Lee would have been the most valuable auxiliary she could have found; in claiming to be her equal, for a time," Lee "lost ground; yet her career has been a profitable one."

Eventually, each girl traveled abroad to study at the Paris Opera. Durang reflected, "Augusta Maywood really was a prodigy. . . . At one bound this talented girl stood beside the best terpsichorean *artistes*" in the United States.[79] He shrewdly noted, "With the furore this precocious child of dance had elicited, it would have proved good policy, while the excitement raged, to have starred her through the country." Instead, her parents hastened her to Paris, "losing the pecuniary rewards which a tour in the United States would clearly have gained." Yet manager Maywood apparently saw this as the moment to propel Augusta into the highest international ranks of balletic achievement, given her youth, talent, and success: with the polish of French training and the luster of an Opera debut, she would be unbeatable. In Paris, "her improvement was wonderful," Durang wrote, and her Opera *début* "a brilliant triumph." Philadelphia's *National Gazette* reported that an American correspondent had gained entry to the dance practice room at the Opera, which he exoticized as a "carefully guarded temple," to see "the little prodigy who had aroused such just admiration" in her U.S. debut.[80] He extolled the "exhibition of her highly developed powers, that attracted," on the stage, "the zealous admiration of her graceful associates, and excited, naturally enough, the vanity of her skilful master, M. Corallie [*sic*]." He noted "the great improvement" in the "graceful flexibility of limb—the soft pliancy of motion, of that young, but inspired creature." This modest American girl indulged "no vulgar display of person, no attitudinizing appeals to the coarse sensualist; she moves in a region far beyond this—where all is grace and beauty," revealed in "the soft, swelling movements of a buoyant and exquisitely formed girl, whose look of youthful innocence dispels every unchaste vision." With orientalist musings, the author added, "My brain is yet heated with the soft visions and graceful images that have slept there, since I read the Arabian tales when a boy. . . . When I want another bright illusion, instead of eating opium, I shall go see the dancing of La Petite Augusta."

Paris critic Théophile Gautier racialized Augusta differently in comments on her debut of November 25, 1839, in the ballets *Le Diable boiteux* and *La Tarantule*. He noted the international cadre of dancers appearing at the Opera: "Danes, Germans, Americans, and English—a real Babel with sixty-one tongues but happily the language of the dance can be understood everywhere, and feet do not speak with an accent."[81] Or do they? Maywood's "distinctive type of talent," Gautier found, revealed "something brusque, unexpected and fantastic that sets her utterly apart" from others he observed. She "has now come to seek the sanction of Paris, for the opinion of Paris is important even for the barbarians of the United States in their world of railroads and steamboats." Americans—be they "Indians" or entrepreneurs—were, to the refined continental viewer, all "barbarians," but, Gautier admitted, "for a prodigy, Mlle Maywood really is very good." Blending his conceptions of American industrial drive and barbarism, he found Augusta "very near to being pretty," with her "wild little face . . . sinews of steel, legs of a jaguar, and agility not unlike that of a circus performer." Contrasting with her wild animal qualities was her tranquility facing the Paris audience: "You would have thought she was simply dealing with a pit full of Yankees." Gautier also detailed Augusta's technique, including "almost horizontal *vols penchés* [leaning flights]," aerial turns, and "*tours de reins*," her "small legs, like those of a wild doe," striding like Marie Taglioni's.

The wildness Gautier claimed to perceive in young Augusta won out in her nature over the "innocence" American commentators projected onto her. In 1840, still a teenager, she eloped with Paris Opera dancer Charles Mabille, bore a child, abandoned husband and baby, then toured as a star through Europe. Augusta reached La Scala, Milan, in 1849, rising there to *prima ballerina assoluta*. Yet she kept abreast of doings back home: among her triumphs in Italy was staging a balletic *Uncle Tom's Cabin*, created soon after the book's U.S. dramatization (see Chapter 5).[82] Once U.S. commentators recognized Augusta's independent streak, they turned viciously on their former darling, condemning her abandonment of parents, husband, and child, and her infuriating capacity, nonetheless, to be rewarded by success. As manager Wemyss wrote, lamenting his dashed hopes for an American theatrical model, "She has deserted her husband, and the heartless letter in which she recommended her child to the care of its father . . . proves that her heart is even lighter than her heels. The very brilliance of her opening in life has been her ruin; the stage again pointed at as impure and immoral"[83]—perhaps, to Wemyss, the greatest of her sins. Augusta, "who would have been the pride" of the stage "as an American artiste—who had gained the highest honors abroad—has become its shame"; should she seek to "appear upon the stage of her native country again, . . . her countrywomen, whose character for purity she has disgraced, will drive her from it indignantly." It would be the women, of course, who would shun and shame the deviant danseuse. Durang's equally indignant condemnation concluded, "Let us draw the veil of oblivion over our regrets, over her and her crimes. In her lovely villa on the beautiful banks of the Arno, . . . where she resides in seeming happiness, she may yet die in the conscientious throes of a guilty heart."[84] Other American theater and dance aspirants would absorb the American public's affections.

Mary Ann Lee took longer than her former rival to cross the ocean for studies in Paris, probably because her family's poverty meant she must work to pay her way. In late summer 1838, she moved from Maywood's unwelcoming Chestnut Street Theatre to the warmth of manager Wemyss's Walnut. There, the dancer Mr. Amherst "wrote a very neat little ballet," *Queen Lily of the Silver Stream*, "in which Lee figured with much grace as the heroine."[85] Durang recalled "one very pretty scene" set amidst "a vast lot of lily vases, arranged pyramidically, from which sprung a *corps de ballet* of very beautiful girls, a chubby Cupid, with bow and love dart; and, from another everspreading lily—a Victoria Regia—arose the Lily Queen." As England had a year earlier crowned Victoria its queen, the United States crowned Lee its ballet favorite, a young woman of talent *and* pure heart. Reaching Paris in late 1843 or 1844, Lee studied at the Opera school, returning to the United States in October 1845 "much improved."[86] She toured the states to adoring acclaim, as a university student in North Carolina confessed in his diary: "Mary Ann Lee, a dancer, has a benefit tonight. There was a great impatience manifested in the society tonight so anxious were the members to see the last exhibition of the pretty little actress. . . . Some of the most lascivious [students] have fallen dreadfully in love with her."[87] Durang recalled, "The winning arch smile that wreathed her features, while reclining into attitudes at the end of every strain, ever won applause, and harmonized with the excellence of her very neat *pas*." Lee became the first American ballerina to star in the ballet *Giselle* (Jan. 1846).[88] In November 1847, she married Philadelphia merchant Edmund Van Hook[89] and was little seen on stage after 1853, perhaps owing to motherhood. "Mary Ann Vanhook" was listed in the 1860 city directory as running a "dancing academy." While Augusta Maywood proved susceptible to "foreign luxurious climes" and was "soon converted into affected and vitiated moral manners," Our Mary Ann[e] lived in civic grace until 1899, when she died in her home city. As well as making her balletic debut at the Chestnut Street Theatre in *La Bayadere*, Lee closed her career there with that work in her final season, September 1853.[90]

As noted earlier, the orientalism of *La Bayadere* is evident, given its supposed setting in India, but we can also glimpse possible African racialized elements. A performance of the Scribe/Auber *Bayadère* in Paris in 1837—the year of the Maywood/Lee debut in Philadelphia—brought blacking up into the picture, according to Gautier, who wrote that the temple dancers were "subdivided into flesh-coloured bayaderes and coffee-coloured bayaderes. The latter . . . wear *filoselle* [silk] stockings over their arms and . . . gloves of an indefinable colour on their hands. Their faces are carelessly daubed with ochre or liquorice juice, which makes them look more like chimney-sweeps than those voluptuous charmers, gilded by the sun, who tinkle the silver bells on their bracelets" at temple doorsteps.[91] Gautier offered his solution to staging "Eastern" exoticism: creation of "a dye of a warm enough pallor to convey the lovely amber-yellow colour of oriental complexions in which the eyes open like black flowers"; then, "that awful chocolate colour and those *filoselle* stockings that offend even the most short-sighted eyes could be dispensed with. Or, simpler still, it could quite simply be agreed that negresses are white." Telling is Gautier's conflation of what he perceived to be Indian and African complexions and representation. No mention of skin tones arose in U.S. reviews I studied, nor do the much-distributed images of Celeste and other ballerinas in the lead role show hints of blackface. These idealized prints depicted only the solo dancers; was the corps de ballet, invisible in such images, so darkened in American productions? No evidence survives on this matter, although that choice would likely be noted by viewers attuned to racial depictions.

T. D. Rice's Rise to Blackface Stardom

There was no question that racial depiction was at the heart, as well as on the skin, of T. D. Rice's Jim Crow. Like the American artists arising in the ballet world, U.S. showman T. D. Rice proved the lure of homegrown talent; W. T. Lhamon argues for Rice's Jim Crow as "a character who stitched filiation across class, region, even nationality, and race," although "what this never-quite-melded alliance saw in Jim Crow remains unrecorded,"[92] making later readings of Rice's work and reception challenging. Rice, born in 1808, grew up in working-class, racially mixed—largely African- and Irish-American—lower Manhattan. There, at markets, along the docks, and in dance halls and saloons, men, women, people of different races, and workers of all trades—including sailors carrying cultural material from port to port—assembled. The sketch "Dancing for Eels, 1820, Catharine Market," depicting a mixed-race encounter among dancers, musicians, and b'hoys enjoying the show, suggests the entertainment world familiar to young Rice, and the movement material and performance intimacy his acts embodied.[93]

As a young actor in New York, Rice watched George Washington Dixon's blackface hit, "Coal Black Rose";[94] then, Rice toured as a minor player on the western and southern U.S. circuits, observing fellow performers' acts and watching workers whose musical-movement rhythms accompanied their labor as haulers, drivers, and vendors. Despite the story Rice broadcast of building his act on an encounter with a limping African American stable hand, he in fact assembled all that he collected through the course of his youth and travels to create his embodiment of a ragged, vibrant "Black" laborer who, in the early 1830s, began to sing/dance "Jump, Jim Crow" (Figure 1.1). As his popularity swelled, Rice moved from song and dance acts to Crow-based skits and full-fledged "Ethiopian operas" as a solo star. These increasingly complex theatrical works gave scope for Jim Crow's appeal to different audiences.

The Sambo-the-servant type of earlier blackface characterization in standard, mostly English, theatrical fare had presented African Americans "as marginal, laughable, and ephemeral," while Rice elevated Jim Crow to a "central, comic, and durable" characterization.[95] Rice invented neither the figure nor the name; traditional African stories and symbolism of buzzards and crows fed long-standing references to Jim Crow among African Americans through stories, music, and dance. Jim Crow's crystallization into "the African American trickster" preceded the nineteenth century. By then, movement that Rice/Crow would adopt had shaped a recognizable Crow song and dance, known to Black workers like those of the Georgia Sea Islands and to established Caribbean Black "nations" among the enslaved.[96] Elements of disguise and disorder in mumming, carnivals, and working-class social protests in the British Atlantic world were well established, constructed in part from centuries-old and ongoing Black-white exchanges of rhythms, music, and movement. These substrata supported "the incredible vitality"[97] of nineteenth-century U.S. blackface performance, including its appearances in works by Rice, whose successes earned him the title of "father of the Aethiopian drama."[98]

What made Jim Crow/Rice such a standout among other blackface performers? Rice stirred together just the right stew of elements drawn from the ancient *commedia dell'arte*, working-class callithumpian antics, U.S. racial anxieties, Jacksonian-edged class tensions, and clever performance choices.[99] His shrewd assemblage of costume, posture, movement, music, and text projected a fluid, multivalent character whose embodiment could be adapted to and read from opposite political stances. Those looking to see African Americans as childlike, deformed song and dance clowns needing guidance and protection in civilized society—as claimed by race scientists—might read those qualities into Jim. Yet, as Lhamon's analyses of Rice's full-length works reveal, "Jim Crow wheels about in these plays, advocating abolition, nixing secession, pushing black pride. He notes where he is barred, where included. He shoves white and black dandies equally hard, talks street jive, mocks elite notions of class history,"[100] creating opportunity, for spectators who chose to read his message this way, for cross-race identification among groups closed out of upper-crust American society, including those struggling under factory "wage slavery" across the rapidly industrializing North.[101] Some American elites sensed these meanings and excoriated Rice's Jim. But for the mostly white, working-class viewers who swarmed Rice's shows, this was *their* theater; they interacted physically and vocally with Jim Crow as Rice created him on stage, motivating new themes, lyrics, and movements that Rice improvised on the spot, or used in subsequent performances.[102]

Commentators lauded Rice's movement skills in dancing and physicalizing his character. Remarking on Rice's performance of the "Jump Jim Crow" song, one wit observed, it "has a feature that belongs to few songs—it is mostly made up of dancing"[103]—unsurprising, given the work's title.

The lyrics specify movements: wheeling (circling), turning, jumping, hand-wagging, and weight-shifting from heel to toe. Other movement elements included tight, rhythmic circling, "a syncopated hop in the flat-footed Shuffle manner," hunched and slanted shoulders, hips swaying "in Congo fashion," and feet performing shuffles, "while the index finger of one hand wiggles shoulder-high at the sky."[104] This dance likely featured sharply accented rhythms, angularity, distortion, and tension alternating with sprawling nonchalance.[105] A reminiscence from 1862 by a Georgia Sea Islander described Black performance of the shout (ring shout), with steps much like those of Jim Crow Rice: shuffling in a circle, turning round oneself, knee-bending, and rocking with alternating toe- and heel-taps.[106]

As the constantly changing song lyrics encouraged improvisation, new movements and attitudes appeared, establishing a vocabulary for subsequent blackface minstrel dancing: energetic use of legs and feet, turns, toe- and heel-slapping, and contorted body positions.[107] Angularity, big gestures, and action drawing attention to the body's vigor and sexuality were typical, reinforcing race-science claims of African-descended people as ungainly in body and barbarous in behavior. These stage acts also appealed to lower-class audiences who saw in them their own work postures, the frenetic release of pent-up energy they sought, as well as characters who, classed beneath these viewers, managed nonetheless to mock, escape, and best their masters.[108]

Mocking class pretensions and elites' efforts to define "American," Rice drew also on the European music, theater, and dance forms these elites embraced, creating send-ups of the social and political control that he and working-class audiences contested. Later blackface minstrels, many of immigrant origins, followed Rice in targeting classism.[109] As Pennsylvania legislators debated humanity and citizenship, Rice offered his own commentary, bringing Black-derived movement and creativity forward for admiration or derision, as viewers chose. An 1837 article, published in Ireland during Rice's overseas tour and reprinted in New York, highlights such varied readings, referring to internationally renowned ballerinas and to the grotesqueries ascribed to lower-class movement:

> Mr. Crow's agility in describing the evolutions that the words enjoin ... is truly magnificent. He has all the velocity of a dancing master, with the quaint capers of a cleave-boy [butcher's assistant]—the bewitching grace of Douvernay, in partnership with the sylph-like movements of Taglioni. He varies his jumpings to an infinite extent, starting with different steps, and terminating with different positions each verse. Then there are eight verses to the song, and it is encored six times; which

draws deeply upon Mr. Crow's ingenuity to vary the pantomime, and remodel the extravagance of this grotesque transaction. And so he does; for each bound he gives is other than the last.[110]

Like Celeste, Rice was a font of energy, creativity, and ambition. Like her, he broke boundaries, and he far more openly commented on current social-political fault lines: the American intellectual elite that embraced Celeste was within Rice's scope for lambast and burlesque.

Rice had close connections to Philadelphia. Aside from the story, in Chapter 1, of his introducing child-star Joseph Jefferson to the stage in the city, Rice chose to premiere several of his "operas" not in New York, but at Wemyss's Walnut Street Theatre, where the young American Mary Ann Lee also felt at home after leaving Maywood's Chestnut Street. Wemyss wisely sensed the popular mood for "American"-themed acts and performers in his hosting Rice and Lee and in calling the Walnut the "American Theatre," redecorated with patriotic banners and images.[111] Rice's premieres under Wemyss included *Oh! Hush!* (July 1833), *Virginia Mummy* (June 1835, after one benefit performance in Mobile, Alabama), and the now-lost *Discoveries in the Moon, or Herschel our Herscheled* (Sept. 1835), the latter two works exemplifying Rice's direct employment (and burlesque) of popular scientific themes—here, Egyptology and air-ballooning—in his plots. Later, Rice's remarkable *Otello* would premiere under Wemyss in Philadelphia, when he managed the Chestnut Street Theatre.

Bone Squash Diavolo was also intended to premiere at the Walnut, where Rice and the stock company developed it through the summer of 1835 while performing other Jim Crow works. Owing to the play's complicated scenography, Rice ran out of time, and ultimately premiered it in Boston, then showed it in New York before its Walnut Street debut in December 1835. When he did see *Bone Squash Diavolo*, Wemyss commented on the child he helped birth: "'Bone Squash' was an amusing affair, the music truly delightful, and ably executed."[112] A journalist for the *Dramatic Mirror*, typically no fan of Rice, also admitted that the work's music was "beautiful." Durang agreed, adding, "In the collection of the airs" that Rice sang in this and other works, "he received great assistance from John Clemens, who really had a genius, in such arrangements." Clemens, Durang regretted, never got his due, since "he was only an humble Philadelphian," and such British-born theater managers as Wemyss showed, Durang felt, "contempt for all things American in his own profession." Yet the popularity of Stephen Foster's sentimental, European-based music in blackface minstrelsy presents another counterexample to Durang's complaint, for Foster, born and raised in Pennsylvania, was widely acclaimed for his compositions.[113]

Bone Squash Diavolo and Ethiopian Opera

Bone Squash Diavolo marked a change in Rice's blackface expression: unlike his previous plays, it populated the stage with only "Black" (blackface) characters, except for the devil—the betailed white Yankee, Sam Switchell (Uncle Sam?), popping in and out of hell, but failing to haul Bone Squash along. In fact, Bone repeatedly outwits white Yankee Sam, and Bone's "Black" friends always aid his escapes. In his plays, Rice rechristened Jim Crow variously—Cuff (*Oh! Hush!*), Ginger Blue (*Virginia Mummy*), and Bone Squash—but Rice's Jim was under each character's corked-up skin. Choosing a title that pointed to the hit opera *Fra Diavolo* (1830; music, as for *Bayadere*, by Auber, libretto by Scribe), Rice ascended the holy ground of Italian opera, dear to U.S. Europhiles. A contemporary recalled, "Dandy Jim and Tom Rice became, in the U.S., the avowed rivals of Auber and Mendelssohn,"[114] figures of high European musical taste. But Rice's libretto had little to do with Scribe's, drawing rather on Douglas Jerrold's hit play *Beau Nash* and on Clay's satiric print "A Dead Cut," while employing the ballad-opera form of John Gay's *The Beggar's Opera*. Jerrold's play attacked Beau Nash, dandy and social arbiter in fashionable Bath, England, but, Lhamon notes, "What Jerrold abuses, Rice organizes" as "the American Punch and Judy, sweeps and slaves devising their own backtalk that might at times rise to counterpunches."[115] *Bone Squash*'s connection to the Clay cartoon bears further consideration.

"A Dead Cut" (Figure 3.5) appeared in Clay's popular series *Life in Philadelphia*,[116] mocking social aspiration by white and Black people, with particularly ludicrous scenes of supposed African American high society. As noted earlier, Clay constructed his "Black" figures as hideous, hopeless fools "aping" (a term knowingly used) white elite behavior but revealing what he projected as their inevitable inferiority through the laughable speech, overblown dress, and ungainly bodies and movement he assigned them. White spectators' enthusiasm for such mockery is evident in its ubiquitous publication by cartoonists on both sides of the Atlantic.

African American viewers understood the cartoons' messages perfectly. Connecticut clergyman Hosea Easton, writing in 1837, published his outraged reading of these images as teaching "contempt" for Black people's supposed "deformity of person" and proving them an "inferior race." He called out features made ludicrous in verbal and graphic depictions: "N——r lips, n——r shins, and n——r heels, are phrases universally common among the juvenile class," for "they are early learned to think of these expressions, as they are intended to apply to colored people, and as being expressive or descriptive of the odious qualities of their mind and body."[117] Easton, thus, drew connections to the scientific observation of racial markers that publications broadcast.

Figure 3.5. "A Dead Cut," from "Life in Philadelphia collection," Edward W. Clay. *(Library Company of Philadelphia, Life in Philadelphia [Philadelphia Set] [5656.F.39]. Accessed June 19, 2024. https://digital.librarycompany.org/islandora/object/Islandora%3A60193)*

He astutely pointed out that "this kind of education is not altogether oral. Cuts and placards descriptive of the negroe's deformity, are everywhere displayed to the observation of the young, with corresponding broken lingo, the very character of which is marked with design"—with ludicrous mockery. Bookstores and barrooms lined their walls with such prints, creating "a display of American civility [that] is under the daily observation of every class of society," a "kind of education" that is "not only systematized, but legalized."

Such imagery traveled from bookstores to barrooms to theaters. Did Easton also see blackface stage acts? He does not say, although it is known that audiences for such shows sometimes included African Americans.[118] Might some such spectators have seen minstrelsy not as "a venue where racial science was simply represented (or, re-presented) to a mass audience and recycled into various popular entertainments," but as "a kind of public laboratory, a vital space of experimentation where alternative theories of race, and resistance to them, were . . . negotiated through performance"?[119] Perhaps, although entertaining displays of phrenology and other current scientific novelties in theaters and museums were also available to meet such curiosity.

Comments from the African American population are few regarding their attendance at blackface shows.[120] But in December 1837, a pivotal point in Pennsylvania's voting rights debate, a statement by editor Samuel Cornish of the nationally read *Colored American* newspaper denounced theater attendance, particularly at blackface shows: "There can, or ought to be but one sentiment concerning those *theatres*, where plays are presented which hold up to ridicule the foibles or peculiarities of an already too much oppressed people"—now facing legal disenfranchisement—"and but one feeling of disgust towards those actors who represent such characters" as "characteristics of the whole people."[121] Cornish, excoriating the ongoing dehumanization of African Americans, pointed to a speech published in the *Sun* (Baltimore), attributed to "that most contemptible of all Buffoons, Thomas D. Rice, alias 'Jim Crow' who has completely put down abolitionism in England . . . so that not an abolitionist will ever again 'cross the Atlantic.'" He concluded with the fervent wish that "no colored American will ever again so disgrace himself, or his people by patronizing such performances, nor even the *theatres* where they are exhibited." I have found no other confirmation of Rice's speech. However, his operas were widely performed, adopted by later blackface troupes, and published. Clearly, Cornish understood not only Rice's reported speech but his performances much the way Easton read Clay's cartoons.

In act I, scene 2 of *Bone Squash*, Rice renamed the characters from Clay's cartoon but kept its text verbatim, drawing attention to the well-known, insulting caricatures. While Lhamon reads Rice's use of the cartoon's imagery and language as inversions of Clay's intent, we have no evidence that audiences saw it as such. The cross-race "filiation" that Lhamon reads into Rice's work did not occur to Cornish, nor, apparently, to many of the white working-class men who dominated Rice's audiences. Rather, the targeted violence of that class against Philadelphia's Black residents—violence that swelled in the mid-1830s, when Rice played there—suggests that, on the streets of the City of Brotherly Love, racial antagonism overwhelmed any sense of cooperation that Rice may have sought to express, were that his intention.[122]

Why was *Bone Squash Diavolo* understood as an "opera"?[123] Rice overtly mocked and appropriated high-art productions like European opera, with its classist appeal, as he generated "American" cultural forms and themes. Like Italian and French opera, Rice mixed music, singing, dancing, acting, and spectacle to tell a story in several acts and scenes. In both European and "Ethiopian" operas, plots were contrived, often comic, derivative, and melodramatic, the music featuring catchy melodies and virtuosic turns, along with showy dance numbers. *Bone Squash* had up to thirteen named characters (listings vary) and a chorus. In the 1840s, with blackface performance dominated by self-contained troupes, all characters were played by men, in travesty for female roles, but Rice's 1830s productions put women in female parts. His 1838 Philadelphia bills list his cast: *Bone Squash*, Mr. Rice; *Paganini Brown*, Mr. Vache; *Spruce Pink*, Mr. Myers; *Major Sam Switchel* [the devil], Mr. Hadaway; *Mose Sharpshins*, Mr. Grierson; *Pompey Ducklegs*, Mr. Collingbourne; *Junietta Ducklegs*, Mrs. Rogers; *Rose*, Miss E. Price; *Snowball*, Miss Price.[124] Bone is a chimney sweep, Brown a musician, and Mose a bootblack—familiar employments for African Americans in the limited job choices open to them—while Spruce is an uppity dandy, Pompey a "Black" gentleman, and Junietta his daughter and object of Bone's pursuit.

The libretto reveals that Rice tapped timely political, social, and scientific themes. In act I, scene 1, before Bone appears, Brown and Mose exchange dialogue that takes off on the age's phrenological frenzy. Pertinent to the script is an 1833 newspaper article on renowned violinist Nicolò Paganini, reporting his virtuosity and wealth, and informing readers that "the whole man bespeaks the soul within. His pile of forehead is, if phrenology be true, an index to the highest mental faculties in excess. The organs of the poet, the musician and the philosopher, stand prominently out, and give a commanding breadth to the upper part of the countenance."[125] The opening of Rice's play, as musician Brown brags of his talents to bootblack Mose, would have been perfectly understandable to audiences of the day:

> BROWN: Hear what de great doctor of Physgne Combobologist say: he says, dat on de back ob de head, just in de middle ob de craneum, de organ ob music am very strongly enveloped in de great Paganini. Now, I've got a bump dar, big as de great watermelon.
> MOSE: How did yu get dat bump? Buttin' down de fence?
> BROWN: No, natur gibe em to me. Buttin' down de fence?—what you take a musiciana for, you saucy N———r? Now, leff me feel your head; you isn't got no bump like de one I is. You is got a berry big bump, just oder de ear. And dat's de sign you black de boots. (All laugh)[126]

This phrenology send-up leads into the show's first song, "I Am de Paganini"; its chorus bears the stage instruction "All dance the shuffle," a step prominent in Clay's earlier "Shippen Street" image from *Lessons in Dancing*. The shuffle was both low-class and minstrel-related.

Once Bone Squash enters, he wishes aloud that he could sell himself to the devil to get some money. Presto!—the devil appears, his banter referring to then-current U.S. negotiations with Russia, to hellfire-and-brimstone preachers, and to temperance societies (plentiful in Philadelphia) as he and Bone bargain for the latter's worth. Bone demands a high price for his soul, insisting he is no lowlife "roun de market and de wharfs. I'm a gemman of color" (p. 185), pointing to urban sites of cultural exchange between Black and white people, and satirizing such "gentlemen of color" as Philadelphia's wealthy, refined, outspoken abolitionist James Forten.[127] In their bargaining, Bone lauds the politically volatile lower-class news sheet, the *Hawk and Buzzard*, while putting down its higher-class competitor, the *Mirror* (p. 186), which had tangled with Rice some years before. Digging into the moneyed white elites, the devil pays Bone not in cash, but by check, assuring Bone the bankers "all know me" so "any of 'em will take old Nick's check in less time than you'd light a match." After this dig to the monied class, Bone and the devil sing, "I'm beginning for to fill, Like a Baltimore Clipper," a song about drinking, Wall Street "shell[ing] out de treasure," and Bone's anticipation of the high life (pp. 186–87). At its end, "Chorus and dance," although the script offers no choreography.

The next scene (act I, sc. 2) enacts the "Dead Cut" cartoon, assigned to Mose, Spruce Pink, and Junietta, as the uppity and showily dressed Spruce and Junietta refuse to recognize bootblack Mose, pretending they are, and always were, of a class far above him. Alluding to the custom of fine ladies, white and Black, keeping journals and friendship albums, Rice precedes the "Dead Cut" text by Junietta's remark, on spotting a man smoking a cigar on the corner, that she regularly records in her journal "ebery 'diculous custom of de white folks" (p. 188),[128] suggesting Junietta's allegiance to elite behaviors, as well as the gaze of Black people on white people. Act I, scene 3, transpires at Junietta's home, where her father, Pompey Ducklegs, agrees to Bone's proposal to marry Junietta. Lhamon explains the choice of Ducklegs as surname based on a slang term for knock-knees.[129] Here, Rice employs perceptions of elite African American customs, Clay's insulting cartoon, local slang, and derogation of Black bodies and movement. Despite Junietta's fainting refusal to marry Bone, a crowd of "Black" characters enters to celebrate the anticipated nuptials, singing "Come, saw upon de fiddle now." The audience is treated to another song and dance "during the symphony" (probably the music between the sung verses) when "they all dance" (p. 192). At the song's end, the characters "dance, as before. The following is the order of dance. Amos advances with Janza and Milly, who dance to Mose, etc. The others dance without precision, following down to lights, to begin chorus" (p. 193)—giving the performers scope for wild, expansive movement, out of character for proper social dancing, but displaying the perceived disordered qualities expected of African American dancing, and allowing performers to show off their movement specialties. More dancing likely ensues when Bone proposes marriage, in act II, scene 1, to a different lady, as celebration is suggested in the open-ended stage instruction, "Business" (pp. 196 and 430, n. 17).

Adding to the play another location widely associated with African American sociality, Rice places act II, scene 2, in a cellar bar of Manhattan's raucous Five Points district, where Bone sings the blackface hit "Sich a gittin' up stairs." Here, his lyrics recount his recent escape from the devil's clutches (pp. 197–98) and allude to dancing at an upcoming ball. Scenes 3 and 4 take viewers to another Black-associated location, a barbershop—barbering being among the professions open to African Americans—where Bone again meets and escapes the devil, but not before he sings a "farewell" song regretting his departure from the life of friends, gambling, and "fancy balls" (p. 203). In the last scene, Bone again faces off with the white devil, but the final moments send Sam Switchell down to hell's flames, while Bone ascends in a balloon, amid fireworks, as he tosses out his recently acquired fine clothing and his class aspirations. As the devil sinks, Bone floats skyward (p. 209), having outwitted the devil—the white man—again. Lhamon reads Bone's ascent as a "a slow, gaudy ejaculation shown as a blobular balloon rising, flares exploding, and long choruses danced out in a friskiness that crosses gender,"[130] although the script includes no dancing reference. Theatrically, however, it seems a likely choice. Lhamon adds, "This is not death, not transcendence, not a trip to heaven; it is too vulgarly lively for that. This is life released, a seeding of attitude." This ending releases Bone from his devilish vows and ambition for "respectable" status marked by fancy clothes and marriage. If spectators understood the sexual innuendo Lhamon implies in this climactic scene, they might have felt confirmed in widespread white anxieties about Black men's alluring sexuality, which pointed to the much-feared "amalgamation" of Black men with white women—a fear that motivated the riotous burning of Pennsylvania Hall in 1838, as well as Clay's cartoon "An Amalgamation Waltz," showing Black men embracing their white lady loves.[131]

Bone Squash Diavolo, thus, engaged themes of politics, class, race, and science, spiced with then-appealing (to some) humor, tunes, dancing, and scenic spectacle, delivering a range of messages that audiences could read and interpret as suited their positions. Rice adapted this work, like others in his repertoire, to different audiences and changing political circumstances. An example of the latter occurred a few years past the 1830s, offering evidence of the production's flexibility in responding to political events. The instance discussed later refers to appearance of a "coon" in act I, scene 3, of *Bone Squash Diavolo*, which I believe was inserted in fall 1844. Toward the opening of the scene, Pompey Ducklegs greets his daughter as he arrives home from market with purchases including a lobster and "anoder ting dat my old gums smack togedder at, like a cellar door leff off de hinges. It is de emblem ob Old Virginny, never tire: it am de coon" (p. 191). The dialogue continues:

JUNIETTA: Dis de coon?
POMPEY: Dat same old coon.
JUNIETTA: It are de coon.
POMPEY: It is de coon. (*Chord. Shows it.*) It puts me in mind ob de many moonshiney nights, when I used to go out wid de old Sancho, and kill 'em. I buy dat coon for your wedding supper.

For Rice's viewers, raccoons might have brought to mind, as the text suggests, the small game that enslaved African Americans savored to supplement their diets, when they had liberty to trap prey. Audiences might also have linked the "coon" to blackface stage character Zip Coon, which preceded and likely inspired Rice's Jim Crow character.[132] But in 1844 this insertion of dialogue and action into this "opera" likely arose from that year's presidential contest pitting Whig Henry Clay against Democrat James Polk. The Whig party took the raccoon as its symbol, relating itself thus to frontiersmen, though its politics embraced commercial interests and national banking, mocked in *Bone Squash*. Henry Clay, retaining the Whigs' raccoon symbol, was often depicted in that guise in political cartoons and banners, with the text, "The [or 'That'] Same Old Coon."[133] Campaign songs for and against him grasped the slogan and sang it, with lyrics appropriate to each party, to the tune of—what else?—"Old Zip Coon."

A report in the *Public Ledger* (Oct. 30, 1844) on *Bone Squash Diavolo*, just before election day, reveals the political fissures resulting in Clay's defeat.[134] It also illuminates Rice's career-long perspicacity in grasping such tensions to vary his acts, make cutting points, and stimulate spectator engagement. The article "Excitement at the Theatre" reported on the Chestnut Street's production of "the burlesque Opera of 'Bone Squash Diavolo'" two days earlier, when an innovation threw spectators "into a state of political excitement by introducing a fat live Coon into the piece." The raccoon's appearance stimulated cheering and hissing, reflecting viewers' political allegiances, and brought the show to a halt. After the animal's removal, Rice stepped to the footlights to address the crowd—such performer-audience interaction being a staple of his shows. He "stated that the play was written some ten years ago, that the Coon was a portion of the play at that time, and that its introduction now had no political reference whatever." But no such performance choice is recorded in earlier reports of this show. As Rice faced the noisy spectators, some engaged in loud crowing, perhaps in support of Jim Crow Rice but more likely for the Democrats' rooster symbol.[135] To reclaim attention to the show, "the players proceeded to a lively part of the piece"—probably the song and dance "Come saw upon de fiddle now," the play's next "lively" number. While this "quieted the disturbance," Rice liked his audience to respond actively—surely just what he expected with the live coon appearance. When the play ended, the spectators "came rushing from the pit and boxes into the street, some crowing like chicken-cocks, and others giving vent to their feelings . . . according to the party to which they were attached." Given Philadelphia's riotous history in this period, this minor outburst "appeared to be a mere struggle of the lungs without any angry or malicious spirit," the *Public Ledger* reported. That "malicious spirit" was amply expressed in ongoing anti-Black violence and, peaking in the period of this theater incident, anti-Irish nativist riots.

From High to Low: Social Dance

A wide range of entertainments that Philadelphians enjoyed in the 1830s focused on the human body itself: political debates about who qualified as human, phrenological readings of moral and intellectual traits, opera ballet, and operatic blackface. Social occasions too called forth bodily display at balls, private parties, and informal gatherings that, like stage works, reflected political and social tensions in the city and nation. Dancing masters' advertisements in mainstream newspapers for lessons, balls, and academies addressed white Philadelphians only. The polish such behaviors afforded proved the civility and elevation of those who practiced them—a polish, cartoons and stage acts inferred, inaccessible to Black people.

The social-dance sphere intersected with the theatrical: several city dancing masters had theater connections, including P. H. Hazard, teacher of Philadelphia's current and aspiring social elites and of U.S. ballet starlets Augusta Maywood and Mary Ann Lee.[136] His story draws this narrative back to the stage, while it also addresses the ballroom. Hazard has been credited as a member of the Paris Opera corps de ballet, and his wife as a ballet dancer from Brussels; they toured Germany before moving to Philadelphia. Hazard was clearly a remarkable teacher, for Maywood and Lee had each studied with him for barely two years before their astounding debuts. Since Hazard connected them to the center of European ballet culture, it made sense to advertise his name as dancing master and stager on bills for the debutantes' performances, establishing their credentials to take on *La Bayadere*. The girls' successes reflected back to their master, who had accomplished so much so quickly. He taught other stage aspirants in Philadelphia, the U.S. city with the most homegrown ballet entrants;[137] among these Philadelphians were the lovely Emma Ince, the four Vallee sisters, and George Washington Smith. After the successes of Maywood and Lee, Hazard advertised leading a complete French ballet company, but aside from the principal ballerina, Mlle. Joséphine Stéphan, and M. and Mme. Hazard, "the new French corps de ballet"[138] turned out to be Hazard's U.S. pupils. Failing to achieve the standards Philadelphians then knew to expect from European ballet dancers, the enterprise foundered. Still, during the troupe's season at the Chestnut Street Theatre (Nov. 1838–Jan. 1839), Hazard staged major European ballets, including *La Déliverance des Grecs*[139] and *La Fille mal gardée*, while giving precious stage experience to students and receiving praise for his own performance skills. A reviewer lauded him as "a muscular and elastic dancer, scientific and very graceful" with "fine" *pirouettes*, while another crowned him "the best male dancer on the stage in our country."[140] Within a few months, Hazard was outshone by the dancing of Paul Taglioni, who appeared at the Chestnut with his ballerina wife, Amalie Galster Taglioni. Yet, owing to an economic depression that affected theaters, these "two very splendid dancers" played to poor houses and kept their visit short.[141]

After this disappointing theatrical season, Hazard turned attention fully to teaching, welcoming social-dance pupils. Probably assisted by his wife, Hazard apparently earned a substantial living, teaching members of society, holding elegant balls, and composing popular ballroom dances, named for him.[142] He had one more stage stint, in November 1846, as "Albert of Silesia" in "the Grand Ballet of Gizelle," supporting French ballerina Mme. Blangy at Philadelphia's Arch Street Theatre.[143] *Giselle* had played in the city a few months earlier (Apr. 1846) with Hazard's pupil Emma Ince as the lead, while another Hazard student, Mary Ann Lee, was the first American to dance that ballet (Boston, Jan. 1, 1846), partnered by George Washington Smith. Hazard left the stage after the brief partnership with Blangy. His notices as a dancing master also cease after this time, when Mme. Hazard alone is listed as "teacher of dancing"; she was then, perhaps, a widow.

The field for dancing masters was crowded in the 1830s, suggesting the city could sustain many teachers. Those of different classes showed off dance training, as noted by wealthy farmer-lawyer Sidney George Fisher, who attended private balls among the city's elite, as well as public charity balls raising funds for civic projects. The latter gatherings, he remarked, "have a good effect in bringing the different classes together occasionally, & tend to produce a more kindly feeling on both sides."[144] His side ("the higher order"), he felt, "are impressed with respect" at such cross-class sociality, "by witnessing the multitudes of decent, good-looking people" *not* of the "higher order"—remarks highlighting class consciousness and the importance of bodily presentation for the young republic's citizens. The other side ("the lower") Fisher felt certain "are gratified by being in the same room with persons whom they consider above them, by having an opportunity of seeing and observing their appearance and manner, & by feeling that they do not disdain to mingle with them and partake of the same amusements with themselves." Fisher also attended a "revival" of the "old" City Dancing Assembly, of which he wrote, "I like a public ball—I mean a select one." Cross-class pleasure stretched only so far.

Among those, aside from the Hazards, identified as "dancing master" or the like in this decade were William Albright, Mr. August, Mr. Badger, Anthony Bonnaffon, D. L. Carpenter (who occasionally appeared with his students on city stages), Thomas and Tobias Fries, Victor Guillou, F. C. Labbe, F. D. Mallat, Frederick Pohlman, and Henry Whale (a stage dancer in his youth).[145] Classes, private lessons, practicing balls, public balls, and demonstrations by the master or his best students were part of the social whirl. Although Frances Trollope disdained Americans' behavior, finding that even the wealthy lacked "refinement," Philadelphians and others in cities and towns eagerly sought access to dancing masters, assemblies, and courtesy texts.[146] Opportunities to learn proper deportment and refine one's physical expression, combined with the formality and excitement of a ball, drew those who could afford lessons and, if required, tickets to such gatherings.[147] For those who found private or class lessons too costly, the price of a magazine might be manageable; periodicals like *Godey's Lady's Book* disseminated the fundamentals of etiquette and dance performance, as did American-flavored etiquette books. Such forces for sociality and refinement had their detractors; the perceived immodesty of the waltz, the expense and showiness of ballroom garb, and the intermixing of people from different classes were seen by some as dangers to the social order, particularly for women, whose delicacy needed protection and whose prudence must be nurtured.[148] Thus, lessons for ladies were often separate from gentlemen's.

The dancing masters listed earlier catered to white society. Did other masters serve the African American community? No such Philadelphia advertisements from this period have come to light. The cartoon "A Five-Points Exclusive" (1833) suggests that Black ladies in New York City were investing in dancing lessons with Frenchman "Mr. Boeyfong," the dancing master named in Clay's *Lessons* depiction.[149] The African ball discussed earlier is another clue to elite Black social dancing. Writing in 1896, W.E.B. Du Bois listed three "dancing masters" in the category "Clerks, Semi-Professional and

Responsible Workers" among the city's African American population, but I have found no documentation of these teachers' professional forebears sixty years earlier,[150] although cartoons based on Clay's "Life in Philadelphia" series broadcast degrading depictions of African American social-dance aspirants. In addition to those already mentioned, such satires included "A black ball: La pastorelle" and "The Lady Patroness of Alblacks," demonstrating white satirists' imagined, mocking views of society among elite and aspiring Black city dwellers.

Responding to the political tensions, anti-Black violence, and dehumanizing categorizations that characterized the city during this decade, African American leaders urged Black residents away from frivolities and toward strict morality, hard work, and education for improving their lot and avoiding attention elicited by behaviors construed as loud, disorderly, or ridiculous.[151] There is but one oblique reference to the ballroom in Joseph Willson's detailed *Sketches of the Higher Classes of Colored Society in Philadelphia*, published in 1841, reflecting his familiarity with elite African American society from his arrival in the city in 1833.[152] Whether taught by dancing masters or not, one Philadelphia "gentleman of color," James Forten, was known not only for his industry, honesty, wealth, and dedication to his people but also for his "correct deportment" and "genuine politeness,"[153] which surely required Forten's immense self-control, given the rampant mockeries of Black behavior.

Was this avoidance of dancing (at least, of its mention) unique to Philadelphia's upper-crust Black society? Samuel Cornish, in the *Colored American*, argued against theater and dance attendance, a fact suggesting his readers—literate African Americans throughout the nation—required such warning.[154] He noted that even "Christian parents often quiet their consciences, while they indulge their children" in dance's "gay pleasure" because they find "that genteel manners can be acquired nowhere but in the dancing school and in the assembly room." Yet Cornish was "well convinced, that *there is more real good breeding and true politeness out of the ballroom than is found in it*." Apparently, some in the upper echelons of Black society arranged such instruction for themselves and families, prompting Cornish's article.

White perceptions of African American dancing as depicted in the city's major papers spread the embarrassments of perceived Black misbehavior before a wide readership. In 1836, a *Public Ledger* column, "Immitation of High Life," suggested the kinds of antics the city's African American leaders so urgently proscribed. The author also insinuated the primate connection of his subjects: "The blacks who are noted for their apish propensities are faithfully following the example of their betters"—white people—in gambling, drinking, dancing, and resorting with "kept mistresses," a remark raising the specter of amalgamation.[155] Such behavior, the report proceeded, resulted in arrests of a "collection of the sable fashionable rabble" (intermixing race, class aspiration, and unsavory behavior) arising from disorders at a "noted dance, gambling, and bawdy house . . . where a ball and card party" was announced. This den of sin on Pine Street "above Sixth," was abhorred by "the neighbors, respectable colored persons," who "testified that the house was a nuisance, a vile recepticle of vice, where the gambler, the drunkard, and the prostitutes, white and black, nightly assembled." Such gathering sites were plentiful: newspapers often reported "negro dance" parties or "frolics" that created "disturbances," "violations of the peace," noise, and brawls in dance halls, taverns, and streets, often in the heavily African American neighborhood between South and Locust Streets from Front to Eighth.[156] A report from within the Black community confirms that such disturbances drew attention of African American arbiters of morality.[157] In this case, Robert Sippel was found "guilty" by a Bethel A.M.E. Church committee "of a Breach of Discipline in the following cases: first, by beating his Wife. 2nd by visiting improper places such as Dance houses," and "getting drunk," as witnesses testified. Sippel "remains impenitent & is accordingly Dismissed." Such flagrant violations were cause for expulsion from the circle of Black respectability.

Churches themselves might provide vibrant movement opportunities of dancing that sustained aspects of African spirituality, built community among Black Philadelphians, and directed full-bodied physicality into socially managed channels. Du Bois reported on a small, "old order . . . Negro congregation" located in "the slums of the Fifth Ward" (Chestnut to South Street, Seventh Street to the waterfront) in the 1830s.[158] The congregation would work itself "to a fervor" that drew attendees from their seats toward the pulpit, where "the most excitable of their number entered the ring," clapping hands and contorting their bodies. Others joined, with "clapping of hands and wild and loud singing, frequently springing into the air, and shouting loudly . . . for hours, until all were completely exhausted, and some had fainted." Earlier in the nineteenth century, John Fanning Watson decried the vigorous singing and dancing he witnessed at camp meetings in Pennsylvania, when "the illiterate *blacks* of the society" participated in—to Watson's mind—the "most exceptionable error" of singing, dancing, and rhythmic movement, lasting hours into the night.[159] Apparently, white attendees, in separate tents, were inspired by such practices. Watson witnessed some Black celebrants falling into "the jerks," a kind of dancing that resulted in "very great deadness of mind" (trances?). In that period, "Black Methodists Holding a Prayer Meeting" (Svinin/Krimmel) depicted an outdoor Philadelphia setting where congregants leapt, flung arms high, and fainted as the minister, guiding them from a doorway, gesticulated. Clay's

1836 caricature of such camp-meeting enthusiasm among Black and white Americans highlights the preacher's vigor, as he sends his emotional listeners into fits of weeping and remorse. While some Black ministers decried physically exuberant religious practices, such rhythmic, musical, and movement-based expressivity persisted, an enduring link to the spirituality of forms like the African ring shout.[160]

Like their white neighbors, African American residents sought their own opportunities for expression, entertainment, and theatricality. Thus, we return to this chapter's starting point, the Philadelphia theater in the 1830s, to note one more newspaper report, the column "City Police" for March 27, 1837—just as the disenfranchisement debate began. "Theatrical Mishap—A disappointed audience"[161] named John Bailey and Lewis Hamer, "gentlemen of color," who "were brought up this morning charged with a breach of the peace.... Messrs. Rhodes and Little, two colored men, issued a Bill, informing the ladies and gentlemen of color, that they had opened a Theatre, in Pine St above Sixth." This may have been the same hall mentioned earlier as a "bawdy house." The bill advertised performances of "the Indian Hunter, the Sailor's Dream, with other interesting pieces," a project that proved appealing: "The audience were on the ground at an early hour in the evening." Hamer served as "door-keeper, when John Bailey, who was to be one of the principal performers, came up to the door and wished to pass in—the door-keeper objected, not having knowledge of him; but John could not brook such indignity." A brawl, involving "a mob," ensued. The constable appeared, both men were brought "to the watchhouse," and "the play was postponed until a more convenient season." Who these individuals were is unknown;[162] no further notices about this intended and unusual African American theatrical endeavor have appeared.

City authorities, apparently, would not countenance a true African American theater enterprise, and this performance's irregularities provided opportunity to obstruct it. Documented performances and indications of saloon entertainments suggest that the most visible theatrical representations of Black people in 1830s Philadelphia were "delineations" by white men in blackface—"Jim Crow" Rice and imitators. While African American performers likely appeared at saloons, fairs, and street markets, these were little recorded and remain obscured from archival records. Such bodies of perceived difference—here in race, but elsewhere in gender, class, ethnicity, and behavior—were the everyday stuff of life in Philadelphia, determining prohibitions, privileges, opportunities, and portrayals.

4

Dancing "Philadelphia in Slices"

The 1840s

George G. Foster's newspaper serial "Philadelphia in Slices" placed fine slivers of the Quaker City, its people, and their society under the author's journalistic, literary microscope.[1] Foster had written for Philadelphia's *North American* newspaper before moving to New York in 1848. He filled his "slices" with common folk—workers, loiterers, men, and women—depicting different classes, races, employments, and tastes, including those who danced or watched dancing. Foster's references, supplemented by dance commentary from other texts, guide this chapter's discussion, *linking dance to publication and print culture.* Joellen Meglin has pointed to the "particular fascination" of the early nineteenth century "with the way narrative structures might be represented in dance,"[2] which was indeed in conversation with literary and other published works.

Some articles in Philadelphia's many and wide-ranging newspapers addressed dance and dancers—reporting, puffing, critiquing, condemning. Newspapers became "democracy's favorite medium of print,"[3] with increases also in publication of books, magazines, and graphic images. Steam presses, railroads, steamboats, catalog sales, and bookshops disseminated print matter to readers of all classes.[4] Philadelphia's *Public Ledger* was among the nation's earliest penny papers (1836); it competed with the *North American*, for which Foster wrote, eventually swallowing it. Dance culture, as revealed and highlighted in such sources, also saw significant forward momentum in the 1840s, beginning with a high point of antebellum U.S. theater.

Elssler in America

Fanny Elssler, the most renowned dancer of the period to appear on American stages, made her U.S. debut, in New York, on May 17, 1840. A Philadelphian played a significant role in bringing the star to these shores.[5] Henry Wikoff, son of a wealthy Philadelphia physician, was living in Paris, admiring Elssler at the Opera, when Stephen Price, manager of New York's Park Theatre, sought his assistance in attracting Elssler for a U.S. tour. Wikoff's introduction of Elssler to the American colony in Paris convinced her that not all was savagery in the United States, and that a tour could be advantageous. When renowned dancer Lucien Petipa declined to join as her tour partner, Elssler chose the French-trained Irish dancer James Sullivan, performing as James Sylvain, listed at times as "Maitre de Ballet et Artiste de L'Academie Royal de Paris."[6] When Price died in the midst of negotiations, Wikoff assumed Elssler's management, for her ladylike behavior reassured him that his name would not be sullied by association with "an opera dancer." He later proved adept at sullying his own reputation.

Those prominent Americans in Paris who met Elssler wrote letters home praising her, creating a stir before the ballerina arrived. Wikoff also courted New York's popular newspapers, particularly the *Herald*, demonstrating the press's publicity power.[7] Elssler's success at New York's Park, prepared by lengthy newspaper puffs, was sweeping. By mid-June 1840, she was packing the Chestnut Street Theatre in Philadelphia. The neighborhood around that building was so thronged for her opening that Elssler made her way into the theater only by subterfuge.

In Philadelphia, Elssler presented two ballets, *La Tarentule* and *L'Amour; ou, La Rose Animée*, and the national dances "la Cracovienne," "la Cachucha," "la Smolenska," and "el Jaleo de Jeres," with *pas seuls* and *pas de deux*. *La Tarantule* was a two-act comic ballet (choreography Coralli, libretto Scribe, music Gide) that Elssler premiered at the Paris Opera in June 1839. The work, a complicated contrivance about the effects of a tarantula bite and the romantic designs of the doctor treating the lovely patient, gave Elssler and Sylvain opportunity to dance a vibrant tarantella—spoofed as "La Mosquito" by the chubby, tutu-clad comedian William Mitchell at New York's Olympic Theatre.[8] In *L'Amour*, created by Sylvain in 1839 when he was ballet master at London's St. James Theatre, Elssler danced Flora to his Zephyr; this and Elssler's other balletic choices, remarked Durang, "were mere zephyrs in substance; as flimsy as the gauze wings affixed to theatrical Cupids."[9] But Sylvain proved a good choice of partner for Elssler's tour: he spoke English, staged works, whipped American dance choruses into presentable shape, taught aspiring U.S. dancers, and spread among them Elssler's repertoire, bestowing her tour with longevity beyond her presence on U.S. shores.[10] Sylvain's dancing was praised as "light and graceful" by New England Transcendentalist Margaret Fuller, although she lamented that he was no match for Elssler's dazzling presence.[11] James Rees, a discerning critic, praised Sylvain as "an artist . . . of the first order," while dancing master Durang considered him "a clever artiste and a capital ballet drill master—industrious, ambitious." Chronicler John Fanning Watson described Sylvain as "the impersonation of Perrot": he "leaps about as if his feet were made of India rubber, and spins around upon the point of his toe like a top. He joins the figurante, and they twirl away and glide along, holding eloquent discourse with their pliant limbs, after the manner of waltzing"—in close embrace. "He, wonderful for grace and beauty of person, is as much the idol of the ladies, as is the other the goddess of the gentlemen."[12] But Watson insisted that any virtuous lady unaccustomed to such displays "instinctively hides her head from a sight" so shocking to her sense of decency, for "there is no affectation here. It is nature out." Audiences loved it.

Elssler's "national" dances, particularly those of eastern Europe and Spain (Figure 4.1), thrilled Philadelphia audiences. Elssler and Sylvain could present these short folkloric works without assistance, but for longer ballets, Elssler needed a corps de ballet. In Philadelphia, Sylvain engaged the Vallee sisters—Elisa, Henriette, Julia, and Amelie—whose French parents had settled in the city, where the sisters were performing by 1838.[13] Even before Elssler arrived, one "Miss Vallee" had "danced 'The Cachucha' very well; then a new affair." Also joining Elssler's company was Philadelphian George Washington Smith, who had earlier danced hornpipes, and perhaps more, at the Walnut Street Theatre.[14] Smith attested, years later, to Elssler's enduring impact: "no one who ever knew Fanny Elssler could forget her. She was the queen—the matchless queen—of the ballet." Also in Elssler's corps, at times, were English comic mime Charles Parsloe, American dancer Julia Turnbull, and European performers Jules and Egerie Martin, Pauline Desjardins, and Madame Arraline (Brooks), already performing on U.S. stages when Elssler appeared.[15]

Philadelphia print media reported on Elssler before her arrival there. The *Public Ledger* reprinted a statement by New York publisher-politician Mordecai Noah, informing readers that "the Park was jammed to overflow" for Elssler's Spanish *cachucha* there.[16] Noah declared she "made a more ethereal, graceful and meaning thing of this splendid dance than any of her predecessors on the stage have done. It was a brilliant display of most ornate and finished posture, such as one might well imagine the Medician Venus would make, were that wonder of the sculptural art to descend from her pedestal, and move to the music of the castanets." But Philadelphia's *Public Ledger* critic

Figure 4.1. "Fanny Elssler in the favourite dance La cachucha," Napoleon Sarony (early 1840s), Washington, D.C. *(Jerome Robbins Dance Division, New York Public Library Digital Collections, Public Domain. Accessed June 19, 2024. https://digitalcollections.nypl.org/items/f89398a0-8c36-0131-55fc-58d385a7b928)*

dismissed as "burlesque" such efforts to raise a castanet dance to the heights of classical art: "Elssler should not be commended for discovering 'much meaning' in her dances, unless she means *well*, which we think is improbable." The *Public Ledger* accused the New York newspapers of having been bought by the advertising largess of Elssler's management. Once she appeared at the

Chestnut, however, the *Public Ledger* conceded that she performed "before the largest audience that has greeted a player at that house for a long time, and with great success," and ballet lovers predicted "she will dance down any opposition in two nights."[17]

The newspapers fought on in the Elssler wars. One opinion, signed "An Amateur,"[18] fumed that Elsslermania had seized the city before the ballerina even appeared, although Amateur conceded that "these plaudits were renewed" at the Chestnut "upon the first simple *pas*, elegant indeed," for Elssler "cannot move without elegance." But, Amateur asserted, she lacked "any extraordinary skill." He pondered the grounds for what he scorned as unwarranted enthusiasm: "The spectators, owing probably to the want of opportunities, are unable to appreciate real excellence"—thus dismissing such fine dancers as the Ravel troupe and Celeste in educating Philadelphia audiences. Tellingly, Amateur stated, these outbursts of Elssler enthusiasm "indicate that want of national pride and self-esteem, too prevalent in the present day, that leads us to give unhesitating approbation to whatever may have enjoyed the patronage of fashionable society in our own or in foreign countries." This shameful failure of national pride prompted "the metamorphosis of the human figure into those apish appearances . . . a servile mimicry of the manners and costumes of foreign nations." Such airs Amateur found especially "disgraceful" in Philadelphia, renowned "for the beauty and elegance of its ladies and for the air of respectability, propriety and gentility, that distinguish its inhabitants." This rational world, Amateur felt, was threatened by Elssler's blinding popularity. George Foster, sardonically slicing up Philadelphia, also remarked on the city's famed orderliness: "Of course the reader is aware that the streets in Philadelphia are as regularly balanced as a merchant's ledger, and that they always faithfully perform their promise," with regularity, conformity, and "but one way to go anywhere or to do anything,"[19] dictated by the city's staid "bourgeoisie." Like "Amateur," Foster noticed the many "very pretty" women of the town, including its "gay Quakeresses" who, dressed in "drab gowns" and "angular bonnets," he compared to "exquisite statues done up in brown paper," yet out enjoying the city's shops and entertainments. Elssler, liberated of any drabness or angularity, ultimately captivated even reluctant "Amateur"; he admitted he could not restrain his enthusiasm when Elssler's dancing ended, "for so pleased was I with the performance, concluded by her artless little speech," thanking the audience in accented English for their reception, "that my feelings . . . discharged through the palms of my hands; which yet tremble from the effects of this *involuntary* though not *unwilling* exertion." Elssler pierced even scrupulous defenses.

Two days later, the *Public Ledger* took up the American ballet cause: "Miss Emma Ince takes her Benefit this evening, at McArann's Garden, and appears in FOUR different dances. She has the services of Master Diamond, the unparalleled Negro Dancer, and Mr. Whitlock, the Banjo Player." Blackface performers Diamond and Whitlock were later associated with early minstrel troupes. The author continued: "Those who wish to patronize native talent will no doubt be much delighted with the performance of this extraordinary little Danseuse," Emma Ince.[20] Pleasure gardens, even more than regular theaters, intermixed entertainments to draw the broadest audiences; apparently, McArann found ballet and blackface, presented together, perfectly consonant. As minstrelsy would, in the 1840s and thereafter, be widely proclaimed as the U.S. contribution to world culture, the placing of "native talent" like Miss Ince beside blackface stars Diamond and Whitlock made sense. Ince was just twelve years old at this time, with but brief study under P. H. Hazard.[21] She must have been delightful to watch; Philadelphia editor James Rees published a lengthy encomium to the young dancer in his *Dramatic Mirror and Literary Companion*, one of the first U.S. magazines "Devoted to the Stage and the Fine Arts." Rees compared Ince to the unforgettable Elssler: "The impressions produced by Elssler, are still vivid in the recollection of the writer, and has enabled him to test with severity" any *faux pas* "discernible in the dancing of Miss Ince, and in her conception of those identical *chef d'ouvres* of that celebrated *danseuse*. These were few," and—significant for Philadelphians—"what has appeared worthy of particular notice, was the modesty of deportment and dress peculiar to herself, which adds materially to the beauty and perfection of the art."[22] Rees assured readers that he had no personal connection to Ince, who drew "this 'passing notice,' from the display of her talents alone." Ince married young and retired from the stage, departing the lists of enduring U.S. ballerinas. Yet, in her brief career, she danced *La Bayadere, La Sylphide,* and *The Fawn's Leap* (created especially for her), along with Elssler-associated national dances—the *cachucha, smolenska, cracovienne,* and *jaleo de Jeres*.

The German-speaking community of Philadelphia heartily championed Elssler. She graciously offered her services at the Arch Street Theatre for "the benefit of [dramatist] Herr R. Riesse, her Countryman," dancing "a Divertisement" with Sylvain and Emma Ince.[23] The native child-dancer and the international star shared the stage. A few days later, "a number of German gentlemen, professors and amateurs of music," "paid a compliment to Fanny Elssler, the celebrated dancer, . . . by performing several airs from the opera of *Der Freischutz*, &c., in front of her hotel," along with a crowd of onlookers. Although it was past midnight, Elssler appeared at her balcony to "acknowledged the compliment by a graceful curtsey."

Ince was but one of the U.S. dancers benefiting from Elssler's presence; among others, Mary Ann Lee studied with Sylvain when she was in the same city with the star; and G. W. Smith danced in Elssler's troupe, improving his technique and stage presence by training with Sylvain and observing Elssler.[24] The tour had further economic and cultural impacts. Theater managers saw houses packed after a low spell, but they complained bitterly of the high costs of presenting Elssler, resulting, they claimed, in net losses. Manager Ludlow, of the nation's southern circuit, found Elssler "a magnificent creature in form," but "without a soul"[25]—a claim at variance with Margaret Fuller's perception when, the story goes, Ralph Waldo Emerson turned to her as they watched Elssler in Boston. He exclaimed, "Margaret, this is poetry," to which Fuller responded, "No, Ralph, this is religion."[26] But, to businessman Ludlow, Elssler was "avaricious to an excess, and so exacting that, if she could have had her will, she would have taken the entire receipts of every night's performance." William Wood, Philadelphia's Chestnut Street Theatre manager, agreed: Elssler had drawn huge crowds, leaving many with the impression that she "must have been profitable to the management, when in truth she broke it."[27] Durang, reporting financial figures for the star's shows in Baltimore, bemoaned that, for U.S. theaters, "this Fanny Elssler incident is but a fair sample of the ruinous starring system." Such claims gain credence in light of Elssler's own response to news that the Chestnut Street Theatre had lost money on her fall 1841 run. Manager L. T. Pratt requested that Elssler assist him in a benefit to recoup some of the losses, to which she replied, in a letter read from the stage, that, despite the "inconvenience, and a considerable pecuniary sacrifice" this service would cost her, she would perform and "decline all renumeration [*sic*] ... in acknowledgement of the extreme good faith and punctuality" of manager Pratt.[28]

Money and morality overlapped in some published comments. Editor of the vituperative *New York Polyanthos* newspaper, George Washington Dixon—himself a popular blackface singer in an earlier professional incarnation—ripped into Elssler for luring Americans to spend dollars watching a "gilded, glittering, shameless creature," a "guilty outrage of the laws of society and of God" whose "fallen spirit is in truth a scoff at female virtue and an impulse to female degradation."[29] Fanny was dancing her triumph, Dixon claimed, while, "in an obscure hovel" in the city, "without fire, alone sat a poor woman, holding to her bosom, her sick and dying babe" (Figure 4.2). Dixon deployed his theatrical lessons well: "As the keen wind came through the crevices," and the mother "clasped the dying child to her bosom; at that moment, a dancing woman, a stranger, with her wealth of thousands, and her ingots of gold and silver, made her last graceful bow," laughing at the duped Americans. Dixon's

Figure 4.2. Front-page cartoon for "Elssler and the Dying Babe," *New York Polyanthos* v. 6, n. 11 (June 19, 1841). *(General Research Division, The New York Public Library Digital Collections, Public Domain. Accessed June 19, 2024. https://digitalcollections.nypl.org/items /4732d310-a888-0131-140a-58d385a7bbd0)*

accompanying cartoon depicted the shivering mother and babe beneath the *grand battement* of Fanny's revealing leg, moneybags hanging from her limbs, as the satisfied lowlives in the audience turned their backs on the tragic scene.

Elssler's second season in the Quaker City was to open November 10, 1840; by mid-September, the *Public Ledger* was condemning Elssler, her dancing, and her perceived immorality. Introducing his wordy complaint, the anonymous author turned—perhaps with a wink—to science: "All animals that have any legs to walk upon love play, and man loves it particularly; and the phrenologists tell us that all playing animals have an *organ of play*. . . . Hence we are playing animals, and rendered such by *nature*."[30] Thus, the author did "not quarrel with stage dancing *in the abstract*," for "dancing is a salutary exercise. . . . perfectly innocent when properly regulated." Yet, on questions of morality, French-imported ballet aligned with the devil:

> While admitting the propriety of dancing, on or off the stage, when properly conducted, we must decidedly condemn the stage dancing imported from Europe within the last twenty years, and of which we have had specimens in Hutin, Vestris, Celeste, Augusta, Lecompte, Elssler, and Satan knows how many others. This dancing, in expression of countenance, attitude, movement and dress, violates the rules of propriety observed in social intercourse by the respectable portion of the American population. It is immoral in *itself*, and immoral in *tendency*; . . . it is accompanied with an exposure that would be positively indecent, and therefore immoral, if the dancer stood still, and its movements and attitudes are intended to express feelings and passions of which any public expression is sinful, because corrupting.

Elssler and her ballet sisters were guilty of offense in displaying *movements* and *attitudes* intended "to expose the person; and, aided by the dress, they do it as effectually as if the performer were naked." The female body was revealed—and offensive. Its movements in dance were "intended to express ideas," inciting "licentious passions." To this writer, the body could express no "ideas" with other meaning.

A second installment published in the same paper expanded on movements and meanings in theatrical expression: "All the intellectual and moral feelings . . . may be properly represented upon the stage; and of such representations we have examples in the sublime or beautiful conceptions of Shakspeare [*sic*], Corneille, . . . and others"[31]—drama, not dance. Women like Celeste, Elssler, and other stage professionals employed costume and movements with the intention to "exhibit mere animal instinct with revolting significancy." The author asked if any woman, "however guarded in conduct off the stage, can be pure in principle and modest in feeling, who, for any purpose, and more especially for gain," displays herself in "an indecent exposure?" The *Public Ledger* was shocked to report that Elssler had offered a substantial sum to the Boston women's committee for erecting a monument at the Revolutionary War site at Bunker Hill, which terribly flustered the New England ladies.[32]

Still, when Elssler returned to Philadelphia in May and June of 1841, the public clamored to see her in *The Maid of Cashmere* (*La Bayadere*), *Dew Drop* (*La Sylphide*, choreography Taglioni, 1832), and the ballet-pantomime *La Somnambula* (1827, choreography Jean-Pierre Aumer, libretto Scribe, music Ferdinand Hérold). Elssler remained a publication subject: an unauthorized but supposedly "Correct Sketch of the Life of Mad'lle Fanny Elssler," published by the pseudonymous "Peter Pindar" of Philadelphia, detailed her ascribed string of love affairs with courtiers across Europe.[33] Even the sheet music for Elssler's ballets was condemned by one writer, for it was "publish[ed] . . . with pictures of Fanny Elssler and other public dancing women, in costumes that insult the dignity of female nature."[34] Yet the music flew off the shelves, prompting the despairing author to ask, "Will mothers, daughters, and teachers take a hint?" It was the women who must resist; the men were lost under Fanny's spell.

One such entranced viewer, "Dramaticus," implored the Chestnut Street management to procure Elssler's services for another run,[35] but she would not dance again in Philadelphia after September 1841. That season, she repeated her earlier repertoire, adding *Nathalie, ou la Laitiere Suisse* (1821, libretto Taglioni). Durang gave the U.S. cast: Elssler danced *Nathalie*, Mme. Desjardins, *Leda*; Sylvain, *Le Count*; Charles Parsloe, *Simkin*. Houses were full, and at each evening's end, Elssler addressed the audience, stirring warm applause. "Indeed," Durang noted, "Elssler understood the diplomatic art very well. She didn't go to royal courts for nothing." Still, "the beautiful skill and grace of the 'Cracovienne' and its kindred national dances failed to keep pace with the nightly expenses," Durang claimed, causing Elssler to bring out "the more imposing ballets of 'La Sylphide' and 'La Bayadere,'" but her "novelty . . . had ceased." As a theater man, Durang may have been backstage to witness the star's response: "She was evidently chagrined, got the *pouts*, was quite uncolloquial behind the scenes, where she was wont to be so merrily talkative, although the stage was nightly converted into . . . a floral homage through which she had to vault knee-deep" to exit. Sadly, "the attraction, which was to have saved the Chesnut from bankruptcy, only hastened the crisis of its fate," although Elssler did close the season "with brilliancy."[36]

Despite Durang's reading, the intellectual and social elite flocked to the theater and also defended dancing as art, countering moralists' condemnations. In personal diaries and published statements, Elssler's admirers expressed rapturous enthusiasm. Philadelphia farmer-lawyer Sidney George Fisher attended her New York opening; he described "her light, airy and graceful movements" that "far surpassed anything I have ever seen." He found her costume "tasteful," her performance "arch, sportive & piquant."[37] Fisher followed her seasons; in fall 1840 she was "quite intoxicating. Her attitudes would form a series of studies for a painter & sculptor & the effect of her floating motions & her exquisite, piquant & artless manner is inconceivable 'till witnessed." Philadelphia magazine *Alexander's Messenger* defended her: "Never has there been a *danseuse* so much abused as Fanny Elssler, and never has one visited this country who so little deserved abuse."[38] Moreover, "all France and Germany look up to" her profession "with admiration." While "her enemies have endeavored to set down" her dancing "as lascivious," the writer asserted that "in fact, such feelings are only experienced by men of corrupt feelings." Elssler, a "lady-like and reserved woman," was "kind and beneficent"; the elegant thank-you dinner she gave to the Chestnut Street Theatre's orchestra, with a charming speech and generous gifts, was offered as evidence.

Rees's *Dramatic Mirror* proffered more praise: Elssler was so "distinguished and fascinating" that the author succumbed to "the witchery of her graceful movements."[39] The "heterogeneous" audience included "some of the loveliest female countenances, we ever beheld," who watched the dancer "with eyes lit up in resplendent loveliness, glowing with admiration at the grace and elasticity of step." He felt sure the ladies saw their own loveliness in Elssler, as audiences she drew to the theaters included more women, and of respectable classes, than typical at the time. Another commentator considered Elssler's U.S. audiences "the most intelligent" viewers, finding in her dancing "latent ideas of grace and harmony" not seen since "ancient Greece gave birth to the most exquisite proportions in sculpture, architecture, the severe graceful form of literature itself."[40] Elssler could "embody abstract qualities," pushing women's capacities beyond the physical and the spiritual, to encompass the intellectual.[41] Women might have appreciated Elssler for her beauty as well as her expressions of female independence, creative depth, and physical prowess,[42] but the *Dramatic Mirror* insisted on her ethereality: "Who could witness the *aerial* flights of the charming Fanny, and not be moved with their transcendent beauty," for "'*She moves a Goddess, and looks a Queen.*'"

The astute Charles Durang evaluated Elssler corporeally: she was "tall," "symmetrical," and with "immense muscular power." To her "uncommonly expressive face" she added "agile gracefulness in her 'poses,' attitudes and arabesque combinations,"[43] all revealing "chasteness and elegance, with nothing of the immodest exposure of the French ballet." Her "nether garments were of a proper length, without obscuring her precision of step." On her technique, Durang observed, "Her raising herself on the points of her toes with so much vigor of firmness, and thus bending, were wonderful, forming perfect animated pictures. Her *enjambées* and *entrachats* were neat, yet vigorous," performed "without the least apparent effort."[44] Elssler's pleasingly "light German countenance" was matched by her "affable and ladylike" comportment. Thus, "whatever may be the whisperings of her social life, she certainly received the attentions of those who were fastidious as to the proprieties of life here. The civilities of the polite and intellectual Christian were granted freely to her."

Durang's reference to Elssler's ethnicity as marked in her physique, and the earlier newspaper nod to scientific analyses of the human body at "play," point toward the scientific interest Elssler stirred, including a phrenological study of her skull, capacities, and intellect by one of the "Phrenological Fowlers."[45] Lorenzo Fowler combined his reading of Elssler with phrenological analysis of New York sculptor James Stout, who had created an image of Elssler so excellent that, Fowler reported, Elssler "has bound herself to sit to no other sculptor in Europe for five years ensuing" (p. 15), highlighting her choice of an American over any European artist. Aside from the admirable sculpture, Fowler was drawn to analyze Elssler because her "qualities of mind, combined with her physical powers, have excited so much curiosity . . . for a few years past" (p. iv) that he wished to provide answers to those seeking to understand the exceptional artist. Fowler concluded the pamphlet with a chart of measurements of Elssler's mental "faculties," as "her phrenological developments" (p. 17) merit scientific attention. He found her "well balanced, the faculties giving ambition, management, sympathy, affection, and originality of mind to the body," with "no organ that is quite deficient, and but few that are only average or moderate in their influence." While "amativeness [the faculty of love] is full and active," it had "an inferior influence compared with that exerted by other faculties," for Elssler "prefers the society of the gentlemen to that of the ladies, not in the capacity of lovers, . . . but in order to gratify her intellect" (p. 18). Other "faculties" notable in Elssler were "benevolence and adhesiveness" (p. 20) and, unsurprisingly, "time and tune" (p. 22).

Appended to Fowler's analysis is "A Brief Memoir of Fanny Elssler" credited to "one of her most intimate friends" (Wikoff?), supposedly written "under her own immediate sanction"—unlikely, given Elssler's well-known insistence on privacy. Confirming Fowler's analysis, "intimate friend" asserted that Elssler's "intellect is truly masculine, possessing great force, depth, and variety. Her judgment is . . . elevated, too, by the most refined taste" (p. 28). Thus, Fowler and "friend" aligned Elssler with masculinity, power, creativity, judgment, respectability, and refinement. "Friend" closed: "No woman ever lived, that has been so exposed to every form and variety of seduction" in the form of "rank, wealth, and honors," yet "there have been few, who have sinned so little, or, making proper allowance for the influence of station."—a dig "friend" could not resist—"the tenor of whose life has been more quiet and respectable" (p. 29).

Elssler appeared in print media beyond newspapers, magazines, and scientific pamphlets. The emerging U.S. literary scene drew her into works of fiction, aside from the spurious biographies of "Friend" and "Pindar." Two Philadelphia authors inserted Elssler into their novels close to the time of her U.S. visit. Timothy Shay Arthur, who moved to Philadelphia in 1841, engaged in poetry, journalism, playwriting, editing, magazine publishing, temperance articles, advice books, and fiction.[46] Tracing "The Three Eras of a Woman's Life: The Maiden, the Wife, and the Mother," Arthur wrote a novella for each "era." *The Maiden* novella weaves Elssler into the story of virtuous young Philadelphian Anna Lee, whom the reader first meets in a scene where she chooses to remain home with her sick mother rather than go to a party with a beau. Afterward, Anna encounters friend Florence, who chatters about the party Anna missed and other doings of her set, telling Anna that she and her friends, against their parents' wishes, had wrangled dates to take them to see Elssler at the theater. Shocked, Anna condemns "these public dancers" (p. 43) whom only low-minded fellows would agree to see. The characters of the men attending such allures and the notorious immorality of stage dancers would combine, Anna warned, to "taint" Florence herself. Anna confesses that her father took her to the opera *Fra Diavolo*, in order that she reach, of her own accord, the "rational conviction [to] shun" the theater's "false allurements" (p. 46). Indeed, "the evil he was so anxious to point out" was as glaring to Anna "as a dark spot in the beautiful azure of heaven." Anna had also seen Mme. Celeste—perhaps during the October 1842 season at the Chestnut, when the ballerina played her famous melodramas and danced the *cachucha*.[47] Anna admits, "There was a charming grace and ease in all her motions; and some of her pantomimic performances were admirable. But my cheek burned the whole time. Could a modest woman expose her person as she did? No! nor could a truly modest woman look upon such an exposure without a feeling of deep shame and humiliation" (p. 53). Florence counters that "crowds of the most respectable women" patronized Celeste's and Elssler's shows, but Anna persists: "Depend upon it, the way in which stage dancing is now conducted, is but a tribute to an impure and perverted taste; and no woman . . . can look upon it with pleasure, without parting with a portion of woman's purest and most holy feelings" (p. 54). Indeed, Florence is soon shunned by the young men in her set, who understand her admiration of Elssler as a sign of Florence's low character. Moral fiction like *The Maiden* put dancing women and their admirers in their lowly place.

A few years after Arthur's admonitory novella, Philadelphia writer-muckraker George Lippard published *'Bel of Prairie Eden: A Romance of Mexico* (1848), far more lurid than *The Maiden*.[48] This swashbuckling spectacle of revenge, lust, and piracy tracks a fugitive Philadelphia family to the Texas prairies, the wars with Mexico, and back to the Quaker City, where Lippard plops the protagonist and his Mexican bride in the midst of the Walnut Street Theatre audience. Lippard here had opportunity not only to lambast theatrical and literary critics—whose blasts he had felt strongly—but also to depict the audience's ostentation and classism, from the "elegant" gents and "beautiful" bejeweled ladies of the first circle to the pit's "hardy sons of toil mingled with the ragged vagabonds," and "the third tier festering with the painted prostitution of the good Quaker City" (p. 185). "What," Lippard asks, "is the sight that enchains the gaze of the sinless girl and the painted outcast of shame" at this theater? "A half-naked woman whirling over the stage, her form clothed in flesh-colored hose that clings to the skin, a piece of white gauze fluttering from her waist, her arms and bosom bare!" No ballerina's name is stated, but the text conjures a mix of G. W. Dixon's portrayal of Elssler and French critic Gautier's rapture over Elssler's sensual *cachucha*,[49] as Lippard describes this "half-naked woman, . . . now standing on one limb, while the other is poised in the air, on a line with her shoulder; now trembling along on tip-toe, as in the ecstasy of lascivious frenzy; now crouching near the foot-lights, her head bowed until her naked breast is revealed . . . to the eyes of the sinless girl, the painted outcast, the old man, and the ragged boy" (p. 185). This exposure "rivets the gaze of the crowded theater—a woman floating along the stage and trafficking her nakedness for bread." Like Arthur's Anna Lee, Lippard insisted he had no "prejudice against the drama," which "may be made the voice of genius, the music of religion" (p. 186). But dancers—"these half-naked women on the stage, tossing in lascivious transport"—were one with "these painted ones in the third tier, bargaining in pollution."[50] Elssler and other ballet stars typically danced at the Chestnut Street Theatre, but Lippard knew the Walnut better, its taste for presenting melodrama matched his own writing, and it presented much ballet—even "Our Mary Ann[e]"—although it had not then captured the imported stars.

Ballet beyond Elssler

The Walnut was among the Philadelphia theaters that gave U.S. dancers a stage for artistic development; it soon would host touring European ballet stars and imported troupes. All such dance acts drew commentary in published sources. Among the emerging American ballet dancers featured in interlude acts at the Walnut and elsewhere were Lee, Ince, Miss E. Moore, Master William Reed, G. W. Smith, Anna Walters, dancing-master D. L. Carpenter and students, along with blackface dancers, discussed shortly, like "Master Diamond," "Mister Vantine," and J. Sanford. Given Elssler's draw, U.S. ballerinas attempted her national dances as soon as they got wind of them—Lee in the *cachucha* (Mar. 26, 1840, even before Elssler's arrival in the United States), Ince in the *cracovienne* (July 8, 1841) and *jaleo de Jeres* (Sept. 17, 1841), Moore in the *cachucha* (Apr. 17, 1845), and others throughout the decade. Occasionally, Americans gained roles in full ballets, as did Ince in *La Sylphide* (Dec. 4, 1841) and *The Fawn's Leap* (May 1842). Philadelphian Anna Walters danced *La Bayadere* for her benefit at the Walnut on April 9, 1844.

Walters was an example of a now-forgotten American ballerina with a dedicated audience. She "displayed infinite grace and immense agility," wrote Durang. "Her style was the French operatic"—ballet.[51] She "had great natural powers for the art," but "had never been regularly trained and taught in that graceful school"—not having availed herself of teachers like P. H. Hazard, James Sylvain, or Durang himself. He saw Walters's dancing as "crude at times and quite unfinished, showing that her acquirements were had through aptness and tact for imitation"—typical of many U.S. ballet aspirants. "Miss Walters, however, pleased; and that now-a-days is quite enough." Like other U.S. dancers, she sometimes shared the stage with European-trained ballet professionals, surely sharpening her skills by observation: she appeared at the Walnut in 1845 with one of Elssler's former partners, M. Martin, in *The Revolt of the Harem* (libretto and choreography F. Taglioni, Paris 1833), a work Celeste introduced to Philadelphia in 1838. For the work's large cast, Martin—the stager in 1845—placed a notice in the *Public Ledger* that he was preparing "a Grand Ballet of Action, aided by several Dancers of acknowledged reputation. Wanted, fifty Young Ladies to assist in the Ballet. Mons. Martin will be prepared to receive them at the Theatre this day, preparatory to rehearsal."[52] While many such "young ladies" did little more than marching drills in picturesque groupings, such experience might open the way to the stage as a livelihood—meager, but something.

Revolt of the Harem, with its complicated plot set in Muslim Spain, appeared in Paris in 1833 and London in 1834, its popularity enduring on the English stage, despite and because of scenes of "nakedness" and armed female warriors, sure to both offend and titillate audiences.[53] While the work might be seen as one of many overblown orientalist ballet concoctions, it could also be read as sympathetic toward nascent feminist movements, questioning such assumptions as marriage being a woman's only choice in life, women's timidity and weakness, and man's power to control and even abuse his wife. The work's complex social narrative, which ultimately weds the heroine to her true love though not to true independence, sidestepped the most radical feminist proposals of the age, but the ballet featured powerful female leads, like Celeste, representing women who took action against oppression. The "radical" nature of ballet included not only its bodily exposure and sensational spectacle but also plots about ideologies of control and expressive powers, featuring technological developments like ballet technique and the pointe shoe.[54] U.S. feminism was fermenting at this moment, between the 1833 founding of the Philadelphia Female Anti-Slavery Society and the 1848 Seneca Falls Women's Rights Convention. Did audiences perceive feminist sympathies in *Revolt of the Harem* as similar to ideas circulated among Philadelphia's vocal feminists?

A few years after *Revolt* appeared on the Philadelphia stage, Lucretia Mott published her powerful "Discourse on Woman," decrying the oppressive domination by husbands, social strictures, and laws that then barred women from political and professional action.[55] While Mott, a strict Quaker, would not attend theater, she approved women's aspirations for strength and health through bodily exercise; responding to her younger feminist friend, Elizabeth Cady Stanton, who expressed shame for her attraction to "dramatic performances, and dancing," Mott responded, "I regard dancing a very harmless amusement." Commentary has not survived to support a claim that Philadelphia women saw *Revolt* in a feminist light, but the increasing presence of homegrown ballet dancers and of women in audiences for ballet performances suggests that the art spoke to both women's sense of beauty and their expressive yearnings.

Such interest and possible readings of works like *Revolt* might be seen as responses to claims of doctors like Charles Meigs, who published statements on woman's place in relation to "her master and lord" (her husband): "The great administrative faculties are not hers. She plans no sublime campaigns, leads no armies to battle, nor fleets to victory. The Forum is no theatre for her silver voice, full of tenderness and sensibility. She discerns not the courses of the planets," which "are naught to her but pretty baubles set up in the sky. . . . She composes no *Iliad*, no *Aeneid*. The strength of Milton's poetic vision was far beyond her fine and delicate perceptions."[56] Yet dancers like Elssler, Celeste, and their European and U.S. sisters, performing *The French Spy, The Revolt of the Harem*, and even gauzy fairy ballets, showed women's strength, creative powers, and independence before the same kinds of "promiscuous" (mixed-sex) audiences that feminists of the day were lambasted for addressing, and sometimes from the same theatrical stages that hosted these dancers. Meigs's remarks were published in the year the Seneca Falls Conference, at which Mott was a guiding light, occurred. That event might have prompted an October 14, 1848, article in the *Public Ledger*, in which the indignant author, overlooking Mott's participation, asked readers, "Whoever heard of a Philadelphia lady setting up for a reformer, or standing out for woman's rights?"—unlike the pushy Boston and New York ladies at whom this author pointed, who aspired to "contend for the rights of women . . . to mount the rostrum, to do all the voting, and, we suppose, all the fighting too." Rather, Philadelphia's ladies "are resolved to maintain their rights as Wives, Belles, Virgins, and Mothers, and not as Women." Many such Philadelphia women—wives, belles, and those with reformist sympathies—were drawn to watch Elssler and other ballerinas dance.

In early 1842, Elssler departed with Jules Martin, having dropped Sylvain as her partner, for a season in Cuba. Sylvain formed a ballet troupe with others from Elssler's former company—Parsloe, Turnbull, and Joséphine Petit-Stéphan, who had performed with ballet master Hazard in 1838.[57] Rees praised their February 1842 performances of *Nathalie* at the Walnut Street, playing to "full and fashionable audiences" eager to support Sylvain, "whose merits as an artist are of the first order," while "the music, costume, scenery, and dancing" were "truly admirable."[58] Petit-Stéphan was "destined to rank with the world's divinity, the graceful Elssler" for her lovely appearance, "her saltatory performances," and her "modesty both in dress and deportment." Julia Turnbull, Rees wrote, falling short of top professional standards, "acquitted herself, however, cleverly," while "Sylvain danced superbly, and Parsloe was inimitable in his drollery."

Like Martin, French ballerina Mme. Eugenie Lecompte had been in the United States for several years and had appeared in Philadelphia (Feb. to Mar. 1838; Nov. 1840) dancing *La Bayadere*, Auber's opera *Masaniello* (*La Muette de Portici*), and the ballet scene from *Robert le Diable*.[59] She was among those foreign dancers accused by the *Public Ledger* article on "Stage Dancing" (1840) of "impropriety" and "sinful" exposure. At the Walnut Street Theatre in November 1842, supported by a cast including the Vallee sisters, Lecompte again presented *Bayadere* and the sensational nun's ballet from *Robert le Diable* (choreography Filippo Taglioni, music Giacomo Meyerbeer). Praised by some critics as "modest, . . . lovely and amiable," an 1837 lithograph of Lecompte by Clay depicts her bare breasted with loose hair (Figure 4.3). The nun's scene, drawing on a range of social anxieties—anti-Catholicism, fear of women's organizations and sexuality, bodily passion upending orderly authority—may have suggested such lasciviousness, but the image surely did not represent

Figure 4.3. "Madame Lecompte. Principal danseuse at the Theatres Royal Paris, London, St. Petersburg in the character of the abbess, in Robert le diable," Edward W. Clay (1837). *(Jerome Robbins Dance Division, New York Public Library Digital Collections, Public Domain. Accessed June 19, 2024. https://digitalcollections.nypl.org/items /510d47e2-0bde-a3d9-e040-e00a18064a99)*

Lecompte's actual performance; main stages like the Walnut would not have permitted such exposure. Yet, aside from the scene's allure, Lecompte was judged a powerful technician who "draws down wonder and surprise," but who "fails to fascinate and fix admiration," for her performance was "all professional, and none of it is feminine": her power set her outside feminine propriety.[60] As a contrast to Lecompte's showy virtuosity, the Walnut brought in European dancer Mme. Augusta, whom Philadelphians had seen in 1838 and 1839 in the *cachucha* (prior to Elssler's arrival).[61] Her repertoire—*Nathalie, La Sylphide, La Bayadere*—offered safe choices; she returned a year later, with "a clever second" dancer, M'lle. Dimier, presenting *Giselle*. Contrasted often with Lecompte, Augusta was praised as "modest," "unstagey and ladylike," "a lady of elegant manners and courtly address."[62]

The Arch Street Theatre offered ballet post-Elssler with an Italian contingent, led by La Scala–trained Giovanna Ciocca and Gaetano Morra (Jan. 1847).[63] Their season was successful enough to warrant the Arch's presenting Paris Opera ballerina Hermine Blangy, with Philadelphia's M. Hazard in April 1847, in *Giselle*. "Gaslight" Foster worked Blangy into "Philadelphia in Slices," placing her at "the famous Franklin House, that *bijou* hotel, . . . a great favorite with artists, musicians, editors, and all that sort of 'trash,'" where they dined luxuriously, enjoying "fashionable" Philadelphia society between shows.[64] Blangy's performances drew praise from Charles Durang, who recalled her as a "splendid dancer" with "a sylph-like figure," yet with "all the vigor of execution in her firm, but finished steps, of the most muscular dancer. There was a finish, an exquisite grace, a delicacy and a *fraischeure* about this artiste, that we have seldom seen."[65] She drew crowded houses including the fashionable and wealthy. Durang added, "These ballets, from Ellsler's [sic] time to the present, are *soup meagre* things" but "this danseuse was a host within herself." Frenchman M. Bouxary, Blangy's partner for her Philadelphia seasons (Apr.–May 1847, Feb.–Mar. 1848) drew commentary too. Durang noted that Bouxary, an artist "of great cleverness," "very agile and firm," married one of the Vallee sisters.[65] But he "inclined to obesity; and, in order to keep down his superfluous flesh, he had to practice several hours every day; real dray-horse labor. . . . Truly, a theatrical life is one of pains, labor and disappointments, both physically and mentally." Durang, in the theater since childhood, knew that life well.

Large-scale ballet troupes appeared in Philadelphia this decade. "Les Danseuses Viennoises," children aged five to twelve, toured the United States under direction of ballerina Mme. Josephine Weiss, of the Viennese theater. Child actors and dancers had long been popular on U.S. stages, for children of theater personnel apprenticed in performance from their early years. James Rees wrote in 1841 of Philadelphians "*Master Reed, Emily Reed, and Misses*

Kinloch" as "Lilliputian votaries of the science of Terpsichore . . . who occasionally charm us in some favorite dance at the Walnut street theatre."[67] Reed danced "manfully," despite his youth, and with sister Emily did an impressive jig, while the Kinloch sisters' "youthful attempts, and graceful efforts in several ballet dances, have attracted attention." But nothing like the fifty well-drilled children of the Viennese troupe had appeared in the United States, where they drew good houses.[68] Their divertissements—"Pas Rococo," "The Grand Peasant Dance," "Le Pas Des Moisseneurs," "Pas des Sauvages," and their famous "Pas de Fleurs"—Durang assessed as "wonderful," noting their "picturesque" dances "were very beautiful and novel."[69] Yet, "there were no solo dancers among them of any excellence. Their steps were few; their powers confined to attitudes and groupings, with garlands, flowers entwined on hoops, scarfs, streamers, ribbons, &c." Their youthfulness, large number, synchronicity, and astute staging were the winning formula for Philadelphia audiences.

The Ravels, having played the city for over a decade in regular seasons, returned to the Chestnut Street in October 1841, but were then absent from Philadelphia until 1847, when they played the Arch with reinforcements from the acrobatic-balletic Javelli, Marzetti, and Wells families. They presented "comic ballets," "vaudevilles," "fairy pantomimes," and "ballets."[70] The classically trained Wells siblings (Henry and Harriet) made the Ravel troupe competitive with other ballet companies. With "a very capital corps de ballet," they showed *La Sylphide* and *Giselle*, the latter featuring Henry Wells as Albrecht, Harriet as Giselle, and François Ravel as Hilarion. Rees found the Ravels' 1841 shows "excellent"; their ballet-pantomime, *M. Dechalameau ou la fete au village* was "all *au fait*"; they "nearly convulsed the audience with laughter by the drollery" of Gabriel Ravel.[71]

To compete with ballet companies at the Chestnut and Arch Street Theatres, the Walnut presented the Monplaisir troupe in June 1848, featuring Hippolyte Monplaisir as director and dancer, with wife Adèle Monplaisir as ballerina.[72] Both were trained in French and Italian academies and danced throughout Europe before their U.S. tours. This "troupe of brilliant dancers," mostly French, but absorbing such local talent as Miss Walters, were judged by Durang to be "most perfect as a body," with the leads the "equals, if not superior, to those who had already appeared on our boards in all the grace, repose and agility of opera artistes"—high praise, given the ballet riches of the day. They presented the "grand Asiatic ballet" *D'Almée, or an Oriental Dream*, staged by company dancer (and Adèle's father) Victor Bartholomin, and *Les Deux Roses*, an Andalusian-flavored "fête" by Bartholomin (Lyon, 1838). Returning to the Walnut in November 1848, the Monplaisirs presented two Philadelphia firsts: *La Esmeralda* (1844, choreography Perrot, based on Hugo's

Notre Dame de Paris, music Pugni) and *Le Diable a Quatre* (1845, choreography Mazilier, music Adam). Durang found *Esmeralda* "a most dramatic subject," danced elegantly and with fine pantomime. *Diable* was rich in "the *demi caractere*," mixing "the serious and comic," in which the "dancing was at all times brilliant."[73] In the troupe's August 1849 season, they produced a topical "patriotic ballet," *The Independence of Hungary*, in support of Hungary's nationalist movement, which garnered U.S. news coverage and sympathy.[74] Also presented were *La Fille mal gardee* and *La Rêve d'un Peintre*, likely a version of *Le Délire d'un Peintre*, created by Jules Perrot for Elssler in 1843, after her U.S. tour.

Beginning the decade with Elssler and closing with large-scale companies, Philadelphia theaters in the 1840s were rich in ballet performance, which became a subject of U.S. print commentary, as American dancers made their ways into imported troupes and absorbed their European repertoires.

Blackface Minstrelsy Emergent

At just this time, Americans were forging distinct cultural expressions, some taking aim at those imported performances sweeping U.S. stages. Elssler and ballet's upper-class appeal were subjects not only of published commentaries, but also of blackface acts that transgressed racial, gender, and class lines in both appropriation and offense. Blackface jigger John Diamond danced "á la Elssler" when the Viennese star first appeared in New York,[75] much as T. D. Rice had grasped the appeal of Italian opera in his biting "Ethiopian operas." Solo acts like Diamond's, along with Rice's enlistment of a theater's stock players to support his plays, typified blackface performance in the early 1840s. Solo blackface dancing was all over Philadelphia stages, as painter-lithographer Mathias Weaver, a theater regular, complained in his diary in April 1840, revealing his own prejudices, that the Walnut stage hosted enough blackface dancing "to last me a year."[76]

A major shift in blackface performance came early in 1843 when the quartet of Dan Emmett (banjo, violin), Frank Brower (dancing, character acts), Billy Whitlock (banjo), and Dick Pelham (bones, tambourine) coalesced into a single act, comprising the Virginia Minstrels, at New York's Bowery Theatre.[77] These performers had shared stages before coincidentally, not as a coordinated company. Among the claims to earlier "troupes" of blackface performers are Eph Horn's 1837 performances in Philadelphia; the Walnut's "Negro 'extravaganza'" (Feb. 1842) with singing and dancing that foreshadowed minstrel shows; and "imitative negro performances" (June 1842) by clusters of players active in early minstrelsy—Diamond, James Sanford, and Richard Myers.[78]

Compared to Elssler's and Celeste's coverage in U.S. publications, blackface acts received less commentary in print media, perhaps because they initially fell beneath the notice of literati. Yet blackface minstrelsy blossomed just as the penny press made newspapers available to readers of all classes, an appeal similar to that of blackface acts.[79] "Philadelphia in Slices" hints at city types who frequented such shows when Foster mentions the volunteer fire companies that sometimes devolved into violent, competitive gangs in neighborhoods contiguous to the city limits. This "set of the most graceless vagabonds and unmitigated ruffians" was "tolerated by the [populist Democrat] authorities because their votes were necessary to keep them in office" (p. 35). Thus, Foster added, "That most odious and disgusting of all characters, the B'hoy," flourished, with "actually a lower and more thorough development of debasement in Philadelphia than in New York." Such "b'hoys" were the working-class, anti-authoritarian, often nativist-leaning young white men, in fire companies and other gangs, who boosted blackface shows. Print commentary on minstrelsy percolated later in the 1840s, along with publication of minstrel music and graphic images of blackface performers in action. Philadelphia-based minstrel and manager Frank Dumont (1848–1919) later took to print to publish his "histories" of the form's gestation, evolution, and Philadelphia connections.

Dumont's 1896 retrospective article, "The Origin of Minstrelsy," presents several linked assertions: first, the unprecedented success of minstrelsy as an enduring entertainment form, from its founding to Dumont's time; and second, minstrelsy's homegrown roots—"purely of native American growth," "originated and fostered by Americans" depicting "scenes in song and story of American life."[80] Dumont admitted that minstrelsy's "America" concerned "Southern life, 'tis true, redolent of the cotton field, the plantation and of slavery, but withal it was American, and as such it grew in favor and was and has been endeared to us ever since." From that tragic vision of slavery defining Americanness, Dumont quickly pivoted to humor: early blackface performers grasped "that their patrons sought laughter," which shaped the form's acts—songs, jokes, and "short farces or burlesques upon topical subjects." Rather than linking this last point to his opening claims, which might lead to uncomfortable analysis, Dumont's attention to minstrelsy's humor pointed to his third thesis: minstrelsy originated in the circus where, before the iconic troupes of the early to mid-1840s, solo blackface acts appeared along with whiteface clowning, acrobatics, and dancing.[81] He stressed Frank Brower's associations with Philadelphia, giving the city claim to blackface formation. Pointing to the frequent credit of T. D. Rice as "the father of minstrelsy," Dumont argued that Rice "did not properly have anything to do with minstrelsy as we know it, but as a singer of negro songs," he admitted, "he was the most famous and best known."[82] In fact, Rice's masking, dancing, songs, humor, political commentary, and plays remained elements of blackface minstrelsy throughout its history.

The banjo, Dumont asserted, was a factor in the Americanness of blackface minstrelsy, as it was introduced by "the darkies of the South," perhaps influenced by the popularity of the Spanish guitar and castanets (related to bones-playing in minstrelsy) in Texas,[83] a "slave state" that entered the union in 1845, as minstrel acts blossomed. The Virginia Minstrels and other early troupes scored successes across the United States and in London, primed by T. D. Rice's previous tours. Jig dancing was embedded in the minstrel formula, along with singing, instrumental virtuosity, and burlesque skits. Philadelphia contributed an early blackface company—the Virginia Serenaders, led by Jim Sanford (Cool White), Richard Myers (Ole Bull Myers, violin virtuoso), and Robert Edwards, playing the Chestnut Street Theatre, often with other players.[84] Tracking these troupes is dizzying, given the constant shifting of personnel among them, the ready creation of new troupes, and the fact that names of famous performers, like dancer John Diamond, were snatched by up-and-comers, so that several such-named minstrels might be on widely distant stages at once.

By the late 1840s, the minstrel formula was coalescing, including the players' semicircular formation on the stage as an opening act, with the troupe dressed, as Dumont recalled, "in plantation costume, checked shirts, striped pants, straw hats, etc. This jolly slavery display, called 'Plantation darkies of the South,'" was followed by "Dandy negroes of the North," with the performers "in full evening dress," continuing the demeaning mockery of Black "refinement" familiar from Clay's cartoons.[85] In a later essay, Dumont revisited this two-part programming, flipping the acts' sequence: for the opening "Dandy Negroes of the North," the players dressed in "black swallow-tail coats, with brass buttons; white vest, tight black pants with straps that passed under the shoes. This was supposed to be the refined part of the bill."[86] In the second part, "Plantation Darkies of the South," players dressed as "field hands"—"checked shirts, with large collars, striped pants and big shoes," performing "plantation songs, grotesque dancing, banjo songs, 'Lucy Long,' 'Old Bob Ridley,' 'The Cachuca' dance, 'Banjo Lesson,' and wound up with a festival dance for the whole troupe, called a 'walk around.'" The emphasis on costuming might reflect observation by northern white minstrels of the colorful, pattern-contrasting clothing worn by free Black people in their promenades and at work, as well as white perceptions of the unusual clothing choices of those enslaved in the South, in part owing to secondhand castoffs they gathered from plantation owners and homemade articles of dress constructed from available materials.[87] On the stage, costuming enhanced the minstrels' theatricality and ridicule, adding opportunities for exaggerated behavior and movement, culminating in a lively all-cast walk-around. Performers who specialized in musical or comic acts also needed dance skills sufficient to support such numbers.

Dumont's 1914 essay underscores the role of dancing in minstrel shows, linking the transvestite figure "Miss Fanny"—the well-known Lucy Long character from the popular song of that name—and *la cachucha*, famously associated with Elssler.[88] The specialty "wench" role in minstrel troupes opened doors to female parody as well as to homosexual representation otherwise banned on stages. These characters and their dancing demonstrate the mixtures of high and low cultural material, cross-dressing titillation, sociopolitical commentary, and racial insult that depictions of such blackface figures represented—a combination that made the *cachucha* particularly rich for minstrel parody and transgression.[89] Like the *cachucha*, blackface spoofs, often skillfully performed, of Italian opera and Shakespearean drama drew on viewers' familiarity with elite cultural delicacies. *Som-Am-Bull-Ole* was a minstrel version of the opera *La Sonnambula* (1831, libretto Scribe and Aumer, music Bellini), presented by Palmo's Ethiopian Opera Company; it included a ballet featuring caricatures of well-known European ballet stars: Md'le Heele-sir [Elssler], Carrotty Greasy [Carlotta Grisi], Say-least [Celeste], Messrs. Mutton [Martin], Tallow knee [Taglioni], and Silly Vain [Sylvain].[90] A commentator wrote, "The burlesque evinces considerable ingenuity in the writer, and the skilful translation from the well-known airs of 'Somnambula' to several of our popular negro [blackface] extravaganzas as choruses, frequently convulsed the audience with laughter." Other opera-ballets spoofed by the Palmo company were *Shin de-heel-a!!: The Virginian Fairy, or the Gum Elastic Slipper*, and *Buy-I-Dare: Or, the Revolt of the Wool-Heads*, with "burlesques on the celebrated Shawl Dance" from *La Bayadere*, and a "Pas Seul, Pas de Trois, Ballet Dance, and a Grand and Imposing Tableau." For many in U.S. audiences, blackface burlesques transformed European works into "American" products by casting "delineations" of the most socially excluded figures in the new nation to represent what these audiences regarded as highfalutin' pretentiousness.

The most dominant minstrel dance was the jig, Dumont wrote: "With the early troupes, the jig dancer was monarch of all he surveyed. He posed about attired in a velvet coat, flashy, flowing necktie, glazed cap, tight pants, patent leather shoes with old copper pennies fastened to the heels"—an early tap-dance shoe. That dancer was so critical that, "if he signified his intention of quitting the show the entire troupe would almost upon their bended knees beg him to remain," for, "without the champion jig dancer the minstrel show was a ship without a rudder." Among Dumont's list of star jiggers were several who appeared in Philadelphia in the 1840s: John Diamond, Jim Sanford, and Billy Birch, with Dick Sliter and Pete Lane arriving in the 1850s. Jig dancing absorbed different cultural traditions; Constance Valis Hill points to its merging "both the upright, on-the-balls-of-the-feet jig" of white performers, "and the flat-footed, buck-and-wing danced by blacks."[91] These "derived from an early form of percussive stepping (later called tap dance) that had evolved from a three-hundred-year musical and social exchange" among Irish and African bondsmen in the Caribbean, exemplifying the dance's "shared biracial roots." Such "racial slippage," Hill notes, flavored the brewing U.S. cultural stew, even as segregationist, scientific, and social forces worked to harden strict racial separation. "'Jigging' became the general term for this new American percussive hybrid," understood as "a 'black' style of dancing." Such dancing had long been performed and exchanged at public markets, river and ocean docks, and interracial saloons where Black and white performers entertained popular audiences—all sites available to the northern urban-based players generating blackface minstrelsy.[92] Also contributing to minstrelsy's stew were contests sponsored by Southern plantation owners, encouraging the enslaved to compete for prizes, feeding the minstrel show's emphasis on competitive "trial" dances designed for spectators to cheer their favorite blackface jigger. "Negro" dances might also be labeled "breakdowns," listed often in advertisements for minstrel shows.

Dumont acknowledged this range of sources to support his claims to the "American" nature of the blackface stage where, he claimed, "everything was a close imitation of the Negro'"—as perceived by white performers and expected by their audiences: "dialect," outlandish costuming, and "grimaces, contortions, shuffling walks." While these insulting mockeries were understood by performers and audiences as "comic," Dumont claimed a serious theme underlying blackface minstrelsy: "About this time the slavery agitation placed the Southern slave prominently before the Northern public and his sighs for freedom and his lost love sold into slavery to other cotton states created a sympathy" that "made minstrelsy a little more attractive as the 'underdog' in then gathering controversies fanned by agitators, North and South." Dumont claimed to see minstrelsy as making an antislavery case. On the other hand, Lhamon points to "proletariat youth" who, rather than supporting blackface out of sympathy for the enslaved, rallied to the minstrel show's "signs of akimbo insurrection against the conventions of control" of the increasingly stratified, industrialized nation.[93] Thus, varied political implications could be read into these shows, as audience members chose: mocking satire and insult for those disdaining African Americans and their claims to freedom and rights; sentimental support for freeing them from oppression; working-class nose-thumbing at parodied white elites; or nationalist pride in the unique elements "Americans" could claim as contributions to transatlantic theater.

The movement material of blackface jiggers and breakdown dancers featured consistent elements: speed, rhythmic syncopation, limbs sharply angled and often revealing the body's core, "vigorous leg- and footwork, twists, turns, and slaps of toe and heel," with "the body . . . always grotesquely contorted," and expressive facial gestures.[94] While some minstrel moves involved air steps, the overall tendency was toward groundedness, with percussive footwork, shuffling or sliding steps, and relaxed knees. Those, like Durang, who preferred the long lines, lightness, and feminine-flavored ballet saw blackface dancing as "a most vulgar exhibition of the elegant art of dancing," although "it was much applauded" owing to "the ever-changeable taste of the public."[95]

The search for truly "American" cultural forms led the author of an article, "American Humor," to assert that "the Aethiopian drama" (blackface entertainment) was indeed a native theatrical form—even if "the lowest description of American farce," below such native themes and characters as "the scheming Yankee, the wild Kentuckian, the generous Virginian, the aristocratic Carolina Planters," and even "the fashionable clergy."[96] Like ethnologists of the day, this author could not resist hierarchy, and anything associated with "Africa" landed at the lowest rung. In the blackface "line," T. D. Rice was "the best," even a "genius," although the article's author claimed that "there are many clever break-down dancers and minstrels from every Southern State"—perhaps an effort to assert the material's authenticity; in fact, minstrel performers were overwhelmingly Northerners, several being natives of Philadelphia. The other characters mentioned earlier also had their physical qualities, as did "national types"—Irish, Dutch, Italian, Chinese, and more—also "delineated" by minstrels in blackface.

The purity of such "American" expressions was defended—satirically, yet, in this age of "literary nationalism," with some claim to truth—by antislavery New Englander James W. Kennard in his essay "Who Are Our National Poets?"[97] He surmised that the surest way to produce a truly "national" art was to "keep our poets at home, give them a narrow education, and allow them no spare money by which they might purchase books, or make excursions into other ranks of society than their own" (p. 332). Thus had Burns and Shakespeare become their countries' national poets. In the United States, "what class is most secluded from foreign influences, receives the narrowest education, travels the shortest distance from home, has the least amount of spare cash, and mixes least with any class above itself? Our negro slaves, to be sure." And, conflating the imitators with their subjects, Kennard declaimed, "from that class [have] come the Jim Crows, the Zip Coons, and the Dandy Jims, who have electrified the world. From them proceed our only truly National Poets." This observation caused Kennard to reflect on American print culture: "Alas! that poets should be ranked with horses, and provided with owners accordingly! In this, however, our negro poets are not peculiarly unfortunate. Are not some of their white brethren owned and kept by certain publishing houses, newspapers, and magazines?" Kennard acknowledged "that while James Crow and Scipio Coon were quietly at work on their master's plantations, all unconscious of their fame, the whole civilized world was resounding with their names" in blackface entertainment. Although "they themselves were not permitted to appear in the theatres, and the houses of the fashionable," the songs of the nation's enslaved Black people "are in the mouths and ears of all; white men have blacked their faces to represent them, made their fortune by the speculation, and have been caressed and flattered on both sides of the Atlantic" (p. 333). Noting the theft of blackface material from its sources, Kennard added a further irony: "Meanwhile, the poor author" of such music and verses "digs away with his hoe, utterly ignorant of his greatness" (p. 340). Such "retiring Samboes" humbly "allow sooty-faced white men to gather all the honors and emoluments!"—an allowance the enslaved were, in fact, denied. Finally, Kennard warned aspiring U.S. poets, "write no more English poems; write negro songs, and Yankee songs in negro style; take lessons in dancing of the celebrated Thomas Rice. . . . Who then will dare to say that America has no National Poets?" (p. 341).

The vicious exclusion Kennard highlighted of African Americans from U.S. main stages had a famous exception, noted earlier: William Henry Lane/Juba, the truly champion dancer Dickens described as a whirlwind of loose-limbed motion from toes to fingers to face, tossing off leaps, shuffles, and capers that gleefully put to shame "a million of counterfeit Jim Crows."[98] Juba's performance delighted the crowd at the cellar dance hall in Manhattan's notorious Five Points where Dickens and his guide had made their way. That dance hall had counterparts in Philadelphia.

Black Writers: Black People and Blackface

Given the daily insult of minstrelsy, in print and performance, it is no surprise that, in the 1840s, American Black leaders also employed print media to publish and share their views on the state of the nation, its culture, and its stages.⁹⁹ In the *North Star*, Frederick Douglass excoriated "the 'Virginia Minstrels,' 'Christy's Minstrels,' the 'Ethiopian Serenaders,' or any of the filthy scum of white society, who have stolen from us a complexion denied to them by nature, in which to make money, and pander to the corrupt taste of their white fellow-citizens."¹⁰⁰ He wrote in 1849 of another troupe, "said to be composed entirely of colored people,"¹⁰¹ but Douglass seemed uncertain of crediting true Blackness to these performers, who "had recourse to the burnt cork and lamp black, the better to express their characters and to produce uniformity of complexion. Their lips, too, were evidently painted, and otherwise exaggerated." Their characters and capacities further belied their claim to the race: "Their singing generally was but an imitation of white performers, and not even a tolerable representation of the character of colored people"—Black people imitating white people imitating Black people. "Their attempts at wit showed them to possess a plentiful lack of it," giving spectators "a very low idea of the shrewdness and sharpness of the race to which they belong." Douglass noted "exceptions" in this "poor set" of performers: "Cooper" had a "really fine voice, who, with a company possessing equal ability with himself, would no doubt, be very successful in commanding the respect and patronage of the public" for African American accomplishment. The bones player, "Davis," was excellent, "but the *Tambourine* was an utter failure." The troupe's dancing drew Douglass's scrutiny: "B. Richardson is an extraordinary character. His Virginia Breakdown excelled anything which we have ever seen of that description of dancing. He is certainly far before the dancer in the Company of the Campbells"—a popular white blackface troupe.¹⁰² Apparently, Douglass saw enough blackface minstrelsy to make such judgments. His essay then took a remarkable turn:

> We are not sure that our readers will approve of our mention of those persons, so strong must be their dislike of everything that seems to feed the flame of American prejudice against colored people; and in this they may be right, but we think otherwise. It is something gained when the colored man in any form can appear before a white audience; and we think that even this company, with industry, application, and a proper cultivation of their taste, may yet be instrumental in removing the prejudice against our race.

Douglass offered a path toward uplift, not debasement, through theatrical performance, if this troupe would "cease to exaggerate the exaggerations of our enemies; and represent the colored man rather as he is, than as Ethiopian Minstrels usually represent him to be. They will *then* command the respect of both races." If the capable performers Douglass named were to join with "persons of equal skill, . . . relying more upon the refinement of the public, than its vulgarity . . . they may do much to elevate themselves and their race in popular estimation." I found no further word of these performers.

Other Black performers, their names now mostly lost, were seen outside main theatrical venues by spectators, like Dickens and his guide, who frequented "low" stages in taverns and dance halls of rowdy neighborhoods.[103] Nearly invisible in the print media of the time, which favored the literati and cultural venues that bought newspaper advertisements, these poorly documented acts surface through descriptions like Dickens's or images like "Dancing for Eels." Foster, in "Philadelphia in Slices," described the "dark and loathsome haunts of infamy and wretchedness" where the city's poor lived, loved, and fought in the "rottenest and most villainous neighborhood ever peopled by human beings. It is the Five Points of Philadelphia" (pp. 38–39). It was also a place, bordering the city's official boundaries, where the poor found housing and society, including in taverns and dance halls where those unwelcome (or unable to pay) at the Chestnut Street Theatre and other respectable venues could perform and applaud in their own ways.

"Uptown" main-stage theaters still had to lure ticket-buyers; they too hosted blackface minstrelsy and sought to attract audiences across class divides. In the early 1840s, Philadelphia theaters offered designated sections of "Colored Seating" for shows blackface and otherwise. Although Durang remarked that "Colored Tiers," "Colored Galleries," and the like "never paid," African Americans took advantage of such opportunities to spectate the same shows as did their white neighbors, from dancing to drama to blackface burlesque.[104] Was it the actors' often skillful performances, the send-ups of elite white culture, or some kind of interracial, cross-class "filiation," as Lhamon has argued, that drew Black spectators to pay scarce cash for burnt-cork shows?[105] Certainly, the Irish, who lived in the same neighborhoods as poor African Americans, became major players in blackface entertainment, allowing them to mock the white elites who stigmatized them and their Black neighbors, from whom they also sought social and political distance.

Douglass rightly anticipated other African American writers' objections to the kind of theater he envisioned as a possible emergence from the blackface stage. Samuel Cornish, editor of the *Colored American*, repeatedly cited theater as "the nursery of vice in every form."[106] He had, in the 1830s, offered choice words condemning blackface shows and the actors performing in them.[107] A few years later, Cornish published a friend's report of attending a theatrical performance in an unnamed U.S. city, where this friend was horrified to view "a burlesque upon the colored people. The actor" was "lost to all self respect, and sunken in the lowest depths of degradation and vice, with his face painted to represent a colored man," performing "scenes, the like of which, no human being, but someone as lost to all sense of honor as himself, ever acted." Worse yet was the composition of the audience, for Cornish's informant "never saw so many *colored persons* at the *theatre* in his life, hundreds were there, and among whom were many very respectable looking persons. O shame! paying money, hard earned, to support such places and such men, to heap ridicule and a burlesque upon them in their very presence, and upon their whole class." White-led abolitionist publications too denounced theater: a *Pennsylvania Freeman* article praising the "intellectual and moral exhibitions" of paintings by Black Philadelphian Robert Douglass Jr. in 1841 urged that the public turn to such "useful and intellectual recreation," instead of "the demoralizing representations of the stage."[108] By 1846, that newspaper named minstrelsy directly: "The Ethiopian Minstrels" performances "tended to degrade the colored population.... Such exhibitions may be 'sport' to the audience of white people, but they are 'death' to a sensitive colored man."

The ludicrous physicalization of Black people—exaggerating and demeaning their bodies, behaviors, and speech—pointed to a candescent current issue at this historical moment. American ethnologists were in full persuasive force by the 1840s, advising U.S. politicians and engaging with European intellectuals. In his 1844 book *Crania Aegyptiaca*, Samuel Morton used his analyses of skulls from the world over to prove that the true "Negroes" found in the archeological remains of ancient Egypt were, by biological determination, "servants and slaves." This issue mattered to Morton for, as he wrote, Egypt was "justly regarded as the parent of civilization, the cradle of the arts," a position surely not attributable to "the lower class of people" there—the darker-skinned Africans enslaved, Morton claimed, to Egypt's elites.[109] He shaped understandings of bodies as visible containers of moral and intellectual characteristics through both his publications and his positions in leading scientific institutions like Philadelphia's Academy of Natural Sciences, where, in the 1840s, Morton served as secretary, vice president, then president.[110]

Morton's theories were disseminated by other U.S. and European scientists in print, lectures, and museum exhibits at the same time that audiences could see such ascribed distinctions played out by blackface performers, who excelled at "making the invisible"—perceived internal anatomy, brain size, morality—"visible" and entertaining.[111] As Sylvia Wynter noted, minstrels "representing the identity of Sambo"—a widely understood reference to a Black servant—"as childlike" on U.S. stages forwarded "processes of infantilization" justifying suppression, paternalism, and violence.[112] While Morton concentrated on skulls and brain size, his follower Josiah Clark Nott added to what he claimed were the races' corporeal distinctions. Responding to a critic, Nott wrote, "Left to propagate in the natural state, . . . the brain of the Negro would not expand, nor his heel contract."[113] Mockeries of Black peoples' protruding heels abound in minstrel songs, as in the line from "Dandy Jim of Caroline" about "lubly" Miss Dinah producing babies who take after Jim: "Dar heels stick out three feet behind, / Like Dandy Jim of Caroline." Southern politicians like Governor James Henry Hammond and Senator/Vice President John C. Calhoun grasped Morton's assertions as incontrovertible evidence for what they claimed as the God-given moral rightness of slavery.

African American writers continued publishing responses to the mounting arguments of U.S. ethnologists justifying slavery as the natural order. Some authors cited in the ensuing discussion lacked direct connections to Philadelphia, but the nationally interconnected group of African American leaders in the antebellum United States circulated publications among Black literary, social, and political societies throughout the nation and abundant in Philadelphia.

Benjamin Lewis, a sailor and whitewasher born in Maine of African/Native American ancestry, initially published his *Light and Truth* in 1836, expanding it in 1844 with support from "A Committee of Colored Gentlemen."[114] These supporters published, in the edition's introduction, their intention that "this volume of collections from sacred and profane history" serve to provide "a correct knowledge of the Colored and Indian people, ancient and modern" (p. iii). The long volume opens with Lewis's placement of the Garden of Eden in Ethiopia (p. 10). Having reviewed a wide range of sources on the Ethiopians, Egyptians, Greeks, Carthaginians, Abyssinians, Syrians, and Native Americans, Lewis ascribed physical beauty and cultural refinement to people from Africa, India, and the Americas. Addressing the same theme as did Morton's *Crania Aegyptiaca*, Lewis claimed *Blackness* for ancient Egyptian rulers (p. 63), whose capacities for government, arts, sciences, technology, philosophy, and morality were, he argued, well known.

Other works addressing the Black body, history, and achievement, written by African Americans, were published between 1841 and 1844, responding to Morton's *Crania Americana* as well as to the flawed and deleterious 1840 U.S. census. That census was the first to count the "insane," with a result—contested by some Northern politicians, physicians, and statisticians—that claimed to show free African Americans had far higher incidences of physical and mental illness than did those held in slavery, thus substantiating the proslavery argument that Black people could not healthfully handle freedom.[115] Among the Black authors publishing in this period, James Pennington addressed that claim in his *Text Book of the Origin and History, &c. &c. of the Colored People*. Escaping slavery in Maryland, Pennington lived for some years in Adams County, Pennsylvania, where a Quaker family supported his independence and education.[116] He later studied at Yale Divinity School and led congregations in Connecticut. Pennington's aim in his *Text Book* was "to direct these [his readers], as to unembarrass the origin, and to show the relative position of the colored people in the different periods among the different nations." Study of human diversity mattered, Pennington wrote, so that "prejudices ... be uprooted, false views ... corrected, and truth ... unveiled" (pp. 6–7). He addressed at length accusations of Black intellectual inferiority (ch. VI) and reviewed the "nonsense" and contradictions of religious and scientific arguments put forth by such notables as Buffon, Blumenbach, Gall, and Rush to explain Africans' dark complexion (ch. VIII). Avoiding the trap of racialism, Pennington flatly declared, "No man is anything more than a man, and no man less than a man" (p. 54).

Similar themes emerge from Dr. James McCune Smith's works, rooted in the author's medical training: he received the M.D. at the University of Glasgow, completed further studies in Paris, and mastered classics, literature, languages, and statistics. In his 1843 "The Destiny of the People of Color," McCune Smith condemned the "learned men" who "have brought the human species under the yoke of classification, and having shown to their own satisfaction a diversity in the races, have placed us in the very lowest rank."[117] The author noted that, were African-descended people as low as monkeys or dogs, no laws would be needed to hold them in their place, since brute animals function at their appropriate level without imposed legal barriers. These learned men's "opinion of our *manhood*, then, may be measured by the severity of their laws" (p. 54). Citing statistics, the author astutely declared as "law" that "an oppressed minority shall ultimately obtain a ruling influence over their oppressors"; this, he forecast, would befall the people of color in the United States by means of such "abstract pursuits" as literature: "We are destined to write the literature of this republic, which is still, in letters, a mere province of Great Britain" (p. 57). Reclaiming the sources of blackface performance, McCune Smith noted, "We have already, even from the depths of slavery, furnished the only music which the country has yet produced. We are also destined to write the poetry of the nation," as Kennard so differently predicted, "for as real poetry gushes forth from minds embued with a lofty perception of the truth, so our faculties, enlarged in the intellectual struggle for liberty, will necessarily become fired with glimpses at the glorious and the true, and will weave their inspiration into song." Art—even, but certainly not only, that tarnished by its counterfeit expression in minstrelsy—would forward African American dominance of the nation's cultural voice.

In the last year of the decade, Black businessman William Whipper, from Columbia, Pennsylvania, and with strong ties to Philadelphia, published his "Appeal to the Colored Citizens of Pennsylvania." A founder of the American Moral Reform Society, he issued his call as part of Black leaders' decade-long efforts to repeal the state's 1838 disenfranchisement law, which Whipper declared "a blow at our manhood."[118] While white detractors were convinced that Black people are "too low in the scale of creation to be reached by the heavenly light" (p. 14), in fact, wrote Whipper, "the Almighty having clothed us with the attributes of human nature, we are placed on an equality with the rest of mankind" (p. 20). Thus, racial science demanded responses not only from Black leaders but from all African Americans, given widespread demeaning representations in science, cartooning, and performance.

Another writer, disgusted with white misunderstandings of Black life, culture, and humanity, alluded at the start of the 1840s to expectations of white readers that African Americans could never achieve respectability or refinement. Joseph Willson published *Sketches of the Higher Classes of Colored Society in Philadelphia* in 1841, soon after the 1838 disenfranchisement vote. His stated intention was to reveal to white readers the respectable and utterly human state of the city's elite Black residents, but he recognized that for many readers, "the idea of 'Higher Classes' of colored society" would be "a novel one; and will, undoubtedly, excite the mirth of a prejudiced community on its annunciation."[119] Some "like to see their neighbors' merits caricatured, and their faults distorted and exaggerated"—an allusion to minstrelsy on page and stage. Such readers "will expect burlesque representations, and other laughter-exciting sketches, and probably be thereby led to procure this little volume for the purpose of gratifying their penchant for the ludicrous." Such readers "indulged in a very erroneous impression": the book's goals were serious—politically and personally. Pointing to the role educated whites played in racial subjugation, Willson noted that African Americans and other non-Caucasians were ill-treated as a result of "the insatiable desire which pervades the reading classes, for productions of a defamatory character, [such] as the 'Journals,' 'Diaries,' &c., of those writers who visit countries foreign to their own, for the purpose of collecting together a worthless compilation of ridicule and personal abuse" (p. 10). Turning to Philadelphia's Black "higher classes," Willson described their engagement with family, churches, jobs, schools, literary societies, music, poetry, "ornamental arts" (particularly the "young ladies," p. 30), and social life, which included the "follies and vices" (p. 37) typical of any elite class. This description led Willson to his one comment touching on dance: when reviewing the "fashionable foibles" of elite Black youth, he reported that anyone "not an adept in such matters, is looked upon as a 'simpleton,' or a 'flat;' or is otherwise regarded in the light that one would be who should appear in a ball-room and offer to lead in the dance, with brogans [work boots] upon his feet—a grossly ignorant and unfashionable fellow!" (p. 50). At the dance gatherings elite African American youth attended, such a mistake would be unthinkable. Willson revealed no more, leaving the dance in darkness. In contrast, a few years later, "Ethiop" in *Frederick Douglass' Paper* wrote of Brooklyn's "polished colored circles," describing "a nice cozey little cotillion or country dance" after a ladies' sewing circle, as well as formal gatherings of "handsome women and fine looking men" who joined in "the merry dance" of elegant, joyous Black society.[120] Did Philadelphia's free Black community enjoy such occasions? No clues have yet come to light. Alas, for Willson's efforts to disentangle free Black people from parody, the blackface stage was on the rise.

Dance and Sociability

As Willson was acutely aware, the pressures under which the free Black community lived in this period caused elite African Americans to keep their social lives and aspirations hidden from observation and mockery. An example of such ridicule in the 1840s was the popular blackface song "De Color'd Fancy Ball," with lively enactment, performed in Philadelphia.[121] The lyrics in the sheet music (1848) send up dance crazes sweeping white ballrooms, with polka and waltz steps named as "chassez," "croisez," "prombernade," and "ballensays"; the text also reinforces mockery of the ascribed physical and moral character of the "Black" dancing couple: their "dark eyes" in flirtatious glances, "dat lubly Juno wid de luxurant head ob wool" who devours a dish of ice cream in a gulp, and Juno's partner, a cock-proud "gobbler," just out of jail for pilfering at the docks, whose heel is "sticking out a foot."

As noted earlier, dancing was discouraged by some African American spokesmen, but others appreciated it; Frederick Douglass championed dance for "exercising so many muscles otherwise little used." Practiced in proper settings, with "the cheering influence of music," as "a daily, not nightly, exercise among the people of all classes," such dancing would increase life's "healthiness" and "happiness."[122] Dance practices of upper-class Black Philadelphians remained carefully cloaked, but allusions to lower-class dancing are more available: published sources record "dance houses" as sites of performance and sociality for "colored people" and for interracial conviviality. Newspaper police logs reported such places as generating brawls and noise—although objections may have also been to such persons having any opportunities for leisure and pleasure.[123] Dickens facetiously labeled the Five Points saloon, where he saw Juba's performance, "Almack's," a reference to fashionable dancing-assembly rooms in London. Dickens remarked on the couple-dancing that preceded Juba's solo: "The corpulent black fiddler, and his friend who plays the tambourine, stamp upon the boarding of the small raised orchestra in which they sit, and play a lively measure. Five or six couple come upon the floor, marshalled by a lively young negro, who is the wit of the assembly, and the greatest dancer known"[124]—thus, Dickens foreshadowed the brilliant dancing of Juba, initially the dance floor's manager. On that floor, "every gentleman sets as long as he likes to the opposite lady, and the opposite lady to him," the dance proceeding until Juba takes the floor, dominating all attention.

Although Philadelphia recorded no dancer of Juba's stature, the crowd at the dance houses of the Lombard-South Street corridor likely followed dance practices similar to those of Manhattan. In "Slices of Philadelphia," Foster asserted, "The colored people are naturally strongly addicted to music and dancing, a propensity which will one day be developed into the most astounding results" (p. 62)—a notable prediction denigratingly voiced. Foster's pointed parody suggests that his remarks applied to Black elites:

> The "dance houses" of these people are numerous and always well attended. The "Astor House" and other similar high-sounding establishments in Baker, Small and Mary-streets, are the earthly paradises upon which are fixed all the waking hopes and midnight dreams of the belles and gallants of the dark hue. There, on Saturday nights gather the ivory-toothed ranks of smiling Afric's daughters, and the perfumed and excruciating dandies of "the first colored circles," to exchange vows and protestations, imbibe soft nonsense and lemonade . . . and to chase the glowing hours with flying feet. Everything here is of course conducted with the most elaborate and pompous ceremony. The smallest requisite of the most fastidious etiquette is observed with as much grave rigor as at the Queen's Drawing-Room. But after the ice is once broken, there is nothing to equal the spirit and abandon with which it is entered into.

The musicality, energy, and "power of sympathy" (p. 64) the "African" displayed in such dance settings would, according to Foster's mixed admiration, disdain, and essentialism, become the means for U.S. Black people to rise: "People may laugh if they please; but that will not prevent us from saying that we believe the stage in all its departments, except perhaps the very highest walks of tragedy, will be eventually occupied by colored actors and actresses, singers, dancers and instrumental performers," bringing a different perspective to Douglass's and McCune Smith's visions of Black people leading American arts. In closing, Foster added,

> It is through this channel that the African mind will first rise to power over the souls of the other races and acquire the fame awarded to unquestioned yet practically useless genius. The abstract love for the beautiful is much stronger and more universal with the African than any white race except the modern Italians and the ancient Grecians; while the intellect and judgment are at present far inferior to all. In short, we believe that, after the African race has become purified from the horrible stains and pollutions of centuries of blood, slavery and oppression, and has found power to rise to its natural level, it will be discovered to correspond to the female sex or the minor key in the grand analogy of the universe.

Could higher praise be offered? Thus would the predictions of race science work out, Foster anticipated with both anguish and admiration, to the elevation of African-descended people—on the stage.

At dance houses, interracial sociality offered opportunities for white men to relax in company with Black workers and, in particular, Black women—a society "proper" white men might wish to enjoy secretly. Foster, in "Slices," wrote that even Philadelphia's white "barrooms are generally not so public as in other places, and the dram-drinker usually slips through a long passage or up a dark alley, before he reaches the goal of his desires," owing to "the still-remaining sense of propriety, at least in outward respects, among nearly all classes of our population, some from a remnant of inward decency, but the greater from motives purely interested and selfish"—avoidance of public scrutiny (p. 49). Foster's claims were echoed in Lippard's best-selling novel of the 1840s, *The Quaker City; or, The Monks of Monk Hall: A Romance of Philadelphia Life, Mystery, and Crime*, rich with scenes of prostitution, seduction, drugs, drinking, and wild dancing. Foster, like Dickens, penetrated sites of vicious sociality, including one that might have been the model for Lippard's novel. "Dandy Hall" was at Fourth and South Streets, an interracial neighborhood of low-class, struggling souls, which Foster deemed "a moral Golgotha of civilization,"[125] where not only the city's "b'hoys" but also higher-class men gathered to carouse and consort with loose women. In the second-floor dance hall, an "old negro fiddler" (p. 39) played for the rowdy, drunken crowd:

Having taken their places and saluted one another with the most ludicrous exaggeration of ceremony, the dance proceeds for a few minutes in tolerable order; but soon . . . the dancers begin contorting their bodies and accelerating their movements, accompanied with shouts of laughter, yells of encouragement and applause, until all observance of the figure is forgotten and everyone leaps, stamps, screams and hurras on his or her own hook. Affairs are now at their height. . . . The dancers, now wild with excitement, leap frantically about like dervishes, clasp their partners in their arms, and at length conclude the dance in the wildest disorder and confusion. (p. 40)

Foster's disparaging description does suggest that some elements of African-sourced dancing—rhythmic accents, individual expression, full-body action, and leaping movement—were absorbed by every dancer on the interracial floor.

While Foster identified Dandy Hall as "the center of the most extensive region of white prostitution in Philadelphia" (p. 41), it had competition. So abundant and nuanced was the brothel business in Philadelphia that by 1849, a directory was needed: *A Guide to the Stranger, or Pocket Companion for the Fancy, Containing a List of the Gay Houses and Ladies of Pleasure in the City of Brotherly Love and Sisterly Affection* was available to gentleman visitors upon request at city hotels. Its published motive was beneficent: "With this book in his hand a man will be enabled to shun those low dens of infamy and disease with which the city abounds."[126] Although brothels were found throughout the city, the "good" houses congregated around Tenth, Eleventh, and Twelfth Streets, the "bad" ones in the alleys at the southeast of the city, Foster's "Golgotha." Other houses were interracial or featured "yellow" (mixed-race) women, who, reported the *Guide*'s anonymous author with deprecating surprise, "meet with more custom than their fairer skinned [white] rivals in the trade of prostitution" (p. 17).

Some gents who secretly frequented such "gay houses" were also part of Philadelphia's elite or aspiring white culture and, when not busy in "Golgotha," could attend dancing academies, public balls, and private assemblies. Newspapers advertised dancing academies, balls for pupils, and public balls where those sufficiently trained might join the terpsichorean festivities. The best pupils, or even theater dancers, might perform a demonstration at such balls, as did Mary Ann Lee, in a "cachuca" at a ball held by dancing masters M. and Mme. Hazard in January 1841.[127] Hazard had prepared Lee for the stage and perhaps she continued studying with him during her professional career. Apparently, even at well-regulated gatherings like Hazard's ball, disturbances might erupt, for the notice assured readers that "an efficient police is engaged."

Dancing master D. L. Carpenter remained active this decade, offering dances that suggest possible theatrical aspiration or influence: "Pas Seuls, Pas de Deux, Pas de Trois, Minuets, a new Double Cotillon by 16 Children, a Symbol Dance by 8 Children, Hornpipes, Highland Flings, and a Double Hornpipe for two Young Men who have not their superiors."[128] Carpenter advertised his "Grand Examination Ball," where attendees could view his students' progress in his "dancing saloon," fitted for showy social dancing. Other schools offered to teach students "fancy dances," gavots, allemandes, German dances, waltzes, the bolero, gallopades, and—should these listings not cover a student's interest—"any Dance from any part of the world" as requested. Dancing masters competing with Carpenter and Hazard included Mr. F. Pohlman, who also taught violin and would provide a band for any ball, and Hungarian dancers Mons. and Mme. Gabriel De Korponay, who could employ French, German, and English to teach the mazourka and polka dances. Listings in city directories for the 1840s name dancing teachers Mrs. Beech, William Bleakly, D. J. Dorney, Thomas Hoffland, Jos. E. Maguire, Miss R. Mallett, theater dancer Jules Martin, Emile Petit, Henry Whale, and Charles Durang. Aside from teaching familiar and new dances, these masters helped sustain the deportment and behavior that, according to Sidney George Fisher, gave to Philadelphia's elites a "much higher tone of manners, character & culture" than he encountered elsewhere. He added, with wistful snobbery, "We are gradually losing it no doubt from the influence of the general causes which control the country, but still we are far superior to New York."[129] Dickens, too, appreciated the "taste" and "genteel discussions" he encountered in Philadelphia society, which he esteemed above that of other U.S. cities.

This abundance of social dancing drew religious groups' scrutiny, published in print media. The Presbyterians, according to an article in 1843, had "uttered a condemnation of *dancing*" to which an anonymous author responded.[130] Such "tyranny," the respondent felt, must be addressed, for "dancing is universal. No race of men ever existed without it." Dancing was "a natural propensity, like laughing. . . . God put it there, and both reason and revelation say that it should be *regulated*, not *suppressed*." In a subsequent article, the dance-defender invoked science: "By references to anatomy and physiology in all animals, as well as to all human history, do we prove that man dances naturally," a "hypothesis fully sustained by phrenological investigation. An eminent phrenologist," unnamed by this anonymous author, has discovered that the human brain contains a *dancing* organ, the *terminating* point of which is in the lower region of the legs. Every organ of the brain . . . requires some point at which stimulation enters, and some other point at which action ends. Then as men dance with their legs, and principally with the lower portion of them, the terminating point of the dancing organ ought to be in or near the feet; and near them is the very spot where phrenology has discovered this point. The phrenologist who has made this discovery calls it the organ of *buffoonery*: and though we dislike the term, it serves our present purpose. He finds it relatively the most powerful in man, and next in the monkey, a fact harmonizing with all human history so far as dancing is concerned, and with all human experience of monkeys.

Thus, science proved "that man is a *natural* dancer" and dancing "one of his *instincts*" which, God-given, is "intended to be gratified," for otherwise, "Supreme Wisdom has *created in vain*"—unthinkable. Among the few references in phrenological publications to an "organ of buffoonery" is one in *The Botanico-Medical Recorder* (1843) by "A. Curtis, professor of medicine at the College of Ohio."[131] Describing an experiment he observed on a woman suffering from melancholy (depression), Curtis wrote that "Dr. B," the experimenter, "touched the organ of buffoonery" on his subject's head, "and promptly roused her; she broke out, laughingly, with the song, 'Take Your Time, Miss Lucy'"—a popular blackface-stage tune of the time, with lyrics satirizing *cachucha*-dancing, Black women's sexual appeal, and wifely shrewishness. Our Philadelphia dance-defender would not likely have appreciated that experiment's result. A London phrenology journal placed "buffoonery" under the "organ of Wit," not linked to dancing.[132]

The Fowlers addressed a related "organ" in their essay "Mirthfulness,"[133] remarkably observing that "the size of Mirthfulness is not always proportionate to what might be called 'Ha-ha-ha-ativeness'" (p. 181). If exercised under a knowing phrenologist's guidance, with "moral faculties and intellect," mirthfulness can yield "good feeling" and "good sense" (p. 182). Struggling to reconcile the Fowlers' liberal views with their strict morality, the article went on: "The jokes of the circus clown are not the jokes for Phrenology. Nor are the burlesques of the Museum; nor the grotesque antics of negro dancers, Jim Crow, etc.; nor many of the farces of the stage," for these are "deficient in the required moral, or thought. Still, they could be made useful," Fowler added, perhaps reluctantly, through "the merry song and dance united," since the organs of "Mirth, Time, and Tune, are located adjoining each other, thereby even requiring their conjoint action." Stammeringly, the article concludes,

"Of all forms of amusement, dancing and singing united furnish probably about the very best; still, dances, as now conducted, Phrenology condemns. At least, it suggests important improvements," undetailed in the essay.

The dance-defending *Public Ledger* columnist was not finished. Later in June, an article appeared titled "The Deacon and the Dancing Master," a dialogue between Dancing Master Quiver, with a faux French accent, and a Presbyterian Deacon, represented unflatteringly as the barkeep in the tavern where the conversation occurs.[134] When the Deacon urges Quiver "to set at nought the grace of the heels . . . and covet aright the more excellent grace . . . of divinity," the dancing master asks, "vy should I give up de danse, de vare poetry of motion, before I can be receive into de church? Does dat divine grace of vich you speak refuse to visit de heart because it see some grace in de heels?" The deacon's liquor-dispensing, the dancing master notes, stimulates far more dangerous vice than dancing. Later that summer, another column offered not just a defense but a history and anthropology of dance, culminating in praise of the art of ballet and quoting "Monsieur Noverre."[135]

Carpenter, who I posit authored these unsigned 1843 articles, did respond in his own name a few years later to yet another religious attack on dancing.[136] Following the newspaper notice for his dancing school for ladies and gentlemen, the master added a *nota bene*: "To inform the gentleman inquisitor who called on D. L. Carpenter, at his school room, last Saturday, and who condemned all Dancing Masters to everlasting punishment hereafter," to "please call again, . . . and if he will find one passage in the Scripture, condemning this healthy art, then will I give up dancing forever. As for its evil propensities," Carpenter added, "I can say with truth and honor, that I have taught no less than eight Ministers of the different denominations, to walk and use the arms gracefully, for the pulpit." He concluded, "I think good of all religious denominations, of churches, &c . . . but do not believe in the superstitions of the present age—[n]or do I believe in private inquisitors, or the ancient mode of bringing us to the rack, in this our beautiful country of lawful freedom." Carpenter invited anyone "ignorant" of a "respectable Dancing School" to witness the "rules and style" of his lessons.

Later, Carpenter also published dance manuals, but in the 1840s, other masters contributed to Philadelphia's burgeoning print output with texts for dance students, or for those who could not take lessons but might learn movement skills using these publications. Such was the objective of an 1827 manual published in New York by Edmund Conway, who had danced on Philadelphia stages: *Le Maître de Danse, Or, The Art of Dancing Cotillons* was subtitled "*By which Every One May Learn to Dance Them, without a Master.*" Of course, the student would progress far more quickly with both text and teacher. Durang published three works, some reproducing portions of the same text.[137] His 1847 *Leaflets of the Ball Room* featured dances Durang and daughter taught at their academy, including eastern European dances then in favor—the *polka, mazurka,* and *redowa,* along with waltzes and Spanish-style dances. Drawing on European models, particularly Carlo Blasis and Jean Georges Noverre, Durang began his next volume, *Durang's Terpsichore, or, Ball Room Guide,* with a flowery statement of purpose, then a brief history of dancing, justifying its usefulness to all classes of people, and an exposition of the "laws" (p. 23) on which his teaching was based. He pointed to dancing as healthy exercise for girls and women, given their "delicate constitutions" (p. 18). Step illustrations show use of a barre-type support for practice, while verbal descriptions link theatrical and social dancing through such movements as positions of the legs/feet, *battements, pirouettes, ronds de jamb,* and arm placement. Durang then described cotillions, quadrilles, polkas, a gallopade, a "palonaise," waltz, redowa, reel, pas de matelot (hornpipe), "miscellaneous dances," and "Ethiopian Cotillions." These latter choreographies, rather than including steps from either African American dances or from blackface minstrelsy, featured "Figures Arranged to the Most Popular African Airs" (p. 85). While the steps are familiar from other American and European dance manuals of the time—ladies' chain, *balancé,* turn, *promenade, chassé,* dos-a-dos—the tunes are from the minstrel stage, including "Miss Lucy Long," "Dandy Jim," and "Old Zip Coon," although the text states, "These figures may be danced to any of the negro [minstrel] airs" (p. 92).

Farewell to Francis Johnson

I close this discussion of the 1840s with a farewell to a Philadelphia figure who exemplified concerns key to this investigation, including his engagement with publication. Francis Johnson (Figure 4.4) was one of the most widely published composers in the early United States, championed by leading Philadelphia publishers George Willig, Benjamin Carr, and others.[138] A superb musician, composer, bandleader, orchestral conductor, and teacher, Johnson died in April 1844, ending an era when his musical leadership was a light to all Philadelphians and a particular pride of African Americans. Known for marches commissioned for civic processions and local military units (led by Philadelphia's white elites), performed by his all-Black band, Johnson also wrote, arranged, and performed music he associated with theatrical works—the *cachucha, cracovienne,* and selections from *La Bayadere, La Sonnambula, The Lady of the Lake,* and *The Swiss Cottage.* In 1824, Johnson

Figure 4.4. *Francis Johnson*. Undated, no artist ascription. Joseph Muller collection of music and other portraits. *(Music Division, The New York Public Library, Digital Collections. Accessed June 19, 2024. https://digitalcollections.nypl.org/items/510d47df-e2fb-a3d9-e040-e00a18064a99)*

and band performed at the Circus, soon to be the Walnut Street Theatre; as they marched onto the stage during the spectacle *The Cataract of the Ganges*, they brought true African Americans onto otherwise all-white stages before blackface minstrelsy's inundation.[139] Later, Johnson arranged and played tunes popular on the blackface stage—"Dandy Jim," "Miss Lucy Long," "Sam of Tennessee," "Old Dan Tucker"—perhaps a concession to public demand or a reclamation of these as Black-sourced music.[140]

Johnson was closely connected to social dance, playing for the city's best dancing masters, for the elite Philadelphia Dancing Assembly, civic balls, and the toney summer resorts of Saratoga Springs and Ballston Spa in New York, where Johnson's compositions, orchestra, and dance-calling enlivened fashionable white society. Johnson and band reportedly played for Philadelphia's

"African" Ball in 1828, and perhaps for other unrecorded balls by his community. His "Recognition March of the Independence of Haiti" and "The Grave of a Slave" held special meaning to Black Philadelphians. Johnson's stature and value to powerholders in white society protected him from some miseries of African American life, but he encountered racial prejudice. When Philadelphia militia units joined parades with companies from outside the city, some units' all-white bands refused to play with Johnson's musicians.[141] Burlesque cartoons of a "Raccoon Band" ridiculed Johnson. His departure with his all-Black ensemble for Europe in 1837 raised concerns for the group's safety as they were denied U.S. passports and, thus, assurance of citizenship protection.

A member of St. Thomas African Episcopal Church, Johnson brought his compositions and those of Haydn, Mozart, and others to listeners at church concerts and beyond, introducing promenade concerts to the city after he observed them in Europe. Johnson's death and dignified funeral were reported respectfully by Philadelphia's mainstream newspapers: some white mourners attended, with a numerous Black congregation and Johnson's band playing black-draped instruments. In a memorial article, *Public Ledger* music critic William Henry Fry wrote that Johnson taught his students and band members "to meet the standards of excellence expected and demanded from them in the world of music." Johnson's service to his city, state, and country "caused an overflow of public gratitude for the contribution he had made to humankind by the time of his death."[142] Johnson's all-Black band, led by musicians he trained, continued to play for Philadelphia assemblies long thereafter. In the view of George "Gaslight" Foster, Francis Johnson, the musicians he nurtured, and the audiences who appreciated his music were proof of "the progressive development of the colored race,"[143] which would bring future generations the gifts of American culture, shaped so significantly by African American creative genius.

5

Order and Entropy

Science, Stage, and Society, 1850–1860

By the 1850s, questions arising in the nation's earliest years had driven—and riven—deeply into the fabric of the United States. Could a national union hold, based on principles expressed in founding documents? How should expressions of society (in unity and variety) appear in national culture? In this decade, Philadelphia's entertainment venues cemented the nation's emerging social stratifications into bricks-and-mortar edifices: Sanford's Opera House and the Academy of Music each aimed to entertain the city's different populations.[1] The former featured blackface minstrelsy, the workingman's stage form; the latter, imported opera and ballet to satisfy elite connoisseurs. Divisions hardened across the political landscape too: North and South faced off over slavery in newly admitted states; laws touching fugitive slaves inspired resistance, fear, bounty-hunting, and literary-dramatic expression. Women, employing the very strictures of their ascribed social sphere, pressed for rights and opportunities. Yet classificatory rigidities not only hardened but also collapsed into one another, a turbulence reflected on the stage.

Developments in science led the drive toward classification and separation. As Frederick Douglass observed, his was "an age of science, and science is favorable to division."[2] Douglass named the major exponents of those divisions—"the Notts, the Gliddons, the Agassiz, and Mortons," whose ethnological claims undergirded social, political, and economic ranks. This chapter focuses on science's *categorization as a methodology for understanding the world*. Ethnologists, through observation and analysis, established hierarchies that placed certain groups (their own) at the apex of human development, and others (those whom some powerholders sought to divest of land, agency, and freedom) at descending rungs. These elites claimed superiority not only corporeally, but also in their capacity for "civilization" and culture. That cultural achievement embraced the serious dramatic stage, European opera, and—with some doubts—the ballet. Culturally, the Black presence in the United States was seen by such elites and many classed below them as a source of curiosity, humor, sympathy, danger, and abhorrence—attitudes mined by blackface performers from the nation's lower entertainment ranks. Yet such cultural distinctions, like those of science, proved difficult to sustain, crumbling and bleeding into one another.

Types of Mankind in Print and Performance

A capstone of racial, corporeal "scientific triumphalism" appeared in Philadelphia in 1354.[3] Spearheaded by Dr. Josiah Clark Nott, written with Egyptologist George Gliddon, the massive tome (over eight hundred pages) had a massive title (see the Bibliography), which I will hereafter refer to as *Types of Mankind* or *Types*. Conjoining science, art, and religion, the work was dedicated to Samuel Morton, hailing Philadelphia's world-renowned authority as the founder of this "new science" (p. 50). Sadly for Nott and Gliddon—who had supplied Morton with skulls from the Middle East[4]— Morton died in 1851. However, with Mrs. Morton's permission, Nott and Gliddon included some of the scientist's unpublished work, which would bolster the book's respectability. The volume had both scientific and political intentions: in Nott's introduction, he touted use of Morton's work by Senator John Calhoun to justify the extension of slavery into new states (pp. 51–52). The book also addressed "the liberality and thirst for information, so eminently characteristic of American republicanism," proving that, as Gliddon's preface claimed "in our own age and land"—unlike Europe—"scientific works can be written and published without solicitation of patronage from Governments, Institutions, or Societies; but solely through the co-operative support of an educated and knowledge-seeking people" (p. xi).

Widening North-South political schisms drew *Types of Mankind* into cultural and sectional rifts: a New Orleans newspaper decried the North's intellectual condescension, exemplified in a reviewer's contemptuous question, "'Who reads a southern book?' We answer, by placing before the eyes of these Pharisees the greatest ethnological work of the age, the 'Types of Mankind,'" which "neither Great Britain nor the North, can rival . . . as a scientific production."[5] The book's introduction forwarded ethnological classifications and aesthetic criteria of Nott's and colleagues' categorizations, describing the "African, with his black skin, woolly hair,[6] and compressed elongated skull; the Mongolian of Eastern Asia and America, with his olive complexion, broad and all but beardless face, oblique eyes, and square skull; and the Caucasian of Western Asia and Europe, with his fair skin, oval face, full brow, and rounded skull" (p. 52).

Harvard professor Louis Agassiz's prefatory "Sketch" to *Types* established a classification system on which Nott and Gliddon based their hierarchical racial claims. Agassiz parsed humankind, and all flora and fauna, into eight "realms"—"Arctic," "Asiatic," "European," "American," "African," "East Indian," "Australian," and "Polynesian." Significantly, all animals, including "man," were subject to "laws" ordering their "diversity" and "distribution," which were "directed by the All-wise and Omnipotent, to fulfil the great harmonies established in Nature" (p. lxxvi). Social hierarchy was, thus, presented as immutable, justified as divine beneficence, and embraced by such powerholders as Sidney George Fisher, whose review of works by Agassiz, Morton, and Nott led him to comprehend that "the difference and natural inequality of the two races, white and black, . . . govern what is called the slavery question. . . . The negro is the inferior—born for subordination and servitude, which has been his lot in all ages, when brought within the sphere of the white race," the highest example of the latter being "the Saxon."[7] Thus, "what position of inequality the negro shall hold, is for the Saxon to determine, . . . guided by his interest, his safety, his pride, and also by his sense of justice and benevolence."

Types reviews each racial group, devoting chapter VI to "African Types," of interest "not simply because they present an opposite extreme from the Caucasian" but also because of "their early communication with Egypt" (p. 180), a focus of this tome. According to Nott, across Africa's geographic span "there exists a regular gradation, from the Cape of Good Hope" in the south, "to the Isthmus of Suez," closest to Europe, "of which the Hottentot and Bushman" of the south "form the lowest, and the Egyptian and Berber types," in the north, "the highest links." The Hottentot and Bushman "are but little removed, both in moral and physical characters, from the orang-outan" (p. 182), owing to facial and bodily features. Further, Hottentots had humped backs, droopy genitalia, and a language "rapid, harsh, shrill," made possible only by "the peculiar construction of the vocal organs of this race" (p. 183).

Moving northward through Africa, Nott found a few groups more appealing physically and morally, though he saw many as "hideous," "barbarous," "superlatively savage" (p. 184), failing in intellect owing to "a cephalic conformation that renders all expectance of their future melioration an Utopian dream" (p. 185). This review inspired Nott's political musings on Liberia, which was founded as a U.S. Black colony around 1820, declaring independence in 1846: "Much as the success of the infant colony at Liberia is to be desired," Nott lamented, "we cannot divest our minds of melancholy forebodings" (p. 189). Morton's research claimed to prove "that the Negro races possess about nine cubic inches less of brain than the Teuton" which, Nott claimed, meant that "the Negroes in Africa must remain substantially in that same benighted state wherein Nature has placed them, and in which they have stood, according to Egyptian monuments," as he read them, "for at least 5,000 years." This groundwork underlay the next chapter, "Egypt and Egyptians," often citing Morton's *Crania Aegyptiaca*: with "genealogical tablets and papyri to guide us, as to the ancestral origin of Pharaonic families," the trained scientist perceives "a family-contour about them all, which at once indicates to the observer that they were of high 'Caucasian' caste, with but little African of any grade" (p. 228). The social order present in the United States at *Types*' publication, thus, descended from the civilization of ancient Egypt, coeval with the Bible, sustained by nature's ascribed racial rankings as elucidated by Morton and Nott. Such supposed physical and intellectual traits shaped vicious perceptions of Black people in the United States, enacted in staged "delineations" throughout the nation.

A few white intellectuals objected, on theological grounds, to *Types of Mankind*, but Black leaders were especially outspoken against its claims. Frederick Douglass chose ethnology as his topic when he had the rare opportunity as a Black man to address graduating scholars at Case Western Reserve University in 1854.[8] Citing expert scientists, he argued that those "technically called the negro race, are a part of the human family, and are descended from a common ancestry," deserving the freedom to exercise every human capacity, despite scientists' claims to the contrary. James McCune Smith had, in the 1840s, pointed to the "rage for classification" among those scholars whose "reprehensible spirit" had twisted science to support racial prejudices.[9] In the 1850s, the situation worsened, he astutely wrote, homing in on race scientists' aesthetic denigrations: "The negro 'with us'"—in the United States—"is not an actual physical being of flesh and bones and blood, but a hideous monster of the mind, ugly beyond all physical portraying" known to "frighten reason from its throne" among "American republicans!"[10] That "hideous" figure brings to mind not only Nott's disparaging language for Africans, but also the outlandish caricatures trotting across blackface stages, eliciting laughter and wonder from audiences across the nation. Thus, "the black man as human" became a "fantasy" of ludicrous impossibility, displayed in the grotesque behaviors of minstrelsy.[11] The author responded with his own parody of ethnological-phrenological claims in "Heads of the Coloured People," showing an entirely different—"hardworking, enterprising" and "heroic"[12]—view of Black crania than that proclaimed by Nott and colleagues.

Douglass's and McCune Smith's writings were familiar to Philadelphia's Black intellectuals through newspapers and societies; others in African American literary circles—Martin Delany and John S. Rock—had medical training as well as Pennsylvania connections. Delany (1812–1885), of Pittsburgh, apprenticed to a physician there and opened a medical practice. In 1852, he self-published *The Condition, Elevation, Emigration, and Destiny of the Colored People of the United States*, calling for the return of African Americans to Africa, for Delany saw no possibility of their fair treatment in the United States. In "Political Destiny of the Colored Race, on the American Continent," Delany addressed science and race: "Our friends in this and other countries"—white abolitionists—"anxious for our elevation, have for years been erroneously urging us to lose our identity as a distinct race, declaring that we were the same as other people," even while some "representatives" of the Caucasian race were "traversing the world and propagating the doctrine in favor of *a universal Anglo-Saxon predominance*."[13] The physician in Delany saw this contradiction as "the great political disease with which we are affected"; his solution was "Emigration." Differing with Douglass and McCune Smith, Delany asserted, "The truth is, we are not identical with the Anglo-Saxon or any other race of the Caucasian or pure white type." Black people bore "inherent traits . . . and native characteristics, peculiar to our race—whether pure or mixed blood." Thus, while Delany grappled directly with *Types of Mankind* in his *Principia of Ethnology*, published in 1879, his views took shape earlier.[14]

Delany's Black contemporary, New Jersey-born John S. Rock (1825–1866), practiced as a dentist in Philadelphia while undertaking medical training.[15] Rock delivered such speeches as "The Unity of the Races" (to the Massachusetts legislature, Apr. 1856), "Races and Slavery," and "The Varieties in the Human Family." None of these texts survive, but the *Liberator* published a transcript of a talk in which Rock argued that "Mother Nature" intended all racial groups eventually to mix, demolishing the categorizations propounded by white ethnologists.[16] Such mixture would benefit Caucasians, he wrote, for "the fine tough muscular system, the beautiful rich color, the full broad features, and the gracefully frizzled hair of the Negro," would improve "the delicate physical organization, wan color, sharp features and lank hair of the Caucasian." The latter group was created, Rock stated with sharp satire, when "nature was pretty well exhausted—but determined to keep up appearances, she pinched up his features and did the best she could under the circumstances." When Black people could access the "avenues of wealth" determining status in the United States, Rock predicted, "we will then become educated and wealthy, . . . and black will be a very pretty color."

As Delany's 1879 response demonstrates, Nott and Gliddon's *Types of Mankind* was influential well beyond the Civil War. Despite the tome's length, detail, and technical language, it achieved wide circulation among readers of all classes and interests.[17] It also alluded to the U.S. blackface stage: in chapter VIII, "Negro Types," Nott linked ancient Egyptian enslavement of Black Africans to contemporary U.S. servitude and entertainment, reproducing an illustration that, as he described it, depicted "some Negroes 'dancing in the streets of Thebes,' by way of archeological evidence that, 3,400 years ago, (or before the Exodus of Israel, B.C. 1322), 'de same ole N——r' of our Southern plantations could spend his Nilotic sabbaths in saltatory recreations, and 'Turn about, and wheel about, and jump Jim Crow!'" (p. 263). Should readers fail to grasp the minstrel show's message, as Nott understood it, he spelled it out for them.

From Mummies to Minstrelsy

Large-scale blackface minstrel troupes abounded in Philadelphia and across the nation by the 1850s, presenting full-evening shows with songs, skits, dances, and burlesques. These performances morphed into variety shows, swallowing up imitations of "others" beyond African Americans—Irish, Germans, Chinese, Japanese, even Shakers;[18] they mocked operas and burlesqued reform movements, particularly women's rights—all in blackface. Troupes remained overwhelmingly male; women sometimes took minor roles in skits, but the few all-female blackface troupes, like the Sable Sisters and the Female Minstrels, were not enduring.[19] White men, blacked up, sometimes in travesty, "delineating" "others" appealed to this entertainment's growing audiences.

Given the flexibility of blackface works, new troupes adapted acts developed by previous performers, creating a malleable minstrel repertoire. Among the plays minstrel companies "franchised" was *The Virginia Mummy* (*The Sarcophagus*), which T. D. Rice based on William Bayle Bernard's 1833 farce, *The Mummy*.[20] In Rice's version, he played the only blackface character, Ginger Blue, but whether later minstrel troupes used blackface for other characters in the work is unclear. Because the script lacked set songs and dances, the physical embodiment of character and action had to be particularly rich, drawing on skills akin to pantomime. Later troupes playing *Virginia Mummy* inserted songs into the play, including the famous dance-song "Jump Jim Crow," and dancing by Ginger Blue.[21] Although the show premiered in 1835, the play rose notably in popularity in the 1850s.

Americans' interest in mummies—a strain of the orientalism that, as earlier discussions revealed, also affected ballet—soared in the 1850s. *Types of Mankind* often cited recently discovered mummies in supporting its claims about racial anatomy and ranking (i.e., pp. 132–33, 212–14, 428–29, 454, 672, 688)—incidentally increasing audience interest in *Virginia Mummy*. Yet Rice's play skewered science, Egyptology, and white society (with allusions to temperance, Irish naivete, racial amalgamation, and "Eastern" exoticism), featuring jokes on and by the "Black" lead, Ginger Blue. The plot involves encasing servant Ginger Blue in a sarcophagus, in which he is instructed by one "Capt. Rifle" to pose as an ancient mummy. Having read "Dr. Galen's"[22] newspaper notice seeking mummies on which to test Galen's purportedly life-renewing elixir, Rifle plans to use the "mummy" as a wedge for entering the doctor's home to woo Galen's lovely ward, Lucy. Eager to try his restorative on a revered figure of antiquity, Galen fails to note that the mummy's "owner," disguised in "Persian" regalia, is the very Capt. Rifle whom the doctor had previously refused as Lucy's suitor. Blinded by his fantasies and ambitions, Galen fails also to notice that, as he addresses the supposedly three-thousand-year-old mummy in wonder at what he imagines to be its august history, that very mummy (Ginger Blue) answers him with physical tricks and witty put-downs in "Black" dialect. During the show, Galen and his "domestics" attempt to perpetrate violations on the body of mummy-Ginger—snipping off a finger, sewing his mouth shut—perhaps allusions to the corporeal terrors visited upon enslaved Africans. Yet Ginger counters each attack with tricks, kicks, and comments that save him from all but Galen's alcoholic "life-restoring" elixir, which Ginger swallows eagerly, coming to vibrant life in mocking exchanges with the assembled characters. Ginger so enjoys the intoxicating elixir, the breakfast he snatches from Galen's tray, and the tricks he plays on educated white society that he announces, in closing, "Should any ob de faculty hab occasion for a libe mummy again, dey hab only to call upon Ginger Blue; when dey'll find him ready, dried, smoked, and painted, to sarb himself up at de shortest notice." Rice's Ginger not only kicks Galen and his associates bodily, but he lands solid punches on the entire enterprise of ethnological science.

The mania for mummy-unwrapping was familiar to audiences watching *Virginia Mummy*. Since the early 1820s, mummies had been displayed and unwrapped by men of science across Europe and the United States, inspiring Rice's *Virginia Mummy* spoof.[23] In the early 1850s, renewed interest in mummies was stimulated by the tour of Egyptologist George Gliddon, former U.S. vice-consul to Egypt and soon coauthor with Nott of *Types of Mankind*. Gliddon's spectacular "Panorama of the Nile" opened in November 1849 in New York to ecstatic reception. He learned from museum-entrepreneur P. T. Barnum that educational lectures presented with exotic props, colorful transparencies, lighting effects, and moving music drew large, respectable audiences.[24] This his show did, appealing even to religious sectors that saw it as an opportunity to uncover biblical history. After New York, Gliddon played Boston in April 1850, where he heightened the excitement by offering three special lectures, culminating in unwrapping one of the four ancient mummies traveling with his show. With stellar men of science, including Professor Agassiz, as expert observers in his first two June lectures, Gliddon identified the mummy to be unwrapped, based on hieroglyphics and other indicators, as the daughter of an Egyptian high priest. Lecture three—the opening of the case and the mummy's unwrapping—was sold out. But, as the last of its swathing was removed—the piece covering the mummy's pelvis—the body was revealed to be that of a male, whose genital potency the ancient embalmers had carefully sustained. The audience's uproarious laughter was barely calmed by Gliddon's hasty explanation that ancient drunken embalmers had, he insisted, put the wrong body in the case. The national press published send-ups of "the blundering coffin makers / In the Theban shops of mummies" who "Proved themselves a set of dummies, / And misplac'd the lady's body / By this base-born male tom-noddy."[25]

Gliddon soon exited Boston, taking his Panorama—its popularity undimmed by the mummy fiasco—to Maine and then Philadelphia. His warm relationship with Morton and the Academy of Natural Sciences, to which he had donated Egyptian artifacts, surely encouraged him. Eager audiences thronged his show in late September 1850. Undaunted by his Boston embarrassment, Gliddon offered to unwrap not one, but two of the remaining mummies in his show in Philadelphia—likely as an honor to Morton's hometown. His lectures on the soon-to-be-revealed mummies began on December 30, 1850, the unwrapping occurring on January 17, 1851. A reported encounter of some learned viewers with one of the mummies brings *Virginia Mummy*'s Ginger Blue to mind: the gentlemen, strolling through Gliddon's pre-lecture display, heard a voice issuing from the mummy case, demanding they "open the box" and informing them that he, the enclosed mummy, was "a descendant of the Pharaohs." One gentleman, after posing questions about antiquity to the apparently awakened mummy, asked its name. The reply was,

"Bobby." "Bobby who?" asked the astonished inquirer. "Bobby Blitz;" and a little man with a peculiar head of hair glided out of the hall and disappeared into the lecture room of the museum. The . . . word "sold" was audibly heard coming from the box, as if the dried descendant of Mizraim [Egypt] was laughing in its sleeve at the credulity of science, which could not tell a living ventriloquist from the fried remains of burnt rags and a monkey's skeleton.[26]

English stage performer/magician Antonio Blitz (b. 1810) spent many years in Philadelphia, where he died in 1877. A ventriloquist, he named his dummy Bobby, and he too included a "mummy" in his show.

From 1850 to 1860, as Gliddon's Panorama and coedited tome, *Types of Mankind*, traversed the nation, versions of *Virginia Mummy* abounded. It appeared at least thirty-two times in Philadelphia, from major halls (the Arch, Chestnut, and Walnut Street Theaters) to less formal sites (Frank Rivers's Melodeon and Long's Varieties).[27] The city's dedicated minstrel hall, Sanford's Opera House, played it together with Frank Brower's "Happy Uncle Tom Dance," discussed later. Sanford's *Mummy* production included all the characters from Rice's play, following its basic script, but unlike Rice's performance, even the female figures were played by men; this choice suggests that they, and perhaps other characters, might have also blacked up.[28]

Before his Philadelphia move, Sam Sanford had been with Buckley's Minstrels, then performed with and managed the blackface New Orleans Opera troupe. His first Philadelphia "Opera House" (1853) was at Twelfth and Chestnut Streets, thus creating a dedicated minstrel hall in the city; after that site burned, Sanford moved to Cartee's Lyceum on Eleventh Street. To promote that hall's opening (1855), he advertised his distribution of toys and bread to the poor—Black and white together—by the novel means of tossing the handouts from the building's roof to the crowd in the street, causing the mayor to accuse Sanford of inciting a riot.[29] Sanford, a shrewd publicist, flipped the controversy, accusing the mayor of elitist indifference while presenting himself as a champion of all people, just as he skewered them all in his satires. He repeated the bread-tossing stunt at least once, as reported on January 2, 1860.

Sanford's naming his hall an "opera house" expressed the cultural aspiration of blackface minstrelsy to raise its appeal from the working-class audience it initially lured to respectable middle-class viewers, challenging the social-class categories of republican America. Sanford's strategy included ludicrous burlesques of actual European operas and ballets. A newspaper puff targeted class consciousness in reporting Sanford's May 1853 shows:

"The success of Sanford is unprecedented," as his performers "are all gentlemen of decided merit, and possess first class voices, while their dancing, whether of the refined ballet or the genuine breakdown cannot be approached by any similar company in the world"[30]—highlighting his embrace of high- and low-class movement genres. Sanford, "the indefatigable and gentlemanly Manager of this Company," is thus "deserving not alone of the patronage but also of the thanks of the public for catering so liberally for their entertainment and elevating and refining the growing taste for Ethiopian Burlesque until it has become a standard fashionable amusement of the day." Thus Sanford targeted the perceived sweet spot in U.S. entertainment taste.

An example of such programming was Sanford's bill of August 22 and 23, 1853; his version of Bellini's opera *La Sonnambula* included a Highland Fling, a "Tamborine Dance," and the minstrel song and dance "Lucy Long."[31] On that bill Sanford announced, "In Preparation, a Ballet, in which a Burlesque will be given of the Ravel Family," whose ever-successful seasons in Philadelphia made them both familiar to audiences and targets of burlesque. Promising his company of eighteen performers in "Opera every evening with singing and dancing" (Sept. 1853), or "Burlesque Operas, Extravaganzas and Ballet such as were never before introduced in Minstrelsy" (Aug. 9–Sept. 8, 1855), Sanford offered a range of high-culture satires: *Cinderella* (Sept. 1853, Jan. 1857), *The Bohemian Girl* (Oct. 1853), *La Bayadere* (or, *Lah-Buy-it-Dear*, Dec. 1853), *Robert Macaire* (a Ravel staple, Sept.–Oct. 1856), *Fra Diavolo* (Nov. 1856), *Jocko, The Brazilian Ape* (a "Laughable Pantomime" with an all-male, blacked-up cast, Oct. 1859), and, in 1857, *Xlanties; or Forty Thieves*,[32] with burlesques of well-known ballet stars Mme. Celeste, Fanny Elssler, Yrca Mathias (leading ballerina with the Ravel troupe), and Lola Montez (on whom, more later). That Elssler remained a presence on U.S. stages over a decade after her tour is further evident in blackface minstrel Dan Gardner's balletic spoof *Fanny Ellsler* [sic] "with the Spanish Dance" (*la cachucha*), at Sanford's on November 27, 1857. Sanford also franchised Rice's plays, including *Virginia Mummy* and *Oh! Hush!* (Sept.–Oct. 1856; Feb. 15, 1860).

Capitalizing on his operatic-blackface mixtures, Sanford joined the book-publishing tide with his volume of *Melodies* (1856), a thank-you to Philadelphians "for the very liberal manner in which they have appreciated his efforts, to establish in their midst a permanent place of amusement, devoted almost exclusively to the delineation of Ethiopian characters,"[33] keeping his eye on the audience at the heart of blackface appeal. Still, Sanford shrewdly wrote, his "novelties" were "moral, instructive, and amusing," and "suited in style, tone, and exposition to the public taste"—including the respectable middle class. He sought stability and respectability for himself and family, perhaps a motivation for establishing his Opera House. His son and daughter danced straight balletic interludes on his stage in alternation with blackface acts—thus, the "almost exclusive" presentation of "Ethiopian" "delineation," cited earlier. To distinguish non-blackface acts from minstrel parodies, the young Sanfords' dances bore elevated titles like "Grand Pas de Deux," "Terpsichorean melange," "Operatic Ballet Divertissement," and "Pas de Brilliant," along with national dances—highland flings, Irish lilts, *la manola*, and Elssler's *cachucha* and *cracovienne*.[34] Such opera and ballet elements appealed to higher-class spectators, whom Sanford lured to his "drawing room entertainment with new songs, dances, etc." (Sept. 1853), where "the Strictest Decorum will be Enforced" (Jan. 1856). He boasted, in *Melodies* (p. 2), that his establishment was "patronized by the Elite and Fashion of the Quaker City," owing to its "unsullied reputation." Sanford proclaimed that he "has endeared himself to every right-minded and honorable-thinking citizen by his many acts of benevolence and liberality to the Poor—his purse is ever open in the cause of Charity," wringing extra mileage from his bread-tossing spectacle.

Fugitives from the *Cabin*

The nature of Sanford's and other minstrel shows altered as the decade passed, responding to national developments. The Fugitive Slave Act, part of the Compromise of 1850, admitted new states to the union as "free" or "slave"—continuing the categorization (and its concomitant disorder) with which the nation struggled.[35] Further exacerbating North-South rifts was the Kansas-Nebraska Act, again grappling with new states' status regarding slavery, enacted in 1854, as *Types of Mankind* was published. "Evidence," disseminated in *Types*, of supposed biologically based inadequacies of African-descended people brought the weight of science to politics and law. In December 1856, the Supreme Court's decision in the Dred Scott case denied "rights or privileges" to African Americans, ruling that the nation's founding documents treated them as "a subordinate and inferior class of beings" who, enslaved or free, "remained subject" to white authority.[36] Between the Compromise of 1850 and the 1854 publications of the Kansas-Nebraska Act and *Types of Mankind*, Harriet Beecher Stowe's *Uncle Tom's Cabin; or, Life Among the Lowly* appeared.

Stowe's blockbuster novel enflamed the most sensitive nerves in U.S. politics and culture, stimulating both abolitionist activity and vitriolic attacks on the book, its characters, and its author. *Uncle Tom's Cabin* was quickly adapted for the stage. Durang identified the National Amphitheatre version

(Sept. 8, 1853) as the first Philadelphia production of *Uncle Tom's Cabin; or, Life among the Lowly*, dramatized by S. E. Harris.[37] The staging, with songs by G. C. Howard, "was received for weeks and weeks with unbounded approbation by crowded houses"—"a most signal incident in theatrical annals" and a relief to the theater's distressed finances. Among the cast was dancer Rose Merrifield as Topsy, with songs and "a characteristic dance." Harris's version was "ingeniously and dramatically concentrated without tediousness," Durang opined. He also felt that G. L. Aiken's version of *Uncle Tom's Cabin*, at the Chestnut Street Theatre (Sept. 26, 1853), "opened a new dramatic era" on that esteemed stage. Aiken's play opened with Mr. Mueller's "new Ethiopian overture," an ascription suggesting the composer drew on popular blackface tunes to support the singing and dancing.[38] The play, as Durang saw it, "did, perhaps, as much as any other instrument of antislavery tendency to stimulate public sentiment against the 'peculiar institution.'" With a nod to minstrelsy's class-crossing appeal, Durang noted, "The negro airs, ever pleasing to all classes, gave it infinite *ad captandum* [appealing] aid." Aiken's play filled the entire evening, so that no other works appeared with it, until it was cut from six to three acts, though it later reverted to its full length. At times, versions of *Uncle Tom* played simultaneously at several theaters—for example, at the National and the Chestnut, while Sanford's presented a minstrel parody version, to be discussed.[39]

What explains the sweeping success, in Philadelphia and elsewhere, of a stage work of such length and so serious a theme? A contemporary magazine suggested, "There is nothing that so certainly commands the tears of an audience, as the undeserved calamities of the innocent. One of our theatres has been reaping a harvest of nightly benefits by exhibiting the untimely death of a little girl, and the hardships of a virtuous slave."[40] This enthusiasm, the author felt, "takes us back to the days of Aeschylus, and convinces us that the love of the drama is as strong as it ever was. . . . The descent from Prometheus to Uncle Tom, dramatically considered, is not a very violent one, nor," he punned, "so low as some may imagine." Aiken's play combined a then-appealing blend of moral values—Christian justice, perseverance, duty, temperance, and common sense, while reinforcing Black/white and abolition/proslavery binaries.[41] These values variously crossed classes and races; the National Theatre advertised a separate seating section for "colored" viewers attending the show.

Uncle Tom dramas, with music and dancing, appeared through the 1850s at Philadelphia theaters from the City Museum to the Chestnut Street Theatre to the Academy of Music.[42] It was quickly adopted by blackface minstrels, whose pro-slavery versions dominated city stages as the decade passed. Just as the city saw the first serious dramatizations of Stowe's novel, Sanford brought audiences *Uncle Tom's Cabin, Or, Real Life in Old Kentuck!*, assuredly "not taken from the Novel of Mrs. Beecher Stowe, but founded on a life-like representation of the merriment and pastimes of the glories of the South."[43] Sanford advertised his version as "portraying the happiness of the Negroes of the South, introducing the Harmony that prevails upon Plantations, their Holiday Festivals, Marriages, Congo Dances, &c." The all-male cast featured such characters as Aunt Chloe, Uncle Tom (Sanford's role), Liza, George Harris, Topsy, Lame Jake, Cassy, and Mose. The scenes included "Uncle Tom's Cabin," "Aunt Chloe very industrious," "A Tale about the abolitionists," "Aunt Chloe don't like Cincinnati: 'I'd radder be on de Old Plantation,'" "White folks dat don't own N———rs very good to talk," "Making Love by Moonlight," and the wedding of Liza and George when "Dey Both Jump de Broom! Such a Happy Time." Thus, Sanford presented his view of fugitives from slavery. The play featured "Congo Dances, Reels, Camp Meeting Chants," and a "Finale and Chorus, Corn Shucking Reel." Versions were sometimes advertised as *Happy Uncle Tom*, with its "pictures representing slavery in its true light!"[44] Minstrel jokester Dan Rice (unrelated to T. D. Rice) published in Philadelphia his "Uncle Tom's Cabin, Entitled Wait for the Wagon," where the singer recounts the cheating, fleecing, and jail time he experienced as a "free" man in the "Nordern States," with a nostalgic chorus, "But gib me de plantation," where, the character assured audiences, life was so much better.[45] In Sanford's and others' versions of Stowe's plot, all family members reunited, lovers married, and deaths were averted. The "Black" characters found themselves duped by slimy Northern abolitionists and, once tasting "freedom" in the North, the fugitives fled back to what was presented as their happy Southern enslavement, to sing and dance, "Den hand de Banjo down to play, / We'll make it ring both night and day; / And we care not what de white folks say, / Dey can't get us to run away."[46] Sanford attributed his frequent showing of *Uncle Tom* to "the many requests of our Southern friends," alluding to the numerous Southern students at the University of Pennsylvania and to Philadelphia merchants' close ties with Southern production networks.

"Happy Uncle Tom" also appeared as a stand-alone dance act, a specialty of minstrel dancer Frank Brower, appreciated in Philadelphia for his long-standing connections to the city. He danced "Happy Uncle Tom" for the Chestnut Street Theatre's Christmas and New Year's shows (Dec. 1854–Jan. 1855) and in other city theaters.[47] Brower's act, aside from its title, had little to do with Stowe's work, instead featuring a dialogue between "Jeff" and "Tom" about playing banjo for a white folks' ball and concluding with the "Happy

Uncle Tom" dance.[48] Other blackface troupes played longer versions of the show, including Boyd's Minstrels at Star Hall in March 1854, presenting "*Uncle Tom's Cabin*—Not the great National (Libel) Slander on the character of the South, but Happy Uncle Tom—the only version which faithfully portrays the real condition of Southern Slavery"; and Myers & Landis Star Troupe of Ethiopian Vocalists and Delineators in *Uncle Tom at Home; or, Southern Life as it Really Is*, in September 1856 at Philadelphia's Melodeon. These Happy-Tom shows exemplified theater managers' alignment with the fractious categories shattering national unity and inciting violence in politics, society, and culture. Sanford, for example, operated in a famously liberal and pro-abolition city, yet catered to "Southern" tastes—tastes with apparently wide appeal in the City of Brotherly Love.

As Sanford nudged his shows toward what he saw as education and refinement, other venues filled the vacuum for lower-class amusement. Among these, the "free and easy"—an entertainment concept borrowed from England—appeared in the early 1850s.[49] According to critics, such taverns catered primarily to working-class men, encouraged "intemperance" through "smoking and drinking," and featured entertainments intended "to gratify a vulgar and indecent taste, rather than to mend the morals and improve the heart."[50] Some free and easies (along with "concert saloons") hosted *tableaux vivants* (essentially still-life nude shows), circus and ballet performers, and blackface acts.[51] A reporter from Philadelphia writing in a New York newspaper regretted the dearth of good music in his home city, except for "many so-called concerts nightly given to red-faced and boozy lager-beer customers, by musical creatures of the lowest talent."[52] The Melodeon, a developed version of the concert saloon, often produced minstrel shows (including *Uncle Tom* plays) and some "dry" family matinees. While music dominated these shows, jigs and breakdowns often appeared, as did some ballet dancers. Venues called "dance houses" or "dance halls," on the other hand, emphasized social dancing rather than stage shows. Offering working-class men opportunity to partner with the houses' female habitués, they were frequent sites of prostitution, gambling, and brawling. Some dance houses had stage shows, just as some concert saloons offered social dancing. It is possible that performers at some of these less publicized sites were Black, although documentation is lacking. Certainly, some of the women available for dancing and other interactions at dance halls were Black; a dominant feature of these venues was women entertaining men, on the dance floor or stage.

Some women, discussed next, came to the stage through a very different route.

Women and Medical Education

Philadelphia's Musical Fund Hall, typically a site for concerts, balls, and, eventually, minstrel shows, hosted the first commencement of the Female Medical College of Pennsylvania (FMC) on December 30, 1851. FMC, founded in 1850, was the first and longest enduring institution dedicated to educating women as physicians.[53] The commencement speaker, Quaker physician Joseph Longshore, hailed the eight women graduating with the M.D. as initiating "an eventful epoch in the history of your lives, in the history of woman, in the history of the race"—the human race. The commencement reflected social and philosophical splits fracturing the city and nation, particularly categorization by sex: a contingent of male medical students from University of Pennsylvania, attending the FMC graduation, engaged in boisterous ridicule, prevented from reaching riotous levels by a conspicuous police presence.

As women were denied admission to Penn's medical school, their alternative at FMC was hailed at women's rights conventions; at a national gathering in Philadelphia (Oct. 1854), a delegate praised it as "the first city, not only in the United States, but in the world, to establish a Medical College for Women."[54] The school offered professional opportunities through medicine and created the possibility for women to consult doctors of their own sex on matters that made exposure to male doctors awkward, even unthinkable, in this age of extreme propriety. FMC enrolled not only those seeking degrees, but also those following courses for their own information, and it provided an imprimatur to female lecturers who sought to educate women, beyond the consulting room, about their bodies and health.

Many FMC enrollees rejected the prevailing view of women's separate spheres, but the college's second-year catalog pointed to the ways that ascribed innate qualities of "woman" made her not only suitable but ideal as a medical doctor. Her "innate" capacity for sympathy gave woman a wedge that opened doors to the healing arts—just as female corporeal lightness and beauty made her ideal for ballet. Initially, FMC's professors were male physicians, but once women graduated the college, they became its teachers.[55] Textbooks for FMC courses included leading publications, despite those texts' views of women; in the required obstetrical work, *Females and their Diseases*, author Charles Meigs asserted that woman "reigns in the heart; her seat and throne are by the hearthstone," for "the Forum is too angry for her. The Curia is too grave and high, and the Commitia too boisterous and rude. . . . Home is her place."[56] Meigs pointed to the "Venus de Medici," an example of womanly perfection, with "a head almost too small for intellect but just big enough for love."

The carnage of the surgical theater was beyond woman, for "she melts at the spectacle of human distress." Yet even prominent obstetricians of the day, like Meigs, admitted the "delicacy" of women in childbirth and other exposing situations when faced with a strange man, though a physician, accessing their bodies.[57] At FMC, women made inroads in the field and proved themselves against accusations that they were too fragile for such work, incapable of intellectual challenges, and "desexed" by earning a living, particularly one so intimately associated with the body.[58]

While dancers like Mme. Celeste and Fanny Elssler challenged such matters with their expressive performances on public stages and their appeal to audiences, those attending FMC argued with public lectures and treatment of patients. The highly regarded Black teacher and scientist Sarah Mapps Douglass attended FMC lectures in 1852, then shared her knowledge with African American women through public lectures on physiology and anatomy and her teaching at the Institute for Colored Youth.[59] As Britt Rusert notes, Douglass's lectures not only provided vital information to her listeners, but they also allowed Douglass to counter demeaning scientific claims and minstrelized performances of Black females by presenting her own person—body and mind—as she lectured.

Lecturing was a popular, respected form of entertainment, competing for audiences with "refined" stage productions—choral and orchestral music, opera, ballet, and Shakespeare—and often hosted in the same halls.[60] Gliddon took advantage of this popularity for his Egyptology lectures. Newspaper "Amusements" columns listed lectures alongside stage performances. One observer saw the lecture as "the American amusement which is most congenial to our habits and tastes," since "the opera is always an exotic with us; the theatre is a reproduction of the English . . . and the dramas we have ourselves produced, are either adaptations of the French, or mere *spectacles* of the lowest and most prurient sarcastic scandal."[61] These "spectacles," exemplified by "negro minstrelsy," had "degenerated into coarse burlesque and sentimental buffoonery"—both of which were used in satirizing, in blackface, the craze for lectures. Some popular speakers, including O. S. Fowler lecturing on topics like "Woman's Phrenology, Woman's Sphere, Woman's Rights, as well as her Duties, Treatment and Perfection," were hailed for having "vastly amused us."[62] That commentator then turned attention to women's "reform dress," adding, "The subject of Bloomerism, we presume, Mr. F. will well consider; perhaps he will denounce the pantaloons." Fowler was more interested in heads than legs, but minstrels, certainly, found pantaloons hilarious. Women's "reform dress"—called "freedom dress" or "Bloomers" after feminist Amelia Bloomer—was seen by one journalist as "a sort of ballet-girl costume,"[63] as the knee-length full skirt and fitted leggings resembled the dancer's tutu.

Female physicians found lecturing a means of gaining additional income and attracting patients, particularly given the refusal of male medical organizations to admit women practitioners to their associations or hospitals. Women physicians lecturing publicly carefully presented themselves as professionals offering practical, science-based information for women's health and knowledge, shunning Gliddon's taste for spectacle. Yet, given the penetrable border between education and entertainment, even displaying themselves as professional women in public—whether to all-female or to "promiscuous" audiences—was itself a daring, exposing choice, faced also by women's rights speakers and, of course, by ballet dancers.

Female lecturers and reformers were targeted in blackface parodies. In February 1855, "Mr. John W. Landis, the Greatest Ethiopian Delineator extant," was announced to "appear as Miss Lucy Soap Stone and deliver his Great and Original *Lecture on Woman's Rights*," mocking Massachusetts feminist Lucy Stone (1818–1893), and perhaps reminding Philadelphians of their own outspoken Lucretia Mott; Landis's send-up was followed on the bill by "the celebrated Burlesque Opera of *Happy Uncle Tom*,"[64] making explicit the blackface stage's linked denigration of the interconnected reform movements, abolitionism and feminism. At Sanford's Opera House, Dan Gardner played in *Seven Ages of Woman*, also billed with "the great Moral Drama of *Uncle Tom's Cabin*" in blackface. Sanford later linked Brower's "Happy Uncle Tom Dance" with Cool White's "Lecture on Woman's Rights."

Women were the primary audience for lectures on the female body by FMC graduates and were dominant at women's rights gatherings. Some women surely attended minstrel mockeries, and women were certainly recorded among ballet audiences. If these female spectators also attended lectures on women's anatomy, they had occasion to see that anatomy in vivid action on the ballet stage in costumes and movements beyond the scope of everyday modesty—a factor in ongoing controversies about the propriety of ballet, the women who performed it, and the audiences that enjoyed it.

Lola Montez: Crossing Oceans, Classes, and Performance Genres

One exceptional woman, who raised and complicated categorization of women's roles and capacities as she created and re-created her own identity, crossed the Atlantic to perform in the United States in the 1850s. She also crossed performance genres during her career, embracing ballet, parody, and lectures. The remarkable Lola Montez—who broke behavioral rules, traversed political borders, and slid among social classes and national identities—first appeared in person in Philadelphia in January 1852. Theatergoers had likely read about her already, as sensational European news coverage traveled to the United States about Montez's theatrical, political, and amorous life.[65] Philadelphia theater audiences had already seen a character bearing her name, though with little relation to her actual story; in June 1850, Conner's Theatre presented the "laughable farce" *Lola Montes* (by J. S. Coyne).[66] The play's dance numbers included a "Burlesque Pas Seul" by Mrs. Junius Brutus Booth Jr. (married name of dancer Clementine De Bar), and "La Cachucha" by Julia Turnbull. By 1852, the real Montez "appeared as the representative of herself" in *Lola Montez in Bavaria*, by New York playwright C.P.T. Ware, in which she played "the characters of *Danseuse*, the *Politician*, the *Countess*, the *Revolutionist*, and the *Fugitive*"—drawn from her life story.[67]

Who was this exceptional woman? Montez, born in Ireland of Irish parents around 1818, was named Marie Dolores Eliza Rosanna Gilbert. Her youth was complicated by her father's death (in the British military in India, where Montez spent her infancy) and by her alienation from her mother, but she was well educated in English private schools that included social-dancing appropriate to proper young ladies. A disastrous youthful marriage, her need for money, her fierce independence and anti-authoritarianism, and her striking beauty inspired the soon-to-be Lola to turn to the stage, particularly toward highlighting her body and dramatic capacities through dance, although she lacked ballet training. With her dark hair and flashing eyes, she lighted on an identity as an expatriate Spanish noblewoman. It worked well enough: in dances titled as "El Olano," "La Sevilliana," and "the popular Spanish dance, 'La Lassaleada, or the Spider Dance,'"[63] viewers in England and elsewhere read into her performances what they considered authentic Iberian fire, despite accomplished Spanish dancers having graced European stages, and non-Spanish dancers'—Elssler's and others'—skillful versions of that nation's dances.[69]

Montez finagled her way not only onto English and continental stages but also through European aristocratic courts in a swath of pistol-pointing, horse-whipping, and amorous intrigue. Along the way, she landed sensational love affairs with Franz Liszt and King Ludwig I of Bavaria, whom she claimed to have inspired toward democratic reforms. Ludwig granted her the title Countess of Landsfeld, one of the many odd mixings—here, of aristocratic status and democratic firebrand—that Montez sustained in her tumultuous life. Post-Ludwig, her taste for high living, unsavory lovers, and scandal emptied her purse, necessitating a return to the stage. Although few critics praised her dancing, she attracted enthusiastic audiences and big enough box office yields. Perhaps lured by news of Celeste's and Elssler's earnings, Montez turned to America's vast theatrical territories, preparing herself to conquer this New World by studying with Auguste and Charles Mabille (abandoned husband of American-born ballerina Augusta Maywood). These Paris Opera dancers knew the balletic character-dance repertoire, which they taught Montez, creating her signature "Spider Dance."

Montez presented these dances for her debut season in New York, but American audiences also expected to see full ballets. She hired Philadelphia dancer, choreographer, and former member of Elssler's troupe George Washington Smith, who had partnered American ballerinas Mary Ann Lee, Julia Turnbull, and Anna Walters, and danced with European stars Giovanna Ciocca and Leon Espinosa during their U.S. tours.[70] He performed and staged new and classic works across the United States and served as ballet master at New York's Bowery Theatre and Philadelphia's Arch. Smith had the remarkable ability to make ballets for Montez, a dancer of little capacity, by highlighting her beauty and histrionics, while avoiding the outright immodesty or lewdness that many in her audiences initially anticipated.

Montez's New York debut (Dec. 29, 1851) in Smith's *Betly the Tyrolean* received mixed notices: "Some three thousand 'men about town' were crammed between the walls of the theatre . . . while not more than a dozen feminines, except in the 'colored row,'" reportedly attended.[71] The columnist, familiar with high-quality ballet, admitted Montez was beautiful, but "dancing is evidently not her vocation." Her muslin bodice appeared "almost transparent" and her bonnet "saucy." Still, the column assured readers that Montez's "style of dancing is rigidly modest—her greatest angles"—her leg openings—"not exceeding 45 degrees"—perhaps reflecting limited technique rather than modesty. The audience enjoyed Montez but, to her annoyance, more loudly applauded the virtuosity of her Italian partner, Gaetano Neri.[72] The ballet featured a "Tyrolienne" solo for Montez, a *pas de deux* with Neri, a "Mountaineer Dance" by the corps, and a Hungarian dance with Montez leading the corps in drill patterns. The *Morning Herald* reported, "As a danseuse, she is decidedly inferior to Cerrito," an Italian ballet star of the period who never danced in the United States, "to Augusta, and others," but "there is a nameless grace about her person and movements which, with her history, gives her an attraction which a better artist could not command." Montez's allure was concocted of her beauty, her dynamism, her performance vehicles, and her notorious personal history. Figure 5.1 shows Philadelphia cartoonist David Claypoole Johnston's satire of her stage presence, her "take" (the

Figure 5.1. "Lola has come! Enthusiastic reception of Lola by American audience," David Claypoole Johnston (c. 1852). *(Library of Congress. Photograph. Accessed June 19, 2024, https://www.loc.gov/item/93511938)*

"manager" has pocketed her "agreement" for "half the house"), an audience member's half-ashamed leer, and a critic's (or readers') astonishment.

For Montez, Smith also created the ballets *Un Jour de Carneval a Seville* and *Diana and Her Nymphs*, along with divertissements like the "Sailor's Hornpipe" and a duet version of Montez's "Spider Dance" that he performed with her. In *Un Jour*, Montez was in her element—fiery "Spanish" dances including a "Pas de Andalusia," a "Pas de Sivigliana," and a "Pas de Matelot."[73] In *Diana*, Montez presented herself as "a partly unclothed woman to the gaze of a crowded auditory,"[74] eliciting "a gasp of astonishment at the effrontery. . . . Men actually grew pale at the boldness of the thing; young girls hung their heads"—clearly, women were among Montez's audience—and "a death-like silence fell over the house. But it passed; and, in view of the fact that these women were French ballet-dancers, they were tolerated." Montez was neither French nor a ballet dancer, but this critic lumped stage dancers into one unsavory category. Durang noted the irony of Montez playing "*Diana*, the Goddess of Chasteness,"[75] a theme on which the near-nude tunic may have been Montez's commentary.

Montez opened in Philadelphia on January 19, 1852, with Smith's ballets and the ensemble he trained. The Walnut Street Theatre's manager raised ticket prices, pointing to the extensive costs of her productions, including Lola's high fees.[76] To encourage attendance, a *Public Ledger* article wondered at what the author claimed were misrepresentations of Lola, concluding that "scandal is always busy with the reputation of women who assume so bold an attitude in public" as had Montez.[77] The author expounded that, if "the exhibition of the talent . . . is proper of itself, the public would appear to have but little to do with any other facts in relation to them. They go to see the exhibition, not to endorse the moral character of the performer." After all, this author opined, many an artist with "splendid abilities . . . does not reach the average standard of morals which gives a free passport to social intercourse," yet their talents were appreciated. Yet most critics acknowledged Montez's meager dance capabilities; it was her colorful past and person that drew interest. Lola had no difficulty with her "passport to social intercourse" in the United States, where she was admitted to elite circles (she was, after all, a countess). The author then rallied ethnological tropes to assert Montez's worth: "Lola's appearance . . . is exceedingly light, airy and delicate—light complexioned, dark hair, dark and heavy eyebrows, aquiline nose, large prominent eyes," not "the tiger she has been represented to be." Even this pro-Montez author admitted, "there is nothing remarkable in her dancing," but rather "her *manner* and *motion* and *carriage*," all "exceedingly elegant," earned her "universal admiration." One critic noted that the house was full, mostly but not only with men, who found her "pretty and full of grace in her movements," with "a lady-like carriage."[78]

Although Montez enjoyed hobnobbing with well-heeled socialites in each U.S. city, she sustained her reputation as a political liberal and woman of the people—evidence of her savvy boundary-crossing. In gratitude for her benefit performance for the Philadelphia Association of Disabled Firemen, trustee Colonel Wallace offered an onstage tribute: "M'lle Lola Montez, I address you by the name you have made renowned as an artist, in preference to the title of nobility, which is your due"—acknowledging her complicated categorization and appeal.[79] He thanked her for her "generous sympathy" for the city's firemen and presented her "a medallion" of George Washington, for, "to a lady of known liberal and republican principles and sentiments, like yourself, I feel that nothing could be more acceptable." Montez replied, "You could not have conferred upon me a greater honor," endearing her to the city's working classes, who manned the fire companies. Barnum's Museum added Montez's image to its "extensive collection of Wax Statuary."

Montez did not charm all. Durang uncharacteristically referred to her in his commentary as "Lola," while he called every other performer, of whatever theatrical rank, "Mr. X," "Miss Y," or "Mme. Z." When Montez was at the Chestnut Street Theatre (Oct. 1852), playing herself in *Lola Montez in Bavaria*, Durang found the play "in harmony with the stupendous humbuggery of the heroine. It however subserved curiosity," he sniffed, "and made money for the Countess of Rhodomontade," crowning her with what he saw as her empty boasts and claims, as well as her pecuniary motivations.[80] In short, "her dancing and pantomime were of the la-la species. It was bold artificiality."

Montez then presented herself as an actress, rather than dancer, perhaps owing to her loss in June 1852 of Smith's collaboration and inspired by the genre-crossing and earning power of dancer-actress Mme. Celeste. Montez commissioned H. J. Conway's *Charlotte Corday; or, Jacobins and Girondists*, starring herself as Corday, revolutionary heroine and assassin of Jean-Paul Marat. Again, Durang assessed Montez a failure, "lack[ing] most woefully dramatic ability and declamatory powers."[81] Rather, she employed "a kind of namby-pamby energy, like the forced plant of the hot-house. . . . Instead of being the 'Martyrdom of Charlotte Corday,' the effort should have been named the *decollation* of the Countess of Lansfeldt," he sneered, for Montez attempted to substitute her personal endowments for her dramatic (in)abilities. Dismissing her "clap-trap drama," *The Maid of Saragossa*, he added, "Lola" was a "bold nonentity," and "certainly not an operatic dancing artiste. Those who have studied the principles of that graceful art," as had Durang, had "perceived that her knowledge of theatrical dancing . . . violat[ed] all its rules and fundamental bases as prescribed by the Academy." Yet Durang was fascinated by her: after these dismissive remarks, he devoted several columns to her wild, rule-breaking life.

Many others in the United States, from Boston to Buffalo, Washington, D.C., to New Orleans, were drawn to Montez and her shows, despite their own expressed misgivings. During her tours, her temper and impudence sustained her reputation as a "virago," adding piquancy to her appearances.[82] By May 1853 she was mining new theater territories—the California gold fields—with successes theatrical and personal: she married (and divorced) a respected journalist, bought a home, became a local celebrity, then longed for a return to the stage and wider admiration. Montez departed for Australia in June 1855 but, failing to gain attention or income there, she returned to New York in late 1856. Now beyond the blush of youth, she crossed into new performance territory: lecturing.

Reports of Montez as lecturer appeared in Philadelphia before she did. Articles on her Canadian lectures about "beautiful women" called Montez *"charmante"* and inoffensive, though others excoriated audiences who paid to hear someone "who does not deserve to be called by the 'sacred name'" of "Woman."[83] By November 1857, Montez was at Philadelphia's Musical Fund Hall, her lectures advertised as "brilliant in their character and enriched with anecdotes and incidents, of which the reading and the experience of the lady furnish an abundant supply." To assure Philadelphians that nothing too shocking would be revealed in the talks, notices stated that "In Boston," a city as buttoned up as Philadelphia, "they were well attended" and "much admired."

The *Public Ledger* (Nov. 13, 1857) reviewed Montez's "Gallantry" talk, which "brings in Greek gods, medieval chivalry, Charles II and Louis XIV," as well as her "intimate acquaintance with the court gossip and social life of most of the capitals of Europe." The talk "was listened to with marked attention, and applauded throughout." The *Press* (Nov. 16) puffed Montez's lectures as "the most praise-worthy laurel that gems the chaplet of her heroism. Of the fact that she is a heroine, there can be no mistake, although," the newspaper added ambivalently, "but few would probably willingly endorse the character of all her conquests." The science of mind and body, the commentator argued, could help the reader appreciate Montez, given the "*density and compactness* indicated in her appearance which few persons possess." Further,

> her temperament is so strictly of the *mental* cast as to banish at a glance every idea of grossness. Her brain is massive for one of her size, and prodigiously developed in the region of what is phrenologically denominated the *observing, knowing,* and *knowledge-seeking* organs, giving a sharp prominence to her brow, that even overshadows her full, intellectual eye. But then, there is such a mastery of soul, that seems to beam from every muscle of her face . . . adding to this, the silvery sweetness of her liquid voice . . . and we have some clue to the capabilities of Lola Montez.

That she could cross lines of propriety and still garner praise was evident in the *Press* reporter's remarks that Montez's descriptions of beautiful women were not the "chief merit" of her talk; rather, her merit lay in "that noble sentiment, . . . that the only true and enduring beauty of woman was to be found in those accomplishments that adorn the mind and heart." Of course, it did not hurt her lectures' appeal that *she* was a beautiful woman, though no longer a girl. She shared her "recipe for the preservation of physical beauty—temperance, exercise, and cleanliness," which the Quaker City newspaper found "sensible." But the *Public Ledger* offered a column on the categories of lecturing as an American entertainment form, pointedly stating, "Last, though not least numerous, are the lectures of private individuals, for their own benefit," citing the "trashy lectures upon love and gallantry," from which Lola Montez profited.[84] Public display, moneymaking, and her personal history combined to drop her into that author's dustbin.

In Montez's "Heroines of History and Strong-Minded Women," a critic found "the most amusing" portion was when she "suggest[ed] a *Men's*-rights Convention": she spoke "with dramatic effect, such a speech as might have been delivered on such an occasion by one of the injured *harder* sex."[85] Like blackface minstrels who mocked women's rights in burlesque reform speeches, Montez—a strong, independent woman herself—could indulge in parody, as she was also parodied on the blackface stage.[86] In June 1858, Montez promised publication in Philadelphia of *The Autobiography and Lectures of Lola Montez (Countess of Landsfeld)*.[87] The book would be rich in "spicy anecdotes and piquant reminiscences," although based on "careful reflection and research," even expressing "a highly moral tone," appealing to readers of different classes, sexes, and interests.

Montez lectured again in Philadelphia from December 1859 through January 1860, this time featuring her talk on England, "John Bull at Home." The *Press* noted the high social status of attendees—many women, as well as the usual strong turnout of men—and their approval of her remarks.[88] But by August, newspapers were reporting her illness, probably a stroke, and her convalescence in New York; by late January 1861, she was dead, aged forty.[89] After a dashing review of her remarkable history, the article closed, "Her life was a bold defiance of the rules of society, but her death was an amend": now religious and "chastened," she suffered her "bodily pain without a murmur," donating her remaining money to needy women. Another obituary, recognizing and eulogizing her boundary-trespassing boldness, hailed Montez as "the last, perhaps, of that extraordinary class of talented, emancipated women," who, like "Sappho and Aspasia . . . has been a puzzle and a grief to the disbelievers in woman's capacity for bold thought and free action."[90]

Ballet beyond Lola

Such women were exemplified by Montez and by Celeste, Elssler, and Mathias, whom Sanford parodied in *Xlanties*, his "Musical, Satirical and Quizzical Burlesque," pointing to Philadelphia's busy ballet world beyond Lola. While

Elssler remained only in memory and influence, Celeste performed at the Walnut Street Theatre in November 1851 and May 1852.[91] By then, she was a mature woman and manager of London's Adelphi Theatre, proving further her capacity to succeed outside prescribed female spheres. On stage, she presented herself less in ballets and more in pantomimic-dramatic roles like *The French Spy*, *The Wept of Wish-ton-wish*, and *Masaniello, the Neapolitan Fisherman*. But she closed her May 1852 season with *La Bayadere*, the role that had motivated Augusta Maywood and Mary Ann Lee to debut on that stage fifteen years earlier. Durang enthused that, in *The Miami, the Huntress of the Mississippi* (Nov. 10, 1851), "the great artiste, . . . after an absence of seven years, . . . was received with rapturous applause," for "Celeste, 'the divine,' appeared as fresh and youthful as ten years before"; indeed, she remained "that ever-green hue of Terpsichorean grace and agility."[92] In Celeste's comedic *Taming a Tartar; or, Magic and Mazurkaphobia*, she played *Mrs. Mazurka* (wife of a basket-maker "devoted to dancing"). Other figures participated in the work's comedic dancing: *Count* and *Countess Crackovienski*, the character *Kickerwiski*, *Mazurka* the dancing basket-maker, *Ivan* dancing a *pas de matelot*, and French dancing master *Mons. Coupée*.

The Ravel family, crossing genres among acrobatics, pantomimes, and ballets, was supplemented in the 1850s by fine acrobats including Joseph Marzetti, the Lehman family, and Leon Javelli, along with French dancer Paul Brillant as ballet master and Mlles. J. Bertin, *première danseuse*. Durang praised the troupe's professionalism, virtuosity, and taste in their Walnut season (Jan.–Feb. 1850), noting the "very splendid dancing and grouping" Brillant and Bertin led in a new ballet, *Zaida, or the Queen of Flowers*.[93] The troupe produced familiar ballets, including *Jocko* and *Giselle*, in which Brillant, Durang opined, lived up to his name, an "agile and graceful dancer—a perfect artiste." The Ravels' 1852 season was equally "fresh" and "brilliant," with the fine French danseuses Mlles. Celestine and Victorine Franck, the Martinetti family, and a large corps de ballet. Brillant danced a "polka cotillion," a "mazourka waltz," and a "new saloon polka" in Jerome Ravel's original and superbly executed ballet-pantomime *The Elopement; or, A Return to the Village*.

In their 1854 season at the Walnut, the Ravels introduced the fine French-born dancer Yrca Mathias, crowned at the St. Petersburg Opera as "the 'Queen of Dancers,'" according to Durang.[94] On January 9, she made her Philadelphia debut in the "grand ballet" *Paquita* (choreography Joseph Mazilier, music Édouard Deldevez), originally presented at the Paris Opera in 1846 with Carlotta Grisi and Lucien Petipa. Philadelphia had seen its "grand pas de deux" when Paris Opera ballerina Nathalie Fitzjames and Giuseppe

Carrese of Naples' San Carlo Theatre performed at the Chestnut Street in January 1851.[95] Durang praised Mathias as "an exquisite pantomimist" and "a most splendid dancer—not so much in elegance and refinement as in spirit, agility and passionate expression." She was the particular ballet favorite of the critic for one Philadelphia arts and culture magazine, who praised her agility, grace, expression, and novel steps as representative of a new, Russian-influenced ballet technique.[96] But Philadelphia theater aficionado William Meredith found the Ravels "the same tiresome humbugs they were five or six years ago. . . . Yrca Mathias danced very well," but he failed to appreciate "the *furore* . . . she has excited. She has very nice legs and a good bust, but her beauty is not extraordinary"; he preferred Louise Ducy-Barre, French ballerina in the troupe, who danced "Donna Anna" in *Paquita*.[97] Later, Meredith moved beyond assessments of ballerina beauties to concede that the Ravels' *Jocko* was "a most entertaining performance," adding the interesting note that the ballet was followed by "gymnastic performances by all the troupe as Ethiopians." The Ravels, perhaps in blackface, is a theme I have encountered nowhere else. Were they expanding their theatrical genre-coverage to embrace this popular U.S. form? The Ravels played Philadelphia's Walnut in 1855, '56, and '57. By autumn 1859, they would be elevated to the elite Academy of Music (see later).

In November 1852, another star, Josefa ("Pepita") Soto (Aranda), graced Philadelphia's stages—the first truly Spanish dancer in the city, despite earlier Spanish-style dance performances. Soto's appearances challenged claims to Spanishness made not only by Montez but also by all prior *cachucha* dancers, even Elssler. After a hit New York run, "Signorina De Soto" appeared at the Chestnut, star of a troupe of "French and Spanish dancers"—mostly French.[98] A Sevillian, Soto had danced in Madrid, Paris, and London and studied ballet in Paris with Sylvain. Soto's 1853 performances of ballet and Spanish dances impressed Durang in her "executing some very brilliant *pas*," while her 1854 partnership with George Washington Smith showed exemplary "*éclat*."[99] Again, William Meredith found her disappointing, although he noted that the audience wildly applauded her.[100] Perhaps he mistook her more Spanish movement qualities for faults, distinct as they may have been from the more familiar French school. After tours south and west, Soto returned to Philadelphia in January 1859, leading the ballet in *Robert le Diable* at the Academy of Music.[101] A truly Spanish ballet troupe, under José Maria Llorente, performed in Philadelphia in November 1855, although they gleaned little newspaper commentary.[102] They presented *The Vintage of Xeres, The Seashore at Malaga, La Madrillenne, San Juan de Alfa Rache*, and *The Siege of Saragossa*.

Challenging another categorization—that of ballet as European—was the growing number of U.S. ballet artists claiming the imported art as their own. Among those in Philadelphia in the 1850s were veterans Julia Turnbull as well as Mary Ann Lee who, after some years away, returned to the stage, perhaps owing to a change in marital or financial status. A benefit was offered at the Chestnut Street Theatre to "Mrs. Van Hook, late Mary Ann Lee" on May 28, 1852.[103] For this honor (and income), she danced a scene from her 1837 debut, *La Bayadere*. Lee, under her own name, danced with Smith in *La Manola*, *La Sicilienne*, and other national dances in late summer and autumn at the Walnut, and again in spring 1853, presenting balletic works such as *Undine* and *Nathalie*. Many other U.S. ballet dancers appeared on Philadelphia stages, often in interludes or in supporting roles in ballets. Names appearing with some regularity include the young dancers Gertrude Dawes, Mary Ann Denham, E. V. Foulkrod, Fanny Mowbray, Clara Reed, Sam Sanford's children, the Vallee sisters, Anna Walters, Ellen Warren, Louise Wells, Henrietta Wilks, Mr. and Miss Wood, Mr. Calladine, and Samuel H. Hemple.[104]

High Class: The Academy of Music

In September 1851, the Chestnut Street Theatre, Philadelphia's "Old Drury," offered a taste of the operatic art, with Max Maretzek and company,[105] soon to be highlighted at the Academy of Music. Yet, despite its history as "the once favorite resort of the fashionable and intellectual society, . . . the resort of elegance and refinement," the Chestnut was losing its cachet.[106] Its last lessees seemed "more interested in liquor sales than drama," sneered a commentator, hinting at the class of audience the hall then attracted.[107] As it spiraled downward, managers brought in light pantomime, dancing, and blackface minstrelsy, but the theater was "in bad odor" with higher-class audiences and performers, as Durang lamented after visiting the Chestnut's green room during a blackface troupe's run: "What a scene of burnt cork, red paint, drinking liquor bottles and tumblers!"[108] In that hallowed green room, Durang mourned, the chair that once gave rest to "Jefferson, Warren and Francis" and the clock "that erst directed the labors of the best regulated theatre we ever saw; the old mirror, where the old Thespians adjusted their robes, now reflected the drama's shame—its degradation!" After its last show on May 1, 1855, the Chestnut was demolished. Other city theaters, a commentator wrote, had also become scenes of increasingly raucous audience behavior, not only among "the lower classes" but even by "people who dress like gentlemen, and therefore ought to know how to behave themselves."[109] Class distinctions and behaviors proved difficult to maintain.

Philadelphia's elites sought their own theatrical enclave: in March 1852, a board of successful merchants, some from the city's oldest families, chartered a "Prospectus' for "An Opera House, or American Academy of Music." In part an edifice to elitism, it still had to straddle class categories, with a practical eye to popular appeal both to balance the anticipated books and to meet U.S. claims to a democratic society. The Academy would not be named for the street on which it would stand (like the Chestnut, Walnut, or Arch Street Theatres), nor for its home city, but rather for the entire nation, staking its claim to *American* music and taste. Oddly, its charter then called for it to feature "Operas, English and Italian, promenade and other concerts, the pure drama" (*not* blackface minstrelsy, then touted as *the* American contribution to world culture), "pantomime" (alluding to the imported art of ballet), and "French Vaudeville."[110] The incorporators asserted that "an establishment of the kind is an acknowledged want of the community," although precise evidence to that claim was not offered; previous failures to establish such a site resulted from poor planning (p. 3). An Opera House could succeed, the Prospectus argued, if it avoided costly tickets, long periods of inactivity, an "expensive" in-house company, and demanding "stars." Rather, these merchant gentlemen would run it like "our railways, telegraphs, postage and newspapers," ruled by a "policy of numbers, low prices, and a superior character of average performances," by means of which, they claimed, "the opera can be made to pay for itself" (p. 4). Not only the city's nearly half-million residents but visitors "would resort to a place of cheap and elegant amusement" (an odd pair of descriptors), whether they were "possessed of a taste for music or not."

These visionaries might have been encouraged by shifts in the city's sociality, noted in a newspaper article of February 1854: "Everyone must have noticed the rapid increase, during the past two seasons, not only of our places of amusement and entertainment, but also of the disposition on the part of the community to patronize these establishments. Only a short time ago our principal theatres were almost deserted," except when expensive stars appeared, but now, "theatres are nightly filled," while "the Circus and the Menagerie, . . . the Ethiopian Minstrels, . . . fat women and grizzly bears, dwarfs and six legged sheep, wax statuary and living boa-constrictors" each attracted "various classes of community"—acknowledging the gradations and varied appeal of entertainment types.[111] "Old and young, male and female, grave and gay, resort to their respective favorite haunts," keeping the streets busy until the late hours. This theatrical boom reflected "the increasing disposition" of Philadelphians to step away from "business, and indulge in recreation," a marked change in a city famed for "sobriety, and a rigid adherence to the old-fashioned rules of propriety." The commentator philosophized, "Well, so long as harmless amusements only are sought, this disposition is rather a blessing than otherwise." The proposed Academy of Music would ensure that blessing.

The hall (anticipated in the charter at five thousand seats, but seating fewer than three thousand when built) would have superior ventilation, so that those unable to escape the city's summer would find the Academy a refuge from the heat, while "the lover of music will be amply cared for during the winter or operatic season" (p. 5). For the high class of audience the managers sought, they promised, "Care will also be taken so to conduct the house by the exclusion of all improper characters, and of intoxicating drinks, as to meet the approbation of those who have been driven from our theatres by past bad management." Access and egress would avoid a "crush" in the lobbies, "boxes with elegant drawing rooms" would be provided, and all seats would offer fine sight lines and acoustics (p. 7). Lest this plan suggest exclusivity unacceptable in a nation where "aristocracy was the enemy of the republic,"[112] the prospectus promised "the intended low prices of admission"—fifty cents for orchestra seats and twenty-five cents for the balcony (competitive with the better minstrel halls) "will enable persons with limited means and large families" to attend (p. 5). Yet, the prospectus promised that the "magnificent amphitheatre" would be so splendid that "no theatre of the world would afford a parallel" (p. 6). And the "stage department" would run "upon the general plan of the Académie Royale of Paris"—of course.

The Academy would draw visitors to Philadelphia, the prospectus declared, as had theatrical enterprises in New York and Paris, since "the eastern cities are naturally regarded by the citizens of the rest of our country as the seats of superior refinement and enjoyment" (p. 8). Philadelphia's easy access to "the western and southern merchants" would make its opera house a destination for such visitors and a boon to hotels, shops, and restaurants. This view of the city's cultural weight was not just self-aggrandizement, for, as Richard Bushman highlights, Philadelphia was among "the mythic cities in the United States in 1850" where "country people thought fashionable life" and "cultural authority" "reached the pinnacle."[113] While the Academy of Music was intended to "meet the tastes and means of all," the Prospectus targeted "those of independent means" who desired "a comfortable and refined place of amusement." Advancing Philadelphia's history of education and beneficence, the Prospectus writers saw the institution as "a rallying point for musical art throughout the country," calling for the founding of a music school, justifying the name "Academy of Music."

Several years passed in completing fundraising and construction of the building, still standing at Broad and Locust Streets, housing operatic and ballet offerings. Designed by Philadelphia native Napoleon LeBrun, with Gustavus Runge, the plan acknowledged La Scala, Milan.[114] U.S. President Franklin Pierce attended the groundbreaking in 1855 at what was then the westerly side of town. When opened, the opera house—"most perfect" of any in America or Europe—shone as "a credit to Philadelphia, nay, the country at large, a model in truth, from which all might derive benefit."[115] The Academy's interior gleamed with gold paint, crystal chandeliers, and red plush, as images of Europe's revered composers, Greek gods, and muses gazed upon the audience. A grand ball opened the edifice in January 1857; the second-floor ballroom hosted select social gatherings for years thereafter. The Academy's first operatic production was Maretzek's mostly Italian company in the U.S. premiere of Verdi's *Il trovatore* (Feb. 1857). In September, the city saw the Academy's imported ballet troupe, the Ronzani Ballet (Figure 5.2), created for this U.S. engagement by Domenico Ronzani, a leading mime, choreographer, and ballet stager, closely associated with La Scala, who had worked in many European capitals and with stars like Fanny Elssler and Augusta Maywood.

Figure 5.2. View from the stage of Ronzani's ballet troupe at the Academy of Music, engraving (Oct. 1860). *(Historical Society of Pennsylvania small graphics collection [V63], Ba 09 Ac12a, DAMS #693. Published with permission)*

Ronzani, choosing his lead dancers from his extensive European contacts, featured Louise Lamoureux and Filippo Baratti, with members of the Pratesi family and, as principal mimes, Cesare and Serafina Cecchetti, who brought along their seven-year-old son, Enrico.[116]

Anticipating that Ronzani's "*ballet* will burst upon us like some splendid oriental story,"[117] the once-beloved Ravels were treated by commentators as embarrassments; their "efforts were weakly esteemed by us to be rather extraordinary, but one dash of Ronzani's creatures will obliterate all recollections of Matthias [*sic*], Robert, Marzetti, and the others of the French *corps*." The reality would prove otherwise. Publicity for the Ronzani troupe was typified by a puff on Philadelphia's claim to cultural eminence: "This world renowned troupe of brilliant dancers and unrivalled pantomimists commence their *first* engagement in America, on Wednesday next, at *our* 'Academy of Music,'" opening with "the grand fantastic ballet of 'Faust,'" which Jules Perrot had premiered with Elssler and Perrot at La Scala (1848), the source for the Philadelphia production.[118] Ronzani staged the work in 1854 in Vienna for once-beloved, now-reviled (in the United States) American ballerina Augusta Maywood. Touting the company Ronzani assembled, the article promised, "the entire troupe of artistes (28 in number) will appear, aided by nearly *two hundred* auxiliaries," this category giving local dance aspirants access to the new stage. "The piece has been one month in active preparation, and . . . we predict that the ensuing engagement will be the most brilliant one on record. Philadelphia ought to feel proud that the debut of this extensive company takes place in their city." This balletic achievement would allow Philadelphia to regain its cultural preeminence.

A preview performance garnered both praise and satire: one critic enjoyed Lamoureux's "nimbleness and elasticity," which brought to mind "such brisk creatures as the gazelle, the fawn, the decapitated chicken, the midnight mosquito," while Baratti displayed "such twirling and twisting, such bewildering aerial flight, and such wrigglings of the body" that could "only be approached by an expiring frog."[119] Another preview commentary compared the appearance of Mephistopheles (played by Ronzani) to that of Egyptology satirist Bobby Blitz, mentioned earlier. Positively noted were the gorgeous scenery and the "sweet music by *two* full bands." A more high-minded commentator remarked on "the delicate, intellectual beauty of the whole story," most vivid in the final act when "the real sentiment, and passion, and pathos of the drama comes out—for a drama it is, though motion takes the part of dialogue," thus elevating *Faust* into higher theatrical echelons than balletic entertainment typically reached. As a reporter from *The Press* wrote after the debut, "It is wrong to call these—*dances*. They constitute *acting*, in many cases, so expressive are they." Another commentator concurred: "Ronzani, the author of the piece, is a genuine poet. He speaks in attitudes, in groupings, what Dante and Goethe, and Byron have done in verse. Lamoureux and her sister graces are the language which Ronzani utters, . . . gracefully charming."[120] Ballet had transcended movement; it was speech.

Faust debuted at the Academy on September 16, 1857. Press reports highlighted the audience, comprising high society in all its "beauty and fashion," along with Philadelphia's "leading *literati*."[121] Of *Faust*, a critic remarked that it was so far above "attempts at ballet heretofore made in the United States, that proper description is totally out of the question," for this work, as other critics noted, was "really a serious drama without words, and not a mere hotch-potch of dances and tricks."[122] Nonetheless, "as a spectacle . . . it was a triumphant success." Given "the multitude of dancers on the vast stage at one time . . . the precision and beauty of their evolution delighted everyone," despite flaws in some scene-changing mechanisms. Even the critic for the *New York Tribune* handed the palm to Philadelphia's Academy: "The ballet has never before been transplanted to American soil in the full vigor of its developed strength and beauty," but "it is yet a question whether it will bear kindly the deportation from its home, and will flourish in an alien soil"—a telling note on ballet's perceived foreignness.[123] The author reflected on earlier "half-blown enterprises" attempting "to introduce the Terpsichorean exotic"—again highlighting ballet as foreign. Ignoring prior decades of U.S. ballet performance, the *Tribune* congratulated Academy manager E. A. Marshall as "the first to make the attempt" at presenting true ballet.

Alas, with all its demonic spectacle and tantalizing temptation scenes, *Faust* was long—running from 8 P.M. until 11:15 P.M.—"a severe strain on the patience."[124] While "the audience started off briskly and was prodigal of its plaudits," eventually the spectators "dozed off—a large number of individuals going away home" after act three. In sum, *Faust* was judged "too extensive and leaden an affair. A *ballet* should be brief, gay and quick." Lamoureux "looked somewhat worn, and . . . did not receive a cheerful guerdon [reward] from the audience," although her dancing was "dazzling." Unfortunately, "her best work was done in the third act, which found everybody . . . inclined to somnolency." Baratti, the reviewer wrote, "was in full possession of his astonishing faculties" and "the *coryphees*, with their gyrating forms and incessantly smiling faces (poor things!), did their duty without faltering or bungling." Doubts about ballet's foreign flavor persisted: "We trust the ballet, as Mr. Marshall has brought it out, will be well sustained. We have our fears, however, that it is not in accordance with the taste of the habitues of the Academy. It is certain the houses last week, after the first night, were only moderate."[125]

The author recommended "shorter ballets" on subjects "less offensive." Whiffs of the Ravels floated through this critic's yearnings. *Faust* was, within a week, shortened.

Ronzani learned quickly for his next ballet: on September 30, 1857, *Il Birrichino di Parigi* debuted at the Academy. A review, highlighting the large and respectable audience, opined that this ballet, being "shorter, lighter, and less tedious than 'Faust,'" was "worth seeing once."[126] The *Press* reviewer agreed: "If the ballet, entitled 'Il Birrichino di Parigi,' had been produced at the Academy of Music before 'Faust,'" the company's success "would have been assured and decided from the first," for "this new and beautiful ballet" earned "oft-repeated applause." *Il Birrichino*, from the Teatro Carlo Felice (Genoa, 1848), premiered in Philadelphia with seven-year-old Enrico Cecchetti as "Ottavio," a child saved from drowning by the orphan "Giuseppe" (il Biricchino), played in travesty by Teresina Pratesi. The complicated story, set in 1820s Paris, was dismissed by one critic as "incomprehensible and absurd"—so much for ballet as speechless drama. Yet, "as a spectacle," *Il Birrichino* was "magnificent, fully equal if not beyond the glories of *Faust*."[127] The plot, with class-crossing lovers as well as cross-dressing dancers, offered much mime and dancing. It opened with a carnival scene and closed with a wedding celebration, the "Grand Ball in Masquerade" featuring a "Grand Tableau of Love and Joy." In between appeared such popular numbers as "La Zingarella," the "Polka," and the "Marseillaise Galop," with Lamoureux, Baratti, the Cecchettis, and the Pratesis.

Il Birrichino was reviewed as "the most complete, perfect, and beautiful dance we ever saw," "a decided success," "nothing at all like it, in this country, until now"—and its U.S. premiere was, proudly, in Philadelphia. Lamoureux, as Giuseppe's sister, "was as versatile as ever. In the variety of her steps, her astonishing command of all the diversities of motion, and in neatness and ease, she is beyond doubt the best dancer seen in the United States for many years."[128] One review praised her "inimitable gentle grace, her neatness of execution together with the expression she throws into every step and attitude," which "confirms us in the opinion that she is to be compared only to the very greatest dancers, Rosati, Ferraris, Marie Taglioni, Cerito [sic], Carlotta Grisi"—none of whom appeared in the United States, though news stories about them did. Baratti too earned accolades as "the best male dancer we have ever seen," while "the *coryphees* were excellent." In sum, "the Ronzani ballet troupe has inaugurated a new era in stage dancing, and created a standard which will hereafter be the only recognized measure of terpsichorean performances." Perhaps.

The Ronzani troupe left for New York and Boston, returning to the Academy in December 1857 having learned its lesson. Although the company did again present *Faust*, described as "half-dazzling, half-dull,"[129] Ronzani also presented less weighty ballets—*L'Illusione d'un Pittore* (credited to Cesare Cecchetti, likely based on Elssler's earlier version), *Alloggio Militare* (choreography Cecchetti), and Ronzani's "Fairy Ballet" *The Golden Horse* (which he had premiered in Genoa), with a "programme of incidental dances."

The perceived failure of U.S. audiences to properly appreciate such elevated ballet art, evident in responses to *Faust*, was analyzed in light of the scientific vision of the day by a writer for *Fitzgerald's City Item*: "It is very doubtful whether the Ballet will be as successful as the Opera,"[130] for "there is a prejudice against it"—its corporeality? "Our appreciations of the Ballet are very limited," as "it is valued as a plaything. . . . We have no artistic perception of its method, nor any scientific knowledge of its law," for "the realities of the Ballet must be studied to be enjoyed," not merely treated as light entertainment. But science could illuminate it: "The eye that would pierce the pleasure of the Ballet must be educated in the physiology of motion, keen to see the principles of a pirouette, to unravel the plans on which two hundred sylphs are floating." More than amusement, ballet was a matter of refined perception and of education that, evidently, U.S. audiences lacked.

The next year's season at the Academy featured little ballet, aside from dance scenes in operas like *Martha* and *William Tell*, not performed by the Ronzani troupe: despite the dismissal of the Ravels by earlier critics anticipating the sweeping success of Ronzani's company, former Ravel ballerinas Celestine Franck and Louise Ducy-Barre took the Academy stage for these roles. January 1859 saw Pepita Soto leading the ballet in operas—*La Traviata, Les Huguenots*, and *Robert le Diable*. But in June 1859, a newly formed Ronzani troupe, with La Scala ballerina Annetta Galletti and Philadelphian George Washington Smith, was back, performing familiar favorites—*La Bayadere, La Maja de Seville* (choreography Smith), *Esmeralda, The Jolly Millers*, and divertissements like "La Manola" and the "Pas de Matelot" (likely directed by Smith). The troupe disbanded soon thereafter, but in September and October 1859, Galletti and Pratesi danced light works at the Academy.

Putting to rest earlier dismissals of the Ravels as failing to meet Philadelphians' balletic preferences, that troupe—combining the families Ravel, Martinetti, and Lehman—unrolled a monthlong Academy season in October 1859. Their run promised, one reporter noted, to "draw immense houses, and greatly amuse thousands in this city, as they have done any and every year during the last twenty-five."[131] The "grand *corps de ballet*," headed by Maria Hennecart and Paul Brillant, presented new repertoire as well as several of the company's well-known ballets, including the ever-popular ballet-pantomime *Jocko, the Brazilian Ape*; the "spectacular, comic ballet" by Jerome

Ravel titled *Kim-Ka, or the Adventures of an Aeronaut*; a one-act version of *La Sylphide*; and such divertissements as Brillant's *Terpsichore, Fete of the Muses*, and the Philadelphia premiere of *The Belle of Madrid*, with Gabriel Ravel. The troupe's promise of success was realized; they opened "to a large audience, thus proving that the beautiful exhibitions of these artists are likely to be more popular than intellectual performances"—a Ronzani put-down.[132] After a week of Ravel shows, another critic enthused, "These astonishing artists continue to draw intelligent and crowded houses" and "are among the wonders of their profession. . . . They are now as popular as they were twenty years ago, and"—noting the Ravels' appeal to viewers of all classes—they "are visited by crowds of young and old, rich and poor," owing to their varied programs, superb skills, and avoidance of "vulgarity or indecency."

Ballet, then, made it into the elite echelons of the Academy of Music, but it succeeded there primarily in support of operas or intermixed with the popular wonders of the Ravels. The more "scientific," "intellectual" productions that Ronzani introduced fell flat.

The Dancing Masters Invoke Science

Ballet's failure to succeed as "intellectual" did not discourage the city's dancing masters from aligning themselves with the academic drive toward disciplinary systemization. D. L. Carpenter claimed in his 1854 *Amateur's Preceptor on Dancing Etiquette* that previous treatises on "private dancing" had failed to clearly state the "principles of the art."[133] Carpenter claimed impeccable credentials for such principle-based teaching, including study under Monsieur G. De Granville, "an artist from the Academy Royal of Paris" (p. 13). As in the sciences, the "theoretical laws" (p. 7) and the means for realizing them, Carpenter wrote, must be forthright and practiced. Fundamentals of social dancing covered deportment, gait, turn-out, the five balletic positions, steps like battements and jetés, arm placement, and bows, followed by teaching of select dances (pp. 8–10)—"cotilions, quadrilles, waltzes, or whatever description of dancing which is in request in good society," avoiding "certain scientific steps and elevated caperings" inappropriate for the "drawing-room" (p. 11). Still, learning "fancy dances," Carpenter asserted, would keep youngsters healthy and amused, but only qualified teachers like himself could judge which dances were appropriate. Titles of some dances he taught alluded to stage works—the "Bolero Waltz," "Esmeralda Waltz," "Shawl Dance," "Pasteryians" (Pas Styrien), "Cachucha," "Double Cachucha," "Minuette de la Cour," "Cracovienne," and even various *pas seuls, pas de deux, pas de trois, pas de quatres*, and *pas de Brilliante*. For those aspiring to become dancing masters, Carpenter advised, "Neither follow the precepts of simple unpractised theorists, utterly incapable of demonstrating clearly the true principles of the art, nor be guided by the imaginary schemes of innovating speculators," whose efforts to modernize dancing were "working its destruction" (p. 74). Quoting Italian master Carlo Blasis, Carpenter encouraged readers to practice dance diligently, since "even the most perfect figure, Apollo Belvedere, for example, would not 'attain excellence' without *study, industry and perseverance*" (p. 76). Nott, too, found the Apollo Belvedere the apt figure for corporeal perfection in "manly beauty."[134]

Like Carpenter, Charles Durang's manuals in the 1850s included ballroom dances referring to stage works from both operatic and blackface repertoires: "Der Freyschutz Quadrilles," "Bohemian Girl Quadrilles," and "Ethiopian Cotillions."[135] His *Fashionable Dancer's Casket* included, under "Supplemental New Dances," the "Serious Family Polka," alluding to Morris Barnett's popular comedy *The Serious Family*,[136] which typically featured the characters in a polka. When the work played the Chestnut Street Theatre (Sept. 13, 1853), this dance was a "Bloomer Polka" by "Miss Dawes" (in "reform" dress); in a later show (Oct. 17, 1853), Durang referred to it as "the original 'Serious Family Polka,' a live quadrille." Like Carpenter, he also pointed to the "laws" governing social interactions.

This overflow of theatricality, as well as systemization, into social-dance teaching paralleled changes in U.S. society, even among the Society of Friends—at least the "Progressive Friends," who took notably liberal stances among Quakers. Oliver Johnson, onetime editor of the *Pennsylvania Freeman* antislavery newspaper, assured the Progressives that true religious belief must embrace the God-given human desire for amusement. He cited the failure of anti-dance prejudices to "discriminate between the amusement itself and those abuses which do not necessarily grow out of it."[137] While dancing at balls wastes time, strength, and money, he claimed, dancing as everyday exercise is both healthful and "gladdening," a fundamental response of "our nature"—thus, scientifically justified. Johnson advised families to dance together regularly for healthy, joyful amusement.

Beyond the Quakers, dancing and theatricality as components of sociality were gaining ground, for 'American middle classes after 1850 were beginning to accept the necessity and legitimacy of social forms they had once condemned as social hypocrisy" and of the theatrical presentation of the self in society.[138] This might help explain the acceptance of Lola Montez into some U.S. social circles, the greater attendance at theaters, and dancing masters' incorporation of theatrical steps, references, and dances into ballroom practice. In a tautological justification, elite high society could be in constant flux, molding itself around the belief that, as physician and ethnologist Samuel Cartwright insisted, in the United States, "equals are on a perfect equality."[139] Gaining access to high status was itself proof of one's belonging there, an understanding stretched, by ethnologists and politicians, to justify racial rankings. Even in the North, African-descended people were, Cartwright argued, as naturally excluded "from the drawing room and parlor" as were "pots and kettles and other kinds of kitchen furniture," because—and as proof that—they were not equals. The U.S. dancing masters whose texts I cite made no such racist claims, but if any in white society sought elegant deportment to prove their fitness for high-class status, dance training with proper masters could be the key, while the minstrel stage and racial cartooning illustrated perceptions of Black people's inevitable failure to achieve bodily refinement.

Making the case for dance education as a kind of corporeal science was New York dancing master Edward Ferrero, whose Italian parents, Edoardo and Adelaide Ferrero, had been stage dancers. The family moved to New York in Edward's infancy, opened a dancing school, and raised their son in the knowledge of fine dancing, which he later taught at West Point's military academy. Edward Ferrero's *The Art of Dancing, Historically Illustrated* (1859) opened with seven erudite chapters on dance history of ancient Greece, Europe, and the Americas, also addressing Native American dance. Ferrero mixed science with poetry: "Motion is the eternal law of nature. Everything dances. The waves of the ocean dance to the music of the winds" and, "according to the philosophers, the sun and moon dance about the earth, the three upper planets about the sun as their centre."[140] Touching on health, Ferrero noted "the physical advantages of dancing," whereby "the shoulders are thrown back, the inferior limbs attain greater strength and elasticity, the muscular masses of the hips, thighs and legs are symmetrically displayed," giving the dancer greater strength and beauty (pp. 77–78). Dancing was especially valuable for women, "whose delicate constitutions require to be strengthened by frequent exercise" (p. 78). But the joy of dancing and the pleasure of refined society gave education in dance its greatest value. Ferrero also noted increased distinctions among social classes: "Formerly, it was not considered improper or derogatory for ladies and gentlemen to attend public balls, and share in their performance," but as the U.S. population grew and "the ball-room habitués degenerated into a mixed assemblage, the more refined portion of the community avoided them. Dancing, therefore, among the most cultivated and *élite*, is confined to parlors and private assembly rooms" (p. 74), avoiding low-class contamination.

The trend toward separating the "refined" class from others on social occasions appeared in Philadelphia. Academy of Music fundraiser Sidney George Fisher supported such social distinctions, offering a cautionary tale touching the esteemed Rush family: Mrs. James Rush (Phoebe Ann Ridgway Rush) "was very fond of society, but had her own notions on the subject, affecting to despise those distinctions of position and birth which produce different circles and separate the persons of a class," he noted.[141] Committed to democratic sociality, "she declared that she found agreeable people in every circle and therefore visited all and invited all to her house," making "her parties . . . very mixed," Fisher felt, and bringing together those "who would not and could not mingle," but "several instances of gross misconduct on the part of some of her guests convinced her at last that she had made a mistake and she restricted her acquaintance very much afterwards." Fisher found this change salutary and inevitable, just as he championed the Academy of Music as a statement of the city's refined tastes and cultural eminence, despite its Prospectus's awkward efforts to embrace all classes. After attending a Dancing Assembly ball that he found "crowded, dull & stupid," Fisher had remarked a few years earlier, "Our society is broken up & degenerated under the influence of democracy, which is destructive at least to all the refinements & embellishments of life."[142] Interestingly, Fisher's observations of the belles at the city's 1850s balls agreed with John Rock's mocking take on the impoverished appearance of the white race; attending a ball in 1856 at the Musical Fund Hall, Fisher recorded that he "was struck by the remarkable deficiency of female beauty" at the gathering: "Small, thin, undeveloped creatures," despite their dancing, "they do not seem fit to become mothers. The race is certainly degenerating here."

Between 1850 and 1860, at least fifty dancing masters taught in Philadelphia for long or short periods, offering classes, practicing balls, and formal soirées. Some teachers had stage-dance experience: Mme. Hazard, Mary Ann "Vanhook" (Lee), Carpenter, Durang, Jules Martin, Henry Whale, and George Zavistowski. Quite a few women were teachers: Mme. Hazard and Mary Ann Lee, along with Mrs. Beech, Mary Campbell, and Mme. Snowden; Charles Durang taught with daughter Caroline, Professor Gaszynski with his daughter; Mrs. and Mr. George T. Sheldon taught together; and Mme. Antonia taught with M. George Zavistowski. M. Mazarin stated in his 1854 notice that Miss Mazarin—his daughter?—would teach children's classes. In 1855, William Duff and wife advertised their "Academy for Dancing Exercises," stressing dance as healthy, much as Francis Naylor and daughter advertised that "exercise promotes health."[143] Masters like Carpenter touted their long-standing respectability and success. Those less familiar to

Philadelphians presented credentials: Mazarin claimed he was "of the Royal Academy of Paris and Professor of Dancing in that city for fifteen years" and Gaszynski was "late of Boston and well known in the most fashionable circles, having introduced many dances used in the Courts of Europe." The appeal to some Americans of somehow partaking in European aristocratic society is evident in such notices, as it was in the thrill of associating with Montez, Countess of Landsfeld.

Philadelphians like dentist Leonard Koecker enjoyed a wide range of entertainments: dancing lessons, balls by dancing masters and in friends' homes, operas, theater (including Montez), magic shows (Sr. Blitz, among others), juggling acts, variety, and "gayeties."[144] The city by this decade offered many amusement choices. Koecker, though not of an established Philadelphia dynasty, was a professional man, and white, allowing him aspiration toward refinement and social ascension. For the city's Black professionals—ministers, teachers, business owners, and others—dancing, if practiced socially, went unrecorded in the 1850s.[145] The academies and soirées of dancing masters listed in newspapers and city directories were closed to African Americans, whatever their income or standing in their communities. However, influential members of Philadelphia's Black society carefully chose occasions for display and pomp, as in the June 1857 parade and rites opening the "New Hall of the Colored Masons," with participation of twenty "African" Freemason lodges and eight "Grand Lodges" from other cities and states.[146] African American elite ladies shared less public social rituals, such as parlor visits with exchanges of friendship albums that recorded their poetic, artistic, and botanical interests.[147] Not all Black Philadelphians embraced these values: class divisions continued between African Americans of established families and recent arrivals from enslavement or rural areas who were struggling to find a place in the urban landscape. These took their pleasure as they could: showy dress, boisterous street and tavern entertainments, and expressive public deportment characterized working-class Black Philadelphians' amusements, as white residents experienced similar divisions in sociality and behavior.[148]

Dance houses remained popular in this decade, as free and easies, concert saloons, "varieties," and "gaieties" offered light entertainment.[149] Surely many unrecorded sites of drinking, gaming, dancing, and socializing hosted Black, working-class, and interracial sociality, as indicated by a journalistic investigation into the groggeries, lodgings, and dance houses of Philadelphia's lowest, most vice-infected neighborhood—Fifth to Eighth Streets east-west, and Lombard to Fitzwater north-south.[150] Poverty, interracial living, criminality, drinking, partying, and dancing might mix together in such sites, as police logs reported concerning "disorderly dancing parties."[151] While details of the danced social life in these settings are little recorded, one source mentions the ubiquitous "old black fiddler behind the stove" ready, for a few pennies, to play any tune requested.[152]

Efforts to solidify class and social categories, foreshadowing entertainment divides later in the nineteenth century,[153] appeared in Philadelphia edifices like Sanford's Opera House, for the blackface-loving locals, and the Academy of Music, for devotees of European opera and ballet. Yet both halls attempted to claim allegiance from classes not typically drawn to their featured offerings: Sanford lured proper bourgeois families, while the Academy boasted its appeal for sweating, cash-poor workers. Women, pushing past the strictures of their ascribed sphere, appeared on city stages in the 1850s as dancers, lecturers, and physicians. Was lecturing education or entertainment? Was ballet a cultivated art or a barely disguised girly show? Did blackface variety burlesque African Americans or mock white elites? Were these entertainment forms "American," or were both derived from imported, appropriated sources? Was science true and immutable or a subject for performance, satire, and defiance? Could categorical distinctions hold—on the stage, in the streets, across the nation?

Bodies—the means of dance expression and objects of dance viewing—carried then, as now, all the weight of corporeal meanings understood in that time and place. Determinations of class, race, and gender—and the barriers created to protect them—were studied by Philadelphia-connected scientists, projected in buildings gracing city streets, and embodied in dancing on stages and in ballrooms. At the same time, these very hierarchies and categories collided, collapsing into one another amid the realities of human behavior and aspiration, of curiosity and experience, and of bodies in motion, shaping an ever-emerging blend of cultural material to meet the tastes of a public in social and political flux.

6

Conclusions

Dance as Discourse in Antebellum Philadelphia

Mythic City, Embodied Citizens

Philadelphia, one of the early U.S. "mythic cities," was noted for its orderly street plan, industrious citizenry, and burgeoning commerce as well as its vibrant culture, rich in theatrical and social dancing. That dancing—entertainment, exercise, protest, religious expression, parody, display, discovery, and more—reflected political, social, and cultural contests in a nation under turbulent formation. The bodies that comprised the U.S. population and enacted its culture(s) came to represent markers of inclusion or exclusion, of power or vulnerability, of humanity or less. Philadelphia experienced, and led, such contests, grappling with perceived binaries: American/European, white/Black, men/women, class distinctions or egalitarianism, refinement or populism. Channels of contest embraced visual and textual depictions, political and scientific systems, and social and theatrical dancing.

Two dance genres that exemplified, expressed, and explored human differences—ballet and blackface "delineation"—emerged as distinct forms through the 1820s and '30s; each expanded in visibility and complexity in the 1840s and '50s; and each responded to political and social concerns engulfing the nation. At theaters—from taverns with rude stages to well-appointed halls with the latest machinery and stars—dancers appeared in song-and-dance acts, interlude entertainment, plays or operas, ballets, and pantomimes. Ballrooms, bars, and homes in Philadelphia hosted public and private social dancing, keeping dancing masters and musicians busy, as were the presses that published dancing manuals, dance music, advertisements, and commentary. Some theatrical dancers hailed from Europe—England and France initially, then Austria, Italy, Hungary, Russia, and Spain—while others were born or raised on U.S. soil. Some wore elegant costumes and danced versions of the latest ballets, and some, daubed in black paint, mocked those ballets and also danced jigs and breakdowns dressed in clownish rags or dandified suits.

Bodily concerns expressed in dance were shaped by national issues, public culture, and science, particularly concerns about slavery and citizenship rights. The body itself was seen as revealing the status of human beings, the corporeal as manifesting an individual's (and group's) intelligence, capacities, emotional makeup, and moral fiber. Defining and ranking humanity became increasingly divisive with national expansion, necessitating decisions about slave or free status of new territories and states. This polarizing issue simmered and boiled amid other developments, including Native American removal, immigration, and demands for women's rights—issues that pointed attention to perceptually different kinds of bodies. Bodies became everyone's business: learning to "read" them, to distinguish ascribed bodily capacities, served to order and navigate U.S. society and culture, establishing allegiances and erasures.[1]

Science provided the metrics and markers of human status, applied to understanding and forwarding the established social and political order. Famed Philadelphia researchers and institutions, advancing influential theories of natural order, biological systemization, and categorical rankings, were sources of pride for many, proving Americans could hold intellectual weight even among learned Europeans. Theories understood as scientific guided the nation's social, political, economic, and artistic unfolding. Danced stage representations attracting Philadelphians and other Americans at this time depicted just those persons demeaned in scientific rankings and excluded from the political stage—Black people and women. In mainstage settings and beyond, the former were "delineated" by white men in what became blackface minstrelsy, the latter by white women in the evolving art of ballet. As lectures, museums, publications, and graphic images ensured public diffusion of the latest intellectual theories, so too did stage depictions. Yet these same performances could also challenge prevailing stereotypes.

Ballet and Bodily Virtuosity

Some ballet scenarios supported tropes of women as physically fragile or socially subservient to men, while they featured real women dancing virtuosic, athletic movement and exposing their bodies in costumes regarded by many as overly revealing the female anatomy. Several prominent dancing women—Mme. Celeste, Augusta Maywood, and Fanny Elssler—took control of their careers and earned big money, manifesting creativity and enterprise far beyond the sphere of proper women's behavior. While women pursuing public careers fell askance of norms in this age, dancers, overtly employing corporeal display, were particularly linked with public, disorderly women. Yet many dancers—from Elssler the star to Emma Ince the American aspirant—were praised for their "modest" public behavior. Their performances came to shock less with the prevalence of bodily displays in museum exhibits, lectures, and theatrical *tableaux vivants* in the antebellum period: Americans were learning to see human bodies anew. Philadelphia gentleman Sidney George Fisher remarked on a *tableau vivant* he observed abroad, where "educated people . . . do not hesitate to look at a statue of a naked man or woman in company with the other sex. Why should they not look at the living figure, why not contemplate the beauty of the actual form," if themes and characters depicted "are chaste, noble & elevated," since "the living figure" would hold even "greater interest than the marble copy."[2] Yet more interesting were living figures in motion—virtuosic motion, on stage. This, the ballet provided.

In the early antebellum period, English dancers like the Parkers and the Hathwells dominated U.S. stages in works like *Little Red Riding Hood, Love Among the Roses*, and *Cherry and Fair Star*, with dancers drawing on British dance forms (hornpipe and clog), pantomime, and harlequinades. As English stages hosted French dancers, British performers also understood French ballet, but they lacked the intensive academic training available in Paris (or other European opera cities) and did not participate in the choreographic projects of French and Italian ballet masters. Technical superiority, distinct choreographic vision, and new works based on romantic themes distinguished what was widely understood in the United States to be the French ballet school, soon also embracing Italian dancers and works. As Durang remarked, "A well-trained dancing eye can discern whether a dancer has been educated in the Parisian Academy the instant he assumes an attitude."[3] "Scientific" training—a systemized, efficient curriculum—molded dancers into technique powerhouses who met the demands of roles from "sylphides" to "Spaniards" to "squaws," as scenarios listed them. Such balletic virtuosity served choreographic inspiration. One U.S. reviewer grasped this point, complimenting Ronzani not only for the elegance of his leading dancers but also for "the completeness of the troupe," which far surpassed stagings by prior ballet stars "ill supported by a corps de ballet, made up of such materials as were hastily gathered in the localities where the stars made their appearance."[4] Drawing on his European training and connections, Ronzani assembled "some fifty female dancers" perceived as "admirably trained." This U.S. critic understood the quality of the dance work as represented in the training of the full *corps de ballet*.

The French dancers with the longest stage lives in the United States were Mme. Celeste and the Ravel troupe. Paris Opera–trained Celeste, an audience favorite in ballets and melodramatic pantomimes, first appeared in Philadelphia in 1828 and made her last appearance in 1852. Celeste was a solo star, performing with stock companies as she toured, while the Ravels were a family-based company of several generations. They trained youngsters from infancy, absorbing other performers who contributed to the troupe's range and brilliance in impeccably rehearsed acrobatics, pantomime, *commedia*-style works, spectacle, and charming, balletic dancing as performed in Paris's boulevard theaters. A savvy Philadelphia theater manager observed, "The admirable discipline, system, and exactness of their corps"—descriptors that brought them into the fold of the scientific—"astonished and delighted quite as much as their rare capabilities."[5]

The Ravels' evening-length programs were weighted toward the light and entertaining. But, alert to the growing U.S. taste for Paris Opera–style ballets, the company employed well-trained professionals to stage and perform works of major choreographers—Charles Didelot, Pierre Gardel, Joseph Mazilier, Jules Perrot, Jean-Antoine Petipa, and Filippo Taglioni.[6] They brought to U.S. stages Paris Opera–trained ballerinas, such as Hermine Blangy and Celestine Franck, and standard balletic repertoire including *Jocko, La Sylphide, Giselle, Le diable a Quatre*, and *Esmeralda*. The Ravels also created their own libretti and hired choreographers like Paul Brillant for new works. Durang, like other Philadelphia commentators, praised the company, noting that its performers and repertoire 'never have been equaled in this country for novelty and general excellence. Their popularity has for thirty years been unbounded."[7] Artists like Celeste and the Ravels set a high bar, familiarizing Philadelphia viewers with ballet excellence.

The balletic world increasingly featured women in this period; defying the scientific ranking of women as below men in intellectual and physical potential, American women, like their European ballet sisters, took on the challenges of stage dancing. Lacking academies like those of Paris or Milan, aspiring Americans studied whenever possible with European-trained dancers performing and teaching in the United States, including Philadelphia's remarkable P. H. Hazard. Publications by European ballet masters were familiar to U.S. dancing masters. In the United States, as elsewhere, women came to dominate ballet performance, particularly in use of pointe technique.

Romantic themes grappling with social anxieties and longings made effective use of the ambivalent and dramatic potential of the female body as pure but enticing, subservient but powerful, restricted but willful. As women seeking entry into the medical profession noted that their ascribed capacities for sympathy and caring made them suitable as physicians, so could women dancing on theatrical stages highlight their supposed innate grace and bodily lightness. The revealing/obscuring use of white tulle, the qualities of gas lighting, and the thematic interplays of otherworldliness (the *ballet blanc*) and exoticism (national dances) in ballet narratives accentuated not only women's lightness but also their allure and capacity to express visions both enticing and uplifting.

Scientific evaluations of women's physical and intellectual limitations suggested that those who—by choice, force, or necessity—lived outside these strictures could not be considered true women; those enslaved, laboring, appearing on public stages, or seeking educational and professional access were beyond the sphere of true womanhood. Yet stage dancers, showing women's bodies as strong and expressive, could also be understood as models in motion of female capacity. This may have drawn some women to ballet audiences, although few had access to publishing their views.[8] Dancers' exposed flesh also drew some eyes with gazes other than the scientific. Alluring foreign-born ballerinas might be dismissed as products of lax European morality—particularly the supposedly debauched, overly refined French[9]—but when U.S. dancers began achieving balletic success, the threat of moral contamination from within arose: either these dancers, as true Americans, would bring newly chaste standards to the art, or they would be dragged into ballet's moral swamp.[10] The case of Augusta Maywood proved the latter outcome to many, while "modest" U.S. dancers like Mary Ann Lee modeled ballet as not only morally harmless, but *American*.

How did these dancers move? No one moment marks the beginning of what has been called the Romantic ballet, but knowing viewers recognized that something new, closely tied to French theaters and training, was afoot.[11] Durang, for example, remembered the introduction of "an entire corps de ballet" from Paris at the Chestnut (Feb. 1827), including Achille, Barbiere, Hutin, and Celeste. Initially, the audience received the performance coolly, but they were soon won over by the group's graceful dancing, brilliant footwork, and enchanting "classic attitudes." Their technique included dancing on pointes, elevated jumping moves, limb extensions, multiple turns, and stage "magic" of flying performers aerially, all built on centuries-old foundations of bodily positions and control that held the torso pliantly stable and allowed the limbs range and intricacy in steps and beats.[12] The ballet shoe of the time did not permit long-sustained pointe-balances, and the height of leg extensions might not have far exceeded 90 degrees, yet this pointework and expansiveness of movement were new and astonishing.

As European dancers staged works in the United States, Philadelphians saw ballets, in some versions, soon after they appeared in Europe, including works central to dance romanticism: *La Bayadere* (1830 Paris) was danced in December 1834 and throughout the antebellum period in Philadelphia; *La Sylphide* (1832 Paris) appeared in late 1837 and remained in the U.S. ballet repertoire; *Robert le Diable* (1831 Paris) was at the Chestnut in February 1838; *Giselle* (1841 Paris) appeared in April 1846; *The Devil's Violin* (1849 Paris, choreography Arthur Saint-Léon), April 1850. American dancers learned these works: Mary Ann Lee was not only the first American (with Augusta Maywood) to dance a lead in *La Bayadere* (Dec. 1837) but also the first U.S. ballerina to dance *Giselle* (Jan. 1846), with fellow Philadelphian George Washington Smith as Albrecht. To this performance, Lee brought the polish of studies in Paris, where she learned major romantic ballets (*La Fille du Danube*, choreography Filippo Taglioni; *La Jolie Fille de Gand*, choreography Ferdinand Albert) that she presented in the United States. The "national" dances essential to such ballet works were much interpreted by Americans: Lee danced the *cachucha* as early as May 1839, and the Vallee sisters by December of that year; Lee took on the *pas styrien* in 1840; and Ince danced the *cracovienne* in 1841, probably having observed Elssler or studied with Sylvain.[13] Techniques and tastes revealed in balletic works were understood by U.S. commentators as imports, as European products that "spoke French,"[14] but they served some theater lovers and many professionals as models for U.S. aspiration, interpretation, and response.

Philadelphia contributed significantly to the lists of ballet performers, stagings, teachers, choreographers, and chroniclers. P. H. Hazard, an apparently superb teacher, trained young Philadelphians in the demanding art, staged works, and also danced in the Chestnut Street season of 1838 to 1839. Mary Ann Lee, Augusta Maywood, and Emma Ince are Hazard's best-known pupils, but many others—recorded in playbills by such sobriquets as La Petite Celeste (1839), La Petite Gertrude (1844), and La Petite Taglioni (1844)— might have been his students. George Washington Smith was well enough trained to perform with Elssler and Ronzani and became a highly visible dancer, stager, and choreographer from the 1840s onward. These dancers typically started on stage in small parts, observing the polished European performers from the wings, alert to opportunities to dance in the spotlight.

Blackface Bodies

Also awaiting their turn for the spotlight were U.S. dancers (and musicians, actors, and comedians) who sought to express what they experienced and could embody from their own world of work, social encounter, and national tensions. Blackface acts in the early nineteenth-century U.S. were promulgated by working-class white men, typically of little status initially in theatrical ranks, among whose intentions were to draw audiences to burlesques of the low and the high, and to earn their livings as showmen.[15] The fact that audiences—primarily (but not entirely) white, working-class men—found these shows to be their entertainment of choice speaks to the racial, class, political, and economic pressures that viewers saw displayed by these corked-up, irreverent, often downright insulting actors, including Philadelphians Frank Brower, William Kelly, and Anthony Winnemore. The city was a creative home for T. D. Rice's development of new works in the 1830s and by the 1850s had its own dedicated minstrel hall, under Sam Sanford. As the national union frayed, the rise in performance of jolly plantation scenes, rebutting Stowe's *Uncle Tom's Cabin*, expressed pro-Southern allegiances. Such choices, highlighting the city's fractured politics, surely infuriated Philadelphia's vigorous abolitionists, Black and white.

Blackface Ballet and Exoticism

Those fractured views informed U.S. actors touring the nation's minor circuits,[16] sniffing the political and social winds as the nation struggled with what it meant to be "American." These actors found funny, and worth satirizing, the snooty acts of European opera and its associated movement form, ballet. They landed on just the disguise to clothe their mockery: burnt cork, distorted dialect, and their versions of songs and dances they picked up watching African Americans and others at docks, railroad stations, and towns these actors toured. Such was the case with T. D. Rice who, with works like "Jump Jim Crow," *The Virginia Mummy*, and *Bone Squash Diavolo*, established a stage type that subsequent minstrels imitated in skits and operatic spoofs: Winnemore composed "Stop Dat Knocking" (1843), a parodic Italian operatic scene for the Ethiopian Serenaders and performed by other troupes, while Campbell's Minstrels published their versions of the "operatic choruses" from *Ernani* (Verdi, 1844).[17] Playbills (not from Philadelphia) list the Christy's Minstrels spoof of pantomime-ballet *Jocko*, titled *Weffo, the Mischievous Monkey* (or variations), in which George Christy's Weffo, one commentator wrote, "rivals that of Marzetti," a renowned Jocko interpreter with the

Ravels.[18] The polka, staged by many ballet dancers when it surged as a popular social dance, graced the Ethiopian Serenaders' satire, *The Virginian Girl*, of Baife's *The Bohemian Girl*; it featured a "Burlesque Polka in imitation of Monsieur Martin' (who partnered Elssler in the United States) and American ballerina "Miss Turnbull."[19] Sanford also spoofed *The Bohemian Girl* and other operatic and ballet works, allowing him to claim success in "elevating and refining the growing taste for Ethiopian Burlesque" to "a standard fashionable amusement."[20] How closely blackface performers imitated ballet technique surely varied, but they intended that audiences "read" their spoofs as ballet, according to their advertising images. One minstrel performer, the fine singer and dancer Francis Leon (Patrick Francis Glass, Figure 6.1), clearly took his ballet act seriously—in blackface and travesty—throughout his career of the 1850s and '60s with Leon's Ethiopian Opera Troupe, among others.[21] In the early 1860s, he billed himself as "the Ethiopian Cubas," in admiration of the Spanish star ballerina Isabel Cubas, then in the United States.

Satires of specific performers also fed minstrel humor, as in the "ballet" dancers presented by Palmo's Ethiopian Opera Company in 1845: Mme. Heels-sir (Elssler), Mme. Carotty-Greasy (Carlotta Grisi), Mme. Say-Least (Celeste), M. Tallow-knee (Taglioni), M. Mutton (Martin), and M. Silly-vain (Sylvain).[22] The Virginia Serenaders offered *Shin-de-Heel-La—La Cenerentola/Cinderella* at the Chestnut Street Theatre; its "Fairy Land" section featured "Signora Nicolai" as "the Very Green Fairy Queen," and a group of "Sprites" played by "Colored Ladies of high standing in every suburban direction of this large city"—alluding to racially mixed neighborhoods like Moyamensing and Northern Liberties. The "Sprites" were, surely, blackface travesty roles, given the personnel listed in the bill, which promised music by "the favorite and famous Rossini," in "a world of African Songs, Duets, and Concerted Music."

The burnt-cork disguise cut in every direction: mocking both those who had no power to prevent the mockery and the classy Europhiles who saw themselves burlesqued in these acts by those they considered the lowest stratum in the nation—rather, by those appropriating that status for their stage parodies, "delineating" and thereby erasing Black presence on those stages.[23] Given that the ballet dancers imitated or spoofed were mostly Caucasian females, the travesty ballerina acts by blackface white men added layers of then-perceptible humor, insult, and suggestion to such "delineations." Omnivorously collecting cultural elements from different directions, classes, and genres, U.S.-born minstrels concocted a stew of offense, humor, and physical-musical virtuosity that many recognized as a new national entertainment form;[24] minstrelsy would help birth the American musical theater, becoming a source of both pride and shame for the nation.

Figure 6.1. Master Leon, the "Leon Schottisch," Sarony, Major & Knapp Lith. (1861). *(Jerome Robbins Dance Division, New York Public Library Digital Collections, Public Domain. Accessed June 19, 2024. https://digitalcollections.nypl.org/items/54f15690-b199-0133-8c99-00505686a51c)*

Like ballet acts featuring "national" dances, minstrelsy programs rolled out depictions of others beyond African Americans—"Tyrolese choruses," "Swiss bell ringers," Chinese characterizations, and Arab-tinged imitations,[25] along with national dances of the ballet stage. The *cachucha*, for example, was sometimes associated with the blackface wench (and song) "Lucy Long" and *cachucha*-like dancers graced many minstrel sheet-music covers. Mr. LaConta of the Virginia Serenaders, among others, made a specialty of the dance, in blackface and appropriate costume with castanets (bones), flounces, fitted bodice, and hair bun.[26]

Like their burnt-cork competitors, performers in operas and ballets drew on sources far and wide, displaying racialized, stereotypical visions of different "types" of people. These included dances from Spain (the *cachucha, bolero*, and *jaleo*, among others),[27] the Italian *tarantella*, dances from eastern Europe (*cracovienne, polka*, and *pas styrien*) and the Middle East (Arabic, Greek, and Turkish dances), and Far Eastern themes labeled as Indian or Chinese, the latter more common in the 1850s as Chinese immigration to the United States grew. These dance types sprang from ethnic groups that ethnologists like Nott considered tainted by racial "adulteration" or as representing his view of primitive versions of humanity.[28] "Black" and "Indian" (Native American) characters occasionally appeared in balletic characterizations also, although the former delineation was far more the business of minstrelsy, and the latter was represented at times by Native Americans performing their own dances on U.S. stages.

One advertisement for such a demonstration reflects the tragically demeaning view of Native Americans broadcast by ethnological investigations of the period: "Six Indian Chiefs," "Sacs, Foxes, and Iowas," men and women, "will go through with a War Dance, &c., this afternoon and evening, at the Masonic Hall. They are noble looking fellows, and fully represent, we have no doubt, the fast waning race."[29] The group also promised a Hunt Dance, Grand Pawnee Dance, White Bear Dance, Feast Dance, "Squaw" Dance, and Scalp Dance, to "their own Music, and they are all clad in their own Native Costume, of the most costly kind." An educational matinee was offered for "parents and children." Did such "Native" shows inspire blackface performers, as in Sanford and Horn's burlesque "Indian War Dance" at the "Museum Building" in February 1848, and the Virginia Serenaders with Frank Brower in a "Celebrated Burlesque Indian War Dance" in their March 1849 show?[30] Or were they inspired by the likes of American ballet dancer Henrietta Vallee taking on Celeste's hit, *Wept of Wish Ton Wish, or the Indian Girl*, in 1847 and 1848? Surely the "costly" costumes advertised in the Native American show, and the drama of the War Dance—no longer a source of fear to East Coast Euro-Americans after years of Indian Removal, but rather a safe way to package and display "Indianness"—would have appealed, if differently, to both ballet and blackface interpreters.

While "Indians" failed white ethnologists' standards of civilization, Africans fell even lower. Citing French paleontologist Georges Cuvier, Samuel George Morton affirmed that "neither the Gallas (who border on Abyssinia), nor the Bosjesmans, nor any race of Negroes, produced the celebrated people who gave birth to the civilisation of ancient Egypt," from whom "the whole world has inherited the principles of its laws [and] sciences"; these were established by ancient Egyptians of "the same race with ourselves"—Caucasian.[31] "The Negroes" throughout Africa, Morton wrote, had other capacities, being "proverbially fond of their amusements, in which they engage with great exuberance of spirit; and a day of toil is with them no bar to a night of revelry."[32] Thus, as Nott pointed out in *Types of Mankind*, enslaved Black people in ancient Egypt, enjoying their "Nilotic sabbaths," also "jump[ed] Jim Crow," entertaining not only themselves, but the supposedly Caucasian spectators observing them in antiquity, as did American plantation owners and audiences.

Blackface and Black Cultural Products

Was there any relationship between blackface performance material and Black cultural products? Did dance participate in "a yoking across perceived differences" in blackface minstrelsy and/or in "a closing out or a separation"[33] that put white "delineators" on stages and left Black people to low-class dance halls and street acts? Did early blackface minstrelsy, touted as an authentic U.S. cultural invention, steal from African Americans the claim to forming "America's first choreography," insinuating the need for white men to interpret this deeply rooted cultural production?

Some writers find evidence of African-sourced retentions in blackface acts, based on minstrels' close observations of Black people. Such claims arise from the troupes themselves advertising what they claimed as their acts' authenticity: the Virginia Minstrels promised to "introduce not only a chaste and pleasing school of Negroism, but also a true copy of Ethiopian life,"[34] thus educating and entertaining viewers. Theater historian T. Allston Brown pointed to blackface banjo player Billy Whitlock's gaining an "accurate knowledge of the peculiarities of the plantation and cornfield negroes" through visiting, whenever he toured the South, "some negro hut" to observe singing and dancing, "taking with him a jug of whiskey, to make them all the merrier."[35] Eric Lott cites minstrel performers seeking out Black workers in cities and frontier towns—"a white man and a black man becoming," according to minstrel Ben Cotton, "'brothers for the time being.'" Did that Black man feel such fraternity? His opinion is undocumented. Minstrel performer Frank Dumont, reviewing the 1840s to '60s, suggests a sympathetic reading: "The Negro slave of the Southern States, toiling in the fields of cotton, cane or corn, created an interest and sympathy. His songs and peculiar dances appealed to all classes and the white man began to imitate him in his mannerisms," creating an art that was "purely American," being "of our own soil and its institutions"[36]—slavery, a national institution. This American "purity" Dumont contrasted with pretentious imports—French or Italian opera—"patronized, but really not understood," he demeaningly asserted, "by the richer classes." He too noted blackface actors gathering material from plantations and "river fronts or levees," fertile sites for cultural exchange, where Black workers were employed.[37]

Far from underscoring blackface acts as representing African American culture, other scholars point to these stages' odious distortions, with depictions "unlike any concept of the plantation black or even the Sambo stereotype" of earlier Euro-American stagings [38] Brenda Dixon Gottschild condemns minstrelsy as "a white conceit having little to do with African American anything and, on the other hand, a genre that expropriated and imitated bona fide Africanist expressive forms," including movements "aped," burlesqued, and utterly "misinterpreted" by minstrel performers.[39] Such blackface buffoons were blind to the "acts of defiance conducted under the cover of nonsense, indirection, and seeming acquiescence" that the enslaved practiced at great peril—acts legible to those engaged in "subterfuge" and "abrogation" of established power hierarchies through music, song, dance, and praise.[40] As noted earlier, Black leaders like Samuel Cornish abhorred blackface minstrelsy on page and stage, admonishing readers to shun such demeaning depictions. Yet the need to issue such warnings substantiates the attendance of African Americans at these performances, raising the question of what drew them. I have found no surviving remarks on this subject by Black audience members, but these viewers apparently read the show's messages differently than did minstrelsy's denouncers, perhaps appreciating the display on professional stages of elements they recognized from their own songs and dances or enjoying minstrelsy's mockery of white elites.[41]

Other scholars argue that questions of "authenticity"—a standard that, Lhamon points out, "is not establishable anyway"—are irrelevant to understanding the minstrel genre, which was not about any pretended or "faux anthropology" of supposedly realistic representation.[42] Rather, its concerns were entertaining a paying public and mocking social and political elites as well as African Americans in the clownish, discomfiting, and insulting disguise of blackface.

In the subsequent analysis, I ask what, if any, relationship *in movement* can be traced, through antebellum blackface minstrelsy, to African American sources and to other sources shaping minstrel dancing.

Minstrelsy's Movement: Sources and Evolution

By the time of blackface minstrelsy's emergence, African-descended peoples had been living in North America for centuries, often in mixed groupings of different African nations, European-descended people, and Native Americans. After U.S. congressional prohibition of the transatlantic slave trade (effective 1808), illegal importation from Africa and, primarily, natural increase among the enslaved nearly tripled the number of persons in bondage in the South up to the start of the Civil War, when Pennsylvanians (and other Northerners) no longer held enslaved persons.[43] As the nineteenth century unfolded, most Black Americans—Northern or Southern, free or enslaved—were U.S.-born, distancing them from direct African sources. African American clergyman Hosea Easton decried this history of alienation: "The injury sustained by the colored people, is both national and personal," for "they are lineally stolen from their native country, and detained for centuries, in a strange land" where "their blood, habits, minds, and bodies, have undergone such a change, as to cause them to lose all legal or natural relations to their mother country."[44] Yet they did not lose all cultural connections, although these were transformed by the pressures of new environments. Culturally and spiritually, African forms and forces endured among African-descended persons held in slavery and by those facing the oppressive conditions threatening free Black people. Although Africans kidnapped to the United States were from different tribes and nations, most were from western or central Africa, so fundamental similarities among enslaved peoples' cultures brought them closer to one another than to European mores and means of expression.[45] Dancing, thus, became a kind of cultural river carrying memory, meaning, and identity among African-descended people in the United States even as these forms were influenced by contact with non-Black populations.

By the antebellum period, African American movement practices were distinct from, yet strongly shaped by, African dance. For example, the forward-angled torso typical of African dance was maintained in much African American dancing, but sometimes alternated with an upright stance, perhaps influenced by Irish- and British-jig verticality (or other European dancing) and/or responding to the flexibly vertical spine necessary for bearing loads on the head, which the enslaved experienced. The much-noted bent-knee posture of enslaved Black dancers brought them lower to the ground, enabling asymmetry, initiation of action at the hips, and isolation of body parts in motion—elements of African movement.[46] Spatial use retained such Africanisms as ring formations, encircling a soloist, and dancers responding to one another's expressive movement, typically without touching. Dancing often included African elements like facial expressions and improvisatory action drawn from a wide movement repertoire—shuffles, turns, leaps, and body-patting, closely attuned to musical rhythms. Adoptions from Euro-American dances—elevation onto the balls of the feet, set dance types, and some partner contact—contributed non-African material to an ever-evolving repertoire.

Other marked continuities with African dance among the American Black population included use of polyrhythms, polycentrism, speedy execution, and rhythmic drive. Dance virtuosity, widely appreciated in Africa, was sometimes expressed through competitions in speed, aerial movements, and endurance—factors noted by observers of African American dancing. Further enduring African elements among American Black dancers included movements related to work actions or inspired by the natural world (birds, rabbits, foxes), humor and satire, contrasting movement and rhythmic textures, an understanding of movement as expressing the sacred, and the pervasiveness of dance in cultural and individual expression. Black rhythms, musicians, and instruments—the banjo, African versions of the violin, and percussion using drums, tambourines, gourds, bones, quills, handclaps, and more—penetrated U.S. cultural practices.[47]

Philadelphia participated in these cultural transformations: in the mid-eighteenth century, when the city had a sizable enslaved population, a chronicler recalled gatherings in Washington Square: "It was the custom for the slave blacks at the time of fairs and other great holydays, to go there to the number of one thousand, of both sexes, . . . dancing after the manner of their several nations in Africa, and speaking and singing in their native dialects." They undertook traditional burial and memorial practices in the square, then a "potter's field" for the deceased poor.[48] Such "jubilees" in Philadelphia can be likened to dances held in New Orleans' Place Congo, to "John Canoe" (Jonkonnu) festivals in the Carolinas, and to Pinkster celebrations in New York.[49] In the early nineteenth century, Philadelphia attracted fugitives from Southern slavery, who contributed new cultural material to existing practices. Increasingly distant from fresh African sources, Philadelphia's African-descended population at this time engaged in movement practices distinct from those of any one nation in Africa, yet in many cases bearing cultural elements that physically archived African sources.[50] These internal identifiers of community appeared within Black work environments such as fields, docks, and markets, and in social settings like taverns, ballrooms, homes, and churches.

The drawing "Dancing for Eels, Catharine Market" (1820, New York) exemplifies the role of markets and wharves in commercial and cultural exchanges among people Black and white, enslaved and free. In such settings, workers, loafers, shopkeepers, sailors, and others mingled, showing and enjoying dance and music for pennies and prestige. At Philadelphia's busy wharves and markets, this same mixture of persons shared and observed the work songs and physicality marking their labor.[51] Other examples of overlap in Black-white practices in antebellum Philadelphia include the elite African ball, discussed in Chapter 2, and reports in city police logs of popular dance houses in Black and interracial neighborhoods where vibrant blendings of Black and white dance elements appeared. While religious congregations like St. Thomas's and Mother Bethel drew from the more circumspect among Philadelphia's African American community, there were apparently Black churchgoers whose practices sustained the physical exuberance of African worship in song, dance, rhythms, and embodied possession.[52]

Black-influenced movement also passed into Pennsylvania through the state's border with the upper Chesapeake region, where early and extensive Black-white cultural exchange occurred.[53] Slavery in what would become the United States took early root there, as did tenacious adherence among the enslaved to forms like the African ring shout.[54] White residents in the region observed and often enjoyed such performances, as elite Southerners eschewed the austerity that dampened Quaker society. Philadelphians knew the Chesapeake region well through social, commercial, and land ties. The evolving African-sourced repertoire was affected by absorption of movement material from white dance practice, encountered among Irish fellow bondsmen and viewed in settings like markets and wharves, or visible to servants in "masters'" homes and assemblies. In Chesapeake Black culture, this European-derived material was "added without obscuring or diminishing what is African, which persists like the generative rhythm at the dance's core."[55] Movement among the region's Black population retained strong Africanist qualities: it was energetic, rhythmically marked and accented, asymmetrical, angular, dynamically varied, virtuosic, and of long duration per performance.

Philadelphia's connection to the West Indies/Caribbean basin was another factor in cultural transmission. Early in European colonization, the Caribbean saw ongoing mixtures among enslaved Native, Irish, and African bondsmen, along with different European national influences.[56] Generations later, owing to the Haitian Revolution (1791–1804), a substantial population of Black people from the Caribbean arrived in the United States, some brought by masters fleeing unrest, others arriving as freemen. They brought with them a rich movement history that reflected interethnic practices, including partnered dancing with "flamboyant exhibition and contest."[57] Black residents in Philadelphia and elsewhere observed and adapted European forms like hornpipes, reels, country dances, cotillons, and quadrilles, often contributing tunes that became popular among both Black and white people, and serving at times as dance callers for the steps performed at white elite balls.[58] Such was the case with influential Philadelphia musician Francis Johnson, possibly born in Martinique.[59] By the antebellum period in the United States, then, white dancers and spectators had been long affected by African-related material through viewing dancing of the currently or recently enslaved and the local free Black population, and dancing themselves to the music and calls of Black musicians—all contributing to a distinctive U.S. social-dance repertoire. Philadelphia, like cities and towns throughout the United States, was deeply touched by "the stereophonic, bilingual, or bifocal cultural forms originated by, but no longer the exclusive property of, blacks" in the interconnected Atlantic world.[60]

Thus, blackface acts in Philadelphia's theaters were part of a thickly woven fabric of movement, in dance and daily activity, shared by residents of different "types." Did any dancing in blackface shows draw from distinctively African American movement material? As noted earlier, features of blackface stage dancing frequently cited by observers included speed, strongly accented rhythms, and high-energy expression, elements with precedents in African-derived dance. Similar qualities, differently realized in movement, could also be ascribed to (and melded with) Celtic dancing, another contributor to blackface performance. While most minstrel dancing was fast and energetic, the slower slides of the "J-bone" or "Essence"—also movements with African American precedents—provided that dancing with dynamic, textural contrast. Speedy or slow, blackface dancing was seen by viewers as loose, free, fluid, and extroverted.[61] Performers typically did not travel far across the stage, but rather moved from bent-legged, grounded placements to aerial jumps and leaps, turning and circling around a spot, as indicated in "wheel about and turn about and jump Jim Crow." Groundedness, typical of African-derived dancing that employed relaxed knees and shuffling footwork (brushing, floor-slapping), was noted by observers of minstrel dances, mentioned in song texts, and depicted graphically.[62] Rocking movements and heel-toe weight-shifting distinguished minstrel dancing from Anglo-Celtic movement, although blackface jiggers could also employ the vertical posture of Irish-derived hornpipes and jigs. The bent-knee posture appeared in the angular, often extroverted movement of minstrel jigs and breakdowns, also featuring flexed feet, hips protruding back or sideward, torso tilted off-center, hands spread and angled, elbows bent "akimbo," and arms flung outward or overhead.[63] Angular movement, much associated with African-based sources, was also visible in popular depictions of leg action in Irish-style jigs. Dancers on blackface stages often exhibited extravagant facial expressions and colorful, sometimes ragged costumes supposedly representing plantation garb or urban dandies' dress.[64] These exaggerations were likely heightened for theatricality and humor, much like circus-clown makeup and dress, another inspiration for minstrelsy.

The relationship of minstrel-dance performances to musical accompaniment could be seen as another link to African American sources, including the instrument choices of blackface players—banjo, violin, bones, tambourine, and clapping.[65] Sources for minstrel tunes have been variously ascribed: some were drawn from plantation melodies, others from riverfront and ocean wharves, some from the blendings and inventions of the frontier, others from street vendors, and much of it written by composers like Stephen Foster who specialized in such music. William Mahar points to the minstrel show as "the first point of intersection between an African American culture with a rich musical heritage that included African retentions and a largely derivative English and Italian stylistic tradition"—these latter sources widely visible and audible in U.S. theaters at the time. On the blackface stage, these elements "mixed occasionally with Anglo-American folk materials."[66] Hans Nathan finds that minstrel musicality, featuring lively tempi and rhythms inspired by African American music, fell short of the "degree of animation" typical of Black music (and its kinesthetic expression), making minstrel performances "tame compared to the real thing." He also points to non-African-inflected traits of such music, including repetition of short phrases, symmetry of phrasing, and use of equal note values, diminishing the rhythmic complexity typical of African-sourced music. However, offbeats, accents, and surprising rhythmical structures appeared in some minstrel tunes, moving them beyond typical English theatrical usage. Efforts to imitate African-related timbres led to use of slides and runs in minstrel-stage interpretations.

Further aspects of blackface performance that connect to African American forms include such broader contextual values as improvisation, satire, competition, and audience-performer interaction. The ever-changing lyrics of blackface songs and skits, whereby they addressed specific communities or political moments, was matched in dance improvisation, where performers could strut their specialties and try out new material according to inspiration, encouraged by boisterously appreciative spectators. Audience reaction was essential to minstrel shows, for which working-class spectators felt ownership: this was *their* entertainment, requiring none of the restraint of more decorous settings. Such immediate responsivity between performers and onlookers would have been familiar to Black Americans, who sustained African understandings of music and dance as communal expressions. Satire, noted earlier, also shaped much African American dancing, often signifying commentary on powerholders; satire also underpinned British burlesque and European forms like *commedia dell'arte*, which fed the English harlequinade tradition, including its black-masked trickster, Harlequin. Satire fed the virtuosity of the plantation cakewalk, which likely inspired the minstrel-show closer, an all-company walkaround of spectacular display.[67] Competitions and challenge-dancing became attractions of blackface jigging.

As noted, non-African American material shaping minstrelsy's music and movement came, in part, through Irish immigration to the Americas. As minstrelsy emerged new influxes of immigrants fleeing harsh conditions in Ireland brought poor Irish and free Black workers tightly together in urban living and work settings, feeding competition and resentment among low-wage workers in these groups. Philadelphians felt the pressure of this immigration and responded in the 1840s with vicious riots. Scholars have noted the substantial presence of Irish performers in blackface minstrelsy, which offered such immigrants a range of opportunities—paid work, mockery of their Black job competitors, occasion to distance themselves from racial others (as the Irish themselves had been depicted), satires of their uppity higher-class employers, and perhaps, for some, identification through the blackface mask of the status they shared with African Americans as despised outsiders.[68] The presence of Irish blackface performers reinforced the Celtic jig posture and vibrant step dancing that both melded and contrasted with Africanist elements of relaxed torso, shuffles, and acrobatic bursts of aerial movement.

Reading Dance

Residents of the early United States learned to "read" bodies—scrutinizing, evaluating, and ranking themselves among different "types" throughout their lives. Understandings of bodies in social, economic, scientific, literary, and political spheres—portrayed in lectures, texts, graphics, museum displays, and performances—prepared audiences and critics to "read" bodies displayed on stages.

Many theater spectators were dancers themselves—in ballrooms, not theaters. They would be familiar kinesthetically with ballet: the common technical basis of genteel social dancing and balletic stage techniques is evident from manuals dancing masters published for home training in ballroom behavior. Thus, many spectators knew the rudiments of techniques they observed on stages and the exercises that allowed their mastery, recognizing professionals' virtuosity in steps, postures, and expression. This knowledge shaped journalistic criticism, emerging in this period, as distinct from "puffs" commissioned by managers or artists to boost ticket sales.[69] Early in the century, a Philadelphia critic had felt inadequate to comment on a ballet performance he saw, since "criticism has little or nothing to do with ballets or pantomimes, for they defy criticism."[70] Yet as more ballet dancers appeared on U.S. stages, critics learned to be more articulate. They often judged female dancers by bodily and facial beauty, but not those features alone: critics remarked on dancers' grace in mastering difficult techniques without showing strain;[71] they noted virtuosity in turns, pointework, and speedy leg action;[72] they comprehended the powerful expressivity of balletic pantomime;[73] and they compared dancers to one another and to pinnacles of balletic art like Marie Taglioni, whom some had seen in Europe.[74] They also noted when dancers failed to meet expectations: one critic remarked that American dancer Julia Turnbull, at the Chestnut in 1842, lacked "the elasticity and finish of step, which would render her performance interesting to a *connoisseur*."[75] Since Elssler—praised for her "grace and elasticity of step"—had recently danced on that stage, this critic felt informed of the highest standard.

Elssler, the most renowned ballerina to grace antebellum U.S. stages, garnered extensive commentary. One observer summed up her technique, qualities, and appeal in a flowery review, typical of the time, praising her "visionary beauty":

> With one leg—no, one *articulated extremity* . . . midway between heaven and earth, the other scarcely touching the ground—her white arms, like rays of light, thrown upwards—her small classical head crowned with fragrant flowers—her full, beautiful and speaking eye—her beaming smile—her dazzling teeth—the arch playfulness of her whole manner—it was too much for the susceptible audience, who once more testified their excessive admiration of extravagant contortions, in a tremendous and prolonged burst of applause.[76]

He continued, enraptured, yet able to detail something of Elssler's technique and brilliance:

> Not a whisper—not a breath—not a sound; you might have heard the fluttering of a moth! Look! with what intensity is every eye fixed

on the form of that light and fairy-like creature, as she moves before them in a wonderful succession of classically elegant attitudes.

She floats! she flies! she melts!—she is the air! A flower would not bend beneath her feet! With what beauteous smiles she now rewards the spell-bound audience. . . . But stay! what is she about to do now? With one limb flung out upon the air, as if disdaining to associate with its companion . . . she commences an astonishing rotary motion. Round and round, and round she flies—she whirls faster and faster—she is invisible! . . .—she is lost in a mist! . . . Ah! 'tis over; and now behold her, firm and motionless, upon the extremest edge of her white satin shoe, while the people worked up to a perfect phrenzy of delight.

Other ballerinas—from modest Philadelphian Emma Ince to convention-breaking Lola Montez, imported star Mme. Augusta to local starlet Augusta Maywood, and the French Mme. Lecompte to the American Mary Ann Lee—were evaluated in the nation's periodicals for beauty, grace, technique, and expressivity. These criticisms, while of their time, indicate American viewers' growing capacity to read, appreciate, and evaluate ballet movement.

Ballet commentary overwhelmingly focused on ballerinas, but male dancers were not entirely overlooked. A long list of accomplished, well-trained dancers (mostly but not all European) graced Philadelphia and other U.S. stages, some receiving critical notice. Frenchman P. H. Hazard adopted Philadelphia as home for his dance-teaching, which might have encouraged the *Public Ledger* to turn attention, if briefly, toward his performance, amid its extensive praise and analyses of ballerinas Hazard partnered in November 1838 at the Chestnut Street Theatre. His dancing was "muscular and elastic," "scientific and very graceful; his *pirouettes* are remarkably fine."[77] "Mr. Mallet," in his staging of *La Deliverence des Grecs* at the Chestnut, was noticed for his "elastic and excellent dancing," which "was warmly applauded." Margaret Fuller critically assessed Elssler's U.S. partner, James Sylvain, as "a light and graceful dancer" who "understood his part" although, whenever Elssler exited the stage, "the light all vanished from the scene, the poetry stopped on the wing. . . . We wanted to see the prince with the princess, but she was escorted by a gentlemanly chamberlain."[78] At the Academy of Music, the Ronzani company's male star, Filippo Baratti, drew considerable notice, even serving for one reviewer as a model of masculinity for too-genteel U.S. youth: "Signor Baratti . . . is a study for our young, pale, slim gentlemen, who are guiltless of physical exercise, and reduce themselves to human lathes by excessive smoking and owling. See Baratti! An incarnation of vigor—a big muscle. How he does spring, twirl, spin, and do everything but turn himself outside in!" Yet even this admirer added, "To see a *man* dance, though is a sad sight and a bore."[79] The remarkable men with the Ravel troupe also drew critical note. Gabriel—acrobat, mime, and dancer—was praised by one critic as a "genuine son of *Momus*"[80] for his comedy, and by another as "that prince of pantomimists." Paul Brillant's ballets for the Ravels were considered "admirably arranged" and "as admirably executed by their composer."[81] Noteworthy, however, is the near-absence in the period of solo print images depicting male dancers, when solo images of ballerinas were numerous. On occasion, ballerinas were depicted with a partner's support, indicating where men belonged in the balletic universe; as soloists, male dancers apparently lacked commercial appeal.

The men, thus, were accepted as company directors, choreographers, and supports for ballerinas, who were understood by U.S. viewers as the center of balletic focus. The techniques, plots, and concerns of the ballet stage were indeed woman-centered. In step with the emerging "woman movement" calling for women's access to political, economic, and professional spheres, ballerinas appeared in increasing numbers on American stages, just as U.S. women were taking to lecture halls and convention podiums as reformers and advocates. Activism in abolition, temperance, and women's rights, among other reform issues, increased through and beyond the 1830s, when the city's women founded their own antislavery societies, attended the Seneca Falls Women's Rights Convention, and entered the first college program dedicated to training female physicians. In this context, while ballets could be appreciated (or condemned) by male voyeurs who saw them as opportunities for half-naked women to expose themselves to public view, some spectators saw different values. The plots of ballets like *The Revolt of the Harem* or *La Sylphide* created opportunities to show women exerting power over men who sought to control them. Yet plot outcomes were often disappointing or even tragic; the single women acting as agents of their own fates in *Giselle* or *Bayadere* often faced dire outcomes within their constrained worlds, outcomes reflecting anxieties about women's roles in contemporary society. Ballerinas' capacities to dance virtuosic and even masculine roles, the bold and knowing employment of bodily allure that made stars of performers like Lecompte and Montez, and the independence of income and professionalism that the ballet stage offered to some dancers made the world of ballet suspect to moralists, physicians, and politicians seeking to keep women in a protected, male-directed sphere. Those same factors and values made ballet appealing to some men and to women seeking to understand their own physical natures and to engage actively beyond the kitchen or parlor—along with those women (and men) who could perceive ballet as an art of elegance, expressivity, and beauty.

Blackface stage acts too could be understood variously: the stereotypical "negro" or "Ethiopian" character, denigrated from earlier English dramatic models, was derisively depicted by white actors as the antithesis of civilized behavior and humanity. Yet such figures as Jim Crow, Bone Squash, and Ginger Blue outwitted every white character they encountered; they landed sharp blows at their antagonists and had the last word in addressing audiences. A critic of the time understood this message and "deprecated" T. D. Rice's "method of introducing the *sable skin*, to the walks of the drama, and investing them with the character of a hero of the piece," which was "plainly observable in all of Rice's productions, thereby attaching much more importance to their '*doings*' than what is the case in real life."[82] Elevating Black characters to heroic, center-stage stardom, even in satires, offended dramatic propriety. So did presentation of all-male casts in travesty roles, typical on the minstrel stage, creating spaces for otherwise-forbidden homosocial expression and for mockery of women, particularly as reformers. Such blackface, cross-gender characterization created a grotesque mirror image of ballerinas in travesty roles with exposed legs and mustachios, bearing weapons, and wooing or waltzing with other ballerinas in a ballet's narrative action.

Their mix of high and low, American- and British-sourced elements allowed blackface performers to display dance familiar to workers and ethnicities of different kinds. Yet, delineations of African American characters and bodies could not sidestep burning questions of slavery and citizenship ever more fractious and explosive through the antebellum decades. As civil war loomed, minstrelsy increasingly depicted the contented, uncivilizable plantation slave, happy with his ascribed songs and dances, reassuring audiences that all was well with the nation's "peculiar institution."[83]

Historian John Stauffer notes the critical importance of Black bodily presentations on public stages for thinkers like Frederick Douglass, who understood this role in his public presentations: "True art for him meant accurate and 'authentic' representations of blacks, rather than caricatures such as blackface minstrelsy."[84] Creating his own "black public persona" endowed "life and humanity" to the race, including those enslaved, through presentation as "a performer or art object"—the performer having his own agency and the art object its own aesthetic appeal, thereby uplifting both performer and spectator. Douglass and James McCune Smith both predicted that African Americans would shape the nation's arts and expressivity, a formation in evidence in their day and borne out by history. Douglass's appeal to the imagination of performer and viewer shaped his imposing lecture style, which engaged elements from the scholarly to the mimetic and burlesque.

Mimesis, burlesque, and "scholarly" parody were, very differently, elements of blackface minstrelsy. Blackface stage acts could be understood as embodiments of depictions that many Philadelphia artists and presses poured forth in this period, showing Black people as apish, unruly, and devious; as ludicrous in their overblown efforts to display elite behaviors; and as low-level creatures connecting the animal realm to the human in gradations of intelligence, beauty, behavior, and morality. Minstrel music cover images often depicted blackface characters with animals: crows, cows, alligators, apes, frogs, and fish cavort with the "Black" characters shown reveling in some of these illustrations. William Thackara and E. W. Clay, among others, graphically mocked African Americans, associating Black men with uncontrolled bodily behaviors and highlighting oversized pelvic and groin areas with strategically placed and overtly phallic props. Such prints, disseminating demeaning interpretations of "Black" bodies, were enlivened in stage spectacles, as in T. D. Rice's use of Clay's "A Dead Cut" in *Bone Squash Diavolo*.

Verbal texts too prepared audiences to "read" the minstrel stage: popular periodicals like the *Philadelphia Monthly Magazine* and scientific tomes such as Morton's *Crania* treatises described African-descended people as inadequate, troublesome, ridiculous, or threatening. Such failings were understood as innate to Black bodies. Like many scientific colleagues, Morton intermixed aesthetic evaluations with analyses of Black and white bodies: whites had skull bones that were "delicate," hair that was "fine," noses "aquiline," and capacious "oval" skulls, allowing them "the highest intellectual endowments."[85] Lorenzo Fowler's phrenological analysis of Elssler called on just such tropes. On the other hand, peoples of the "Ethiopian" race, or "the negro," Morton wrote, had "woolly" hair, noses "broad and flat," heads "long and narrow," "the forehead low," and "jaws projecting." Morton admitted that the "moral and intellectual character of the Africans is widely different in different nations," but his summary assessments featured descriptors like "revengeful," "stupid and slothful," "noted for indolence, deception and falsehood," "proverbially fond of their amusements," and possessing "little invention, but strong powers of imitation,"[86] alluding to their perceived entertainment value. As Hosea Easton protested, African-descended people in the United States were depicted as guilty of "every foul purpose imaginable," contemptuous as "an inferior race" revealing in life, art, and text "their deformity" from head to toe—or, as Easton put it, from "lips" to "heels,"[87] and, he might have added, from inner to outer. It is no coincidence that blackface burlesque arose just as Pennsylvanians debated and acted on disenfranchisement of non-white people, claiming that African Americans were incapable of responsible citizenship and could not be entrusted with the vote. This the minstrel stage highlighted.

Yet Philadelphia was also a city of reformers, including both white and Black leaders of the U.S. abolitionist movement. Whether white reformers regarded African-descended people as equals (as, it appears, was the case with Lucretia Mott and her associates) or as human beings, inferior but deserving guidance and sympathy (as Harriet Beecher Stowe's *Uncle Tom's Cabin* might be understood in both book and stage versions), abolitionists were acutely aware of the injustices and dangers that Black people, enslaved and free, faced. But minstrelsy was not the entertainment of choice for serious, reformist Philadelphians, who abhorred the bodily humor, alcohol consumption, and raucous sociality associated with much blackface performance. Rather, linkage of abolitionism, temperance, Sabbath observance, and women's rights led such reformers to find pleasure in prayer meetings, hymn-singing, coldwater picnics, lectures, and possibly the moral entertainments of select theatrical works.[88] Dramatizations of *Uncle Tom*, however, might bring some from these different publics together, melding minstrel tropes into moralistic melodrama.

Some Philadelphia cultural critics recorded views of blackface shows. Several found such entertainments "low," "awkward," "brute," "coarse," "disgusting," "depraved and degraded."[89] Others appreciated them as "not without originality, considerable invention, and a rich vein of burlesque humor," even praising the companies (Sanford's, here) as "capital," performing with such skill and satisfaction that spectators "go away delighted" by the "strong bill" that ensures the viewer will "get your money's worth."[90] New York critic Y. S. Nathanson recorded the power this form asserted on the public, while also providing rich description of the rocking, "akimbo" movement in an impromptu dance he witnessed: "Of the thoroughly impressive and extraordinary sights" Nathanson beheld, "the most memorable and noteworthy was that of a young lady in a sort of inspired rapture, throwing her weight alternately upon the tendon Achilles"—the heel—"of the one, and the toes of the other foot, her left hand resting upon her hip, her right, like that of some prophetic sybil, extended aloft," a gesture associated with ecstatic African religious expression, and thus appropriate to the author's view of the girl's entranced state.[91] That hand was "gyrating as the exigencies of the song required," while the dancer was "singing Jim Crow at the top of her voice." From this description, invoking the well-known print of "Jim Crow" Rice ascribed to Clay, the author moved to prophesy: "Popularity like this laughs at anathemas from the pulpit, or sneers from the press." Pointing to the cross-class appeal of this act, the writer predicted, "The song which is sung in the parlor, hummed in the kitchen, and whistled in the stable, may defy oblivion."

Nathanson's comments are notable since little remains to document the man- or woman-in-the-street responding to such shows. An 1833 lithograph of T. D. Rice on a New York stage, "thronged to an excess unprecedented in the records of theatrical attraction," shows, perhaps exaggeratedly, the ownership audiences felt in their rowdy attraction to Rice's center-stage characterization.[92] Such stage-devouring responses to Rice are not directly reported in Philadelphia, although he and other blackface acts were big draws there. City customs officer William David Lewis wrote in his diary (Mar. 29, 1845) of seeing "the Negro opera—a white company with their skins blacked—at the Chesnut St. Theatre" (Palmo's Ethiopian Opera Co.), which he judged a "pretty good company,"[93] and he saw enough theater to know. A few years later, Lewis found "the New Orleans troop of 'Ethiopians,'" a blackface group, "quite a talented company." Nothing more; for Lewis, as an educated, modestly upper-class Philadelphian, such performances were just another choice on an extensive menu of entertainment options. Durang understood such acts similarly throughout his *History*; he admired the skill of performers like Rice, whose professionalism Durang observed at close hand, but as a cultivated man of the theater, he regretted that minstrel troupes distracted audiences from what he judged nobler theatrical fare.[94] Yet the appeal of blackface performance reflected the sharp political divides and urgencies then facing the nation. Excoriations by Black writers, admonishing readers to avoid theaters and, especially, those acts that "ridicule . . . an already too much oppressed people"[95] alert us to this perception of blackface performance among African American thinkers. Such writings, however, do not explain the responses of Black spectators who chose to spend their entertainment cash on such shows. Some theaters featuring blackface acts advertised "colored seating," suggesting that Black attendance was desired and expected (in segregated sections),[96] as it was at times for ballets and non-blackface dramas.

The blackface stage never held only one value for all viewers but rather was riddled with "contradictory meanings."[97] One spectator might appreciate the actors' vigorous performance skills; another might laugh at the ludicrous corked-up clowns whose foibles made the viewer feel superior to the "Black" characters "delineated"; someone else might cheer these clownish characters for getting the better of white upper-class authority figures in blackface skits; while another might find curious or moving the depiction of supposed Black life. And many commentators were proud of what they perceived as *their own* entertainment—American-made, arising from hardworking (even enslaved) folk, effectively taking on (and taking off on) the operatic and balletic showpieces so dear to Europhiles, while bringing pleasing melodies, virtuosic jigging, and belly laughs at affordable prices to audiences of different types. In its omnivorous swallowing, reworking, and regurgitating of cultural material, minstrelsy evolved into a flexibly syncretic form, embodying, burlesquing, and dancing out race, class, and gender. It met the entertainment tastes of more Americans, of all classes, than did any other performance genre of the time, weaving itself deeply into the nation's cultural fabric.

In Sum

In this critical period of national formation, dancing was fully in the mix that constituted the U.S. cultural stew, a stew very much on the boil. Stages that drew audiences helped define and were defined by understandings of what the nation was about and who had a right to shape it. Dance acts staged in Philadelphia's varied theaters trotted human beings of all types—and of assumed types—across the boards, demonstrating perceived oddities, capacities, and accomplishments, allowing audience members to recognize, cheer, mock, contemplate, disparage, or otherwise grapple with the different kinds of people in the young nation, all present in cosmopolitan Philadelphia.

Dancing, whether on ballet or blackface stages, in toney ballrooms or rowdy dance halls, created in the antebellum period a space for mobility across divides that threatened the young nation's unity—divides demarcating human status, races, genders, cultures, classes, and moral views. Theaters served as sites not only of diversion and wonder but also of mixture, contest, opportunity, and experimentation with themes troubling the political, social, scientific, and aesthetic ordering of the nation. At stake was the human body itself—its appearance, behaviors, meanings, and opportunities. Philadelphia—a center of both ideas and action, the City of Brotherly Love and of explosive rioting—fielded artists, writers, teachers, thinkers, opportunists, and producers who created and critiqued works featuring bodily representations on page and stage. Dance and dancing confirmed, challenged, and embodied established and emerging views of human capacities and rights, discourses that shaped United States politics and culture, bodies and minds.

Notes

Primary sources from the United States for this research typically did not include diacritical marks in titles for French ballets or names, and are thus presented in that primary-source form throughout this text and notes.

CHAPTER 1

1. Lhamon, *Raising Cain*, 97. William Winter claims that four-year-old Jefferson debuted in this act in Washington, D.C. (*Life and Art of Joseph Jefferson*, 104–5; 158–61). Language in quotations from the period, often highly offensive by current standards, represents choices by those authors, choices that will, over the course of this volume, contribute to revealing the volatile and often violent nature of U.S. cultural, social, and political development with regard to candescent issues of race, ethnicity, gender, and class.

2. Wemyss, *Twenty-Six Years*, I, 206–7. J. Jefferson, as an adult, earned fame for his Rip Van Winkle impersonations.

3. Durang, *History*, v. 4, ch. 23, 73; v. 5, ch. 89, p. 279; v. 5, ch. 109, p. 351.

4. First known performance of *Cherry and Fair Star* was Apr. 8, 1822, London. Philadelphia listings for 1833 in James, *Old Drury*, 540.

5. Quotations: Rees, "Arch Street," *Dramatic Mirror*, 109; Durang, *History*, 2 ser., ch. 22, 71.

6. For example, "American Humor," 215.

7. Durang, *History* v. 4, ch. 23, 73.

8. W. Wood, *Personal Recollections*, 368.

9. Meglin, "Behind the Veil of Translucence," pt. I, 73.

10. Ndiaye, *Scripts of Blackness*, 139–40.

11. Kirtley, "Athens of America," *Encyclopedia of Greater Philadelphia*.

12. Bolster, *Black Jacks*; Furstenberg, *When the United States Spoke French*; Lazo, *Letters from Filadelfia*; Ritter, *Philadelphia and Her Merchants*.

13. Casey, "Limits of Equality," 151–222.

14. Warner, *Letters of the Republic*. On "flesh, existence defined at its most elemental level," as determinant of humanity in the early United States, see Hartman, *Scenes of Subjection*, 4.

15. Dickens, *American Notes*, 39; Wright, *Views of Society and Manners*, 39, 61–62.

16. G. Nash, *Forging Freedom*, 3; for population figures, 137.

17. Bacon and McClish, "Reinventing the Master's Tools," 35; E. Lapsansky, "The World the Agitators Made," 95–97.

18. On early abolitionism in Pennsylvania, see Polgar, *Standard-Bearers of Equality*; on early Black churches, Fordham, *Major Themes in Northern Black Religious Thought*.

19. Gibbs, *Performing the Temple of Liberty*, 181–83, 194; Schrag, *Fires of Philadelphia*.

20. E. Lapsansky, "'Since They Got those Separate Churches'"; G. Nash, *Forging Freedom*, 271–78.

21. Tocqueville, *Democracy in America*, I, 974.

22. Sturge, *Visit to the United States*, 40. See also F. Wright, *Views of Society*, 54. Philadelphia was often called "the Quaker City" and, owing to the egalitarian philosophy of Quakerism, "the City of Brotherly Love."

23. Adams, "Letter from John Quincy Adams to the Pennsylvania Hall Association."

24. I. Brown, "Cradle of Feminism"; "Philadelphia Female AntiSlavery Society," Historical Society of Pennsylvania [hereafter HSP].

25. Sánchez-Eppler, *Touching Liberty*, 20.

26. Early Philadelphia theatrical history is detailed in Brooks, *John Durang*.

27. Brooks, "Against Vain Sports." On Forten attending the theater, see Winch, *A Gentleman of Color*, 170–71.

28. Dillon, *New World Drama*, 4–6.

29. Costonis, "Placide, Alexander," *International Encyclopedia of Dance*, V, 197–99.

30. "Francis, William Bodley," *Biographical Dictionary*, V, 389–92; Furstenberg, *When the United States Spoke French*, 104.

31. Sánchez-Eppler, *Touching Liberty*, 1–2. See also Warner, *Letters of the Republic*, esp. 115–16.

32. For a review of research engaging "body politics" as historical focus or method, see Gouda, "Colonial Encounters, Body Politics, and Flows of Desire."

33. Grosz, *Volatile Bodies*, x. See also Jackson, *Becoming Human*.

34. Ballantyne and Burton, "Introduction," *Bodies in Contact*, 4.

35. Crane, *Performance of Self*, 3. Subsequent quotations, 6.

36. On skin as determinant of early ethnographic rankings, see Wiegman, *American Anatomies*, 27–28.

37. Gottschild, *The Black Dancing Body*, xiii; "Mapping the Territories" is Part III of Gottschild's text. See also Gottschild's *Digging the Africanist Presence in American Performance*, and Hazzard-Donald, *Jookin'*.

38. DeFrantz, "The Black Beat Made Visible," 1.

39. On "public culture" and the "public sphere," see Habermas, *The Structural Transformation of the Public Sphere*; Warner, *Publics and Counter-Publics*.

40. Richardson, *Centennial City*; Cooperman and Sherk, *William Birch*; Gerdts, *Thomas Birch (1779–1851)*; As. Gonzalez, *Visualizing Equality*; Shaw, "Moses Williams, Cutter of Profiles"; M. Snyder, "William L. Breton"; Ward, *Charles Willson Peale*.

41. F. Mott, *History of American Magazines*; B. Stearns, "Early Philadelphia Magazines for Ladies." On daguerreotypes relevant to this research, see Wallis, "Black Bodies, White Science."

42. For example, Hawthorne/Winner, *Stories of Africa*.

43. Chaffee, "A Chart to the American Souvenir Lithographs"; Moore, *Prints on Pushcarts*, 5–6.

44. Easton, *A Treatise on the Intellectual Character, and Civil and Political Condition of the Colored People*, 40–42.

45. G. Nash, *Forging Freedom*, 254.

46. Wiegman, *American Anatomies*, 27. The term "scientist" was proposed by English educator William Whewell in 1833, an alternative to such ascriptions as "natural philosopher" or "man of science" (L. Snyder, "William Whewell").

47. Walsh, "The 'New Science of the Mind,'" 397–413.

48. Henderson, "A Note on the 'Circular Room,'" 158–59. See also Carson, *History of the Medical Department*.

49. Walsh, "The 'New Science of the Mind,'" 398–400.

50. Rush, "Observations Intended to Favour a Supposition," 289–97, quoted in W. Stanton, *The Leopard's Spots*, 7.

51. Erickson, "Anthropology of Charles Caldwell, M.D.," 252. On "anthropology/ethnology," see Goodall, *Performance and Evolution*, ch. 3; Stocking, *Race, Culture, and Evolution*, 44–47.

52. Caldwell letter to George Combe, Aug. 12, 1837, in Poskett, "Phrenology, Correspondence, and the Global Politics of Reform," 417.

53. L. Fowler, *Phrenological Developments and Characters of J. V. Stout . . . and Fanny Elssler*, iii.

54. Dickson, *An Oration Delivered at New Haven*, 7, 39.

55. Dickson, *Remarks on Certain Topics Connected with the General Subject of Slavery*, 27. Subsequent quotation, 27.

56. Dickson, *Remarks*, 26.

57. Quoted in Smedley, *Race in North America*, 232.

58. *Types of Mankind* went through nine editions in the nineteenth century, well past the Civil War (Erickson, "The Anthropology of Josiah Clark Nott," 103–20).

59. W. Stanton, *The Leopard's Spots*, 182. See also "Darwin in America," online.

60. Hall, *A Faithful Account of the Race*, reviews these thinkers' responses.

61. Bolster, *Black Jacks*; M. Jones, *All Bound Up Together*; Washburn, *The African American Newspaper*.

62. Cartwright, "Unity of the Human Race," 130.

63. Fisher, *The Laws of Race as Connected with Slavery*, 7–8. See also *A Philadelphia Perspective: The Diary of Sidney George Fisher*. Fisher later became an emancipationist.

64. Russett, *Sexual Science*, 7; see also Schiebinger, *Nature's Body*, esp. 159–60.

65. Nolan, *A Short History of the Academy of Natural Sciences*.

66. Hodge, "A Lecture Introductory to the Course on Obstetrics," 5; next quotation, 12.

67. Hodge, "An Introductory Lecture, to the Course on Obstetrics," 8, 11, 14.

68. Dewees, *Treatise on the Diseases of Females*, 13; next quotation, 14. On the uterus, 18–22. On "republican motherhood," see M. Nash, "Rethinking Republican Motherhood," and Theriot, *Mothers and Daughters in Nineteenth-Century America*. Meigs mentions "republican daughters" in *Females and their Diseases*, 365. Also see Smith-Rosenberg and Rosenberg, "The Female Animal."

69. Meigs, *Females and their Diseases*, 24.

70. Meigs, *A Memoir of Samuel George Morton*, 21.

71. Comment on Meigs's estimate of women's intelligence by an unnamed reviewer, in "Bibliographical Notices—Females and their Diseases . . . by Charles D. Meigs," 482. Meigs's remark on women's head size: *Females and their Diseases*, 47.

72. E. C. Stanton, *History of Woman Suffrage*, 854. Preston's remarks: "Valedictory Address to the Graduating Class," 8, Drexel University Legacy Center.

73. On treatment of women in dance-history research, see Claire, "Dance Studies, Gender, and the Question of History," 161–88. On women in Romantic ballet, Cordova, "The Romantic Ballet in France"; Jowitt, *Time and the Dancing Image*, chs. 1 and 3.

74. Moody, "Illusions of Authorship," 113–15; McConachie, "American Theatre in Context," 167.

75. Halttunen, *Confidence Men and Painted Women*, esp. chs. 4 and 6.

76. For various reports on this story, see *Bentley's Quarterly Review*, v. 2 (Jan. 1860), 388; S. Harris, *The Philosophical Basis of Theism*, 542; Pattison, "The Relation of Art to Religion," 329.

77. "Editorial Notes," *Putnam's*, 206.

78. Evans, *The Feminists*; Lueck, Salenius, and Schultz, eds., *Transatlantic Conversations*.

79. Dewees, *A Treatise on the Diseases of Females*, 109, 116; Horner, *The Home Book*, 79–80, 133, 431; Meigs, *Females and their Diseases*, 420, 522. On *Giselle* in this light, see Meglin, "Behind the Veil of Translucence," pt. 3, 75–78, 130–39.

80. Halttunen, *Confidence Men*, 92, 97; Rosenberg, "Beauty, the Beast, and the Militant Woman," 562–84.

81. On Lane, see, among others: Dickens, *American Notes*, 36; S. Johnson, *Burnt Cork*, 75–80; M. Winter, "Juba and American Minstrelsy," 28–47. On an African American blackface troupe: Douglass, *North Star* (June 29, 1849). On New York's African Grove Theatre: Hay, *African American Theatre*, 2–17; Hill and Hatch, *History of African American Theatre*, chs. 1 and 2.

82. *Philadelphia Album, and Ladies' Literary Gazette* (Oct. 24, 1827).

83. The phrase "genius for contentment" is in Lhamon, *Raising Cain*, 5. On qualities ascribed to Africans, see Bisco, "Town Amusement," 13–14; Cartwright, "Dr. Cartwright on the Caucasians and the Africans," 53–55; Osofsky, *Puttin' on Ole Massa*, 39–40.

84. Lhamon, *Jim Crow, American*, 26; subsequent quotation, 32.

85. See Brooks, *John Durang*, 90–92, 96–102.

86. *The Caliph of Bagdad*, with M. Ronzi Vestris, M. Achille, and a French dance troupe (Walnut St. Theatre, Sept. 19–24, 1829); *Nathalie*, by Fanny Elssler (Chestnut St., Nov. 19–21, 1840, and Sept. 1–21, 1841); *L'Amour d'Quatre*, child ballet-troupe (American Academy of Music, Sept. 10, 1859).

87. Harlequinades performed in Philadelphia include *Harlequin and Mother Goose*, with Charles Durang (Arch St., Mar. 3, 1832); *Harlequin and the Magic Trumpet*, the Ravel Troupe (Chestnut St., Feb. 1–4, 1837); *Mother Bunch and her Magic Rooster; or, Harlequin in California*, with George W. Smith (National Amphitheatre, Dec. 25, 1849).

88. *The Falls of Clyde* (Jan. 1, 1820, and May 26, 1831, Chestnut and Walnut St. Theatres); *Jocko, the Brazilian Ape* (various theaters, fall 1825 to fall 1860); *The Willow Copse*, by Dion Boucicault (May 24, 1852, to Sept. 11, 1855, at several city theaters).

89. Levine, *Highbrow/Lowbrow*, 85–102; Wilson, *History of the Philadelphia Theatre*, 22, 107, 111; W. Wood, *Personal Recollections*, 456.

90. *Cinderella* (a version of *Cendrillon*?, choreography Albert, 1823, Paris) appeared from Feb. 1824 to Oct. 1859 (Chestnut and National Theatres). Mme. Celeste presented dances from *Gustavus 3rd* (music Auber, choreography F. Taglioni) in Dec. 1834 (Chestnut), and the full work in Jan. 1835. *The Bohemian Girl* (by Balfe, not the later Puccini opera) first appeared in Dec. 1844 (Chestnut Street Theatre).

91. Nathanson, "Negro Minstrelsy," 75.

92. Durang, *Durang's Terpsichore*, 85, and *Dancer's Own Book*, 85–92. Social dancers did not perform in blackface.

CHAPTER 2

1. HSP "An Essay on Dancing," Letter II, p. 17. Subsequent quotations, Letter III, 21, 24; Letter IV, 34. Nearly all U.S. authors at the time were men; the paternal tone toward the "lady" addressed suggests that the unnamed author is male.

2. Chaffee, "A Chart to the American Souvenir Lithographs"; Dini, ed., *Dance: American Art*; As. Gonzalez, *Visualizing Equality*; Moore, "Prints on Pushcarts."

3. M. Harris, *Colored Pictures*, 2.

4. A set of Clay's images is at the Rosenbach Museum and Library, another at the American Antiquarian Society. The latter, with penciled annotations mentioned in my analyses, is used for the sequence of images presented here, while the images here reproduced are from the Rosenbach. See Myers, "Dance and the Performance of Self," on Clay's *Lessons* as "arranged hierarchically" (in Dini, ed., *Dance: American Art*, 55).

5. "Philosophy of Fashion," *Philadelphia Monthly Magazine*, 72.

6. G. Nash, *Forging Freedom*, 254.

7. Quoted in P. Lapsansky, "Graphic Discord," 217–18. See also Otter, *Philadelphia Stories*, 82; White and White, *Stylin'*, 115. I am grateful to Lee Arnold, then Senior Director of the Library and Collections at the Historical Society of Pennsylvania, for clarifying (Sept. 14, 2021) the artist and collection for this cartoon.

8. On "reading" dance images: Dini, "Invitation to the Dance," in *Dance: American Art*; Kosstrin, "Kinesthetic Seeing"; Seebass, "Iconography and Dance Research"; Sparti and Van Zile, "Introduction," in *Imaging Dance*, 1–16.

9. On "elite" and "upper class," see Baltzell, *Philadelphia Gentlemen*, 6–7, 12–13. On the City Dancing Assembly, Brooks, "The Philadelphia Dancing Assembly in the Eighteenth Century."

10. Wright, *Views of Society and Manners*, 27; see also Furstenberg, *When the United States Spoke French*, 131. On the ballroom as ladies' domain, see Aldrich, *From the Ballroom to Hell*, 5–7.

11. Gourdoux-Daux, *Elements and Principles of the Art of Dancing*. I am grateful to Elizabeth Claire, Pierre-François Dollé, and Irène Feste for conversations (Nov. 2020) on this source. Information on Guillou is in HSP "Dance Masters," Claude W. Unger Collection 1860A; LCP, *Poulson's Scrapbook of American Biography*, I (Mar. 11, 1825) and II (Dec. 1, 1826).

12. Gourdoux-Daux, *Elements and Principles*, 5–6; *balancé* on 60, 70, 72.

13. On Francis (Frank) Johnson, see C. Jones, *Francis Johnson*; LaBrew, *Francis Johnson*; Southern, *The Music of Black Americans*, 66, 104–8. On Martinique's cultural dynamism, Manuel, *Creolizing Contradance*, 40.

14. Durang, *History*, v. 2, ch 22, p. 213 and 3 ser, ch. 3, p. 9.

15. Quoted in C. Jones, *Francis Johnson*, 113; analysis of Johnson's music and connections to African and African American musicality is in Hale Smith's Appendix 5, p. 270; and in Szwed and Marks, "The Afro-American Transformation of European Set Dances," 31–32.

16. Pilgrim, "Masters of a Craft," 269–93; designation "epicenter," 273.

17. S. Davis, *Parades and Power*, 34, 104–9, 161. Watson reports masquerades as outlawed from Feb. to Mar. 1808 (*Annals* v. III, 159–60). On the Meschianza, see Brooks, "Emblem of Gaiety, Love, and Legislation," 72–75.

18. *National Gazette* (Jan. 26, 1828).

19. "A Few Reflections upon the Fancy Ball," HSP Am. 3075.

20. Hanson, *The Democratic Imagination in America*, 121–54. The term *soirée dansante* is in the *National Gazette* (July 10, 1824), *Public Ledger* (Jan. 2, 1851).

21. C. Jones, *Francis Johnson*, 60–61.

22. *The Philadelphia Index, or Directory, for 1823*; *Desilver's Philadelphia Directory and Stranger's Guide for 1828* and *1829*.

23. Brooks, *John Durang*, 153, 157, 186.

24. Guillou was born in Saint Domingue, was educated in France, taught a dancing academy for many years in Philadelphia, and retired to Cuba, where he died in 1841 or 1842 (*Poulson's Scrapbook of American Biography*, I, 14; Scharf and Westcott, *History of Philadelphia*, II, 964).

25. *Poulson's Scrapbook of Philadelphia History*, Jan. 28, 1822.

26. On the waltz's dangers, see Aldrich, *From the Ballroom to Hell*, 18–19; Claire, "Imagination, Vertigo, and Contagion."

27. Ewell, *The Medical Companion*, 494, 499, 508, 514, 576; Ewell's text, published in Washington, D.C., includes approbations by Philadelphia physicians (pp. iv–vi). See also *National Gazette*, "Of the Exercises most Conducive to Health in Girls and Young Women" (Oct. 20, 1827).

28. Caldwell, *Elements of Phrenology*, 23–24; next quote, 88–89.

29. *National Gazette* (July 31, 1827) announced Tacon's appointment. See also "Embassies and Legations in Washington," 3. On U.S-Spanish-Spanish American relations, see DeGuzmán, *Spain's Long Shadow*; Lazo, *Letters from Filadelfia*.

30. Mme. Hutin danced with Achille in July 1827 (LCP Playbill Collection, 1827, Phi Che [19] 5761.F77). She also appeared with Barbiere in July 1828 (Durang, *History*, v. 3, ch. 42, p. 254). She was likely related to an actor at popular Parisian theaters, Jacques Antoine Francois [Francisque] Hutin (1796–1842); see Lacauchie, "Portrait de Jacques François-Antoine Hutin"; Chevalley, "Madame Francisque Hutin," 40.

31. *Francis Courtney Wemyss Prompt Book*, Walnut St. Theatre, HSP Am 8363.

32. Brooks, *John Durang*, esp. chs. 5 and 7.

33. Durang, *History*, v. 2, ch. LXV, p. 141; and v. 2, ch. LXXIII, p. 157. Other examples of such interludes are in FLP, Theatre Collection Box 32 (Feb. 9, Mar. 22, 1824); *Democratic Press* (Oct. 3, 7, 1825); *Poulson's American Daily Adv.* (Mar. 7–May 30, 1826).

34. Mayer, *Harlequin in his Element*; Senelick, "Pantomime, English," 837–38 in *Cambridge Guide to Theatre*.

35. A. Davis, *America's Longest Run*, 52. On the Parkers, see Ireland, *Records of the New York Stage*, I, 323, 355, 358, 470–71, 498, 535, II, 155, 387, 414, 478; Swift, *Belles and Beaux*, 7–8, 57, 64. Chaffee, "A Chart to the American Souvenir Lithographs," features the Parker sisters, c. 1820s, in a *pas de deux*, as cover image.

36. Durang, *History*, v. 2, ch. 30, p. 226. The "puff" from the *United States Gazette* (Mar. 10, 1826); the "bollerno," at Philadelphia's Chestnut Street Theatre, in *Poulson's American Daily Advertiser* (May 11, 1826); the discouraging comparison in the *Albion* (Sept. 1, 1827).

37. Durang, *History*, v. 3, ch. 41, p. 253; on Miss Rowbotham with "the French dancers," 3 ser, ch. 5, p. 17. Her "Grand Pas Seul" was at the Chestnut Street Theatre (*Daily Chronicle*, Jan. 10, 1829). On French dancers in English theaters, see Guest, *The Romantic Ballet in England*.

38. These ballets are found in FLP Theatre Collection Box 53; LCP Playbill Collection 1827 Phi Che; James, *Old Drury*.

39. The libretto for this ballet was likely *Cherry and Fair Star; or, the Children of Cyprus: A Drama, in Two Acts*, credited to Mme. d'Aulnoy (London, 1822). The Darleys are listed in James, *Old Drury* (1812, 1820, and 1821); and in Philadelphia City Directories (1829, 1830).

40. Cockrell, *Demons of Disorder*, ch. 1, "Blackface on the Early American Stage"; Nathan, *Dan Emmett*, ch. 1.

41. Dillon, *New World Drama*, 21, addresses "the promiscuous circulation of scripts" for dramatic works, "and the improvisational local revisions of these scripts," throughout "the Anglo-Atlantic world," which would have included the handling of ballet scenarios in Philadelphia.

42. Durang, *History*, v. 2, ch. 23, 215, all italics in text; playbill in LCP Playbill Collection, PB 1825 Phi Che (19)5761.F.76a.

43. Wemyss, *Twenty-Six Years*, v. I, 94.

44. Falcone, "The Arabesque."

45. Chevalley, "Madame Francisque Hutin"; Costonis, "Ballet Comes to America," 264–66.

46. On French dancers in the United States before Hutin and company, see Brooks, *John Durang*, 69–70, 87–89, 93–94, 246.

47. Letter, Apr. 19, 1827, HSP Leaming Family Papers, Collection 0622, box 6, correspondence 1826–1839. On debates over Hutin's costume and on balletic morality, see Lehman, "Virtue and Virtuosity," 162–68.

48. Ireland, *Records of the New York Stage*, I, 528.

49. "Fashion's Mirror," *Philadelphia Album, and Ladies' Literary Gazette* (July 19, 1827).

50. Quoted in Chevalley, "Madame Francisque Hutin," 42; see also p. 83.

51. *Albion* (May 27, 1827) and *Mirror* (Nov. 10, 1827), quoted in Chevalley, 84.

52. Jackson, *Becoming Human*, 49; Russett, *Sexual Science*, 51–52; Schiebinger, *Nature's Body*, 75, 145.

53. Gibbs, *Performing the Temple of Liberty*, 7; Gourdoux-Daux/Guillot, *Elements and Principles of the Art of Dancing*, 14.

54. Costonis, "Ballet Comes to America," 374–81; Hammond, "Ballet Training," "Clues to Ballet's Technical History," and "Steps through Time."

55. Durang, *History*, v. 3, ch. 46, p. 260.

56. *National Gazette* (Jan. 8, 1829). Colley Cibber quote from the *Daily Chronicle* (Jan. 9, 1829).

57. Respectively: LCP Playbill Collection, PB 1827 Phi Che (19) 5761.F.78; the *Daily Chronicle* (both Ronzi Vestris dances); Durang, *History*, v. 3, ch. 54, p. 276.

58. McAllister, *White People Do Not Know*, 92–94. See also Ireland, *Records of the New York Stage*, I, 399.

59. FLP Theatre Collection Box 53, and *Daily Chronicle*.

60. Brooks, *The Dances of the Processions of Seville*, 155–72. On balletic national dances, see Arkin and Smith, "National Dance in the Romantic Ballet," in Garafola, *Rethinking the Sylph*.

61. Durang, *History*, v. 2, ch. 27, p. 221.

62. Durang, *History*, v. 2, ch. 12, p. 191, and ch. 13, p. 195 (Kirby was not in these Philadelphia productions). On *La Perouse*, see Dunmore, *La Peyrouse dans l'isle de Tahiti*; Linnekin, "Ignoble Savages and Other European Visions," 10; "West's Characters," National Library of Australia.

63. Goodall, *Performance and Evolution*; Shepherd, *Theatre and Evolution*, 3–29. On European precedents for "animalization" of Black figures on stage, see Ndiaye, *Scripts of Blackness*, 193, 205–20.

64. De Lurieu, *Jocko; ou, Le singe du Brésil*. Other versions: Lefebvre, *Sapajou, ou Le Naufrage des Singes* (Paris, 1825); Jean-Antoine Petipa, *Jocko ou le Singe du Brésil* (Brussels, 1826); Taglioni, *Danina, or Jocko, the Brazilian Ape* (Stuttgart, 1826; published 1828 as *Jocko, O Sia La Scimia Brasiliana*), premiering with Marie Taglioni as Brazilian "slave" Danina (Goldschmidt, "Marie Taglioni," 112).

65. Goodall, *Performance and Evolution*, ch. 2. A "jocko" in this period was a term for an ape (Schiebinger, *Nature's Body*, 78–79).

66. Chasteen, *National Rhythms*, 3, 13–14, 140, 195–96. On "la chica," see Ayestarán, *El Candombe, la Chica y la Bambula*, 164–69; Manuel, *Creolizing Contradance*, 166, 210, 226; Moreau de Saint-Méry, *Description topographique*, 45.

67. Nolan, *Short History of the Academy of Natural Sciences*, 7–10.

68. Cobb wrote the story and Harry Watkins the play version of *The Pioneer Patriot; Or, the Maid of the War-Path*. See Irelan, *Enacting Nationhood*, 1–23.

69. *The Barber of Seville; or, Almaviva et Rosine*, by "the French corps de ballet," was called a "grand ballet," Walnut St. Theatre, Jan. 1828 (Durang, *History*, v. 3, ch. 46, 260). The "ballet-pantomime" *The Caliph of Bagdad* played the Arch Street Theatre, Sept. 1829, with both the Ronzi Vestris and Achilles (Durang, *History*, v. 3, ch. 48, p. 26). An excerpt from *Nina* was at the Chestnut Street Theatre in Mar. 1828 by ballerina-mime Mlle. Celeste (Durang, *History*, v. 3, ch. 41, p. 251).

70. On Léon and Corby Léon, see mentions throughout Blasis, *Notes Upon Dancing*; Costonis, "Ballet Comes to America," 270, 462; Moore, *Echoes of American Ballet*, 64.

71. Durang, *History*, v. 3, ch. 46, p. 260.

72. Durang, *History*, v. 3, ch. 55, p. 161; Moore, "La fille mal gardée in America"; *Daily Chronicle* (Jan. 21 and 26, 1829). This version of *Fille* may have been choreographed by Aumer, with music by Hérold, as premiered in Paris, 1828.

73. On Union, New Jersey, see "The Beginnings of New Jersey"; "Union, New Jersey, United States," *Encyclopedia Britannica*. On Quakers in New Jersey, Pomfret, "West New Jersey: A Quaker Society." Images of Quaker dress in the period are at "Quaker Dress, 1800–1805."

74. Clarkson, *A Portraiture of Quakerism*, v. 1, 113.

75. F. Wright, *Views of Society*, 36–37.

76. Watson, *Annals*, v. 1, 276. See also C. V. Hill, "In the Eye of the Beholder," in Dini, ed., *Dance: American Art*.

77. These works can be seen at LoC and at the Metropolitan Museum of Art, online.

78. Myers, "Dance and the Performance of Self," in Dini, ed., *Dance: American Art*, 57. The jig as an African American dance is discussed in Gottschild, *Digging the Africanist Presence*, 97–98; C. V. Hill, "In the Eye of the Beholder," in Dini, ed., *Dance: American Art*; Stearns and Stearns, *Jazz Dance*, 37. On "vernacular" dancing "performed to the rhythms of African American music . . . that makes those rhythms visible," in contrast to European academy-derived dancing, see Malone, *Steppin' on the Blues*, 2.

79. *National Gazette* (Feb. 20, 1823).

80. On early Philadelphia street names, "Historic Street Name Index," online. The interraciality of city neighborhoods is a theme throughout G. Nash, *Forging Freedom*.

81. "An Enquiry into the Condition and Influence of the Brothels," 4, 5. See Bushman, *Refinement of America*, 414–24; DuComb, *Haunted City*; Laurie, *Working People of Philadelphia*; Newman, *Embodied History*, 1–15, 140–41.

82. Laurie, *Working People*, 58–61, 151–55; Schrag, *The Fires of Philadelphia*, 52–53.

83. Quotations from a Philadelphia newspaper in G. Nash, *Forging Freedom*, 275; see also Scharf and Westcott, *History of Philadelphia*, I, 624.

84. "Enquiry into the Condition and Influence of the Brothels," 9–10. On the "bonnetless" woman marking a prostitute, see Carlisle, "Disorderly City, Disorderly Women," 11. On associations of stage dancers with "public women," see Lehman, "Virtue and Virtuosity"; Rosenman, *Unauthorized Pleasures*, 93–99.

85. Brooks, *John Durang*, 82–83. Steps for "Pas de matelot—A Sailor Hornpipe, Old Style," are in C. Durang, *Durang's Terpsichore*, 158, and may represent John Durang's version. John Durang's self-portrait of his hornpipe can be viewed at *Jenny Glover's Fiddletails* online. Social-dance versions of hornpipes are in Carpenter, *Amateur's Preceptor*, 71; C. Durang, *The Dancer's Own Book*, 107.

86. Dickens, *American Notes*, 36. Gottschild reference: *Digging the Africanist Presence*, 100. Durang's comment on the shuffle is in *History*, v. 5, ch. 89, p. 279.

87. "Back to Back," graphic, Edward Williams Clay, c. 1829, HSP Life in Philadelphia 7688.F.

88. Morton, *Crania Americana*, 6, 91, *Crania Aegyptica*, 3, 9; Nott, *Types of Mankind*, 184–88, 197, 403.

89. Watson, *Annals*, II, 261.

90. Ndiaye, *Scripts of Blackness*, 187–234; White and White, *Stylin'*, 16.

91. See, for example, DuComb, *Haunted City*, 72; Davison, "E. W. Clay," 60.

92. R. Abrahams, *Singing the Master*, 94–95; Douglass, *My Bondage and My Freedom*, 195; Hartman, *Scenes of Subjection*, 70–76; A. Lomax, *Alan Lomax*, 69–70.

93. L. Brooks, "Race, Rank, and Reform," 147–78.

94. McAllister, *Whiting Up*, 43. On African American balls in New York in this period, see "Journal of a Tour through the Eastern States," 70.

95. Egan, *Life in London*, illustrations by I. R. and G. Cruikshank. On Cruikshank inspiring Clay, see Davison, "E. W. Clay," 58–59, 85; Otter, *Philadelphia Stories*, 81–88. "Life in Philadelphia" series available at LCP or HSP digital collections.

96. Davison, "E. W Clay," 213–17; P. Lapsansky, "Graphic Discord," 225; Nyong'o, *The Amalgamation Waltz*, 103–34; "An Amalgamation Waltz" is in NYPL Digital Collections; "An Amalgamation Polka" at University of Michigan, William L. Clements Library Image Bank.

97. On early "Black" characters and U.S. blackface drama, see Collins, "White-Washing the Black-a-Moor"; L. Hutton, "The Negro on the Stage," 131–33; Nathan, *Dan Emmett*, 3–34; Rehin, "Harlequin, Jim Crow," 683–87.

98. Cockrell, *Demons of Disorder*, 29.

99. G. Nash, *Forging Freedom*, 46, 51–52. On British precedents to U.S. "Black" stage dialect, see Ndiaye, *Scripts of Blackness*, 159–68.

100. Nathans, "Staging Slavery," 204–6. *The Triumphs of Love* and *The Politicians* scripts are in the Oxford Text Archive. On *Robinson Crusoe*, see Brooks, *John Durang*, 60, 65, 97, 101–2, and "Staged Ethnicity," 193–225.

101. Hay, *African American Theatre*, 6–17; Hill and Hatch, *History of African American Theatre*, 26–35; McAllister, *Whiting Up*, 51–61; Warner et al., "A Soliloquy," 1–46.

102. McAllister, *White People Do Not Know*, 94–95; G. Thompson Jr., *Documentary History*, 136.

103. Notice of Hewlett's Philadelphia shows is in *Poulson's American Daily Advertiser* (Jan. 18, 1826). For York performances, *York Gazette* (May 8 and 29, 1827); for Lancaster, *United States Gazette* (Philadelphia, May 22, 1827). See also G. Thompson Jr., *Documentary History of the African Theatre*, 38–39, 167–71, 183–84.

104. T. Davis, "Acting Black," 163–89; McAllister, *White People Do Not Know*, 43, 158, 172–76; Warner et al., "A Soliloquy Lately Spoken," 11–12.

105. Mathews's relationship with Philadelphia is discussed in Nathan, *Dan Emmett*, 44–48. On Mathews's Philadelphia shows (Feb. and Mar. 1823), see Durang, *History*, v. 2, chs. 9 and 10, pp. 183–88, and vol. 4, ch. 35, p. 111; and James, *Old Drury*, 373–74, 382–85. Gibbs links Mathews to later British minstrelsy (*Performing the Temple*, 153–61).

106. C. Mathews, *The London Mathews*, illustrated (Rosenbach Museum and Library).

107. A. Mathews, *Memoirs of Charles Mathews*, 390, letter to James Smith, Esq. (Feb. 23, 1823).

108. Goodall, *Performance and Evolution*, ch. 4.

109. Durang, *History*, v. 2, ch. 14, p. 199.

110. Scharf and Westcott, II, 1080. Durang's claim is in *History*, 3 ser, ch. 17, p. 56. See also DuComb, *Haunted City*, 76–77; Ireland, *Records of the New York Stage*, I, 632; Watson, *Annals*, III, 380.

111. On Krimmel and dance depictions: DuComb, *Haunted City*, 21–22; Myers, "Dance and the Performance of Self," in Dini, ed., *Dance: American Art*, 52–56. Regarding the Krimmel/Svinin prayer meeting watercolor, see G. Nash, *Forging Freedom*, 194. The Metropolitan Museum of Art lists Svinin as artist of this image; the PBS site, *Africans in America*, suggests it is by Krimmel, from a collection Svinin assembled. On Mount and dance: C. Smith, *Creolization of American Culture*.

112. Shaw, "'Moses Williams, Cutter of Profiles,'" 22–39.

113. Lange, *Picturing Political Power*, 36.

CHAPTER 3

1. Dillon, *New World Drama*, 9–13.

2. Gundaker, "Give Me a Sign," in Gross and Kelley, eds., *History of the Book*, v. 2, 486.

3. Walker wrote glowingly of "that truly Reverend Divine (Bishop Allen) of Philadelphia" (*Appeal, in Four Articles* 63–65); subsequent quotations from 7, 68.

4. Gundaker, "Give Me a Sign," 490–91; Malamud, *African Americans and the Classics*, 63–65, 114.

5. "Free Blacks," *Philadelphia Album, and Ladies' Literary Gazette* (Oct. 22, 1831): 341.

6. McCurdy, "Origins of Universal Suffrage," 11.

7. E. Smith, "End of Black Voting Rights," 279–99; Winch, "Free Men and 'Freemen,'" 14–19 (population figure, 16).

8. Boromé, "Vigilant Committee," 320; G. Nash, *Forging Freedom*, 172–73, 275–77. On race riots, E. Lapsansky, "Since They Got Those Separate Churches,'" 54–78; E. Smith, "End of Black Voting Rights," 283–84. On concepts of "citizenship" in the antebellum United States, M. Jones, *Birthright Citizens*, 1–13.

9. On "coloured conventions," Spires, *The Practice of Citizenship*. On African colonization, Bay, *The White Image*, 22–32, 66; G. Nash, *Forging Freedom*, 234–46.

10. M. Jones, *All Bound Up Together*, 47–48; Otter, *Philadelphia Stories*, 7, 108.

11. I. Brown, "Cradle of Feminism," 143–66. See also E. Lapsansky, "The World the Agitators Made," 91–99; Yee, *Black Women Abolitionists*, 95.

12. Kelley, "'A More Glorious Revolution': Women's Antebellum Reading Circles," 189.

13. *Proceedings and Debates of the Convention . . . 1837*, 541 (June 21, 1837), italics in text.

14. J. Parrish, *Present State and Condition of the Free People of Color* (LoC); LCP, *Register of Trades of the Colored People*.

15. I. Brown, "Cradle of Feminism," 157, 158–61; Scharf and Westcott, *History of Philadelphia*, I, 650–51.

16. *Proceedings of the Third Anti-Slavery Convention of American Women, . . . 1839*, 6 (LoC).

17. Dewees, *Treatise on the Diseases of Females*, 13. Subsequent quotations from 14, 15, 18, 21.

18. Hodge, "A Lecture Introductory to the Course on Obstetrics," 15; subsequent quotes, 5.

19. Dewees, *Treatise*, 109.

20. "Author of the American Gentleman's Medical Pocket-Book," *The American Lady's Medical Pocket-Book*, 16–17. Subsequent quotations, 27, 36, 39.

21. Caldwell, *Phrenology Vindicated*, 152. Subsequent quotations, 153–54.

22. Caldwell, *Phrenology Vindicated*, 28–32. On the Caucasian/classical ideal, see Malamud, *African Americans and the Classics*, 180; West, "Race and Modernity," 78–80. Quotes on Caribs in Caldwell, *Phrenology Vindicated*, 70–71. The Carib (Kalinago) people are Indigenous to the Lesser Antilles (Sweeney, "Caribs, Maroons, Jacobins").

23. Dain, *A Hideous Monster of the Mind*, ch. 7, 197–226; Wallis, "Black Bodies," 41.

24. Morton, *Crania Americana* [*Cr Am*], iv, 88; on the "Charibs," 236–40. See W. Stanton, *The Leopard's Spots*, 25, 35.

25. On connections of "scientific racism" to aesthetic values, see Gilroy, *The Black Atlantic*, 8, 76.

26. Quoted in Casey, "The Limits of Equality," 161.

27. Walsh, "The 'New Science of the Mind.'" On phrenology and liberal thinking, see Poskett, "Phrenology, Correspondence, and the Global Politics of Reform"; Russet, *Sexual Science*, 20–22.

28. Sorisio, *Fleshing Out America*, 21, 29.

29. Johnston, *Phrenology Exemplified and Illustrated*.

30. Greenblatt, *Phrenology*, 797–99; van Wyhe, "The History of Phrenology."

31. *Public Ledger* (Nov. 20, 1838; Aug. 13, 1841; Jan. 17, 1849); *Pennsylvania Freeman* (Apr. 27, 1854).

32. "Natural Capabilities of Negroes," *American Phrenological Journal* (1846).

33. "March of Intellect," *Philadelphia Inquirer* (June 1, 1831); later notice, *National Gazette* (Aug. 6, 1831). Mr. Lively's tour, *Public Ledger* (June 25, 1836). Phrenology appeared in Douglass's *North Star* (Feb. 5, 1848; June 18, 1848; Nov. 10, 1848).

34. Rusert, *Fugitive Science*, 125.

35. *Public Ledger* (Dec. 13, 1842; see also June 25, 1844; July 12, 1844).

36. Sorisio, *Fleshing Out America*, 15.

37. FLP Theatre Collection, Box 34, playbills (Dec. 15, 17, Chestnut St. Theatre). On Celeste as Maze's student, Swift, *Belles and Beaux*, 29.

38. Ludlow, *Dramatic Life*, 513; Durang, *History*, v. 3, ch. 37, p. 244, and ch. 41, p. 251. Durang notes Celeste's Paris Opera training in ch. 41, p. 251, and ch. 54, p. 276.

39. On ballet related to melodrama, see Costonis, "Ballet Comes to America," 83, 152, 267, 347; Mates, *America's Musical Stage*, 46–47, 101–7.

40. Durang, *History*, v. 4, ch. 46, p. 133. T. Brown identifies Checkini as English (*History*, 69).

41. See Lehman, "Virtue and Virtuosity," 111–15. Philip Hone commented on an early New York presentation of *La Bayadere* with "singing and speaking" (*The Diary of Philip Hone*, I, 227).

42. Durang, *History*, v. 4, ch. 46, p. 133. In v. 4, ch. 48, p. 139, Durang also describes the musical "drama" *The Maid of Cashmere*, "an alteration of the three-act drama of 'Lurline; or, the Spirit of the Rhine'" (J. G. Burrows and George Dibdin Pitt, *Lurline; Or the Water Nymphs' Revolt*) produced at the Walnut Street Theatre to challenge Celeste's opera-ballet at the Chestnut.

43. "Celeste as the Maid of Cashmere," NYPL Digital Collections.

44. Ludlow, *Dramatic Life*, 513. My database of performances in Philadelphia includes numerous presentations of *La Bayadere* between 1834 and 1860, with varied casts of European and American dancers.

45. Ireland, *Records* II, 119. See also Wemyss, *Twenty-six Years*, I, 153.

46. Ludlow, *Dramatic Life*, 362; subsequent quotation, 513.

47. See Kant, "The Soul of the Shoe," 190–97, in *The Cambridge Companion to Ballet*.

48. Durang, *History*, v. 3, ch. 37, p. 244.

49. Documentation is in LCP PB v. 11 and PB 1832 Phi Che (20) 5761. F. 8a; Durang, *History*, v. 4, chs. 23, 28, and 30; James, *Old Drury*, listings for 1833, 1834.

50. Swift, *Belles and Beaux*, 75–80; Schneider, "Ravel Family," 316–20.

51. Durang, *History*, v. 4, ch. 28, p. 86; subsequent quotation from v. 4, ch. 23, p. 73.

52. Durang, *History*, v. 3, ch. 54, p. 276–77. On Celeste's pointework and "combat," v. 4, ch. 39, p. 117.

53. Durang, *History*, 3 ser., ch. 13, p. 40; Moody, "Illusions of Authorship," 115–16. On female managers in London, see Ridgwell, "City Women: Managers and Leading Ladies at the City of London Theatre."

54. Quoted from the *New York Herald* (Dec. 7, 1836), in Lehman, "Virtue and Virtuosity," 187. On Caroline Augusta Josephine Therese Fuchs, the Comtesse de St. James, see Ireland, *Records of the New York Stage*, II, 176–77, 182; Swift, *Belles and Beaux*, 109–15.

55. *Spirit of the Times* (Dec. 17, 1836), in Lehman, "Virtue and Virtuosity," 220. Manager William Wood complained of Celeste's costliness in *Personal Recollections*, 398, 425; her high earnings were also reported in *United States Gazette* (Nov. 19, 1835, quoted in Wilson, *History of the Philadelphia Theatre*, 97), and by Rev. Robert Turnbull in "Expensiveness of Theatres," *Colored American* (Mar. 21, 1840).

56. Lehman, "Virtue and Virtuosity," 209; on dance linked to prostitution, see Rosenman, *Unauthorized Pleasures*, ch. 3.

57. Ludlow, *Dramatic Life*, 513; Wemyss, *Twenty-Six Years*, I, 153 and II, 332–33. See also Lampert, *Starring Women*, 113–45.

58. *The Celeste-al Cabinet*, probably by Albert Hoffay (New York, 1836), LoC and NYPL.

59. Durang, *History*, v. 4, ch. 46, p. 132. These graphic depictions were not intended to represent photographic exactness but rather were created to lure purchasers. On the travesty dancer in this period, see Garafola, "The Travesty Dancer in Nineteenth-Century Ballet," 35–40.

60. Durang, *History*, v. 6, ch. 112, p. 358.

61. "Stage Dancing," *Public Ledger* (Apr. 15, 1837); next quotations from article of the same title (Sept. 15, 1840).

62. Quotation from Ireland, *Records of the New York Stage*, II, p. 119.

63. Ireland, *Records of the New York Stage*, I, p. 533.

64. See, among other sources, Jowitt, *Time and the Dancing Image*, 49–65, 105–23.

65. Durang, *History*, v. 6, ch. 112, p. 35; Swift, *Belles and Beaux*, 91. In some advertisements, *The French Spy* was called a "grand Historic ['dramatic' or 'military'] spectacle" (*Public Ledger*, Sept. 12, 1836, June 16, 1837, Oct. 24, 1838, Nov. 3, 1838). See Haines, *The French Spy; Or, The Siege of Constantina*.

66. Morton, *Crania Americana*, 12; subsequent quotation Dover, "The Racial Philosophy of Johann Herder," 128. On Western sympathy for the Greek revolt, Gibbs, *Performing the Temple of Liberty*, 187; Malamud, *African Americans and the Classics*, 80–81.

67. *Public Ledger* (Jan. 18, 1840); earlier listings, July 8, 1837, and Dec. 8, 1838.

68. Hall, *A Faithful Account*, 67. Subsequent quotations: Foster, *Corporealities*, 4; Morton, *Crania Americana*, 1.

69. Morton, *Crania Americana*, 18; on "Hindoos," 32–33.

70. Examples are in *Poulson's American Daily Advertiser* (Jan. 1, 4, 1825); *Public Ledger* (Nov. 28, 1837; Dec. 31, 1842; May 26–June 1, 1843). See Deloria, *Playing Indian*, esp. 3–14.

71. Durang, *History*, v. 4, ch. 35, p. 113; *Public Ledger* (Sept. 12, 1836, July 8, 1837, Oct. 29, 1838, Aug. 27, 1839).

72. Morton, *Crania Americana*, 6; subsequent quotations, 74–75.

73. On Celeste in this work in 1851, Durang, *History*, v. 6, ch. 112, p. 358; *Public Ledger* (Nov. 10, 1851).

74. Durang, *History*, v. 4, ch. 50–51; *Public Ledger*; and *Weekly Messenger*.

75. *Weekly Messenger*, "Theatrical Affairs" (Mar. 21, 1838).

76. Durang, *History*, v. 4, ch. 51, p. 148.

77. Gibbs, *Performing the Temple of Liberty*, 213–14, 232–33; Grubbs, "General Trades Union Strike, 1835," *The Encyclopedia of Greater Philadelphia*.

78. Slout, *Olympians of the Sawdust Circle*, 170–71. Letter, *Weekly Messenger* (Sept. 26, 1838), justifies Augusta Maywood as a Philadelphian, despite her New York birth.

79. Durang, *History*, v. 4, ch. 51, p. 147–48.

80. "La Petite Augusta," *National Gazette* (Dec. 18, 1838). Renowned choreographer and dancing master Jean Coralli taught Augusta for a year and a half; she also studied with ballet star Joseph Mazilier (Costonis, "The Wild Doe," 129–30).

81. *Gautier on Dance*, 79–80. *Le Diable boiteux* (1836, Paris, choreography Coralli, music Casimir Gide); *La Tarantule* (1839, Paris, libretto Scribe, choreography Coralli, music Gide).

82. Ekstrom, "Augusta Maywood," in *Notable American Women*, II, 518.

83. Wemyss, *Twenty-Six Years*, II, 293.

84. Durang, *History*, v. 4, ch. 51, 148.

85. Durang, *History*, v. 4, ch. 53, p. 155. Lilies symbolized purity; an Amazonian lily was named for Queen Victoria in 1837. Amherst was at the Walnut (also called the "American" Theatre) from Mar. to Sept. 1838, according to listings in LCP Playbill Collection, PB Phi Cooke 1838(27) 5761.F.32a (McAllister), the *Public Ledger*, and Wemyss, *Twenty-Six Years*.

86. Costonis, "Ballet Comes to America," 282, quoting the *Spirit of the Times*. Swift credits Lee with studies under Coralli in Paris in 1844 (*Belles and Beaux*, 186).

87. Giles J. Patterson, *Journal of a Southern Student*, quoted in Grimsted, *Melodrama Unveiled*, 105–6. Next quote, Durang, *History*, v. 2, ch. 12, p. 195.

88. *Giselle, ou les Wilis* (1841, Paris, libretto Gautier, choreography Coralli and Perrot, music Adolphe Adam). On Lee in *Giselle* (Boston, Jan. 1, 1846), Moore, "Mary Ann Lee," 114.

89. *McElroy's Philadelphia City Directories*, 1844–1860. The marriage date is in Swift, *Belles and Beaux*, 187. Lee is consistently listed as "Miss Lee," but on May 27, 1852, she took a benefit as "Mrs. Van Hook, late Mary Ann Lee" (Durang, *History*, v. 6, ch. 106, p. 341).

90. "Laurel Hill Gravestone Honors Trail-blazing Ballerina" (June 8, 2011); Malinsky, "Lee, Mary Ann." Durang on Lee's closing season (1853): *History*, v. 6, ch. 116, p. 367.

91. *Gautier on Dance*, 30, on the Paris Opera performance (Nov. 1837). See also Ducomb, *Haunted City*, 83. On use of dark sleeves and burnt cork in earlier Philadelphia racial delineations, see Gibbs, *Performing the Temple*, 6.

92. Lhamon, *Jump Jim Crow*, 2, 8.

93. Lhamon, *Raising Cain*, 1–3, 8, 15, 23–28, 34–35; C. Smith, *Creolization of American Culture*, 175–76, 182, 188–89, 208. A description of dancing at the market is in DeVoe, *The Market Book*, 344–45. The image is on the "Creolization of American Culture" Tumblr site. See also C. V. Hill, "In the Eye of the Beholder," in Dini, ed.,

Dance American Art, 36; and Gilroy on "the theorisation of creolisation, métissage, mestizaje, and hybridity" (*The Black Atlantic*, 2).

94. On connections between Dixon and Rice, see Ducomb, *Haunted City*, 77–79; S. Johnson, *Burnt Cork*, 62, 69.

95. Lhamon, *Jump Jim Crow*, 8, for quotations in this sentence and the next; on the Sea Island and other Southern Black versions of "Jim Crow," 8–9. See also S. Johnson, *Burnt Cork*, 5; Jones and Lomax Hawes, *Step It Down*, 55–57; Lhamon, *Raising Cain*, 181–184; L. Parrish, *Slave Songs*, 111.

96. Jones and Lomax Hawes, *Step It Down*, 55–57; Cockrell, *Demons of Disorder*, 13–29; on blackface and disguise by white and Black people, 32–38, 47–53. See also Chasteen, *National Rhythms*, 93–95.

97. Cockrell, *Demons of Disorder*, 56. On the deep roots of Africanist movement in American dance, see Gottschild, *Digging the Africanist Presence*, 1–10, 81–128; Hazzard-Donald, *Jookin'*, chs. 1 and 2.

98. "American Humor," 219.

99. Cockrell, *Demons of Disorder*, 32–53, 73–75; Saxton, "Blackface Minstrelsy and Jacksonian Ideology."

100. Lhamon, *Jim Crow, American*, ix. See also Lott, *Love and Theft*, 6, 35, 68, 72, 94; Mahar, *Behind the Burnt Cork*, 41, 258–59. On elite abhorrence of Rice, see Lhamon, *Jump Jim Crow*, 2–6, 11–13, 20–24.

101. On wage slavery and Southern enslavement, Gibbs, *Performing the Temple of Liberty*, 191, 213–14, 232–33.

102. On blackface audiences, Cockrell, *Demons of Disorder*, 58. On Rice's improvisations, T. Brown, *History of the American Stage*, 310; Lhamon, *Jim Crow, American*, 1.

103. *Cork Herald* (May 13, 1837), quoted in S. Johnson, *Burnt Cork*, 51. See also Nathanson, "Negro Minstrelsy—Ancient and Modern," 72; Cockrell, *Demons of Disorder*, 75. Malone, *Steppin' on the Blues*, 28, notes that a feature of African American culture is to "'dance the song,'" an element Rice grasped for his act.

104. Stearns and Stearns, *Jazz Dance*, 41.

105. Gottschild, *Digging the Africanist Presence*, 96–102; Stearns and Stearns, *Jazz Dance*, 39–41.

106. White and White, *Stylin'*, 73.

107. Lott, *Love and Theft*, 117.

108. Lhamon, *Raising Cain*, 23–28, 62–65, 161.

109. Bean, "Transgressing the Gender Divide," in Bean et al., eds., *Inside the Minstrel Mask*, 246; Gottschild, *Digging the Africanist Presence*, 25; Nowatzki, "Paddy Jumps Jim Crow," 162–84.

110. *Spirit of the Times*, May 13, 1837, reprint from the *Cork Herald*, Ireland, quoted in Lhamon, *Jump Jim Crow*, 40–41. Pauline Duvernay (1812–1894) was a French ballet dancer whose fame reached the United States, although she did not. The "Taglioni" reference was likely to Marie.

111. A. Davis, *America's Longest Run*, 71. On Rice's connection with Wemyss and the Walnut Street Theatre, see Lhamon, *Jump Jim Crow*, 43, 52–54, 415, n. 93; and *Jim Crow American*, xix.

112. Wemyss, *Twenty-Six Years*, 1, 206. Subsequent quotations from *Dramatic Mirror* (Oct. 2, 1841); and Durang, *History*, 3 ser., ch. 22, p. 71. Lhamon, *Jump Jim Crow*, 416, n. 97, confirms Clemens's work with Rice.

113. On Foster, see "Biography," Guide to the Foster Hall Collection, 1800–1952; Cockrell, "Of Soundscapes and Blackface," 66–69; Saxton, "Blackface Minstrelsy and Jacksonian Ideology," 5–8.

114. Bisco, "Town Amusement," 13.

115. Lhamon, *Jump Jim Crow*, 58.

116. LCP, "Life in Philadelphia collection"; Davison, "E. W. Clay," 85–95; Otter, *Philadelphia Stories*, 81–88.

117. Easton, *Treatise on the Intellectual Character*, 40–41; subsequent quotes from 41–42. See also M. Harris, *Colored Pictures*, 9; West, "Race and Modernity," 86.

118. Cornish, "Theatres," *Colored American* (Mar. 6, 1841). In September 1841, for example, "colored" seating was offered for Rice's blackface "operas" at Philadelphia's Arch Street Theatre (FLP Theatre Collection, Boxes 7, 108). Dance halls and saloons, some racially integrated, had entertainment including blackface acts, but did not issue playbills, so the extent of Black viewers' exposure to such performance was likely greater than documentation reveals.

119. Rusert, *Fugitive Science*, 116.

120. M. Jones notes the rarity of comments by "black activists" on "the minstrelsy scene" (*All Bound Up Together*, 100).

121. Cornish, "The Theatre," *Colored American* (Dec. 9, 1837), italics in original. Cornish lived in Philadelphia (1815–1821) before moving to New York. On Rice's Baltimore speech, see Nyong'o, *Amalgamation Waltz*, 121–23.

122. Laurie, *Working People of Philadelphia*, 62–66; E. Lapsansky, "'Since They Got Those Separate Churches,'" 54–78.

123. Rice called *Bone Squash Diavolo* "A Burletta" (Lhamon, *Jump Jim Crow*, 178). It is called an "opera" in 1830s and '40s *Public Ledger* notices; Durang, *History*, 3 ser., ch. 22, p. 71; Ireland, *Records of the New York Stage*, II, 152; Mahar, *Behind the Burnt Cork Mask*, 102–3; Rehin, "Harlequin Jim Crow," 687; and Wilson, *History of the Philadelphia Theatre*, 58. The text of *Bone Squash Diavolo* used here is in Lhamon, *Jump Jim Crow*, 178–209. Subsequent quotations from this source are cited by page number, in-text.

124. Cast listing assembled from advertisements published June 28, 1838 (*Public Ledger* and *Pennsylvania Inquirer*). Overlap with characters given in Lhamon, *Jump Jim Crow*, 178, is inexact, reflecting the fluidity of scripts and practicalities of available performers.

125. *Philadelphia Inquirer* (Oct. 1, 1833). Although Paganini never performed in the United States, his achievements were widely reported (Lhamon, *Jump Jim Crow*, 428, n. 5).

126. Lhamon, *Jump Jim Crow*, 180–81.

127. Winch, *A Gentleman of Color*. On newspapers mentioned next, see Lhamon, *Jump Jim Crow*, 429, nn. 8, 9.

128. On elite African American women's journals and friendship albums, see Armstrong, *A Fragile Freedom*, 120–47; As. Gonzalez, *Visualizing Equality*, 3–4, 29; Rusert, *Fugitive Science*, 203–6.

129. Lhamon, *Jump Jim Crow*, 428, n. 2; Lippard, *The Quaker City*, I, 362.

130. Lhamon, *Jump Jim Crow*, 59.

131. E. W. Clay, "An Amalgamation Waltz," [c. 1839], American Antiquarian Society. See also Collins, "White-Washing the Black-a-Moor," 87–101; Nathans, "Staging Slavery," 213–17; Nyong'o, *Amalgamation Waltz*, 103–34.

132. Cockrell, *Burnt Cork*, 55–62.

133. "Party Symbols," National Museum of American History, online; Hanson, *The Democratic Imagination*, 121–54.

134. Wilentz, *The Rise of American Democracy*, 558–74.

135. Saxton argues for the close identification of blackface minstrelsy with the Democratic party in this period ("Blackface Minstrelsy and Jacksonian Ideology").

136. Hazard was typically listed as "P. H. Hazard"; Costonis, in "Ballet Comes to America," 271, names him "Philippe," as does Swift, *Belles and Beaux*, 112. In Costonis's "'The Wild Doe,'" he is "Paul H. Hazard," and is so named by M. Winter, "Augusta Maywood," 119–37. Philadelphia City Directories for 1837–1845 list a "Philip H. Hazard" (no "Paul"), but state no profession, although other Philadelphia dancing masters are so identified.

137. Costonis, "Ballet Comes to America," 348–54, 359–64, 378, 383–84, 387, and appendices D, E, and F.

138. Wemyss, *Twenty-Six Years*, II, 314. See also Durang, *History*, v. 4, ch. 55, p. 161; Swift, *Belles and Beaux*, 155–58; *Public Ledger* (Nov. 14–Dec. 12, 1838).

139. Likely a version of *Les Grecs, ballet-pantomime en deux actes* (Bourdeaux, Dec. 1827, choreography Alexis Blache, music Hypolite Sonnet).

140. *Alexander's Weekly Messenger* (Nov. 21, 1838); see also Thespis, *Public Ledger* (Nov. 27, 1838); By "scientific," the commentator referred to Hazard's systematic, professional training.

141. Durang, v. 4, ch. 55, p. 164. On the depression, S. Davis, *Parades and Power*, 137.

142. HSP Claude W. Unger Collection 1860A–Box 5, bills. Mme. Hazard is listed as a dancing teacher in the *Philadelphia Directory* (1840–1850 and possibly 1853 [as "Pauline Hazard"]). Hazard's dances are included in Durang, *Ball-Room Bijou*, 137, and *The Ball-room Companion* (NYPL).

143. *Public Ledger* (Nov. 23, 1846). Durang calls the work "*La Gazelle*" and credits Hazard as stager (*History*, v. 5, ch. 85, p. 268). Ince in *Giselle* is in Wilson, *History of the Philadelphia Theatre*, Apr. 15–22, 1846, Walnut Street. On Lee and Smith in *Giselle*, see Moore, "Mary Ann Lee," 146.

144. Fisher, *A Philadelphia Perspective*, entry Mar. 31, 1837, p. 29; on the dancing assembly, Mar. 21, 1838, p. 48. *Public Ledger* notices of such "citizen's balls" and charity balls include Mar. 27, 1837; Mar. 7, 1838; Feb. 22, 1839.

145. HSP Claude W. Unger Collection 1860A, Box 5, Bills, and "Henry Whale's account book 1830–1840," Am.3140; the *Philadelphia Directory* 1820–1829; *Public Ledger*; Poulson's *Scrapbook of American Biography*, I, 14. Name spellings vary among sources.

146. Trollope, *Domestic Manners of the Americans*, 56, 83, 130, 173, 324.

147. On discipline- and class-based movement cultures, see Myers, "Dance and the Performance of Self," in Dini, ed., *Dance: American Art*, 51–63. Examples of dancing advice and description in a popular magazine are articles, all titled "Dancing," *Godey's Lady's Book*, v. I (1830): 25–26, 91–92, 162–63, 209, 260. Among etiquette books published in Philadelphia in this decade: *The Young Lady's Book: A Manual of Elegant Recreations* (1830); *The Laws of Etiquette; or, Short Rules and Reflections for Conduct in Society* (1836); Leslie, *Miss Leslie's Behaviour Book: A Guide and Manual for Ladies* (1839).

148. Aldrich, *From the Ballroom to Hell*, esp. 19, 25, 119.

149. LCP, "Life in Philadelphia" series: "A five points exclusive taking the first steps towards the last Polish" (New York, c. 1833).

150. Du Bois, *The Philadelphia Negro*, 101, 106. Cartoons next cited: William Summers and Charles Hunt, "Life in Philadelphia. A Black Ball" (London, 1833); Charles Hunt, "The Lady Patroness of Alblacks" (London, c. 1834). "Allblacks" spoofed the name "Almack's," a fashionable London assembly room.

151. "The minutes and proceedings of the First Annual Meeting of the American Moral Reform Society . . . August, 1837" (LoC); Fordham, *Major Themes in Northern Black Religious Thought*, 33–53, 74; Jable, "Aspects of Moral Reform," 344–63.

152. Willson, *Sketches of the Higher Classes*, 50; mentions of music on 30, 58–59. See also Winch, *A Gentleman of Color*, 117; Yee, *Black Women Abolitionists*, 13. G. Nash (*Forging Freedom*, 222) remarks that middle-class Philadelphia Black residents attended "elaborate balls supplied sumptuously by black caterers and enlivened by black musicians," but no specifics are given of dates, places, or events so celebrated.

153. Quotes from unidentified author of *Wealth and Biography of the Wealthy Citizens of Philadelphia . . . by a Member of the Philadelphia Bar* (1845), in Winch, *A Gentleman of Color*, 331.

154. Cornish, "Letter on Christian Education," *Colored American* (Dec. 1, 1838), italics in source. He published further anti-dance arguments on Dec. 15, 1838. Antitheater articles appeared often (Mar. 18, Apr. 15, Apr. 22, Sept. 30, Oct. 28, 1837; Sept. 1, 1838; May 18, Oct. 5, 1839; Mar. 14, Mar. 21, Apr. 25, Oct. 17, 1840; Feb. 20, 1841). F. Hutton reports advertisements in antebellum Black newspapers for teachers of music and dance for Black students, but examples do not include Philadelphia (*The Early Black Press*, 94–95).

155. "Mayor's Office," *Public Ledger* (Dec. 10, 1836).

156. For example, *Public Ledger* (Dec. 3, 1836; Oct. 20, 1837; July 26, 1839).

157. *Minute and Trial Book, Bethel A.M.E. Church*, 1822–1835, 1838–1851, entry of Mar. 23, 1830(?), Archive of Bethel A.M.E. Church, Philadelphia.

158. Du Bois, *The Philadelphia Negro*, 220–21.

159. Watson, *Methodist Error*, 29–30, italics in text; subsequent quotation, 159. Clay's "Methodist Camp Meeting" is in the Smithsonian's National Museum of American History.

160. Herskovits, *The Myth of the Negro Past*, 215–19, 265–69, 271; Stuckey, "Christian Conversion," 39–58; Thompson, *Ring Shout*, 2–6, 109.

161. *Public Ledger* (Mar. 27, 1837); see also Southern, *The Music of Black Americans*, 121. The works listed are *The Indian Hunter*, otherwise unrecorded, and *A Sailor's Dream*, a play of that title being performed at the Arch Street Theatre in 1842 (Wilson, *History of the Philadelphia Theatre*, 268), possibly unrelated to this earlier work.

162. *McElroy's Philadelphia Directory, for 1837* did not mark listings by race, as did other directories in this period. Jacob Hamer & Son are listed as tailors, close to the purported site of the performances. Several John Baileys appear: a carpenter, a weaver, and a porter, all occupations possible for a Black worker of the period. Listings of individuals surnamed "Rhoads" and "Little" are numerous.

CHAPTER 4

1. Taylor and Foster, "Philadelphia in Slices," serialized, *New York Tribune* (Oct. 21, 1848–Feb. 15, 1849), in G. Taylor, "Gaslight Foster."
2. Meglin, "Behind the Veil of Translucence," I, 69. On literacy and publication, see Hall, *A Faithful Account*; Gross and Kelley, eds., *History of the Book*; Lynch, "Every Man Able to Read."
3. Gross, "Introduction," in Gross and Kelley, eds., *History of the Book*, v. 2, 9; on Philadelphia as a publication capital, Vogeley, *The Bookrunner*.
4. Green, "Early American Power Printing Presses," 143–53; P. Lapsansky, "Graphic Discord," 202.
5. On Elssler's tour, see Costonis, "The Personification of Desire"; Delarue, *Fanny Elssler in America*; and McCoy, "Fanny Elssler's Reception."
6. Durang, *History*, v. 4, ch. 57, p. 171.
7. Lueger, "Henry Wikoff and the Development of Theatrical Publicity." On Elssler's U.S. reception, publicity, earnings, and controversies, see also Lampert, *Starring Women*, 147–84. Wikoff and the New York newspapers are discussed in Katz, *Humbug!*, esp. 59–80.
8. Guest, *Fanny Elssler*, 133; *Oxford Dictionary of Ballet*, s.v. "La Tarentule."
9. Durang, *History*, v. 4, ch. 57, p. 171.
10. Guest, *Fanny Elssler*, 130.
11. Fuller, "Entertainments of the Past Winter," 66; subsequent quote, "Chesnut St. Theatre," *Dramatic Mirror* (Feb. 5, 1842), 205. Durang quote in *History*, 3 ser, ch. 8, p. 25.
12. Watson, *Annals*, v. II, 582.
13. Durang, *History*, v. 4, ch. 57, p. 170, on Vallee's dancing *la cachucha* on Jan. 1, 1840. See also Swift, *Belles and Beaux*, 158, 216. *Public Ledger* advertisements record the Vallee sisters before Elssler's tour (Nov. 1838–May 1840). The *Dramatic Mirror* lists the Vallees with Elssler (August 28, 1841), 21.
14. Swift, *Belles and Beaux*, 216. Smith's hornpipe was advertised in the *Public Ledger* (May 7, 1840). Guest quotes Smith's recollection of Elssler (*Fanny Elssler*, 136). See also Moore, "George Washington Smith," 139–88.
15. Guest, *Fanny Elssler*, mentions Parsloe, Arraline (130, 147), and Desjardins (181); Costonis reports Desjardins and Arraline "were not first-rate ballerinas" ("Ballet Comes to America," 309). On Turnbull, see Moore, "Notable American Women" III, 484.
16. *Public Ledger* (May 23, 1840).
17. *Public Ledger* (June 19, 1840).
18. *Public Ledger* (June 20, 1840).
19. Taylor and Foster, "Philadelphia in Slices," 27–29. Foster points to the city's "substantial" "bourgeoisie" on 30; its "pretty women," 31; and "gay Quakeresses" as "exquisite statues," 32.
20. *Public Ledger* (June 22, 1840). On Whitlock, see Cockrell, *Demons of Disorder*, 149; Dumont, "Origin of Minstrelsy." On Diamond, see Mahar, *Behind the Burnt Cork Mask*, 19; Nathan, *Dan Emmett*, 61.
21. T. Brown, *History of the American Stage*, 191. Ince debuted in 1839 as Zoloe in *La Bayadere*, the same work in which Lee and Maywood debuted.

22. *Dramatic Mirror* (Nov. 20, 1841, 113). On *The Fawn's Leap*, see Rees, *Dramatic Authors of America*, 125. Durang credits the work to "S. Steele"—perhaps Silas Steele, also a composer of minstrel songs.

23. *Public Ledger* (June 30, 1840); next quotation, July 2, 1840.

24. Lee advertised herself in "Fanny Elssler's Dance of the Smolenska," *Public Ledger* (Sept. 2–4, 1840) at Burton's New National Theatre.

25. Ludlow, *Dramatic Life*, 537.

26. "George Sand," *Bentley's Quarterly Review*, 388.

27. W. Wood, *Personal Recollections*, 397–98. Durang citation, *History*, 3 ser, ch. 8, p. 25. Philip Hone, an admirer, also noted Elssler's high earnings, *Diary*, II, 31 (June 12, 1840).

28. "Fanny Elssler," *Dramatic Mirror* (Sept. 25, 1841), 53.

29. G. W. Dixon, "Fanny Elssler and the Dying Babe," 10. McCoy notes that Elssler as a European, a ballet dancer, and an unwed mother was an offense to U.S. moralists ("Fanny Elssler's Reception," 77–79).

30. "Stage Dancing," *Public Ledger* (Sept. 15, 1840).

31. *Public Ledger* (Sept. 19, 1840).

32. "Bunker Hill Monument," *Public Ledger* (Oct. 1, 1840).

33. Pindar, "A Short and Correct Sketch of the Life of Mad'lle Fanny Elssler," in Delarue, *Fanny Elssler in America*, 120–28.

34. "Something for the Ladies," *Public Ledger* (June 24, 1841).

35. *Dramatic Mirror* (Jan. 1, 1842), 164. Repertoire listed in Durang, *History*, v. 4, ch. 62, p. 189.

36. Durang, *History*, v. 4, ch. 57, p. 172.

37. Fisher, *A Philadelphia Perspective*, 101. Subsequent quotations 102, 107.

38. "Fanny Elssler, Compliments and Kindnesses," *Alexander's Messenger* (Sept. 29, 1841).

39. "Fanny Elssler," *Dramatic Mirror* (Sept. 11, 1841), 37.

40. "The Fine Arts. The Ballet," *Arcturus* (New York, July 1841), 123.

41. Jowitt, *Time and the Dancing Image*, 47.

42. See Rosenman, "Spectacular Women," esp. 40–52.

43. Durang, *History*, 3 ser, ch. 8, p. 25.

44. Durang, *History*, v. 4, ch. 57, p. 171.

45. L. Fowler, *Phrenological Developments and Characters of J. V. Stout . . . and Fanny Elssler*. Stout's "The Gypsy's Dream" sculpture (including its artistic, political, and moral readings at the time by various critics) is addressed in Katz, *Humbug!*, 61–80. This image came from Elssler's performance in *La Gipsy* (choreography by Mazilier), which Elssler debuted in 1839 in Paris, and which she performed in New York and Philadelphia.

46. Bright, "T. S. Arthur."

47. *Public Ledger*, FLP and LCP playbills, and Durang, *History*, v. 5, ch. 66, p. 205.

48. See also Gibbs, *Performing the Temple of Liberty*, 233–40.

49. Guest, "Fanny Elssler's Cachucha," 14.

50. On theaters luring men to drink and brothels, see Dorsey, *Reforming Men and Women*, 106–8.

51. C. Durang, *History*, v. 5, ch. 73, p. 231. See also *Wemyss' Chronology*, 82.

52. *Public Ledger* (Jan. 20, 1845).

53. Engelhardt, "The Revolt of the Harem on the English Stage"; Meglin, "Feminism or Fetishism" in Garafola, ed., *Rethinking the Sylph*. See also Durang (*History*, v. 4, ch. 54, p. 161); Wilson, *History of the Philadelphia Theatre*, 312–13.

54. Cordova, "Romantic Ballet in France," 113–25; Kant, "The Soul of the Shoe," 187–96; Meglin, "Behind the Veil of Translucence," pt. 1, and "Feminism or Fetishism" in Garafola, ed., *Rethinking the Sylph*. On women's enjoyment of female stage performers, see Haitzinger, "Female Bodies as the Other Alterity on Stage," 80–98; Rosenman, *Unauthorized Pleasures*, 87–123, and "Spectacular Women."

55. L. Mott, "Discourse on Woman" (1848). Mott's comments on physical exercise for women are in E. C. Stanton, *History of Woman Suffrage*, I, 374; on dancing, 422.

56. Meigs, *Females and their Diseases*, 40–41. On feminists addressing "promiscuous" audiences, see M. Jones, *All Bound Up Together*, 23; E. C. Stanton, *History of Woman Suffrage*, I, 327, 395. On feminist Fanny Wright speaking from theatrical stages, Gibbs, *Performing the Temple of Liberty*, 153–54, 165–70; Trollope, *Domestic Manners of the Americans*, 212.

57. Durang, *History*, v. 5, ch. 64, p. 201; Guest, *Fanny Elssler*, 181.

58. "Chestnut St. Theatre," *Dramatic Mirror* (Feb. 5, 1842), 205.

59. Durang, *History*, v. 4, ch. 51, p. 148–49, v. 4, ch. 60, p. 183, v. 5, ch. 67, p. 208. Her modesty was praised in *Dramatic Mirror* (1841, date illeg.).

60. *The Albion* (New York, Dec. 16, 1837), quoted in Lehman, "Virtue and Virtuosity," 201; see also 239–40. The *Weekly Messenger* (Feb 19, 1838) also remarked on Lecompte's performances. On the ballet scene in *Robert le Diable*, see Meglin, "The Gothic Rituals of Nuns."

61. On Augusta's 1838 and 1839 seasons, see *Public Ledger* and Durang's *History*, v. 4; on the 1845 shows, *Public Ledger* (Nov. 22–Dec. 5). Swift gives biographical details for "Caroline Augusta Josephine Therese Fuchs, the Comtesse de St. James," *Belles and Beaux*, 109–112. Durang called Dimier "clever" in *History*, v. 5, ch. 87, p. 274.

62. Assessments of Augusta, in sequence, from the *New York Mirror* (July 11, 1840), 21; *Sunday Mercury* (May 17, 1840), quoted in Lehman, "Virtue and Virtuosity," 95; Ludlow, *Dramatic Life*, 66.

63. On Ciocca and Morra (later, G. W. Smith and Gaetano Neri partnered Ciocca), see Swift, *Belles and Beaux*, 297–303. Their seasons are in Durang, *History*, v. 5; FLP Theatre Collection box 11.

64. Taylor and Foster, "Philadelphia in Slices," 59. Blangy's seasons are in *Public Ledger* and Durang's *History*, v. 5. See also Swift, *Belles and Beaux*, 267–80.

65. Durang, *History*, v. 5, ch. 35, p. 268.

66. Durang, *History*, v. 5, ch. 89, p. 277. Blangy's Arch Street seasons are in FLP Theatre Collection Box 115; and *Public Ledger*.

67. *Dramatic Mirror* (Dec. 11, 1841), 143.

68. FLP Theatre Collection, Box 115; *Public Ledger*; Swift, *Belles and Beaux*, 283–93; Wilson, *History of the Philadelphia Theatre*, 32–33.

69. Durang, *History*, v. 5, ch. 88, p. 275.

70. Their 1847 season is in *Public Ledger* and FLP Theatre Collection Vol. 115; 1848 season in *North American & United States Gazette*. Durang commented on the corps de ballet (*History*, v. 5, ch. 85, p. 267); on their mid-June 1849 season, v. 5, ch. 95, p. 300.

71. *Dramatic Mirror* (Oct. 30, 1841), 93. Various libretti for *Monsieur De Chalumeaux* were published, including a comic opera (1806, Paris, text M. Auguste and music

P. Gaveaux) and a ballet version (1834, Italy, choreography Giovanni Galzerani, music Cesare Pugni).

72. Monplaisir seasons are in A. Davis, *America's Longest Run*, 92–93; Durang, *History*, v. 5, ch. 90, p. 281; Moore, *Echoes of American Ballet*, 114–18. The libretto for Bartholomin's *Les Deux Roses* was published by the Lyon Theatre in 1838. Hormigón identifies Hippolyte Monplaisir as a student of Blasis (*El Ballet Romántico*, 54).

73. Durang, *History*, v. 5, ch. 93, p. 291.

74. Durang, *History*, v. 5, ch. 96, p. 300–1.

75. On Diamond "á la Elssler," see Berkin, "Antebellum Touring," 50.

76. LCP, Mathias Weaver Diary, Apr. 4, 1840; also Aug. 14, 1841.

77. Nathan, *Dan Emmett*, 143–58; Nowatzky, "Paddy Jumps," 163.

78. A. Davis, *America's Longest Run*, 83–84; Durang, *History*, v. 5, ch. 65, p. 202.

79. Lott, *Love and Theft*, 93.

80. Dumont, "Origin of Minstrelsy."

81. In "Minstrelsy!" (1902), Dumont provides bills of the original Virginia Minstrels, linking them to circuses (HSP Collection 3054, Frank Dumont Minstrelsy Scrapbook, Box 1). See also Lott, *Love and Theft*, 24–25.

82. Dumont, "Origin of Minstrelsy."

83. Dumont, "Origin of Minstrelsy." The term "minstrel" initially referred to musicians, not specifically to blackface players. For example, in 1837 to 1838, prior to formalization of blackface minstrelsy, African American bandleader Francis Johnson and musicians toured Europe, advertising their truly Black band in London as "The American Minstrels" (*The Morning Post*, London, in Jones, *Francis Johnson*, 159). Johnson's performances featured works of Rossini, Mozart, Bellini, Maurer, Rode, and Johnson.

84. FLP Theatre Collection Box 108 and *Public Ledger* (July 2–12, 1847; Apr. 17–May 16, 1848); Dumont, "Golden Days of Minstrelsy." Berkin discusses appropriation of Diamond's name by other performers ("Antebellum Touring," 53).

85. Dumont, "Origin of Minstrelsy." Examples of acts titled with the word "Darkies" include Bourette & Co. at Franklin Hall (Feb. 25–27, 1847, HSP Dumont Minstrelsy Collection); Virginia Serenaders at Chestnut Street Theatre (May 8–16, 1848, FLP Theatre Collection Box 108); Ethiopian Serenaders at Welch's National Amphitheatre (Aug. 1, 1849, FLP Theatre Collection Box 46).

86. Dumont, "Golden Days of Minstrelsy."

87. White and White, *Stylin'*, 20–36, 90–94.

88. See also T. Brown, *History of the American Stage*, 70; Nathan, *Dan Emmett*, 131; Winans, "Early Minstrel Show Music," in *Inside the Minstrel Mask*, 147–48. On blackface "wench" roles, Bean, "Transgressing the Gender Divide," in Bean et al., eds., *Inside the Minstrel Mask*, 245–56; Mahar, *Behind the Burnt Cork Mask*, 312–18; S. Johnson, "Gender Trumps Race," 224, 232–35.

89. Brooks, "Danza española en la escena americana temprana"; Mahar, *Behind the Burnt Cork Mask*, 10–11 and, on blackface performers' skills, 113, 145, 153–54.

90. *Public Ledger* (Mar. 22–31 and Apr. 8–12, 1845).

91. C. V. Hill, "In the Eye of the Beholder," 29; see also 30–32, in Dini, ed., *Dance: American Art*; Gottschild, *Digging the Africanist Presence*, 97–98.

92. On market sites and cultural exchange, see DeVoe, *The Market Book*, 344; Lhamon, *Raising Cain*, ch. 1, pp. 1–55. On plantation dance contests: R. Abrahams,

Singing the Master, 98; White and White, *Stylin'*, 77–78. On blackface dance contests, Berkin, "Antebellum Touring," 46–47.

93. Lhamon, *Raising Cain*, 44–45.

94. Lott, *Love and Theft*, 117; Nathan, *Dan Emmett*, 61–62,72–75, 87–93.

95. Durang, *History*, v. 5, ch. 76, p. 237, on "Master Diamond in a negro dance," Jan. 9, 1844.

96. "American Humor," 219, 215. On minstrelsy, Northerners, and Philadelphians in blackface troupes, see Saxton, "Blackface Minstrelsy and Jacksonian Ideology," 7–8. On various ethnic "delineations" in minstrelsy, Goodall, *Performance and Evolution*, ch. 4.

97. Kennard, "Who Are Our National Poets?," 331–41. On "literary nationalism," Nowatzki, "'Our Only Truly National Poets,'" 363. On Kennard, see Robinson, "The Agony and the Ecstasy of James Kennard Jr."

98. Dickens, *American Notes*, 36. On Juba in England, see S. Johnson, "Gender Trumps Race," 220–47.

99. On national interconnections among Black intellectuals, see Armstrong, *A Fragile Freedom*; Bacon and McClish, "Reinventing the Master's Tools"; Hall, *A Faith Account of the Race*; M. Jones, *All Bound Up Together*; Martin, "The Banneker Literary Institute of Philadelphia."

100. Douglass, *North Star* (Oct. 27, 1848); subsequent quotations, June 29, 1849. On Douglass's writings on blackface, see also Lott, *Love and Theft*, 36–37; Nyong'o, *Amalgamation Waltz*, 125–33.

101. M. Jones suggests the troupe was Gavitts Original Ethiopian Serenaders (*All Bound up Together*, 100). Peterson reports the all-Black Mocking Bird Minstrels appeared later in Philadelphia, 1855–1856 (*The African American Theatre Directory*, 220); I found no documentation of them.

102. Campbell's Minstrels, claiming to be "the oldest band in the United States," played Philadelphia (*Public Ledger*, Apr. 24, 1849; Aug. 3–21, 1850; Dec. 24, 1851; and beyond).

103. Lhamon, *Raising Cain*, 158. On Philadelphia's poorest neighborhood, see Hartley, "Philadelphia's 'Five Points,'" 10–22.

104. Durang, *History*, v. 5, ch. 98, p. 308. The earliest reference I have for such seating in Philadelphia is at the National Theatre (*Public Ledger*, Sept. 2–4, 1840), when ballet dancing and non-blackface plays were produced. Lhamon discusses Black people as theatrical audiences in this period (*Raising Cain*, 154).

105. Lhamon, *Jump Jim Crow*, 2. On Philadelphia's working-class divides, see Laurie, *Working People*, 62–66, 155–56. On anti-Irish sentiment, Schrag, *The Fires of Philadelphia*. On the Irish, "whiteness," and blackface minstrelsy, see An. Gonzalez, "Navigations," 21–25; Nowatzki, "Paddy Jumps Jim Crow." On anti-Black sentiment among some Irish workers, Scharf and Westcott, *History of Philadelphia*, I, 662.

106. Cornish, *Colored American* (Dec. 1, 1838); among his other theater condemnations: Mar. 18, Apr. 22, 1837; Sept. 1, Oct. 28, 1838; May 18, Oct. 5, 1839; Mar. 14, 1840; Apr. 25, 1840; Feb. 20, 1841.

107. Cornish, "The Theatre" (Dec. 9, 1837). Subsequent quotes from *Colored American* (Mar. 6, 1841).

108. *Pennsylvania Freeman* (Apr. 14, 1841), cited in As. Gonzalez, *Visualizing Equality*, 91–92.

109. Morton, *Crania Aegyptiaca*, 1. See also Bay, *The White Image*, 26–35; Malamud,

African Americans and the Classics, 148.

110. Nolan, *A Short History of the Academy of Natural Sciences*, 11–14. On Black Africans in Egypt, see Morton, *Crania Aegyptiaca*, 11. On public dissemination of these views, Frederickson, *The Black Image*, 74–90; W. Stanton, *The Leopard's Spots*, 1–121.

111. Rusert, *Fugitive Science*, 116.

112. Wynter, "Sambos and Minstrels," 151.

113. Nott, letter to Moses Ashley Curtis, c. 1845, quoted in W. Stanton, *The Leopard's Spots*, 78; see also 52–53. The lyric from "Dandy Jim" is in Mahar, *Behind the Burnt-Cork Mask*, 214.

114. On Lewis's *Light and Truth*, and other African American sources of ethnology and "universal history," see Bay, *The White Image in the Black Mind*, 44–46; Dain, *A Hideous Monster of the Mind*, ch. 5; and Rusert, "Types of Mankind: Visualizing Kinship."

115. Schor, *Counting Americans*, I, ch. 3; W. Stanton, *The Leopard's Spots*, 58–65.

116. Pennington, *Text Book of the Origin and History, &c. &c. of the Colored People*. See Bay, 50–52; Hall, *A Faithful Account*, 58–79.

117. Quoted in Stauffer, *The Works of James McCune Smith*, 53. See also Patterson, "An Archaeology of the History of Nineteenth-Century U.S. Anthropology," esp. 465–76.

118. Whipper, "An Appeal to the Colored Citizens," 12.

119. Willson, *Sketches of the Higher Classes*, 5. See Otter, *Philadelphia Stories*, 124–29; Winch, *The Elite of our People*, 1–64.

120. Ethiop, "From Our Brooklyn Correspondent, Brooklyn Heights," *Frederick Douglass' Paper* (Apr. 14, 1854).

121. Jenkins's Inimitable Ethiopian Serenaders at Peale's Museum (*Public Ledger*, Oct. 23, 1848); sheet music with cover illustration, LoC.

122. Douglass, "Dancing as an Exercise," *North Star* (July 21, 1848).

123. Examples of such reports appear in the *Public Ledger* (May 13, 1840; Oct. 9, 1841; June 3, 1842; Jan. 1, 1849). On dance halls, some hosting African American performance, S. Davis, *Parades and Power*, 29, 44; McAllister, *White People Do Not Know*, 28; White and White, *Stylin'*, 93, 103.

124. Dickens, *American Notes*, 36.

125. Taylor and Foster, "Philadelphia in Slices," 38. On Dandy Hall, see Carlisle, *Disorderly City*, 8–9.

126. LCP, *A Guide to the Stranger*, 8.

127. *Public Ledger* (Jan. 14, 16, 18, 1841).

128. *Public Ledger* (Jan. 9, 1840); "Grand Examination Ball" (Jan. 7, 1839); teaching "any dance" (Oct. 1, 1841). Other listings are from *Public Ledger* and city directories of the 1840s.

129. Fisher, *A Philadelphia Perspective*, 213 (Oct. 1, 1848). Dickens quotations, *American Notes*, 39.

130. "Dancing," *Public Ledger* (June 5, 1843); next quotations, "Call Another Set," Public Ledger (June 6, 1843).

131. A. Curtis, *The Botanico-Medical Recorder*, 388. On "Lucy Long," see Mahar, *Behind the Burnt Cork Mask*, 307; Railton, "Miss Lucy Long."

132. "On the Opinions of Phrenologists Touching the Function of the Organ Called Wit," 383.

133. L. or O. Fowler, "Analysis of Mirthfulness," 177–83.
134. *Public Ledger* (June 27, 1843).
135. *Public Ledger* (Aug. 1, 1843).
136. The *Public Ledger* (Oct. 5, 1849) reported a resolution of "The Baptist Association" that dancing was "opposed to the spirit of the Gospel, and prejudicial to the growth of grace in the soul," and should "be habitually discontinued by Christians." Carpenter responded in *Public Ledger* (Nov. 5, 1849).
137. See de Guardiola, "Bits of *Bijou*: The Missing Middle of Durang's 1848 Manual."
138. Johnson's early publications are at LCP Rare Sheet Music Philadelphia 12373.F; and UPenn Kislak Kurt Stein Collection of Francis Johnson Sheet Music, Folio ML410. J66 S7 and Folio M1.J64.
139. C. Jones, *Francis Johnson*, 94.
140. Day, "Fun in Black," in Bean et al., eds., *Inside the Minstrel Mask*, 46–47.
141. C. Jones, *Francis Johnson*, 212 and 156–58; LaBrew, *Francis Johnson*, 20, 25.
142. Quoted in C. Jones, *Francis Johnson*, 244. See also *Poulson's Scrapbook of American Biography*, II (Apr. 8, 1844), III (Apr. 10, 1844).
143. Taylor and Foster, "Philadelphia in Slices," 64.

CHAPTER 5

1. On increasingly class-based entertainments from the 1840s onward, see McConachie, "American Theatre in Context," 147, 151–60. On Philadelphia's class-conscious entertainment choices, S. Davis, *Parades and Power*, esp. 29–30; for New York, Lott, *Love and Theft*, 66, 69. For the role of class in pre–Civil War and wartime developments, see Varon, *Armies of Deliverance*; and Williams, *A People's History of the Civil War*.
2. Douglass, "Address Delivered by Fred'rick Douglass, before the Literary Societies of The Western Reserve College," *Frederick Douglass' Newspaper* (July 21, 1854). Cornel West notes, "*Observation* and *differentness* are the essential guiding notions in natural history" ("Race and Modernity," 77).
3. The theme of "scientific triumphalism" is explicated in Frank, Gleiser, and Thompson, "An Introduction to the Blind Spot," in *The Blind Spot*; also summarized in "How Human Experience Makes Science Possible," by these same authors.
4. Gliddon and Morton corresponded regularly, developing a warm friendship (Meigs, *A Memoir of Samuel George Morton*, 28; Vivian, "George Gliddon in America").
5. *New Orleans Daily Creole* (Oct. 27, 1856), 2. The book was, however, published in Philadelphia, and Nott graduated from University of Pennsylvania medical school.
6. Philadelphia lawyer-scientist Peter A. Browne ranked human races by hair type in *The Classification of Mankind, by the Hair and Wool of their Heads* (1853). On aesthetics of skull shape, see Levine, *Highbrow/Lowbrow*, 222–24; West, "Race and Modernity," 55–86.
7. Fisher, *The Laws of Race*, 5–14.
8. "Address Delivered by Fred'rick Douglass, before the Literary Societies of The Western Reserve College," *Frederick Douglass' Newspaper* (July 21, 1854), 2. The speech was much revised before and after its commencement delivery (Douglass, *Life and Times*, 455–57). See also Bay, *The White Image*, 66–71; Gilroy, *The Black Atlantic*, 59–60.

9. Stauffer, *The Works of James McCune Smith*, 53.
10. McCune Smith, quoted in Dain, *A Hideous Monster of the Mind*, 246–47.
11. Huggins, *Harlem Renaissance*, 266; also 248–57.
12. McCune Smith's "Heads of the Coloured People" appeared in *Frederick Douglass' Paper* (Mar. 25, 1852–Nov. 17, 1854).
13. Delany, "Political Destiny of the Colored Race," italics in original. See also Bay, *The White Image*, 63–66; Gilroy, *The Black Atlantic*, 19–37.
14. Beatty, "Martin Delany and Egyptology," 78–99.
15. "John S. Rock," *Black History Now* online, and Bay, *The White Image*, 56–57. Bay claims Rock attended the "American Medical College"; no school of that name appears in available sources. The Eclectic Medical College of Philadelphia seems a possibility for Rock's education, since this school appears to have graduated another Black student, James J. Bias, in 1852 ("Dr. J. J. Gould Bias," *Colored Conventions Project* online). See also H. Abrahams, *Extinct Medical Schools of Nineteenth-Century Philadelphia*, 245, and "Extinct Philadelphia Medical Schools," online. I am grateful to Matthew Herbison of Drexel University College of Medicine, Archives and Special Collections, for a discussion of this matter.
16. *The Liberator* (Mar. 12, 1858), in Bay, *The White Image*, 57–58; Herschthal, *The Science of Abolition*, 221–22.
17. Malamud, *African Americans and the Classics*, 178–82; Rusert, *Fugitive Science*, 14, 76–77, 113, 177; W. Stanton, *The Leopard's Spots*, 161–74.
18. Examples of "Black Shakers" acts listed in Philadelphia's *Public Ledger* newspaper: Virginia Serenaders, Jan. 16–17, and Sept. 10–12, 1850; Campbell Minstrels, Kimberley's Operatic Troupe, Aug. 7, 9, 17, 20, 21, 1850; and Myers & Chambers' Great Ethiopian Burlesque Opera Troupe, Feb. 6–16, 1854.
19. Lawrence, *Strong on Music*, I, 286, 420; Dumont, "Golden Days of Minstrelsy"; Mahar, *Behind the Burnt-Cork Mask*, 40, 105, 325. Madison's Female Opera Troupe played Philadelphia, "assisted by Wood & Christy's Ethiopian Minstrels" (*Public Ledger*, Mar. 1, 1855), and then with Myers & Chambers' Ethiopian Minstrels (*Public Ledger*, June 16, 1855).
20. *Virginia Mummy* is discussed in Lhamon, *Jump Jim Crow*, 20, 26, 46–52; script 159–77.
21. Durang mentions Brower dancing in *Virginia Mummy* (*History*, v. 5, ch. 96, p. 306). Lhamon noted insertion of "Jump Jim Crow" (*Jump Jim Crow*, 165).
22. Named for the second-century Greek physician who, Lhamon notes, "was an early voice in scientific racism" (*Jump Jim Crow*, p. 426, n. 8).
23. Day, *The Mummy's Curse*; Wolfe, "Bringing Egypt to America," 1–20, and "From Eternity to Here." Henry Box Brown's 1849 release from the shipping crate in which he mailed himself to Philadelphia from southern slavery might be seen as related to such mummy-unwrapping; Philadelphia did not play a role in Box Brown's later performance life (see D. Brooks, *Bodies in Dissent*, 66–130; Rusert, *Fugitive Science*, 113–48).
24. Branson, "'Barnum Is Undone in His Own Province.'"
25. *Wisconsin Express* (July 9, 1850), quoted in Wolfe, "Bringing Egypt to America," 10.
26. "Gliddon's Mummy vs. Blitz," *Spirit of the Times* (March 1, 1851), quoted in Wolfe, "Bringing Egypt to America," 13. Blitz identically quotes this incident in his autobiography, *Fifty Years in the Magic Circle*, 178–79.

27. Philadelphia performances are in FLP Theatre Collection, Boxes 9, 10, 108 and vol. 12; HSP Dumont Minstrel Collection; UPenn, Kislak Collection 1384, vols. 12, 13; LCP Theatre Collection vols. 1, 21, Box 42; *Poulson's Scrapbook of Philadelphia History*, v. 1; *Public Ledger*; Durang, *History*; Wilson, *History of the Philadelphia Theatre*.

28. UPenn Kislak Collection 1384, "Theatricals in Philadelphia" Scrapbooks v. 12, Mar. 5, 1857.

29. Sutton, "Fellows Find." The bread giveaway is in *Poulson's Scrapbook of Philadelphia History*, v. 8, p. 56.

30. *Public Ledger* (May 25, 1853), 2. On minstrelsy's parody of class stratification, while attempting to reach audiences across class lines, see Cockrell, *Demons of Disorder*, 57–58; Mahar, *Behind the Burnt Cork Mask*, 4–5, 10–11, 18, 25–26. On penetration of minstrelsy into middle-class homes, Dunson, "The Minstrel in the Parlor."

31. *Public Ledger* (Aug. 22, 23, 1853). Versions of this work were played in Jan. 1855 (FLP Box 44), Sept.–Oct. 1856 (*Public Ledger*), Feb. 22, 1858 (HSP Dumont Minstrelsy Collection).

32. HSP "*The Xlanties; or Forty Thieves* . . . Phila. 1857."

33. Sanford, *Sanford's Melodies*, 1.

34. *Public Ledger*; FLP Theatre Collection Boxes 1, 44, 108; HSP Dumont Minstrelsy Collection; LCP Playbills, v. 1; UPenn Kislak Collection 1384, v. 12, 13.

35. Boromé, "The Vigilant Committee of Philadelphia," 328–29; Delany, *The Condition, Elevation, Emigration*, 154–55; Smedley, *Race in North America*, 240–43; Scharf and Westcott, *History of Philadelphia*, v. 1, 701, 734.

36. LoC, Dred Scott vs. Sandford, 404–5. See M. Jones, *Birthright Citizens*.

37. Durang, *History*, v. 6, ch. 129, p. 401.

38. Quotations in Durang, *History*, v. 6, ch. 116, p. 368.

39. Listings in FLP Theatre Collection Box 44, 46; *Public Ledger* (Oct.–Dec. 1853).

40. "Places of Public Amusement," *Putnam's*, 143.

41. Fletcher and Irelan, "Staging 'Americanization,'" 95–96; Frederickson, *The Black Image*, 97–129; Nathans, "Staging Slavery," 219–20. "Colored" seating: FLP Theatre Collection Boxes 44, 46 (Sept.–Oct. 1853).

42. Listings are found in the *Public Ledger* (Jan. 9 and 30, 1855); FLP Theatre Collection Box 1 (Oct. 10, 1856); HSP Academy of Music (Sept. 17, 1859). On *Uncle Tom* stagings and other melodramatic and minstrel works "wed[ding] cruelty and festivity," see Hartman, *Scenes of Subjection*, 25, and 26–32. On William Wells Brown's "sly revision" of *Uncle Tom's Cabin* for the stage, *The Escape, a Leap for Freedom*, see D. Brooks, *Bodies in Dissent*, 1, 12–13.

43. *Public Ledger* (Oct. 10, 1853). This work appeared at Sanford's throughout the decade.

44. LoC Special Collections, Thr. A9 Box 1 no. 7, Sanford's Opera Troupe, Jan. 21, 1861.

45. *Dan Rice's American Humorist & Shaksperian Jester, Song & Joke Book*, 29, HSP Pam PN6161.R5 1860.

46. Sanford, probably Aug. 15, 1861, cited in Meer, *Uncle Tom Mania*, 64; see also 66–78, 99.

47. HSP Dumont Minstrelsy Collection; FLP Theatre Collection Boxes 35, 108. Boyd's ads, *Public Ledger* (Mar. 20–21, 1854); Melodeon shows, *Public Ledger* (Sept. 16, 30, 1856).

48. Brower, "Happy Uncle Tom: A Celebrated Plantation Scene," 5–8.

49. Ellacott, "The Free and Easies"; Rodger, *Champagne Charlie and Pretty Jemima*, 18, 31–34; HSP Campbell Collection v. 2, "Arch St. to Sixth St.," Jan. 25, 1914; *Public Ledger* (Jan. 30, 1854; Apr. 4–May 6, 1854; Oct. 20, 1854; Jan. 9–Feb. 20, 1855); UPenn Kislak, "Theatricals in Philadelphia," Collection 1384, v. 12.

50. "Our Minor Theatres," *Poulson's Scrapbook of Philadelphia History*, v. 10, p. 69 (Oct. 25, 1858).

51. Rodger, *Champagne Charlie*, 49–50. On saloons hosting low-class shows, see Lott, *Love and Theft*, 74–75.

52. "Philadelphia," *New York Musical Review* (Apr. 3, 1858), 101.

53. Peitzman, *A New and Untried Course*; Longshore quote, p. 5.

54. E. C. Stanton, *History of Woman Suffrage*, 379.

55. Peitzman, *A New and Untried Course*, 17–27; see Atwater, *Women Medical Doctors*, 74, 239.

56. Meigs, *Females and Their Diseases*, 41–42; Venus quotation, 47; final quotation, 44.

57. On "delicacy," Meigs, *Females and their Diseases*, 18–19, 36, 43, 50.

58. The terms "desexed" or "unsexed" expressed fears of women stepping into traditionally male spheres. See E. C. Stanton, *History of Woman Suffrage*, 429; Peitzman, *A New and Untried Course*, 8, 35; "Physicians in Petticoats," *The Ledger* (South Carolina; Aug. 20, 1856).

59. Drexel University College of Medicine, Legacy Center, Matriculation Books, FMC (Sept. 13, 1852–Jan. 25, 1853). On women medical lecturers, see Atwater, *Women Medical Doctors*, 259; Morantz-Sanchez, *Sympathy and Science*, 39, 42, 46. Rusert chronicles Sarah Mapps Douglass's engagement with science in *Fugitive Science*, 184–216.

60. Buckley, "Paratheatricals and Popular Stage Entertainment," in *Cambridge History of American Theatre*, 457; Scharf and Westcott, *History of Philadelphia*, I, 700, 710–11.

61. "Lectures and Lecturers," *Putnam's*, 321.

62. *Philadelphia Inquirer* (Mar. 17, 1854), 2.

63. "The Dress Reformers," *Ballou's* (Mar. 21, 1857), 189. See also Lange, *Picturing Political Power*, 44–45; Morantz-Sanchez, *Sympathy and Science*, 37–38; E. C. Stanton *History of Woman Suffrage*, 469–71.

64. *Public Ledger* (Feb. 7, 1855). Gardner's act at Sanford's, *Public Ledger* (Sept. 1, 1856); Cool White's in UPenn Kislak, Theatricals in Philadelphia, v. 12 (Mar. 5, 1857). Mahar, *Behind the Burnt Cork Mask*, 39, notes the prevalence of women's rights parodies in blackface acts.

65. For example, "Singular Debut of Lola Montez at Paris," in *Alexander's Express Messenger* (June 5, 1844), detailing Montez's "piquant eccentricity" in life and on stage. On Montez's self-fashioning, see Strom, *Fortune, Fame, and Desire*, 44–48.

66. The Arch Street Theatre was named for manager Conner in 1850–51 (Wilson, *History of the Philadelphia Theatre*, 38–41). *Lola Montes* played Conner's on June 27, 1850 (Conner's Theatre Playbills, NYPL). On Clementine De Bar, *New York Clipper* (Sept. 8, 1877); on Turnbull in this play, Durang, *History*, v. 6, ch. 101, p. 320. The Chestnut also showed *Lola Montes* (*Public Ledger*, Nov. 18, 1851). Later, Coyne's revised play was titled *Lola Montez, or, Catching a Governor*.

67. Ireland, *Records of the New York Stage*, II, 594–95; see also Gotcher, "The Career of Lola Montez," 75–77, 185–86. Like Gotcher, B. Seymour attempts to cut through fabrications about Montez (many disseminated by Montez herself) in *Lola Montez: A Life*.

68. Gotcher, "The Career of Lola Montez," lists Montez in "La Sevilliana" and "El Olano," p. 20. On "La Lassaleada," Durang, *History*, v. 6, ch. 108, p. 346.

69. On Spanish dancers throughout Europe, see Plaza Orellana, *Los bailes españoles en Europa*. On Montez's manipulation of her image, Jeschke, "Lola Montez and Spanish Dance," 31–44.

70. Moore, "George Washington Smith," *Dance Index*.

71. The *Mirror* (Dec. 30, 1851), quoted in Lawrence, *Strong on Music*, II, 227–28.

72. Moore, "George Washington Smith," *Dance Index*, 110; *Morning Herald* quote on same page.

73. Gotcher, "The Career of Lola Montez," 124–25.

74. Unidentified critic quoted in Moore, "George Washington Smith," *Dance Index*, 111.

75. Durang, *History*, v. 6, ch. 113, p. 360.

76. *Public Ledger* (Jan. 17, 1852).

77. *Public Ledger* (Jan. 19, 1852).

78. *Public Ledger* (Jan. 20, 1852). Philadelphia newspaper *Fitzgerald's City Item* substantiated this assessment (Jan. 24 and 31, 1852), cited in Gotcher, "The Career of Lola Montez," 141.

79. *Public Ledger* (Feb. 2, 1852). Notice of the wax statue, *Public Ledger* (Mar. 18, 1852).

80. Durang, *History*, v. 6, ch. 108, p. 346–47.

81. Durang, *History*, v. 6, ch. 108, p. 347, including Durang's comment on *Maid of Saragossa*.

82. See, for example, Gotcher, "The Career of Lola Montez," 194–95.

83. The favorable report is in *The Press* (Aug. 3, 1857) reprinted from the *Hamilton* [Canada] *Spectator*; the critical report in *The Press* (Sept. 4, 1857). On Philadelphia lectures, *Public Ledger* (Nov. 7, 12, 1857).

84. *Public Ledger* (Oct. 21, 1858).

85. *The Press* (Dec. 5, 1857).

86. HSP *The Xlantues; or Forty Thieves*, act II, sc. 5.

87. Book notice, *Philadelphia Inquirer* (June 7, 1858). The published version was titled *The Lectures of Lola Montez: With a Full and Complete Autobiography of her Life*.

88. *The Press* (Jan. 20 and 26, 1860).

89. *The Press* reported her illness on Aug. 7, 1860; on Jan. 21, 1861, her death.

90. "Lola Montez, Countess of Landsfeldt," *Frank Leslie's Illustrated Newspaper* (Feb. 2, 1861).

91. Durang, *History*, v. 6, and *Public Ledger*.

92. Durang, *History*, v. 6, ch. 112, p. 358, and ch. 114, p. 364; *Taming a Tartar* discussed on ch. 112, p. 358.

93. Durang, *History*, v. 5, ch. 96, p. 303; subsequent quote, same page. Comments on fall 1852 season, v. 6, ch. 120, pp. 378–79.

94. Durang, *History*, v. 6, ch. 127, p. 395. See also Meisner, *Marius Petipa*, 62 and 353, n. 36. I am grateful for email conversations with Alan Jones on Mathias, Jan.–Feb. 2025.

95. *Public Ledger* (Jan. 2, 1851). Durang's comments, *History*, v. 6, ch. 127, p. 395. On versions of *Paquita*, see Meisner, *Marius Petipa*, 55–58.

96. Joseph M. Church edited *Bizarre: For Fireside and Wayside* in the early 1850s and may have authored the comments on Mathias, found primarily in the magazine's January and February 1854 issues, covering the Ravels at the Walnut Street Theatre. This early notice of a "Russian" as opposed to "French" (or "Italian") shaping of ballet merits further investigation. Mathias appears also to have staged several ballets for the Ravel company (with gratitude to Alan Jones for this information).

97. UPenn Kislak, "Philadelphia Theatricals," Apr. 12, 1854; comments on *Jocko*, Dec. 15, 1856.

98. Mora, "Pepita Soto," 189–90, 225.

99. Durang, *History*, v. 6, ch. 121, p. 38 and ch. 117, p. 372. On Smith partnering Soto, see Moore, "George Washington Smith," 115–16.

100. The positive review was in *Spirit of the Times* (1857), 288; Meredith's remarks, UPenn Kislak, Philadelphia Theatrical Commentaries (Jan. 14, 1853).

101. HSP Academy of Music Scrapbook, Jan. 24, 1859; Mora, "Pepita Soto," 220.

102. *Public Ledger* (Nov. 12–21, 1855). The troupe included María Arrego, Josefa Barquera, Marina Cortez, Valentina Rius, Manuela Moctezuma, Josefa Pacheco, Fernando Cabrera, Agustina Llorente, José Arrego, and perhaps other Spanish dancers. I am grateful to Laura Hormigón for clarifying this listing in emails of Nov. 1–3, 2020.

103. Durang, *History*, v. 6, ch. 106, p. 341; see also Moore, "Mary Ann Lee," in *Chronicles*, 117; Wilson, *History of the Philadelphia Theatre*, 463.

104. Identified in sources as American are: Dawes (Durang, *History*, v. 6, ch. 115, p. 365); the Reeds (Durang, *History*, v. 4, ch. 58, p. 172, and v. 5, ch. 64, p. 197); the Vallee sisters (T. Brown, *History of the American Stage*, 365); Walters (Ireland, *Records*, II, p. 387); L. Wells (M. Winter, "Augusta Maywood," in *Chronicles*, 119); William Wood (Philadelphia City Directories, 1850–1859); and Hemple (Philadelphia City Directories, 1856–1860). Other names that, I conjecture, were American appear in newspapers and chronologies. Typically, continental European dancers were listed as "M'lle" or "Signora," or the like. The "Miss" designation was used for U.S. and English dancers. This is likely a fraction of the U.S. dancers with balletic aspirations appearing in the period.

105. *Public Ledger* (Sept. 19–23, 1851).

106. *Poulson's Scrapbook of Philadelphia History*, v. 4 (Apr. 28, 1855).

107. Wilson, *History of the Philadelphia Theatre*, 48.

108. Durang, *History*, v. 5, ch. 89, p. 279, The actors Durang mentioned were Joseph Jefferson Sr. (1829–1905), William Warren (1767–1832), and William Francis (fl. 1793–1820).

109. Meredith, Philadelphia Theatrical Commentaries (Nov. 15, 1854), UPenn Kislak Center.

110. HSP "Charter and Prospectus of the Opera House," 5.

111. "Philadelphia Amusements," *Poulson's Scrapbook of Philadelphia History*, v. 6, p. 89 (*Pennsylvania Inquirer*, Feb. 4, 1854).

112. Bushman, *Refinement of America*, 410.

113. Bushman, *Refinement of America*, 370; see also 409–11.
114. HSP Collection 3150, Academy of Music Scrapbook—programs, playbills, scrapbooks (1857–1860); and Academy of Music, "Our History," online.
115. "Local Affairs, Academy of Music," *Poulson's Scrapbook of Philadelphia History*, v. 9, p. 6 (Jan. 1, 1857), also describing the interior.
116. On the Ronzani troupe, see Celi, "The Arrival of the Great Wonder of Ballet," 165–80, in Garafola, *Rethinking the Sylph*; Scafidi, Zambon, and Albano, *La Danza in Italia*, 36, 109–10, 120–21. Louise/Luigia Lamoureux had danced in London, Madrid, Venice, Naples, and Turin; Baratti in Milan, Turin, London, and possibly Paris, according to European newspapers then tracking ballet and opera. I am grateful for assistance from Francesca Falcone, Jim Fuller, and Patrizia Veroli in tracking these dancers.
117. Undated clipping (summer 1857?), HSP 3150, "Academy of Music Scrapbook."
118. Undated clipping (Sept. 10, 1857?), HSP 3150, "Academy of Music Scrapbook." See also Moore, *Images of the Dance*, 74. Ronzani's troupe, although called "world renowned," was only formed for this U.S. engagement. On Maywood in this work, see Celi, "Borri, Pasquale," *International Encyclopedia of Dance*, online.
119. "Musical and Dramatic" column, *Evening Journal* (Sept. 15, 1857); Ronzani/Blitz comparison, "The Ballet 'Faust,'" *Evening Journal* (Sept. 14, 1857); subsequent criticism, *The Press* (Sept. 15, 1857), HSP Collection 3150, "Academy of Music Scrapbook."
120. "The Ballet," Daily News (Sept. 21, 1857), HSP Collection 3150.
121. *The Press* (Sept. 17, 1857), HSP Collection 3150.
122. "The Academy of Music—The Ballet of 'Faust,'" Evening Bulletin (Sept. 17, 1857), HSP Collection 3150.
123. *New York Tribune* (Sept. 17, 1857), HSP Collection 3150.
124. Undated clipping (probably mid-September 1857), HSP Collection 3150.
125. "The Ballet," Daily News (Sept. 21, 1857); the shortening of *Faust* noted in "Academy of Music," clipping (Sept. 22, 1857), HSP Collection 3150.
126. "Evening Journal. Musical and Dramatic," clipping, (Oct. 1, 1857), HSP Collection 3150. The *Press* quote and review from same date, same collection. Ronzani's libretto was published in Philadelphia (1857) in English.
127. "Academy of Music," *Sunday Transcript* (Oct. 4, 1857), HSP Collection 3150.
128. "Academy of Music," *Sunday Transcript*, and "The Ballet," *Sunday Dispatch* (Oct. 4, 1857), HSP Collection 3150.
129. "Academy of Music," undated clipping (perhaps Dec. 14, 1857), HSP Collection 3150. A version of *Le Délire d'un Peintre* (1843, choreography Perrot, for Elssler) was presented by the Monplaisir troupe, Walnut St. Theatre in Aug. 1849 (Durang, *History*, v. 5, ch. 96, p. 300).
130. "Musical. Academy of Music," *City Item* (Sept. 26, 1857), HSP Collection 3150.
131. *The Press* (Sept. 29, 1859).
132. *Philadelphia Inquirer* (Oct. 4, 1859); subsequent quotation, *The Press* (Oct. 13, 1859).
133. Carpenter, *Amateur's Preceptor*, 7. I have no record of a dancer or dancing master at the Paris Opera of the period named G. De Granville (or a version thereof). Many thanks to Emmanuelle Delattre-Destemberg and Nadine Meisner for assistance in this matter.
134. Nott, *Types of Mankind*, 313.
135. Durang, *Dancer's Own Book*, 80–92.

136. Durang, *Fashionable Dancer's Casket*, 177; on "laws," 17, 44, 45, 70, 188. Barnett's play was at the Chestnut in fall 1853 (Durang, *History*, v. 6, ch. 116, p. 367, and ch. 124, p. 389). A likely parody of this work by Sanford's troupe was *The Frightened Family* (*Public Ledger*, Sept. 17, 1855).

137. O. Johnson, *Amusements*, 12; subsequent quotations, 13.

138. Halttunen, *Confidence Men and Painted Women*, 167.

139. Cartwright, "Dr. Cartwright on the Caucasians and the Africans," 50.

140. Ferrero, *Art of Dancing*, 76.

141. Fisher, *A Philadelphia Perspective*, 283 (Oct. 26, 1857). A different view of Phoebe Rush's social philosophy, including her employment of Francis Johnson for her balls, is in C. Jones, *Francis Johnson*, 58–60, 113.

142. Fisher, *A Philadelphia Perspective*, 233 (Jan. 17, 1850); "deficiency of female beauty," 256 (Mar. 26, 1856).

143. *Public Ledger* (Jan. 14, 1856; Sept. 26, 1854, Mazarin; Sept. 7, 1855, Duff; and Sept. 19, 1854, Gaszynski).

144. Leonard Koecker Diary, LCP 1852: 119921.D; 1860: 119920.D.

145. In comparison, Frederick Law Olmsted writes of elite Black socializing, dancing lessons, and balls in 1850s Alabama and Louisiana (*Journey in the Seaboard Slave States*, 554, 646).

146. *Poulson's Scrapbook of Philadelphia History*, v. 9, p. 59 (June 25, 1857). See S. Davis, *Parades and Power*.

147. Armstrong, *A Fragile Freedom*, 120–46; Rusert, *Fugitive Science*, 181–218.

148. E. Lapsansky, "Friends, Wives, and Strivings," 3–24; G. Nash, *Forging Freedom*, 217–21, 247–52, 265.

149. *Poulson's Scrapbook of Philadelphia History* points to "minor theatres and concert-rooms" where shows "consist of vocal music, dancing, negro minstrelsy, and entertainments of a similar character" (Oct. 25, 1858); that source names McDonough's Gaieties, Thomeuf's Varieties, and Long's Varieties (Feb. 27, 1859).

150. Souder, "The Mysteries and Miseries of Philadelphia," Evening Bulletin, HSP UPA/Ph HN80.P5M97 1853a. On lower-class sociality, sometimes interracial, see Cockrell, *Demons of Disorder*, 82–86; Ulle, "Popular Black Music in Nineteenth Century Philadelphia," 20–28.

151. *Public Ledger* (Nov. 21, 1856; also Feb. 6, Nov. 2, 1850; Jan. 21, 1853; Feb. 24, Oct. 21, 1854). William Bobo's *Glimpses of New York City by a South Carolinian* (1852) describes a saloon/dance house in New York's Five Points neighborhood (to which Philadelphia's Lombard–South Street corridor was compared), where "piebald" (mixed-race) revelers drank, smoked, and danced "cotillions" in what Bobo regarded "a most disgusting and revolting manner" (p. 96).

152. Souder, "Mysteries and Miseries of Philadelphia."

153. Dillon, *New World Drama*, 28; Levine, *Highbrow/Lowbrow*, esp. 206–30.

CHAPTER 6

1. See Dillon, *New World Drama*, 16–17.

2. Fisher, *A Philadelphia Perspective* (Sept. 24, 1847), 200.

3. Durang, *History*, v. 5, ch. 84, p. 264, speaking of Irishman Mr. Bennie's lack of "a thorough schooling and practice in the academies." The association of ballet

with France remained strong, whatever the dancers' backgrounds; Ronzani's mostly Italian troupe at Philadelphia's Academy of Music "produces all the Ballets after the French school" (*New York Herald*, Dec. 23, 1861, quoted in Rodger, *Champagne Charlie*, 48).

4. "M'lle Louise Lamoureux," *Ballou's* (Jan. 16, 1858), 33.

5. W. Wood, *Personal Recollections*, 368.

6. Schneider, "Ravel Family," 319; Swift, *Belles and Beaux*, 75–80.

7. Durang, *History*, v. 6, ch. 132, p. 410, on performance at the Walnut Street, July 9, 1855. Newspapers like the *Dramatic Mirror* and *Public Ledger*, and managers like William Wood, praised the Ravel troupe's quality and appeal.

8. Exceptions are Margaret Fuller, editor of the *Dial* (Boston); and Sarah Josepha Hale, editor of *Godey's Lady's Book* (Philadelphia). See also Rosenman, *Unauthorized Pleasures*, 9–12.

9. Lehman notes that some Americans associated anything French with "corrupt and libertine monarchy, . . . mob behavior and violence" ("Virtue and Virtuosity," 170). The efflorescence of "debauching" dancing schools in Philadelphia was blamed by some on French aristocrats fleeing revolution (Jable, "Aspects of Moral Reform," 347).

10. Halttunen, *Confidence Men and Painted Women*, 156.

11. Ludlow, *Dramatic Life as I Found It*, 362. Subsequent Durang quotations, *History*, v. 3, ch. 37, p. 244. Examples of "Romantic ballet" are found in period sources: Durang, *History*, v. 6, ch. 104, p. 335, and ch. 112, p. 358; and *Public Ledger* advertisement for the Chestnut Street Theatre (Nov. 11, 1840) and for the Arch Street Theatre (Dec. 1–3, 1845). The term is found in more contemporary sources such as Cordova, "The Romantic Ballet in France"; Foster, *Corporealities*, 4–7; Hormigón, *El ballet romántico*; and Kant, "The Soul of the Shoe," 193, 196.

12. Hammond, "Clues to Ballet Technique" and "Steps Through Time"; Jowitt, *Time and the Dancing Image*, 37–40; Kant, *The Soul of the Shoe*, 190–92.

13. *Public Ledger* (Nov. 20 and Dec. 23, 1839; Dec. 12, 1840; July 8, 1841).

14. Chaffee, "A Chart to the American Souvenir Lithographs," 22.

15. Mahar, *Behind the Burnt Cork Mask*, 8–9, 353. Winans argues that "the *real* essence of minstrelsy was *burlesque*" of social classes ("Early Minstrel Show Music, 1843–1852," in Bean et al., eds., *Inside the Minstrel Mask*, 160).

16. On circuits outside major cities, see Berkin, "Antebellum Touring," 44–45.

17. Mahar, *Behind the Burnt Cork Mask*, 22; LoC, "Stop dat knocking at de door" (1847). Winnemore (1815–1851) was born and died in Philadelphia; the Winnemore Serenaders performed in the city often (*Public Ledger*, Nov. 8–27, 1847, and Oct. 14, 1849; FLP Theatre Collection, Box 108, Mar. 1–3, 1849, and Sept. 18, 1849). "Ernani," *Campbell's Melodies, Arranged for the Piano-forte* (1848?), Washington State University Libraries Digital Collection.

18. Harvard Theatre Collection, Christy Minstrels, playbill, n.d.; *New York Herald* (Oct. 1, 1856).

19. FLP Theatre Collection Box 108, July 10, 1845.

20. *Public Ledger* (May 25, 1853).

21. Wittmann, "Kelly and Leon's Minstrels," blog; Bean, "Transgressing the Gender Divide," in Bean et al., eds., *Inside the Minstrel Mask*, 251–53. I have no record of Leon in Philadelphia. On Cubas, see G. Curtis, "Editor's Easy Chair," 849; Mora, "Sounds of Spain," 274.

22. FLP Theatre Collection Box 34, Mar. 26, 1845; *Shin-de-Heel-La*, Box 108, May 8, 1848.

23. Dillon, *New World Drama*, 19; Roach, *Cities of the Dead*, 5–6.

24. Sanford's choice to name his Philadelphia minstrel hall "the American Opera House" exemplifies minstrels' sense of creating an art distinctly *of* the United States.

25. Mahar, *Behind the Burnt Cork Mask*, 23, 37.

26. FLP Theatre Collection Box 108, Sept. 18, 1849; HSP Dumont Minstrelsy Collection, Jan. 21, 1850.

27. On the predominance of Spanish-related themes in ballet's national dances of this period, see Brooks, "Danza española en la escena americana temprana."

28. Nott, *Types of Mankind*, 67, 94, 115, 243, 405, 412.

29. *Public Ledger* (Dec. 31, 1842, and thereafter).

30. Sanford and Horn: FLP Theatre Collection Box 108, May 8, 16, 1848, and HSP Dumont Minstrelsy Collection, Feb. 19, 1848; Brower's version, *Public Ledger* (Mar. 10, 1849); Miss Vallee in *Wept of Wish Ton Wish*, in Wilson, *Philadelphia Theatre*, 709 (Aug. 2–31, 1847, and July 12–13, 1848).

31. Morton, *Crania Americana*, 31; Morton expanded this view in *Crania Aegyptiaca*.

32. Morton, *Crania Americana*, 87. Nott quotation from *Types of Mankind*, 263, illustration figure 185.

33. Lhamon, *Raising Cain*, 2. On African American dance as the foundation of American choreography, see Malone, *Steppin' on the Blues*, 38, also citing Ralph Ellison's lecture at Harvard University, Dec. 1, 1973. Malone notes that dance demonstrates minstrelsy's "strongest debt to African Americans" (p. 52).

34. London playbill of June 19, 1843, quoted in Slout, "Brown's Burnt-Cork History," online.

35. T. Brown, "Early History of Negro Minstrelsy," quoted in Gottschild, *Digging the Africanist Presence*, 95. Lott quote, *Love and Theft*, 51–52; see also 30, 35, 41.

36. FLP Frank Dumont, "Golden Days of Minstrelsy."

37. FLP Frank Dumont, "Golden Days of Minstrelsy." See also Lomax Hawes and Carpenter, *The Georgia Sea Island Singers*, 14.

38. Huggins, *Harlem Renaissance*, 249. See also Cockrell, "Of Soundscapes and Blackface."

39. Gottschild, *Digging the Africanist Presence*, 83, 99, 101. On "signifying" of movement in Black social contexts, see Hazzard-Donald, *Jookin'*, 64; White and White, *Stylin'*, 101.

40. Hartman, *Scenes of Subjection*, 8, 67. See also Gilroy, *The Black Atlantic*, ch. 3.

41. DeFrantz addressed blackface minstrelsy and Black audiences in a presentation to the Columbia Studies in Dance Seminar, Mar. 1, 2021 (video no longer available): "Black people loved minstrel shows, when they were any good," allowing for spaces where versions of minstrelsy might be something other than "a lever towards disavowal and debasement" (1 hr., 27 min., 37 seconds). See also Cornish, *Colored American* (Mar. 6, 1841); *New Orleans Daily Creole* (Oct. 8, 1856; Jan. 1, 1857); Nyong'o, *Amalgamation Waltz*, 120.

42. Lhamon, *Raising Cain*, 44–45; see also 31. Also addressing this topic are Hartman, *Scenes of Subjection*, 57; Mahar, *Behind the Burnt Cork Mask*, 333–35, 349–50; Ndiaye, *Scripts of Blackness*, 187–234.

43. Mintz, "Historical Context"; "Trans-Atlantic Slave Trade—Estimates"; "United States Abolition and Anti-Slavery Timeline."
44. Easton, *Treatise on the Intellectual Character*, 36.
45. Holloway, *Africanisms in American Culture*, 1–17; Malone, *Steppin' on the Blues*, 24–26.
46. Daniel, *Caribbean and Atlantic Diaspora Dance*, 14–15, 42–54; Malone, *Steppin' on the Blues*, chs. 1–3; C. Smith, *Creolization of American Culture*, 180; Welsh Asanti, "Commonalities in African Dance," 144–50; P. Wood, "'Gimme de Kneebone Bent,'" in Myers, ed., *The Black Tradition*, 7–8. See also Chasteen, *National Rhythms*; Gottschild, *Digging the Africanist Presence*; Hazzard-Donald, *Jookin'*; Herskovits, *The Myth of the Negro Past*; Southern, *The Music of Black Americans*; Stuckey, "Christian Conversion"; K. Thompson, *Ring Shout*. On the drive "to locate an originary or definitive point . . . of a particular act" and "to sift through authentic and derivative performances," see Hartman, *Scenes of Subjection*, 57.
47. R. Abrahams, *Singing the Master*, 93–94; Hazzard-Donald, *Jookin'*, 27–30 (on the *susa*, a gourd violin); Nathan, *Dan Emmett*, 153–54; Southern, *The Music of Black Americans*, 171–72. On continuities between African and African American music, see A. Lomax, "Homogeneity of African-New World Negro Musical Style" (LoC).
48. Watson, *Annals*, I, 351–52, and II, 265. G. Nash discusses "differences in language and culture among West African subgroups" of enslaved Philadelphians and the endurance of such distinctions (*Forging Freedom*, 11).
49. Hazzard-Donald, *Jookin'*, 39–41; P. Wood, "'Gimme de Kneebone Bent,'" 9–10.
50. Diana Taylor writes, "Performances [actions, behaviors] function as vital acts of transfer, transmitting social knowledge, memory, and a sense of identity through reiterated . . . behavior" (*The Archive and the Repertoire*, 2). This repertoire, allowing "for individual agency" in the act of live transmission (p. 20), both continues and changes.
51. S. Davis, *Parades and Power*, 35, 44; Ritter, *Philadelphia and her Merchants*, 22; Southern, *The Music of Black Americans*, 149.
52. Du Bois, *The Philadelphia Negro*, 220–21.
53. Heckscher, "Our National Poetry," 19–24; Hinton, "Black Dance in American History," 4; Smedley, *Race in North America*, 109–10.
54. Hazzard-Donald, *Jookin'*, 16–19; Stuckey, "Christian Conversion," 39–58.
55. Heckscher, "Our National Poetry," 27.
56. Daniel, *Caribbean and Atlantic Diaspora Dance*, 3, 47–54; Roach, *Cities of the Dead*, xi; Smedley, *Race in North America*, 61, 96, 108.
57. Heckscher, "Our National Poetry," 24. See also Manuel, *Creolizing Contradance*, 1–50.
58. Szwed and Marks, "The Afro-American Transformation of European Set Dances," 29–32.
59. G. Nash, *Forging Freedom*, 151; Southern, *The Music of Black Americans*, 107; HSP Frank Johnson Portrait, Record Number 2293, Ferdinand Julius Dreer collection 0175.
60. Gilroy, *The Black Atlantic*, 3; also 15, 73–75, 199.
61. Huggins, *Harlem Renaissance*, 251; Nathan, *Dan Emmett*, 71–93.
62. Among songs mentioning the shuffle: "De Long Island N——r" and "The Band of N——rs! From Ole Virginny State" (Nathan, *Dan Emmett*, 84). Shuffling, in

imitation and admiration of William Henry Lane (Juba), is mentioned in Keeler, "Three Years as a Negro Minstrel" (1869).

63. On "akimbo" posture, see Lhamon, *Raising Cain*, 44–45; C. Smith, *Creolization of American Culture*, ch. 6, "Akimbo Culture: Dance and the Participatory Pleasures of the Body."

64. Huggins, *Harlem Renaissance*, 254; Nathan, *Dan Emmett*, 81. On circus influences, Dumont, "Minstrelsy!," HSP Collection 3054; Rehin, "Harlequin Jim Crow," 682–84.

65. Seymour (?), "Amusements: Ethiopian Minstrelsy," 4; Gottschild, *Digging the Africanist Presence*, 83; Nathan, *Dan Emmett*, 123.

66. Mahar, *Behind the Burnt-Cork Mask*, 3–4. Quotations from Nathan, *Dan Emmett*, 19; see also 186–88, 195–205.

67. Gottschild, *Digging the Africanist Presence*, 100; Stearns and Stearns, *Jazz Dance*, 123. On competitive blackface dancing, Masten, "Challenge Dancing in Antebellum America," 605–34.

68. An. Gonzalez, "Navigations," 24–25; Gottschild, *Digging the Africanist Presence*, 25; Nowatzki, "Paddy Jumps Jim Crow."

69. See Gordon, *Prophets, Publicists, and Parasites*. Lehman notes the difficulty in discerning criticism from puffs ("Virtue and Virtuosity," 161), but even puffs helped develop vocabulary for more serious criticism.

70. *Theatrical Censor* (Dec. 13, 1806), 190.

71. *National Gazette* (July 19, 1827) on Mme. Hutin and the Achilles; (Jan. 8, 1829) on Mme. Ronzi Vestris.

72. *New York Mirror* (July 11, 1840), 21, on Elssler.

73. *National Gazette* (Feb. 20, 1838), on Augusta Maywood's New York debut; *Bizarre* (Jan. 21 and Feb. 25, 1854), on Yrca Mathias with the Ravels in Philadelphia.

74. *New York Mirror* (July 11, 1840), 21, comparing Elssler to Marie Taglioni. A critic in *Spirit of the Times* reported his extensive ballerina-viewing in both "the Old World" and "the New," when evaluating "Senorita Rolla" in New York (July 4, 1857, 288); he compared Rolla's version of *La Sylphide* with Taglioni's (p. 304). *The Press* (Sept. 21, 1857) crowned ballerina Louise Lamoureux of the Ronzani Troupe "Queen of Dance—for she equals Cerito [sic], Carlotta Grisi, Maria [sic] Taglioni, and Lucille Grahn," none of whom appeared in the United States.

75. "Chestnut St. Theatre," *Dramatic Mirror* on Turnbull (Feb. 5, 1842), 205; Elssler review (Sept. 11, 1841), 37.

76. "La Danseuse, A Sketch by a Philadelphian," *New York Mirror* (Oct. 24, 1840), 142.

77. Thespis, "Chestnut St. Theatre," *Public Ledger* (Nov. 27, 1838). Comments on Mallet in "Chestnut Street Theatre," *Public Ledger* (Nov. 16, 1838).

78. Fuller, "Entertainments of the Past Winter" (1842), 66.

79. Clipping (Sept.?, 1857), "The Ballet," HSP Academy of Music Scrapbook.

80. *Dramatic Mirror* (Oct. 30, 1841), 93. "Prince" quote, Ludlow, *Dramatic Life*, 513.

81. *Porter's Spirit of the Times* (May 9, 1841), 160.

82. "Arch Street," *Dramatic Mirror* (Nov. 13, 1841), 109. Lott discusses Jim Crow and Zip Coon as "figures of exaggerated strength and overwhelming power" (*Love and Theft*, 23).

83. Term used in Durang, *History*, v. 6, ch. 116, p. 368; Glasgow, *The Harpers Ferry Insurrection*, 46; Hall, *A Faithful Account*, 86; Meer, *Uncle Tom Mania*, 99; W. Stanton, *The Leopard's Spots*, 52, 109.

84. Stauffer, "Frederick Douglass and the Aesthetics of Freedom," 115; see also 117, 130.

85. Morton, *Crania Americana*, 5 (Caucasians) and 6 ("Ethiopians").

86. Morton, *Crania Americana*, 87–88.

87. Easton, *Treatise on the Intellectual Character*, 40.

88. Dorsey, *Reforming Men and Women*, 125–31; S. Davis, *Parades and Power*, 147–52.

89. "American Humor," 219; Seymour (?), "Amusements: Ethiopian Minstrelsy" (1859), 4; *Poulson's Scrapbook of Philadelphia History* (Oct. 14, 1855), v. 4, p. 86.

90. "American Humor," 219 ("not without originality"); "Amusements," *Poulson's Scrapbook of Philadelphia History* (May 8, 1859), v. 1, n.p. (on Sanford).

91. Nathanson, "Negro Minstrelsy," 72. The "young lady" observed was almost certainly white, given the context and description. On arms overhead and African religious ecstasy, see Gottschild, *Digging the Africanist Presence*, 99–100.

92. "Thomas D. Rice, American Theatre Bowery New York" (Nov. 25, 1833), National Portrait Gallery (Smithsonian).

93. HSP William David Lewis Diary, Mar. 29, 1845; subsequent quotations, Mar. 11, 1852.

94. Durang, *History*, v. 1, ch. XXXVII, p. 73; see also W. Wood, *Personal Recollections*, 456.

95. Cornish, "The Theatre," *Colored American* (Dec. 9, 1837).

96. Examples include the Olympic/National Theatre (FLP Theatre Collection Box 46, playbill, Jan. 18, 1843; Sept. 2–3, 1844); Welch's National Amphitheatre (FLP Theatre Collection Box 46, playbill, Aug. 1, 1849); Arch Street Theatre (*Public Ledger*, Apr. 30–May 3, 1850, and UPenn Kislak, Collection 1384, v. 13A, July 10, 1858).

97. Gottschild, *Digging the Africanist Presence*, 88. See also Gibbs, *Performing the Temple of Liberty*, 211; Johnson, "Gender Trumps Race," 223; Lhamon, *Raising Cain*, 171; Lott, *Love and Theft*, 15–17; Rehin, "Harlequin Jim Crow," 689, 693.

Bibliography

ARCHIVES

American Antiquarian Society
Clay, E. W. *Lessons in Dancing, Exemplified by Sketches from Real Life in the City of Philadelphia.* "Attitude Is Everything!, By a Dilettante." Philadelphia: R. H. Hobson, 1828. Call no. Reserve 1828 03.

Bethel A.M.E. Church, Philadelphia
Minute and Trial Book, Bethel A.M.E. Church, 1822–1835, 1838–1851.

Drexel University College of Medicine, Legacy Center,
Archives & Special Collections
"First Annual Announcement of the Female Medical College of Pennsylvania, for the Session 1850–51, Situated in Philadelphia." Accessed Dec. 2, 2020. Available at http://innopac.library.drexel.edu/search/g?ACC-076.
Matriculation Books, Female Medical College.
"Valedictory Address to the Graduating Class of the Female Medical College of Pennsylvania for the Session of 1857–58. By Ann Preston, M.D. (1858–59)." Accessed Nov. 10, 2024. Available at https://drexel.primo.exlibrisgroup.com/view/UniversalViewer/01DRXU_INST/12345017570004721?c=&m=&s=&cv=&xywh=-2377,-206,7352,4111&r=0.

Free Library of Philadelphia (FLP)
Dumont, Frank. "The Golden Days of Minstrelsy." *New York Clipper*, December 19, 1914.
Theatre Collection, Playbills.

Harvard Theatre Collection

Christy Minstrels, Philadelphia. Playbills, 1859–1863. Accessed April 1, 2020. Available at http://nrs.harvard.edu/urn-3:FHCL.HOUGH:10622488.

Historical Society of Pennsylvania (HSP)

Academy of Music Collection 3150.

Campbell Collection, vol. 2.

"Charter and Prospectus of the Opera House, or American Academy of Music." Philadelphia: Crissy & Markley, Printers, 1852. Collection 3150, Academy of Music, Mixed Programs 1857–1859.

Clay, Edward Williams. "Life in Philadelphia" graphics (Philadelphia Set), 7688.F.

"Dance Masters." Claude W. Unger Collection 1860A.

Dan Rice's American Humorist & Shaksperian [sic] Jester, Song & Joke Book [Dan Rice's Original Comic and Sentimental Poetic Effusions]. Philadelphia: Robert F. Simpson, 1860. Pam PN6161.R5 1860.

Dumont, Frank. "The Origin of Minstrelsy: Its Rise and Fall since 1842." *Philadelphia Inquirer*, April 5, 1896, 34. HSP Frank Dumont Minstrelsy Scrapbook.

"An Essay on Dancing, in A Series of Letters to a Lady, Wherein the Inconsistency of that Amusement with the True Spirit of Christianity is Demonstrated." Philadelphia: Thomas and William Bradford, and J. W. Campbell, c. 1814. E* .99, v. 1.

Ferdinand Julius Dreer Collection 0175.

"A Few Reflections upon the Fancy Ball, Otherwise Known as The City Dancing Assembly. By a Representative of Thousands." Philadelphia: G. R. Lilibridge, 1828. Am. 3075, v. 1.

Francis Courtney Wemyss Prompt Book. Walnut St. Theatre, HSP Am 8363.

Frank Dumont Minstrelsy Scrapbook, 3054, including "The Origin of Minstrelsy."

Leaming Family Papers, Collection 0622, box 6, correspondence 1826–1839.

Lewis, William David. Diary, Lewis Papers 1680.

"Philadelphia Female AntiSlavery Society." Accessed July 12, 2019. Available at https://hsp.org/sites/default/files/philadelphiafemaleanti-slaverysociety.pdf.

Playbill Collection 3131.

Souder, Casper. "The Mysteries and Miseries of Philadelphia, as Exhibited and Illustrated by a Late Presentment of the Grand Jury, and by A Sketch of the Condition of the Most Degraded Classes in the City. Dedicated to the Citizens of Philadelphia." Philadelphia, 1853. UPA/Ph HN80.P5M97 1853a.

The Xlanties; or Forty Thieves. A Musical, Satirical and Quizzical Burlesque, in Two Acts, "by the C. A. P. & Co., Performed at Sanford's Opera House, Phila. 1857. Introducing Numerous Original Songs, Dances, Peculiarities & Locales." Philadelphia: M'Laughlin Brothers, 1857. Wt* 29, v. 1.

Library Company of Philadelphia (LCP)

American Theatre Playbill Collection, McAllister 5761.F.

A Guide to the Stranger, or Pocket Companion for the Fancy, Containing a List of the Gay Houses and Ladies of Pleasure in the City of Brotherly Love and Sisterly Affection. Philadelphia: 1849. Rare | Am 1849 Guide 65997.D. Accessed Dec. 22, 2021. Available at https://www.librarycompany.org/shadoweconomy/ipad/stranger/index.htm.

Johnson, Francis. Rare Sheet Music Philadelphia 12373.F.
Koecker, Leonard R. Diary, 1852: 119921.D; 1860: 119920.D.
"Life in Philadelphia Collection." Accessed July 20, 2020. Available at https://digital.librarycompany.org/islandora/object/Islandora%3ALINP1.
Poulson, Charles Augustus. *Poulson's Scrapbook of Philadelphia History* and *Poulson's Scrapbook of American Biography.*
Register of Trades of the Colored People in the City of Philadelphia and Districts (1838). Am 1838 Phi Reg 17163.O.4 (C. A. Poulson).
Weaver, Mathias. Diary, from Ohio History Center, vols. 751–754. Diaries, 1840–1843.

Library of Congress (LoC)
Alan Lomax Collection, Manuscripts, The Homogeneity of African-New World Negro Musical Style, 1967. AFC 2004/004: MS 01.01.12. Accessed July 3, 2024. Available at https://www.loc.gov/item/afc2004004.ms010112/.
"De Color'd Fancy Ball." New York: Wm. Hall and Son, 1848. Sheet music, M1.A12V vol. 29 Case Class. Accessed Dec. 20, 2021. Available at https://www.loc.gov/item/sm1848.441690/.
Digital Image Collection.
Dred Scott v. Sandford, 60 U.S. 393 (1856). St. Louis, MO: Washington University in St. Louis, 2000. Accessed Mar. 11, 2022. Available at https://lccn.loc.gov/2003557474.
"The Minutes and Proceedings of the First Annual Meeting of the American Moral Reform Society: Held at Philadelphia, in the Presbyterian Church in Seventh Street, below Shippen, from the 14th to the 19th of August, 1837." Philadelphia: Merrihew & Gunn, Printers, 1837. Accessed July 3, 2024. Available at https://www.loc.gov/item/91898507/.
Parrish, Joseph, and Edward Needles. *The Present State and Condition of the Free People of Color, of the City of Philadelphia and Adjoining Districts, as Exhibited by the Report of a Committee of the Pennsylvania Society for Promoting the Abolition of Slavery, &c. Read First Month (Jan.) 5th, 1838.* Philadelphia: Merrihew & Gunn, 1838. Accessed Sept. 9, 2020. Available at http://www.loc.gov/resource/rbaapc.22520.
Proceedings of the Third Anti-Slavery Convention of American Women, Held in Philadelphia, May 1st, 2d and 3d, 1839. E449 .A6235. Accessed July 1, 2024. Available at https://www.loc.gov/item/11011784/.
Scribe, Eugène (libretto), D. F. E. Auber (music), and Filippo Taglioni (choreography). *Le dieu et la bayadère: opéra en deux actes.* Paris: 1830. ML48 [S407]. Accessed July 10, 2020. Available at https://www.loc.gov/resource/musschatz.12987.0/?sp=2&r=-0.546,-0.453,2.092,0.907,0.
Theater playbill, Sanford's Opera Troupe, Rare Book/Special Collections Reading Room (Jefferson LJ239). Accessed Jan. 31, 2023. Available at https://catalog.loc.gov/vwebv/holdingsInfo?searchId=15202&recCount=25&recPointer=0&bibId=18295140.
Winnemore, Anthony. "Stop dat Knocking at de Door," for the Virginia Minstrels. Boston, 1847. Accessed July 17, 2022. Available at https://www.loc.gov/resource/sm1847.420280.0/?sp=2&r=-1.216,-0.016,3.432,1.47,0.

National Library of Australia

West, William. "West's Characters in the Grand Historical Ballet, Called La-Perouse." 1824. PIC Drawer 12823 #PIC/18002/1–2. Accessed November 10, 2024. Available at https://nla.gov.au/nla.obj-133878531.

New York Public Library (NYPL)

The Ball-Room Companion. A Hand-Book for the Ball-Room and Evening Parties. Philadelphia: George Appleton, 1849. *MGW Res. 73–333.

Conner's Theatre Playbills, NYPL *MGRZ 76–63.

Digital Image Collection.

Hammond, Sandra. "Ballet Training in the Early 19th Century." Video recording. University of Hawaii, 1997. *MGZIA 4–558.

Princeton University, William Seymour Theatre Collection

Allison Delarue Collection. Accessed July 2, 2016. Available at http://libweb5.princeton.edu/visual_materials/delarue/Htmls/printsE.html.

Rosenbach Museum and Library

Clay, E. W. *Lessons in Dancing, Exemplified by Sketches from Real Life in the City of Philadelphia. "Attitude Is Everything!," the Set Signed "By a Dilettante."* Philadelphia: R. H. Hobson, 1828. Call no. A 828 l.

Mathews, Charles. *The London Mathews, Containing an Account of this Celebrated Comedian's Trip to America, Being an Annual Lecture on the Peculiarities, Characters, and Manners, Founded on His Own Observations and Adventures, To Which Are Prefixed, Several Original Comic Songs.* Philadelphia: Morgan & Yeager, 1824. Call no. A 824 l.

Smithsonian

National Museum of American History. *America on Stone.* The Harry T. Peters Collection: Clay, E. W. "Methodist Camp Meeting." 1836. Accessed Jan. 16, 2023. Available at https://amhistory.si.edu/petersprints/lithograph.cfm?id=326094&Category=Pets&Results_Per=10&search_all=false.

National Portrait Gallery. *Catalog of American Portraits.* "Thomas D. Rice, American Theatre Bowery New York." November 25, 1833. Digitized from the New-York Historical Society. Accessed Jan. 16, 2023. Available at https://npg.si.edu/object/npg_NY302436.

University of Pennsylvania Kislak Center (UPenn Kislak)

Durang, Charles. *History of the Philadelphia Stage, between the Years 1749 and 1855, Arranged and Illustrated by Thompson Westcott.* Philadelphia: Thompson Westcott, 1868.

Kurt Stein Collection of Francis Johnson Sheet Music, Folio ML410.J66 S7, Folio M1.J64.

Philadelphia Theatrical Commentaries by William Meredith, 1854–1857. Ms Collection 61.

Theatricals in Philadelphia Scrapbooks, Collection 1384.

Washington State University Libraries Digital Collection
Campbell's Melodies, Arranged for the Piano-forte. New York: Wm. Hall & Son, c. 1848. Accessed Nov. 10, 2024. Available at https://content.libraries.wsu.edu/digital/collection/rcbutler/id/1239.

NEWSPAPERS AND MAGAZINES

Note: Published in Philadelphia, unless otherwise indicated.

Albion (New York)
Alexander's (Express Messenger; Messenger; Weekly Messenger)
American Phrenological Journal (Philadelphia; New York)
Ballou's Pictorial (Boston)
Bentley's Quarterly Review (England)
Bizarre: For Fireside and Wayside
Colored American (New York)
Daily Chronicle
Democratic Press
Dramatic Mirror, and Literary Companion; Devoted to the Stage and the Fine Arts
Fitzgerald's City Item
Frank Leslie's Illustrated Newspaper (New York)
Freedom's Journal (New York)
The Liberator (Boston)
National Gazette
New Orleans Daily Creole
New York Clipper
New York Herald
New York Mirror
New York Musical Review
New-York Times
New York Tribune
North American & United States Gazette
North Star (later *Frederick Douglass' Paper*; Rochester, NY)
Pennsylvania Freeman
Philadelphia Album, and Ladies' Literary Gazette
Philadelphia Inquirer/Pennsylvania Inquirer
Poulson's American Daily Advertiser
The Press
Public Ledger
Spirit of the Times (New York)
The Sun (Baltimore)
Sunday Dispatch
Sunday Transcript
Theatrical Censor
United States Gazette
Weekly Messenger
York Gazette (York, PA)

ARTICLES, BOOKS, AND ONLINE SOURCES

Abrahams, Harold J. *Extinct Medical Schools of Nineteenth-Century Philadelphia*. Philadelphia: University of Pennsylvania Press, 1966.

Abrahams, Roger D. *Singing the Master: The Emergence of African American Culture in the Plantation South*. New York: Pantheon, 1992.

Academy of Music. "Our History." Accessed Oct. 17, 2022. Available at https://www.academyofmusic.org/about/our-history/.

Adams, John Quincy. "Letter from John Quincy Adams to the Pennsylvania Hall Association" (letter of Jan. 19, 1838). *The Emancipator*, May 21, 1838.

"Africans in America, Pt. 3: 'Brotherly Love.'" *PBS*. Accessed Sept. 9, 2022. Available at https://www.pbs.org/wgbh/aia/part3/3h253.html.

Aldrich, Elizabeth. *From the Ballroom to Hell: Grace and Folly in Nineteenth-Century Dance*. Evanston, IL: Northwestern University Press, 1991.

"American Humor." *United States Magazine and Democratic Review* 17, no. 87 (1846): 212–19.

Armstrong, Erica. *A Fragile Freedom: African American Women and Emancipation in the Antebellum City*. New Haven, CT: Yale University Press, 2008.

Arthur, Timothy Shay. *The Maiden*. Philadelphia: E. Ferrett & Co., 1845.

Atwater, Edward C. *Women Medical Doctors in the United States before the Civil War: A Biographical Dictionary*. Rochester, NY: University of Rochester Press, 2016.

Auguste, M., and P. Gaveaux. *Monsieur De Chalumeaux, Opera Bouffon en Trois actes*. Paris: M. M. Gaveaux, Frères, 1806.

Author of The Gentleman's Medical Pocket-Book. *The American Lady's Medical Pocket-Book, and Nursery-Advisor*. Philadelphia: James Kay, Jun. & Brother, c. 1833.

Ayestarán, Lauro. *El folklore musical uruguayo*. Montevideo: Arca Editorial, 1967.

Bacon, Jacqueline, and Glen McClish. "Reinventing the Master's Tools: Nineteenth-Century African-American Literary Societies of Philadelphia and Rhetorical Education." *Rhetoric Society Quarterly* 30, no. 4 (Autumn 2000): 19–47.

Ballantyne, Tony, and Antoinette Burton. "Introduction: Bodies, Empires, and World Histories." In *Bodies in Contact: Rethinking Colonial Encounters in World History*, edited by Tony Ballantyne and Antoinette Burton. Durham, NC: Duke University Press, 2005.

Baltzell, E. Digby. *Philadelphia Gentlemen: The Making of a National Upper Class*. Glencoe, IL: The Free Press, 1958.

Barnett, Morris. *The Serious Family, A Comedy in Three Acts*. New York: M. Douglas, 1850.

Bay, Mia. *The White Image in the Black Mind: African-American Ideas about White People, 1830–1925*. New York: Oxford University Press, 2000.

Bean, Annemarie, James Hatch, and Brooks McNamara, eds. *Inside the Minstrel Mask: Readings in Nineteenth-Century Blackface Minstrelsy*. Hanover, NH: Wesleyan University Press, 1996. Chapters cited:
  Bean, Annemarie. "Transgressing the Gender Divide: The Female Impersonator in Nineteenth-Century Blackface Minstrelsy."
  Day, Charles. "Fun in Black."
  Southern, Eileen. "Black Musicians and Early Ethiopian Minstrelsy."
  Winans, Robert B. "Early Minstrel Show Music, 1843–1852."

Beatty, Mario. "Martin Delany and Egyptology." *Revue D'Egyptologie et des Civilisations Africaines*, nos. 14–15 (2005–6): 78–99.
"The Beginnings of New Jersey." *Chronicles of America*. Accessed Sept. 5, 2021. Available at http://www.chroniclesofamerica.com/quakers/beginnings_of_new_jersey.htm.
Berkin, Nicole. "Antebellum Touring and the Culture of Deception: The Case of Master Diamond." *Theatre History Studies* 34 (2015): 39–58.
"Bibliographical Notices—*Females and their Diseases* . . . by Charles D. Meigs." *American Journal of the Medical Sciences*, 2nd ser., vol. 15 (1848): 481–86.
"Biography" [of Stephen Foster], Guide to the Foster Hall Collection, 1800–1952, University of Pittsburgh Center for American Music. Accessed July 16, 2022. Available at https://digital.library.pitt.edu/islandora/object/pitt%3AUS-PPiU-camfhc201101/viewer.
Bisco, John. "Town Amusement in Summer: The Ethiopian Music." *Broadway Journal* 2, no. 1 (July 12, 1845): 13–14.
Black Methodists Holding a Prayer Meeting [watercolor and ink], or *Black People's Prayer Meeting*, 1811–1813, attributed to Pavel Svinin or John Lewis Krimmel. Metropolitan Museum of Art. Accessed Aug. 8, 2022. Available at https://www.metmuseum.org/art/collection/search/12733; and *Africans in America*. PBS online. Accessed Aug. 8, 2022. Available at https://www.pbs.org/wgbh/aia/part3/3h253.html.
Blasis, Carlo. *Notes Upon Dancing, Historical and Practical*. London: Delaporte, 1847.
Blitz, Antonio. *Fifty Years in the Magic Circle; Being an Account of the Author's Professional Life*. Hartford, CT: Belknap and Bliss, 1871.
Bobo, William M. *Glimpses of New York City by a South Carolinian*. Charleston, SC: J. J. McCarter, 1852.
Bolster, W. Jeffrey. *Black Jacks, African American Seamen in the Age of Sail*. Cambridge, MA: Harvard University Press, 1997.
Boromé, Joseph A. "The Vigilant Committee of Philadelphia." *Pennsylvania Magazine of History and Biography* 92, no. 3 (July 1968): 320–51.
Branson, S. "'Barnum is Undone in His Own Province': Science, Race and Entertainment in the Lectures of George Robins Gliddon." In *The Cosmopolitan Lyceum: Lecture Culture and the Globe in Nineteenth-Century America*, edited by Tom Wright. Amherst, MA: University of Massachusetts Press, 2013.
Bright, Heather. "T. S. Arthur." Pennsylvania Center for the Book. Updated 2018. Accessed Feb. 9, 2023. Available at https://pabook.libraries.psu.edu/literary-cultural-heritage-map-pa/bios/Arthur__Timothy_Shay.
Brooks, Daphne A. *Bodies in Dissent: Spectacular Performances of Race and Freedom, 1850–1910*. Durham, NC: Duke University Press, 2006.
Brooks, Lynn. "Against Vain Sports and Pastime: The Theatre Dance in Philadelphia, 1724–90." *Dance Chronicle* 12, no. 2 (1989): 165–95.
———. *The Dances of the Processions of Seville in Spain's Golden Age*. Kassel, Germany: Edition Reichenberger, 1988.
———. "Danza española en la escena americana temprana: una perspectiva desde Filadelfia." In *Tras los pasos de la Sílfide. Imaginarios españoles del ballet romántico a la danza moderna*, edited by Idoia Murga Castro. Madrid: Museo del Romanticismo, 2022.

———. "Emblem of Gaiety, Love, and Legislation: Dance in Eighteenth-Century Philadelphia." *Pennsylvania Magazine of History and Biography* CXV, no. 1 (Jan. 1991): 63–88.
———. *John Durang: Man of the American Stage*. New York: Cambria Press, 2011.
———. "The Philadelphia Dancing Assembly in the Eighteenth Century." *Dance Research Journal* 21, no. 1 (Spring 1989): 1–7.
———. "Race, Rank, and Reform in Antebellum Philadelphia Social Dance." *Pennsylvania Magazine of History and Biography* CXLIV, no. 2 (Apr. 2020): 147–78.
———. "Staged Ethnicity: Early American Perspectives." *Dance Chronicle* 24, no. 2 (Fall 2001): 193–225.
Brower, Frank. "Happy Uncle Tom: A Celebrated Plantation Scene." In *The Universal Book of Songs and Singer's Companion*. New York: Dick & Fitzgerald, 1864.
Brown, Ira V. "Cradle of Feminism: The Philadelphia Female Anti-Slavery Society, 1833–1840." *Pennsylvania Magazine of History and Biography* CII, no. 2 (Apr. 1978): 143–66.
Brown, T. Allston. "Early History of Negro Minstrelsy: Its Rise and Progress in the United States." *The New York Clipper* LX, no. 3 (Mar. 2, 1912).
———. *History of the American Stage: Containing Biographical Sketches of Nearly Every Member of the Profession that Has Appeared on the American Stage, from 1733 to 1870*. New York: Dick & Fitzgerald, 1870.
Browne, Peter A. *The Classification of Mankind, by the Hair and Wool of Their Heads*. Philadelphia: J. H. Jones, 1853.
Buckley, Peter G. "Paratheatricals and Popular Stage Entertainment." In *The Cambridge History of American Theatre, Volume One: Beginnings to 1870*, edited by Don B. Wilmeth and Christopher Bigsby. New York: Cambridge University Press, 1998.
Burrows, J. G., and George Dibdin Pitt. *Lurline; Or the Water Nymphs' Revolt*. Holborn, London: John Duncombe & Co., 1834.
Bushman, Richard. *The Refinement of America: Persons, Houses, Cities*. New York: Vintage Books, 1993.
Caldwell, Charles. *Elements of Phrenology*. Lexington, KY: Thomas T. Skillman, 1824.
———. *Phrenology Vindicated, and Antiphrenology Unmasked*. New York: Samuel Colman, 1838.
Carlisle, Marcia. "Disorderly City, Disorderly Women: Prostitution in Ante-Bellum Philadelphia." In *Prostitution*, edited by Nancy F. Cott. Munich: De Gruter, Inc., 1993.
Carpenter, David Lawrence. *Amateur's Preceptor on Dancing Etiquette*. Philadelphia: Lee & Walker, 1854.
Carson, Joseph. *A History of the Medical Department of the University of Pennsylvania from its Foundation in 1765 with Sketches of the Lives of Deceased Professors*. Philadelphia: Lindsay and Blakiston, 1869.
Cartwright, Samuel A. "Dr. Cartwright on the Caucasians and the Africans." *Debow's Review: Agricultural, Commercial, Industrial Progress and Resources* 25, no. 1 (July 1858): 45–56.
———. "Unity of the Human Race Disproved by the Hebrew Bible." *Debow's Review* 4, no. 2 (Aug. 1860): 129–36.

Casey, Marion R. "The Limits of Equality: Racial and Ethnic Tensions in the New Republic, 1789–1836." In *The Columbia Documentary History of Race and Ethnicity in America*, edited by Ronald H. Bayer. New York: Columbia University Press, 2004.

Celi, Claudia. "Borri, Pasquale." In *The International Encyclopedia of Dance*. Oxford University Press, 2005. Accessed May 10, 2024. Available at https://www-oxford reference-com.fandm.idm.oclc.org/view/10.1093/acref/9780195173697.001.0001/acref-9780195173697-e-0266.

Chaffee, George. "A Chart to the American Souvenir Lithographs of the Romantic Ballet 1825–1870." *Dance Index* 1, no. 2 (Feb. 1942): 20–36.

Chasteen, John Charles. *National Rhythms, African Roots: The Deep History of Latin American Dance*. Albuquerque: University of New Mexico Press, 2004.

Chevalley, Silvie. "Madame Francisque Hutin." *Dance Magazine*, April 1957, 40–42, 83–85.

Claire, Elizabeth. "Dance Studies, Gender, and the Question of History." *Clio. Women, Gender, History* 46, no. 2 (2017): 161–88.

———. "Imagination, Vertigo and Contagion." Draft chapter. Columbia University Seminar, Studies in Dance, distributed October 2020.

Clarkson, Thomas. *A Portraiture of Quakerism*. Vol. 1. New York: Samuel Stansbury, 1806.

Cobb, Sylvanus. *The Pioneer Patriot; Or, the Maid of the War-Path*. Published serially in *The New York Ledger*, Fall 1857.

Cockrell, Dale. *Demons of Disorder: Early Blackface Minstrels and Their World*. New York: Cambridge University Press, 1997.

———. "Of Soundscapes and Blackface: From Fools to Foster." In *Burnt Cork: Traditions and Legacies of Blackface Minstrelsy*, edited by Stephen Johnson. Amherst: University of Massachusetts Press, 2012.

Collins, Kris. "White-Washing the Black-a-Moor: Othello, Negro Minstrelsy and Parodies of Blackness." *Journal of American Culture* 19, no. 3 (Fall 1996): 87–101.

Conway, E. H., *Le Maître de Danse, Or, The Art of Dancing Cotillons: By which Every One May Learn to Dance Them, without a Master, Having the Figures Displayed in Drawings for that Purpose*. 2nd ed. New York: S. Van Winkle, 1827.

Cooperman, Emily T., and Lea Carson Sherk. *William Birch: Picturing the American Scene*. Philadelphia: University of Pennsylvania Press, 2011.

Cordova, Sarah Davies. "The Romantic Ballet in France: 1830–1850." In *The Cambridge Companion to Ballet*, edited by Marion Kant. Cambridge, UK: Cambridge University Press, 2007.

Costonis, Maureen. "Ballet Comes to America, 1792–1842: French Contributions to the Establishment of Theatrical Dance in New Orleans and Philadelphia." PhD diss., New York University, 1989.

———. "The Personification of Desire: Fanny Elssler and American Audiences." *Dance Chronicle* 13, no. 1 (1997): 47–67.

———. "Placide, Alexander." In Vol. 5 of *International Encyclopedia of Dance*. New York: Oxford University Press, 2005.

———. "'The Wild Doe': Augusta Maywood in Philadelphia and Paris, 1837–1840." *Dance Chronicle* 17, no. 2 (1994): 123–48.

Crane, Susan. *The Performance of Self: Ritual, Clothing, and Identity During the Hundred Years War*. Philadelphia: University of Pennsylvania Press, 2011.

Curtis, A. *The Botanico-Medical Recorder, or Impartial Advocate of Botanic Medicine*. Cincinnati: Shepard & Co., 1843.

Curtis, George W. "The Editor's Easy Chair." *Harper's New Monthly Magazine* 24, no. 144 (May 1862): 849.

Dain, Bruce. *A Hideous Monster of the Mind: American Race Theory in the Early Republic*. Cambridge, MA: Harvard University Press, 2002.

"Dancing." Published serially in *Godey's Lady's Book and Ladies' American Magazine* I (1830), 91–92, 209, 260.

Daniel, Yvonne. *Caribbean and Atlantic Diaspora Dance: Igniting Citizenship*. Champaign, IL: University of Illinois Press, 2011.

"Darwin in America: The Evolution Debate in the United States." Pew Research Center. Accessed July 17, 2021. Available at https://www.pewforum.org/essay/darwin-in-america/.

d'Aulnoy, Marie-Catherine. *Cherry and Fair Star: A Grand Eastern Spectacle in Two Acts*. London: Hodgson & Co., 1822.

Davis, Andrew. *America's Longest Run: A History of the Walnut Street Theatre*. University Park: Pennsylvania State University Press, 2010.

Davis, Susan G. *Parades and Power: Street Theatre in Nineteenth-Century Philadelphia*. Philadelphia: Temple University Press, 1986.

Davis, Tracy C. "Acting Black, 1824: Charles Mathews's Trip to America." *Theatre Journal* 63, no. 2 (May 2011): 163–89.

Davison, Nancy R. "E. W. Clay: American Political Caricaturist of the Jacksonian Era." PhD diss., University of Michigan, 1980.

Day, Jasmine. *The Mummy's Curse: Mummymania in the English-speaking World*. New York: Routledge, 2006.

DeFrantz, Thomas F. "The Black Beat Made Visible: Hip Hop Dance and Body Power," 2004. Accessed July 15, 2020. Available at http://web.mit.edu/people/defrantz/Documents/BlackBeat.PDF.

———. "Studies in Dance Seminar," dir. Lynn Garafola. Columbia University, Mar. 1, 2021.

———. "The Black Beat Made Visible: Hip Hop Dance and Body Power," 2004. Accessed July 15, 2020. Available at http://web.mit.edu/people/defrantz/Documents/BlackBeat.PDF.

de Guardiola, Susan. "Bits of *Bijou*: The Missing Middle of Durang's 1848 Manual." *Capering & Kickery*. Accessed Dec. 20, 2021. Available at https://www.kickery.com/2008/02/bits-of-bijou-o.html.

DeGuzmán, María. *Spain's Long Shadow: The Black Legend, Off-Whiteness, and Anglo-American Empire*. Minneapolis: University of Minnesota Press, 2005.

Delany, Martin R. *The Condition, Elevation, Emigration, and Destiny of the Colored People of the United States. Politically Considered*. Philadelphia: The Author, 1852.

———. "Political Destiny of the Colored Race, on the American Continent." In *Proceedings of the National Emigration Convention of Colored People, held at Cleveland, Ohio, August 24, 1854*. Cleveland, OH: A. A. Anderson, Printer, 1854.

———. *Principia of Ethnology: The Origins of Races and Color*. Philadelphia: Harper & Brother, 1879.

Delarue, Allison. *Fanny Elssler in America: Comprising Seven Facsimiles of Rare Americana*. New York: Dance Horizons, 1976.

Deloria, Philip J. *Playing Indian*. New Haven, CT: Yale University Press, 1998.
de Lurieu, Joseph Gabriel, and Claude Louis Marie de Rochefort-Luçay. *Jocko; ou, Le singe du Brésil, drame en deux actes, à grand spectacle, mêlée de musique, de danses et de pantomime*. Paris: Chez Quoy, 1825.
Desilver's Philadelphia Directory and Stranger's Guide, 1829–1836. Philadelphia: Robert Desilver, 1829–1836.
DeVoe, Thomas. *The Market Book; Containing a Historical Account of the Public Markets in the Cities of New York, Boston, Philadelphia, and Brooklyn*. New York: The Author, 1862.
Dewees, William Potts. *A Treatise on the Diseases of Females*. Philadelphia: Carey, Lea and Blanchard, 1833.
Dickens, Charles. *American Notes for General Circulation*. New York: Harper & Bros., 1842.
Dickson, Samuel Henry. *An Oration Delivered at New Haven before the Phi Beta Kappa Society, August 17, 1842*. New Haven, CT: B. L. Hamlen, 1842.
——— . *Remarks on Certain Topics Connected with the General Subject of Slavery*. Charleston, SC: Observer Office Press, 1845.
Dillon, Elizabeth Maddock. *New World Drama: The Performative Commons in the Atlantic World, 1649–1849*. Durham, NC: Duke University Press, 2014.
Dini, Jane, ed. *Dance: American Art, 1830–1960*. Detroit, MI: Detroit Institute of Art, 2016. Chapters cited:
Dini, Jane, "Invitation to the Dance."
Hill, Constance Valis. "In the Eye of the Beholder: The Black Presence in the Art of American Dance."
Myers, Kenneth John. "Dance and the Performance of Self in America: 1810 to 1850."
Dixon, George Washington. "Fanny Elssler and the Dying Babe." *New York Polyanthos*, June 19, 1841, 10.
Dorsey, Bruce. *Reforming Men and Women: Gender in the Antebellum City*. Ithaca, NY: Cornell University Press, 2002.
Douglass, Frederick. "Address Delivered by Fred'rick Douglass, before the Literary Societies of The Western Reserve College, at Commencement, July 12th, 1854." *Frederick Douglass' Newspaper*, July 21, 1854, 2.
——— . *Life and Times of Frederick Douglass, Written by Himself*. Rev. ed. (Boston: De Wolfe & Fiske, 1892).
——— . *My Bondage and My Freedom*. New York: Miller, Orton, and Mulligan, 1855.
Dover, Cedric. "The Racial Philosophy of Johann Herder." *The British Journal of Sociology* 3, no. 2 (June 1952): 124–33.
"Dr. J. J. Gould Bias." Colored Conventions Project. Accessed Apr. 11, 2022. Available at https://coloredconventions.org/black-mobility/delegates/dr-j-j-gould-bias/.
Du Bois, W. E. Burghardt. *The Philadelphia Negro: A Social Study*. Philadelphia: University of Pennsylvania Press, 1996. Originally published in 1899.
DuComb, Christian. *Haunted City: Three Centuries of Racial Impersonation in Philadelphia*. Ann Arbor, MI: University of Michigan Press, 2017.
Dunmore, John. *La Peyrouse dans l'isle de Tahiti; ou le danger des présomptions, drame politique et moral en quatre actes*. London: Modern Humanities Research Council, 2006.

Dunson, Stephanie. "The Minstrel in the Parlor: Nineteenth Century Sheet Music and the Domestication of Blackface Minstrelsy." *ATQ* 16, no. 4 (Dec. 2002): 241–56.
Durang, Charles. *The Ball-Room Bijou, and Art of Dancing.* Philadelphia: Turner & Fisher, 1848.
———. *The Dancer's Own Book, and Ball-Room Companion.* Philadelphia: Turner & Fisher, 1854(?).
———. *Durang's Terpsichore, or, Ball Room Guide.* Philadelphia: Turner & Fisher, 1847.
———. *The Fashionable Dancer's Casket, or the Ball-Room Instructor, A New and Splendid Work on Dancing, Etiquette, Deportment, and the Toilet.* Philadelphia: Fisher & Brother, 1856.
———. *Leaflets of the Ball Room, Being a Sketch of the Polka Quadrilles, the Baden, Mazurka Figures, . . . Now First Published in the United States.* Philadelphia: Turner & Fisher, 1847.
"Durang's Hornpipe." *Jenny Glover's Fiddletails.* Accessed Sept. 9, 2021. Available at https://fiddletails.com/2016/08/17/durangs-hornpipe/.
Easton, Hosea. *A Treatise on the Intellectual Character, and Civil and Political Condition of the Colored People of the U. States: and the Prejudice Exercised towards Them.* Boston: Isaac Knapp, 1837.
"Editorial Notes." *Putnam's Monthly Magazine of American Literature, Science and Art*, February 1855, 206.
Egan, Pierce. *Life in London; or, The day and night scenes of Jerry Hawthorn, esq., and his elegant friend Corinthian Tom. . . . With numerous coloured illus. from real life designed by I.R. & G. Cruikshank.* London: Chatto & Windus, 1821.
Ellacott, Vivyan. "The Free and Easies." *An A-Z Encyclopaedia of London Theatres and Music Halls*, 2011. Accessed Mar. 12, 2022. Available at overthefootlights.co.uk.
"Embassies and Legations in Washington." *Godoy's Diplomatic and Consular Review* I, no. 6 (Sept. 1916): 3–4.
Engelhardt, Molly. "The Revolt of the Harem on the English Stage: A Spectacle of Domestic Reform." *Dance Research* 33, no. 1 (Summer 2015): 31–49.
Erickson, Paul A. "The Anthropology of Charles Caldwell, M.D." *Isis* 72, no. 2 (June 1981): 252–56.
———. "The Anthropology of Josiah Clark Nott." *Kroeber Anthropological Society Papers* 65–66 (1986): 103–20.
Evans, Richard. *The Feminists: Women's Emancipation Movements in Europe, America and Australasia 1840–1920.* London: Routledge/Taylor & Francis Group, 2013. Originally published in 1977.
Ewell, James. *The Medical Companion, or Family Physician; Treating of the Diseases of the United States, . . . &C. The Management and Diseases of Women and Children.* Washington, D.C.: Printed for the Proprietors, 1827.
"Extinct Philadelphia Medical Schools." University of Pennsylvania PennLibraries: University Archives & Records Center. Accessed Apr. 11, 2022. Available at https://archives.upenn.edu/exhibits/penn-history/medical-history/extinct/.
Falcone, Francesca. "The Arabesque: A Compositional Design." *Dance Chronicle* 19, no. 3 (1996): 231–53.
Ferrero, Edward. *The Art of Dancing, Historically Illustrated: To which is Added a Few Hints on Etiquette.* New York: The Author, 1859.

"The Fine Arts. The Ballet." *Arcturus, a Journal of Books and Opinion*, edited by Evert A. Duyckinck and Cornelius Mathews (July 1841): 122–23.
Fisher, Sidney George. *The Laws of Race as Connected with Slavery*. Philadelphia: Willis P. Hazard, 1860.
———. *A Philadelphia Perspective: The Diary of Sidney George Fisher Covering the Years 1834–1871*. Edited by Nicholas B. Wainwright. Philadelphia: Historical Society of Pennsylvania, 1967.
Fletcher, Anne, and Scott R. Irelan. "Staging 'Americanization': 'America' on Stage: Theater and National Identity, 1671–1867." *Cercles* 19 (2009): 88–101.
Fordham, Monroe. *Major Themes in Northern Black Religious Thought, 1800–1860*. Hicksville, NY: Exposition Press, 1975.
Foster, Susan. *Corporealities: Dancing, Knowledge, Culture, and Power*. New York: Routledge, 1996.
Fowler, Lorenzo N. *The Phrenological Developments and Characters of J. V. Stout, the Sculptor, and Fanny Elssler, the Actress*. New York: L. N. Fowler, 1841.
Fowler, Lorenzo and/or Orson. "Analysis of Mirthfulness, and its Adaptation to Man's Requisition for Amusement." *American Phrenological Journal and Miscellany* VII, no. 6 (June 1845): 177–83.
"Francis, William Bodley." In *Biographical Dictionary of Actors, Actresses, Musicians, Dancers, Managers and other Stage Personnel in London, 1660–1800*, vol. 5, edited by Philip Highfill, Kalman Burnim, and Edward Langhans. Carbondale, IL: Southern Illinois University Press, 1973–93.
Frank, Adam, Marcelo Gleiser, and Evan Thompson. *The Blind Spot: Why Science Cannot Ignore Human Experience*. Cambridge, MA: MIT Press, 2025.
———. "How Human Experience Makes Science Possible." *Resilience* (Jan. 22, 2025). Accessed Jan. 26, 2025. Available at https://www.resilience.org/stories/2025-01-22/how-human-experience-makes-science-possible/.
Frederickson, George M. *The Black Image in the White Mind: The Debate on Afro-American Character and Destiny, 1817–1914*. New York: Harper & Row, 1971.
A Friend of the Drama. "An Enquiry into the Condition and Influence of the Brothels in Connection with the Theatres of Philadelphia." Philadelphia: Published for the Booksellers, 1834.
Fuller, Margaret. "Entertainments of the Past Winter." *The Dial* III (1842): 49–70.
Furstenberg, François. *When the United States Spoke French: Five Refugees Who Shaped a Nation*. New York: Penguin Press, 2014.
Garafola, Lynn. *Rethinking the Sylph: New Perspectives on Romantic Ballet*. Hanover, NH: University Press of New England, 1997. Chapters cited:
Arkin, Lisa, and Marian Smith. "National Dance in the Romantic Ballet."
———. Appendix, "National Dance in the Romantic Ballet."
Celi, Claudia. "The Arrival of the Great Wonder of Ballet, or Ballet in Rome from 1845 to 1855."
Meglin, Joellen. "Feminism or Fetishism? *La Révolte des femmes* and Women's Liberation in France in the 1830s."
———. "The Travesty Dancer in Nineteenth-Century Ballet." *Dance Chronicle* 17–18 (1985–1986): 35–40.
Gautier, Théophile. *Gautier on Dance*. Translated and edited by Ivor Guest. London: Dance Books, 1986.

"George Sand." *Bentley's Quarterly Review* 2 (Jan. 1860): 369–403.
Gerdts, William H. *Thomas Birch (1779–1851), Paintings and Drawings*. Philadelphia: Philadelphia Maritime Museum, 1966.
Gibbs, Jenna M. *Performing the Temple of Liberty: Slavery, Theater, and Popular Culture in London and Philadelphia, 1760–1850*. Baltimore, MD: Johns Hopkins University Press, 2014.
Gilroy, Paul. *The Black Atlantic: Modernity and Double Consciousness*. London and New York: Verso, 1993.
Glasgow, Jesse Ewing. *The Harpers Ferry Insurrection: Being an Account of the Late Outbreak in Virginia, and of the Trial and Execution of Captain John Brown, Its Hero*. Edinburgh: Myles MacPhail, 1860.
Goldschmidt, Hubert. "Marie Taglioni." *Ballet Review* 46, no. 2 (Summer 2018): 101–24.
Gonzalez, Anita. "Navigations: Diasporic Transports and Landings." In *Black Performance Theory*, edited by Thomas F. DeFrantz and Anita Gonzalez. Durham: Duke University Press, 2014.
Gonzalez, Aston. *Visualizing Equality: African American Rights and Visual Culture in the Nineteenth Century*. Chapel Hill: University of North Carolina Press, 2020.
Goodall, Jane R. *Performance and Evolution in the Age of Darwin: Out of the Natural Order*. New York: Routledge, 2002.
Gordon, Adam. *Prophets, Publicists, and Parasites: Antebellum Print Culture and the Rise of the Critic*. Amherst, MA: University of Massachusetts Press, 2020.
Gotcher, Sara Elizabeth. "The Career of Lola Montez in the American Theatre." PhD diss., Louisiana State University, 1994.
Gottschild, Brenda Dixon. *The Black Dancing Body: A Geography from Coon to Cool*. New York: Palgrave MacMillan, 2003.
———. *Digging the Africanist Presence in American Performance: Dance and Other Contexts*. Westport, CT: Greenwood Press, 1996.
Gouda, Frances. "Colonial Encounters, Body Politics, and Flows of Desire." *Journal of Women's History* 20, no. 3 (Fall 2008): 166–180.
Gourdoux-Daux, Jean-Henri. *Elements and Principles of the Art of Dancing, as Used in the Polite and Fashionable Circles: Also Rules of Deportment and Descriptions of Manners of Civility, Appertaining to That Art*. Translated by Victor Guillou. Philadelphia: J. F. Hurtel, 1817.
Green, Ralph. "Early American Power Printing Presses." *Studies in Bibliography* 4 (1951/1952): 143–53.
Greenblatt, S. H. "Phrenology in the Science and Culture of the 19th Century." *Neurosurgery* 37, no. 4 (Oct. 1995): 790–805.
Grimsted, David. *Melodrama Unveiled: American Theater and Culture, 1800–1850*. Chicago: University of Chicago Press, 1968.
Gross, Robert A., and Mary Kelley, eds. *A History of the Book in America*. Vol. 2, *An Extensive Republic: Print, Culture, and Society in the New Nation, 1790–1840*. Chapel Hill: University of North Carolina Press, 2010. Chapters cited:
    Gross, Robert A. "Introduction: An Extensive Republic."
    Gundaker, Grey. "Give Me a Sign: African Americans, Print, and Practice."
Grosz, Elisabeth. *Volatile Bodies: Toward a Corporeal Feminism*. Bloomington: Indiana University Press, 1994.

Grubbs, Patrick. "General Trades Union Strike, 1835." *The Encyclopedia of Greater Philadelphia*. Accessed Apr. 28, 2022. Available at https://philadelphiaencyclopedia.org/essays/general-trades-union-strike-1835/.

Guest, Ivor. *Fanny Elssler*. Middletown, CT: Wesleyan University Press, 1970.

———. "Fanny Elssler's Cachucha: Its Significance and Its Preservation." In *Fanny Elssler's Cachucha*. With Ann Hutchinson Guest. New York: Theatre Arts Books, 1981.

———. *The Romantic Ballet in England: Its Development, Fulfilment, and Decline*. Middletown, CT: Wesleyan University Press, 1972.

Habermas, J. *The Structural Transformation of the Public Sphere: An Inquiry into a Category of Bourgeois Society*. Translated by T. Burger and F. Lawrence. Cambridge, MA: MIT Press, 1989.

Haines, John Thomas. *The French Spy; Or, The Siege of Constantina: A Military Drama in Three Acts, Partly from the French*. New York: S. French, 1837.

Haitzinger, Nicole. "Female Bodies as the Other Alterity on Stage." In *Les Choses espagnoles: Research into the Hispanomania of 19th Century Dance*, edited by Claudia Jeschke, Gabi Vettermann, and Nicole Haitzinger. Munich: Epodium Verlag, 2009.

Hall, Stephen G. *A Faithful Account of the Race: African American Historical Writing in Nineteenth-Century America*. Chapel Hill: University of North Carolina Press, 2009.

Halttunen, Karen. *Confidence Men and Painted Women: A Study of Middle-class Culture in America, 1830–1870*. New Haven, CT: Yale University Press, 1982.

Hammond, Sandra. "Clues to Ballet's Technical History from the Early Nineteenth-Century Ballet Lesson." *Dance Research* III, no. 1 (Autumn 1984): 53–66.

———. "Steps through Time: Selected Dance Vocabulary in the Eighteenth and Nineteenth Centuries." *Dance Research* X, no. 2 (Aug. 1992): 93–108.

Hanson, Russell L. *The Democratic Imagination in America: Conversations with Our Past*. Princeton, NJ: Princeton University Press, 1985.

Harris, Michael D. *Colored Pictures: Race and Visual Representation*. Chapel Hill: University of North Carolina Press, 2003.

Harris, Samuel. *The Philosophical Basis of Theism: An Examination of the Personality of Man*. Rev. ed. New York: Charles Scribner's Sons, 1883.

Hartley, Benjamin L. "Philadelphia's 'Five Points': Evangelism and Social Welfare at the Bedford Street Mission." *Methodist History* 48, no. 1 (Oct. 2009): 10–22.

Hartman, Saidiya V. *Scenes of Subjection: Terror, Slavery, and Self-Making in Nineteenth-Century America*. New York: Oxford University Press, 1997.

Hawthorne, Alice [Septimus Winner]. *Stories of Africa*. Philadelphia: Charles H. Davis, 1854.

Hay, Samuel A. *African American Theatre: An Historical and Critical Analysis*. Cambridge, UK: Cambridge University Press, 1994.

Hazard, Willis P. *The Ball-Room Companion. A Hand-Book for the Ball-Room and Evening Parties*. Philadelphia: George S. Appleton, 1849.

Hazzard-Donald, Katrina. *Jookin': The Rise of Social Dance Formations in African-American Culture*. Philadelphia: Temple University Press, 1990.

Heckscher, Jurretta Jordan. "Our National Poetry: The Afro-Chesapeake Inventions of American Dance." In *Ballroom, Boogie, Shimmy Sham, Shake: A Social and Popular*

Dance Reader, edited by Julie Malnig. Champaign, IL: University of Illinois Press, 2009.

Henderson, Alfred. "A Note on the 'Circular Room' of the Pennsylvania Hospital." *Journal of the History of Medicine and Allied Sciences* 19, no. 2 (Apr. 1964): 156–60.

Herschthal, Eric. *The Science of Abolition: How Slaveholders Became the Enemies of Progress*. New Haven, CT: Yale University Press, 2021.

Herskovits, Melville J. *The Myth of the Negro Past*. New York: Harper & Bros., 1941.

Hill, Errol, and James V. Hatch. *A History of African American Theatre*. Cambridge, UK: Cambridge University Press, 2003.

Hinton, Robert. "Black Dance in American History." In *The Black Tradition in American Modern Dance*, edited by Gerald E. Myers. Durham, NC: American Dance Festival, 1988.

"Historic Street Name Index." PhillyHistory.org. Accessed Sept. 5, 2021. Available at https://www.phillyhistory.org/historicstreets/default.aspx.

Hodge, Hugh Lenox. *An Introductory Lecture, to the Course on Obstetrics, and Diseases of Women and Children: Delivered in the University of Pennsylvania, November 5, 1846*. Philadelphia: William S. Young, 1846.

———. *A Lecture Introductory to the Course on Obstetrics and Diseases of Women and Children: in the University of Pennsylvania, for the Session of 1835–6*. Philadelphia: J. G. Auner, 1835.

Holloway, Joseph E. *Africanisms in American Culture*. Bloomington: Indiana University Press, 1990.

Hone, Philip. *The Diary of Philip Hone, 1828–1851*. Edited by Bayard Tuckerman. New York: Dodd, Mead & Co., 1889.

Hormigón, Laura. *El Ballet Romántico en el Teatro del Circo de Madrid (1842–1850)*. Madrid: Asociación de Directores de Escena de España, 2017.

Horner, William E. *The Home Book of Health and Medicine: A Popular Treatise on the Means of Avoiding and Curing Diseases, . . . Including an Account of the Nature and Properties of Remedies, the Treatment of the Diseases of Women and Children, and the Management of Pregnancy and Parturition*. Philadelphia: J. Locken, 1842.

Huggins, Nathan Irvin. *Harlem Renaissance*. New York: Oxford University Press, 2007. Originally published in 1971.

Hutton, Frankie. *The Early Black Press in America, 1827–1860*. Westport, CT: Greenwood Press, 1993.

Hutton, Laurence. "The Negro on the Stage." *Harper's New Monthly Magazine* 79, no. 469 (June 1889): 131–45.

Irelan, Scott R. *Enacting Nationhood: Identity, Ideology and the Theatre, 1855–99*. Newcastle-upon-Tyne: Cambridge Scholars, 2014.

Ireland, Joseph Norton. *Records of the New York Stage, from 1850 to 1860*, 2 vols. New York: T. H. Morrell, 1867.

Jable, J. Thomas. "Aspects of Moral Reform in Early Nineteenth-Century Pennsylvania." *Pennsylvania Magazine of History and Biography* 102, no. 3 (July 1978): 344–63.

Jackson, Zakkiyah Iman. *Becoming Human: Matter and Meaning in an Antiblack World*. New York: New York University Press, 2020.

James, Reese D. *Old Drury of Philadelphia*. New York: Greenwood Press, 1968.

Jefferson, Thomas. *Notes on the State of Virginia*. Philadelphia: Prichard and Hall, 1788.

Jeschke, Claudia. "Lola Montez and Spanish Dance in the 19th Century." In *New German Dance Studies*, edited by Claudia Jeschke, Susan Manning, and Lucia Ruprecht. Champaign, IL: University of Illinois Press, 2012.

Johnson, Oliver. *Amusements: Their Uses and Abuses: Testimony of Progressive Friends*. New York: Oliver Johnson, 1856.

Johnson, Stephen. *Burnt Cork: Traditions and Legacies of Blackface Minstrelsy*. Amherst: University of Massachusetts Press, 2012.

———. "Gender Trumps Race? Cross-Dressing Juba in Early Blackface Minstrelsy." In *When Men Dance: Choreographing Masculinities across Borders*, edited by Jennifer Fisher and Anthony Shay. New York: Oxford University Press, 2009.

"John S. Rock." *Black History Now*. Accessed Apr. 12, 2022. Available at http://blackhistorynow.com/john-s-rock/.

Johnston, David Claypoole. *Phrenology Exemplified and Illustrated, With Upwards of Forty Etchings*. Boston: D. C. Johnston, 1837.

Jones, Bessie, and Bess Lomax Hawes. *Step It Down: Games, Plays, Songs, and Stories from the Afro-American Heritage*. Athens, GA: University of Georgia Press, 1987.

Jones, Charles K. *Francis Johnson (1792–1844): Chronicle of a Black Musician in Early Nineteenth-Century Philadelphia*. Bethlehem, PA: Lehigh University Press, 2006.

Jones, Martha S. *All Bound Up Together: The Woman Question in African American Public Culture, 1830–1900*. Chapel Hill: University of North Carolina Press, 2007.

———. *Birthright Citizens: A History of Race and Rights in Antebellum America*. Cambridge, UK: Cambridge University Press, 2018.

"Journal of a Tour through the Eastern States, by an English Woman." *St. Tammany's Magazine* 5 (Dec. 17, 1821): 70.

Jowitt, Deborah. *Time and the Dancing Image*. New York: William Morrow & Co., 1988.

Kant, Marion. "The Soul of the Shoe." In *The Cambridge Companion to Ballet*, edited by Marion Kant. Cambridge, UK: Cambridge University Press, 2007.

Katz, Wendy Jean. *Humbug!: The Politics of Art Criticism in New York City's Penny Press*. New York: Fordham University Press, 2020.

Keeler, Ralph. "Three Years as a Negro Minstrel." *Atlantic Monthly* XXIV (July 1869): 72.

Kelley, Mary. "'A More Glorious Revolution': Women's Antebellum Reading Circles and the Pursuit of Public Influence." *The New England Quarterly* 76, no. 2 (June 2003): 163–96.

Kennard, James K. "Who Are Our National Poets?" *Knickerbocker* 26, no. 4 (Oct. 1845): 331–41.

Kirtley, Alexandra. "The Athens of America." In *Encyclopedia of Greater Philadelphia*. Accessed May 20, 2019. Available at https://philadelphiaencyclopedia.org/archive/athens-of-america/.

Kosstrin, Hannah. "Kinesthetic Seeing: A Model for Practice-in-Research." In *Futures of Dance Studies*, edited by Susan Manning, Janice Ross, and Rebecca Schneider. Madison: University of Wisconsin Press, 2020.

LaBrew, Arthur R. *Francis Johnson (1792–1844)*. Baton Rouge, LA: Southern University, 1974.

Lacauchie, Alexandre. "Portrait de Jacques François-Antoine Hutin dit Francisque Aîné." Paris Musees Collections Musée Carnavalet. Accessed Nov. 10, 2024. Available at https://www.parismuseescollections.paris.fr/fr/musee-carnavalet/oeuvres/portrait-de-jacques-francois-antoine-hutin-dit-francisque-aine-1796-1842.

Lampert, Sara. *Starring Women: Celebrity, Patriarchy, and American Theater 1790–1850*. Champaign, IL: University of Illinois Press, 2020.

Lange, Allison K. *Picturing Political Power: Images in the Women's Suffrage Movement*. Chicago: University of Chicago Press, 2020.

Lapsansky, Emma J. "Friends, Wives, and Strivings: Networks and Community Values among Nineteenth-Century Philadelphia Afroamerican Elites." *Pennsylvania Magazine of History and Biography* 108, no. 1 (January 1984): 3–24.

———. "'Since They Got Those Separate Churches': Afro-Americans and Racism in Jacksonian Philadelphia." *American Quarterly* 32, no. 1 (Spring 1980): 54–78.

———. "The World the Agitators Made: The Counterculture of Agitation in Urban Philadelphia." In *The Abolitionist Sisterhood: Women's Political Culture in Antebellum America*, edited by Jean Fagan Yellin and John C. Van Horne. Ithaca, NY: Cornell University Press, 1994.

Lapsansky, Phillip. "Graphic Discord: Abolitionist and Antiabolitionist Images." In *The Abolitionist Sisterhood: Women's Political Culture in Antebellum America*, edited by Jean Fagan Yellin and John C. Van Horne. Ithaca, NY: Cornell University Press, 1994.

"Laurel Hill Gravestone Honors Trail-Blazing Ballerina." *WHYY*, June 8, 2011. Accessed July 21, 2020. Available at https://whyy.org/articles/americas-first-ballerina-honored-with-gravestone/.

Laurie, Bruce. *Working People of Philadelphia, 1800–1850*. Philadelphia: Temple University Press, 1980.

Lawrence, Vera Brodsky, and George Templeton Strong. *Strong on Music*. Vol. 1, *Resonances: 1836–1850*, and vol. 2, *Reverberations: 1850–1856*. New York: Oxford University Press, 1988.

The Laws of Etiquette; or, Short Rules and Reflections for Conduct in Society, by "A Gentleman." Philadelphia: Carey, Lea and Blanchard, 1836.

Lazo, Rodrigo. *Letters from Filadelfia: Early Latino Literature and the Trans-American Elite*. Charlottesville, VA: University of Virginia Press, 2020.

"Lectures and Lecturers." *Putnam's Monthly Magazine of American Literature, Science and Art* 9, no. 51 (Mar. 1857): 317–22.

Lehman, Rhea H. "Virtue and Virtuosity: America's Vision of the Romantic Ballet, 1827–1840." PhD diss., University of Wisconsin, 1986.

Leslie, Eliza. *Miss Leslie's Behaviour Book: A Guide and Manual for Ladies*. Philadelphia: T. B. Peterson & Bros., 1839.

Levine, Lawrence W. *Highbrow/Lowbrow: The Emergence of Cultural Hierarchy in America*. Cambridge, MA: Harvard University Press, 1988.

Lewis, Benjamin. *Light and Truth Collected from the Bible and Ancient and Modern History, Containing the Universal History of the Colored and the Indian Race from the Creation of the World to the Present Time*. Boston: A Committee of Colored Gentlemen, printed by Benjamin F. Roberts, 1844.

Lhamon, W. T. *Jim Crow, American: Selected Songs and Plays*. Cambridge, MA: Belknap Press of Harvard University Press, 2009.

———. *Jump Jim Crow: Lost Plays, Lyrics, and Street Prose of the First Atlantic Popular Culture*. Cambridge, MA: Harvard University Press, 2003.

———. *Raising Cain: Blackface Performance from Jim Crow to Hip Hop*. Cambridge, MA: Harvard University Press, 1998.

Linnekin, Jocelyn. "Ignoble Savages and Other European Visions: The La Pérouse Affair in Samoan History." *The Journal of Pacific History* 26, no. 1 (June 1991): 3–26.

Lippard, George. '*Bel of Prairie Eden: A Romance of Mexico*. In *Empire and The Literature of Sensation: An Anthology of Nineteenth-Century Popular Fiction*, edited by Jesse Alemán and Shelley Streeby. New Brunswick, NJ: Rutgers University Press, 2007. Originally published in 1848.

———. *The Quaker City; or, The Monks of Monk Hall: A Romance of Philadelphia Life, Mystery, and Crime*. 2 vols. Philadelphia: The Author, 1847.

Lomax, Alan. *Alan Lomax: Selected Writings, 1934–1997*. Edited by Ronald D. Cohen. New York: Routledge Taylor & Francis Group, 2005.

Lomax Hawes, Bess, and Edmund Carpenter. "The Georgia Sea Island Singers (1963)." *The Films of Bess Lomax Hawes*, with information booklet, "The Georgia Sea Island Singers." Late 1960s? Accessed May 25, 2022. Available at https://www.youtube.com/watch?v=a13O54znCCU.

Lott, Eric. *Love and Theft: Blackface Minstrelsy and the American Working Class*. New York: Oxford University Press, 1993.

Ludlow, Noah. *Dramatic Life as I Found It*. St. Louis, MO: G. I. Jones & Co., 1880.

Lueck, Beth Lynne, Sirpa Salenius, and Nancy Lusignan Schultz, eds. *Transatlantic Conversations: Nineteenth-Century American Women's Encounters with Italy and the Atlantic World*. Durham, NH: University of New Hampshire Press, 2017.

Lueger, Michael. "Henry Wikoff and the Development of Theatrical Publicity in America." Master's thesis, Tufts University, 2011.

Lynch, Jack. "'Every Man Able to Read': Literacy in Early America." Colonial Williamsburg. Accessed Sept. 4, 2018. Available at https://research.colonialwilliamsburg.org/Foundation/journal/Winter11/literacy.cfm.

Mahar, William J. *Behind the Burnt Cork Mask: Early Blackface Minstrelsy and Antebellum American Popular Culture*. Champaign, IL: University of Illinois Press, 1999.

Malamud, Margaret. *African Americans and the Classics: Antiquity, Abolition and Activism*. London: I. B. Tauris, 2016.

Malinsky, Barbara. 'Lee, Mary Ann." In *International Encyclopedia of Dance*. Vol. 4. New York: Oxford University Press, 2005.

Malone, Jacqui. *Steppin' on the Blues: Visible Rhythms of African American Dance*. Champaign, IL: University of Illinois Press, 1996.

Manuel, Peter. *Creolizing Contradance in the Caribbean*. Philadelphia: Temple University Press, 2009.

Martin, Tony. "The Banneker Literary Institute of Philadelphia: African American Intellectual Activism before the War of the Slaveholders' Rebellion." *The Journal of African American History* 87 (Summer 2002): 303–22.

Masten, April F. "Challenge Dancing in Antebellum America: Sporting Men, Vulgar Women, and Blacked-Up Boys." *Journal of Social History* 48, no. 3 (Spring 2015): 605–34.

Mates, Julian. *America's Musical Stage: Two Hundred Years of Musical Theatre*. New York: Praeger, 1985.

Mathews, Anne. *Memoirs of Charles Mathews*. London: Samuel Bentley, 1838.

Mayer, David. *Harlequin in His Element: The English Pantomime, 1806–1836*. Cambridge, MA: Harvard University Press, 1969.

McAllister, Marvin. *White People Do Not Know How to Behave at Entertainments Designed for Ladies and Gentlemen of Colour: William Brown's African and American Theater*. Chapel Hill: University of North Carolina Press, 2003.

———. *Whiting Up: Whiteface Minstrels and Stage Europeans in African American Performance*. Chapel Hill: University of North Carolina Press, 2011.

McConachie, Bruce. "American Theatre in Context, from the Beginnings to 1870." In *The Cambridge History of American Theatre, Volume One: Beginnings to 1870*, edited by Don B. Wilmeth and Christopher Bigsby. New York: Cambridge University Press, 1998.

McCoy, Genevieve. "Fanny Elssler's Reception: Gender, Class, and Republicanism in the United States, 1840–42." In *Proceedings, Twenty-fifth Annual Conference of the Society of Dance History Scholars*. Philadelphia: Temple University, 2002.

McCurdy, John Gilbert. "The Origins of Universal Suffrage: The Pennsylvania Constitution of 1776." *Pennsylvania Legacies* 8, no. 2 (Nov. 2008): 6–13.

McElroy's Philadelphia Directory. Philadelphia: Edward C. and John Biddle, 1837–1860 annually.

Meer, Sarah. *Uncle Tom Mania: Slavery, Minstrelsy, and Transatlantic Culture in the 1850s*. Athens, GA: University of Georgia Press, 2005.

Meglin, Joellen. "Behind the Veil of Translucence: An Intertextual Reading of the *Ballet Fantastique* in France, 1831–1841. Part One: 'Ancestors of the Sylphide in the *Conte* Fantastique.'" *Dance Chronicle* 27, no. 1 (2004): 67–129.

———. "The Gothic Rituals of Nuns: *Ballet of the Nuns*, from Diderot to Degas." In *Times of Change: Artistic Perspectives and Cultural Crossings in Nineteenth-Century Dance*, edited by Irene Brandenburg, Francesca Falcone, Claudia Jeschke, and Bruno Ligore. Bologna: Piretti Editore, 2022.

Meigs, Charles Delucena. *Females and Their Diseases: A Series of Letters to His Class*. Philadelphia: Lea and Blanchard, 1848.

———. *A Memoir of Samuel George Morton, M. D., Late President of the Academy of Natural Sciences of Philadelphia*. Philadelphia: P. G. Collins, 1851.

Meisner, Nadine. *Marius Petipa: The Emperor's Ballet Master*. New York: Oxford University Press, 2019.

Mintz, Steven. "Historical Context: Facts about the Slave Trade and Slavery." The Gilder-Lehrman Institute of American History. Accessed July 15, 2022. Available at https://www.gilderlehrman.org/history-resources/teaching-resource/historical-context-facts-about-slave-trade-and-slavery.

Montez, Lola. *The Lectures of Lola Montez. With a Full and Complete Autobiography of Her Life*. Philadelphia: T. B. Peterson & Brothers, 1858.

Moody, Jane. "Illusions of Authorship." In *Women and Playwriting in Nineteenth-Century Britain*, edited by Tracy C. Davis and Ellen Donkin. Cambridge, UK: Cambridge University Press, 1999.

Moore, Lillian. *Echoes of American Ballet*. New York: Dance Horizons, 1976.

———. "George Washington Smith." *Dance Index* IV, nos. 6–8 (July–Aug. 1945): 88–135.
———. *Images of the Dance*. New York: New York Public Library Astor, Lenox and Tilden Foundations, 1965.
———. "La fille mal gardée in America." *Dance Magazine*, Feb. 1961, 45–47, 64–65.
———. "Mary Ann Lee" and "George Washington Smith." In *Chronicles of the American Dance*, edited by Paul Magriel. New York: Da Capo Press, 1978. Originally published in 1948.
———. "Prints on Pushcarts." *Dance Perspectives* 15 (1962): 43.
Mora, Kiko. "Pepita Soto: una historia del sueño americano (1852–1859)." *Revista de Investigación sobre Flamenco* 8 (2013): 177–230.
———. "Sounds of Spain in the Nineteenth Century USA: An Introduction." In *Sounds of Spain in the Nineteenth Century USA: An Introduction*, edited by K. Meira Goldberg and Antoní Piza. Cambridge, UK: Cambridge Scholars Publishing, 2016.
Morantz-Sanchez, Regina. *Sympathy and Science: Women Physicians in American Medicine*. Chapel Hill: University of North Carolina Press, 2000. Originally published in 1985.
Moreau de St. Méry, M.L.E. *Description topographique, physique, civile, politique et historique de la partie française de l'isle Saint-Domingue*. Philadelphia: Pauteur, 1797.
Morton, Samuel George. *Crania Aegyptiaca: Or, Observations on Egyptian Ethnography, Derived from Anatomy, History and the Monuments*. Philadelphia: John Penington, 1844.
———. *Crania Americana*. Philadelphia: J. Dobson, 1839.
Mott, Frank Luther. *A History of American Magazines, 1741–1850*. Cambridge, MA: Harvard University Press, 1938.
Mott, Lucretia. "Discourse on Woman" (lecture, Dec. 17, 1849). Philadelphia: T. B. Peterson, 1850.
Nash, Gary B. *Forging Freedom: The Formation of Philadelphia's Black Community, 1720–1840*. Cambridge, MA: Harvard University Press, 1988.
Nash, Margaret A. "Rethinking Republican Motherhood: Benjamin Rush and the Young Ladies' Academy of Philadelphia." *Journal of the Early Republic* 17, no. 2 (Summer 1997): 171–91.
Nathan, Hans. *Dan Emmett and the Rise of Early Negro Minstrelsy*. Norman: University of Oklahoma Press, 1962.
Nathans, Heather. 'Staging Slavery: Representing Race and Abolition on and off the Philadelphia Stage." In *Antislavery and Abolition in Philadelphia: Emancipation and the Long Struggle for Racial Justice in the City of Brotherly Love*, edited by Heather Nathans, Richard S. Newman, and James Mueller. Baton Rouge, LA: Louisiana State University Press, 2011.
Nathanson, Y. S. "Negro Minstrelsy Ancient and Modern." *Putnam's Monthly Magazine of American Literature, Science and Art* V, no. 1 (Jan. 1855): 72–79.
Ndiaye, Noémie. *Scripts of Blackness: Early Modern Performance Culture and the Making of Race*. Philadelphia: University of Pennsylvania Press, 2022.
Newman, Simon. *Embodied History: The Lives of the Poor in Early Philadelphia*. Philadelphia: University of Pennsylvania Press, 2003.

Nolan, Edward J. *A Short History of the Academy of Natural Sciences of Philadelphia.* Philadelphia: Academy of Natural Sciences, 1909.

Notable American Women, 1607–1950: A Biographical Dictionary. 3 vols. Cambridge, MA: The Belknap Press of Harvard University Press, 1971. Chapters cited:
Ekstrom, Parmenia Migel. "Augusta Maywood."
Moore, Lillian. "Julia Turnbull."

Nott, Josiah Clark, and George Gliddon. *Types of Mankind: Or, Ethnological Researches: Based Upon the Ancient Monuments, Paintings, Sculptures, and Crania of Races, and Upon Their Natural, Geographical, Philological and Biblical History, Illustrated by Selections from the Inedited Papers of Samuel George Morton and by Additional Contributions from L. Agassiz, W. Usher, and H. S. Patterson.* Philadelphia: Lippincott, Grambo, & Co., 1854.

Nowatzki, Robert C. "'Our Only Truly National Poets': Blackface Minstrelsy and Cultural Nationalism." *ATQ* 20 (Mar. 2006): 361–78.

———. "Paddy Jumps Jim Crow: Irish-Americans and Blackface Minstrelsy." *Éire-Ireland* 41, nos. 3–4 (Fall–Winter 2006): 162–84.

Nyong'o, Tavia. *The Amalgamation Waltz: Race, Performance, and the Ruses of Memory.* Minneapolis: University of Minnesota Press, 2009.

Olmsted, Frederick Law. *A Journey in the Seaboard Slave States: With Remarks on Their Economy.* New York: Dix & Edwards, 1856.

"On the Opinions of Phrenologists Touching the Function of the Organ Called Wit." *The Phrenological Journal and Magazine of Moral Science* XI, no. LVII (1838): 381–91.

Osofsky, Gilbert. *Puttin' on Ole Massa: The Slave Narratives of Henry Bibb, William Wells Brown, and Solomon Northup.* New York: Harper & Row, 1969.

Oson, Jacob. *A Search for Truth, or, An Inquiry for the Origin of the African Nation: An Address, Delivered at New-Haven in March, and at New-York in April 1817.* New York: Christopher Rush, "a descendant of Africa," 1817.

Otter, Samuel. *Philadelphia Stories: America's Literature of Race and Freedom.* New York: Oxford University Press, 2010.

Oxford Dictionary of Ballet, under "La Tarentule." Accessed Aug. 15, 2021. Available at www.oxfordreference.com.

Parrish, Lydia. *Slave Songs of the Georgia Sea Islands.* Athens, GA: University of Georgia Press, 1992.

"Party Symbols." National Museum of American History. Accessed Aug. 18, 2020. Available at https://americanhistory.si.edu/democracy-exhibition/machinery-democracy/enduring-popular-images-and-party-symbols-0.

Patterson, Thomas C. "An Archaeology of the History of Nineteenth-Century U.S. Anthropology: James McCune Smith, Radical Abolitionist and Anthropologist." *Journal of Anthropological Research* 69, no. 4 (Winter 2013): 459–84.

Pattison, T. Harwood. "The Relation of Art to Religion." *The Baptist Quarterly Review* VIII (July 1886): 324–37.

Peitzman, Steven J. *A New and Untried Course: Woman's Medical College and Medical College of Pennsylvania, 1850–1998.* New Brunswick, NJ: Rutgers University Press, 2000.

Pennington, James W. *Text Book of the Origin and History, &c. &c. of the Colored People.* Harford, CT: L. Skinner, Printer, 1841.

Peterson, Bernard L. *The African American Theatre Directory, 1816–1960: A Comprehensive Guide to Early Black Theatre Organizations, Companies, Theatres, and Performing Groups*. Westport, CT: Greenwood Publishing Group, 1997.
Philadelphia Index, or Directory, for 1823. Philadelphia: Robert Desilver, 1823.
"Philosophy of Fashion." *Philadelphia Monthly Magazine, Devoted to General Literature and the Fine Arts* II, May 15, 1828, 67–74.
"Physicians in Petticoats." *The Ledger*, Aug. 20, 1856.
Pilgrim, Danya M. "Masters of a Craft: Philadelphia's Black Public Waiters, 1820–1850." *Pennsylvania Magazine of History and Biography* CXLII, no. 3 (Oct. 2018): 269–93.
"Places of Public Amusement." *Putnam's Monthly Magazine of American Literature, Science and Art* 3, no. 14 (Feb. 1854): 141–52.
Plaza Orellana, Rocío. *Los bailes españoles en Europa: el espectáculo de los bailes de España en el siglo XIX*. Córdoba: Editorial Almuzara, 2013.
Polgar, Paul J. *Standard-Bearers of Equality: America's First Abolition Movement*. Chapel Hill: University of North Carolina Press, 2019.
Pomfret, John E. "West New Jersey: A Quaker Society, 1675–1775." *William and Mary Quarterly* 8, no. 4 (Oct. 1951): 493–519.
Poskett, James. "Phrenology, Correspondence, and the Global Politics of Reform, 1815–1848." *The Historical Journal* 60, no. 2 (2017): 409–42.
Proceedings and Debates of the Convention of the Commonwealth of Pennsylvania, to Propose Amendments to the Constitution: Commenced and Held at Harrisburg, on the second day of May, 1837. Harrisburg, PA: Packer, Barrett, and Parke, 1837. Accessed Jan. 16, 2020. Available at https://catalog.hathitrust.org/Record/100676981.
"Quaker Dress, 1800–1805." *An Agreeable Tyrant: Fashion after the Revolution*. Accessed Sept. 5, 2021. Available at https://agreeabletyrant.dar.org/gallery/1800-1810/quaker-dress/.
Railton, Stephen. "Miss Lucy Long." *Uncle Tom's Cabin & American Culture*. Accessed Dec. 20, 2021. Available at http://utc.iath.virginia.edu/minstrel/lucylongfr.html.
Rees, James. *The Dramatic Authors of America*. Philadelphia: G. B. Zieber & Co., 1845.
Rehin, George F. "Harlequin Jim Crow: Continuity and Convergence in Blackface Clowning." *Journal of Popular Culture* 9, no. 3 (Winter 1975): 682–701.
Richardson, Edgar P. *Centennial City*. Philadelphia: Historical Society of Pennsylvania, 1971.
Ridgwell, Stephen. "City Women: Managers and Leading Ladies at the City of London Theatre, 1837–1848." *New Theatre Quarterly* 39, no. 3 (2023): 200–215.
Ritter, Abraham. *Philadelphia and Her Merchants, as Constituted Fifty and Seventy Years Ago, Illustrated by Diagrams of the River Front, and Portraits of Some of its Prominent Occupants*. Philadelphia: The Author, 1860.
Roach, Joseph. *Cities of the Dead: Circum-Atlantic Performance*. New York: Columbia University Press, 1996.
Robinson, Dennis. "The Agony and the Ecstasy of James Kennard Jr." SeacoastNH.com. Accessed July 6, 2024. Available at https://www.seacoastnh.com/the-agony-and-the-ecstasy-of-james-kennard-jr/.
Rodger, Gillian M. *Champagne Charlie and Pretty Jemima: Variety Theater in the Nineteenth Century*. Champaign, IL: University of Illinois Press, 2010.
Ronzani, Domenico. *Il Birrichino di Parigi, A Grand Ballet in Three Acts and Four Scenes*. Philadelphia: F. Rullman, 1857.

Rosenberg, Carroll Smith. "Beauty, the Beast and the Militant Woman: A Case Study in Sex Roles and Social Stress in Jacksonian America." *American Quarterly* 23, no. 4 (Oct. 1971): 562–84.

Rosenman, Ellen Bayuk. "Spectacular Women: 'The Mysteries of London' and the Female Body." *Victorian Studies* 40, no. 1 (Autumn 1996): 31–64.

———. *Unauthorized Pleasures: Accounts of Victorian Erotic Experience*. Ithaca, NY: Cornell University Press, 2018.

Rusert, Britt. *Fugitive Science: Empiricism and Freedom in Early African American Culture*. New York: New York University Press, 2017.

———. "Types of Mankind: Visualizing Kinship in Afro-Native America." *Commonplace: The Journal of Early American Life* 13, no. 1 (Oct. 2012). Accessed Jan. 15, 2022. Available at http://commonplace.online/article/types-of-mankind/.

Rush, Benjamin. "Observations Intended to Favour a Supposition That the Black Color (As It Is Called) of the Negroes Is Derived from the Leprosy, Read at a Special Meeting July 14, 1797." *Transactions, American Philosophical Society* IV (1799): 289–97.

Russett, Cynthia Eagle. *Sexual Science: The Victorian Construction of Womanhood*. Cambridge, MA: Harvard University Press, 1991.

Sánchez-Eppler, Karen. *Touching Liberty: Abolition, Feminism, and the Politics of the Body*. Berkeley, CA: University of California Press, 1993.

Sanford, Samuel S. *Sanford's Melodies, As Sung by his Star Troupe at the American Opera House, Philadelphia*. Philadelphia: McLaughlin Bros., 1856.

Saxton, Alexander. "Blackface Minstrelsy and Jacksonian Ideology." *American Quarterly* 27, no. 1 (Mar. 1975): 3–28.

Scafidi, Nadia, Rita Zambon, and Roberta Albano. *La Danza in Italia: la Scala, la Fenice, il San Carlo dal secolo XVIII ai giorni nostri*. Rome: Gremese, 1998.

Scharf, J., and T. Westcott, *History of Philadelphia, 1609–1884*. Philadelphia: L. H. Everts, 1884.

Schiebinger, Londa. *Nature's Body: Gender in the Making of Modern Science*. 1993; New Brunswick, NJ: Rutgers University Press, 2013.

Schneider, Gretchen. "Ravel Family." In *International Encyclopedia of Dance*, vol. 5. New York: Oxford University Press, 2005.

Schor, Paul. *Counting Americans: How the US Census Classified the Nation*. Oxford Scholarship Online. Accessed Dec. 20, 2021. Available at https://oxford.universitypressscholarship.com/view/10.1093/acprof:oso/9780199917853.001.0001/acprof-9780199917853-chapter-4.

Schrag, Zachary M. *The Fires of Philadelphia: Citizen-Soldiers, Nativists, and the 1844 Riots Over the Soul of a Nation*. New York: Pegasus Books, 2021.

Seebass, Tilman. "Iconography and Dance Research." *Yearbook for Traditional Music* 23 (1991): 33–51.

Senelick, Laurence. "Pantomime, English." In *The Cambridge Guide to the Theatre*, edited by Martin Banham. Cambridge, UK: Cambridge University Press, 1995.

Seymour, Bruce. *Lola Montez: A Life*. New Haven, CT: Yale University Press, 1996.

Seymour (?), Charles Bailey. "Amusements: Ethiopian Minstrelsy." *New-York Times*, Aug. 18, 1859, 4.

Shaw, Gwendolyn D. "'Moses Williams, Cutter of Profiles': Silhouettes and African American Identity in the Early Republic." In *Portraits of a People: Picturing African*

Americans in the Nineteenth Century. Seattle & London: Addison Gallery of American Art with the University of Washington Press, 2006.

Shepherd, Kirsten. *Theatre and Evolution from Ibsen to Beckett*. New York: Columbia University Press, 2015.

Slout, William L. "Brown's Burnt Cork History." Circus Historical Society. Accessed July 28, 2022. Available at http://www.classic.circushistory.org/Cork/BurntCork2.htm.

———. *Olympians of the Sawdust Circle: A Biographical Dictionary of the Nineteenth Century American Circus*. San Bernardino, CA: The Borgo Press, 1975.

Smedley, Audrey. *Race in North America: Origin and Evolution of a Worldview*. Boulder, CO: Westview Press, 2011.

Smith, Christopher J. *The Creolization of American Culture*. Champaign: University of Illinois Press, 2013.

———. "The Creolization of American Culture." *Creolization* (blog). Tumblr, May 8, 2013. Accessed May 30, 2022. Available at https://creolization.tumblr.com/post/49913259248/dancing-for-eels-1820-catharine-market-iconic.

Smith, Eric Ledell. "The End of Black Voting Rights in Pennsylvania: African Americans and the Pennsylvania Constitutional Convention of 1837–1838." *Pennsylvania History: A Journal of Mid-Atlantic Studies* 65, no. 3 (Summer 1998): 279–299.

Smith-Rosenberg, Caroll, and Charles Rosenberg. "The Female Animal: Medical and Biological Views of Woman and Her Role in Nineteenth-Century America." *Journal of American History* 60, no. 2 (Sept. 1973): 332–56.

Snyder, Laura J. "William Whewell." In *Stanford Encyclopedia of Science*. Accessed Aug. 4, 2021. Available at https://plato.stanford.edu/entries/whewell/#SciInd.

Snyder, Martin P. "William L. Breton, Nineteenth-Century Philadelphia Artist." *Pennsylvania Magazine of History and Biography* 85, no. 2 (Apr. 1961): 178–209.

Sorisio, Carolyn. *Fleshing Out America: Race, Gender, and the Politics of the Body in American Literature, 1833–1879*. Athens, GA: University of Georgia Press, 2002.

Southern, Eileen. *The Music of Black Americans: A History*. 3rd ed. New York: W. W. Norton & Co., 1997. Originally published in 1971.

Sparti, Barbara, and Judy Van Zile, with Nancy G. Heller and Adrienne L. Kaeppler, eds. *Imaging Dance: Visual Representations of Dancers and Dancing*. Hildesheim, Germany: Georg Olms Verlag, 2011.

Spires, Derrick R. *The Practice of Citizenship: Black Politics and Print Culture in the Early United States*. Philadelphia: University of Pennsylvania Press, 2019.

Stanton, Elizabeth Cady, Susan B. Anthony, and Matilda Joslyn Gage. *History of Woman Suffrage, 1848–1861*. Vol. 1. Rochester, NY: Charles Mann, 1881.

Stanton, William. *The Leopard's Spots: Scientific Attitudes toward Race in America, 1815–59*. Chicago: University of Chicago Press, 1960.

Stauffer, John. "Frederick Douglass and the Aesthetics of Freedom." *Raritan* 25, no. 1 (2005): 114–36.

———. *The Works of James McCune Smith: Black Intellectual and Abolitionist*. New York: Oxford University Press, 2006.

Stearns, Bertha Monica. "Early Philadelphia Magazines for Ladies." *Pennsylvania Magazine of History and Biography* 64, no. 4 (Oct. 1940): 479–91.

Stearns, Marshall, and Jean Stearns. *Jazz Dance: The Story of American Vernacular Dance*. New York: Schirmer Books, 1964.

Stocking, George W. *Race, Culture, and Evolution: Essays in the History of Anthropology*. Toronto: The Free Press of Collier-Macmillan, 1968.

Stowe, Harriet Beecher. *Uncle Tom's Cabin; or, Life among the Lowly*. Boston: John P. Jewett & Co., 1852.

Strom, Sharon Harman. *Fortune, Fame, and Desire: Promoting the Self in the Long Nineteenth Century*. Lanham, MD: Rowman & Littlefield, 2016.

Stuckey, P. Sterling. "Christian Conversion and the Challenge of Dance." In *Dancing Many Drums: Excavations in African American Dance*, edited by Thomas F. DeFrantz. Madison, WI: University of Wisconsin Press, 2002.

Sturge, Joseph. *A Visit to the United States in 1841*. London: Hamilton, Adams, and Co., 1842.

Sutton, Matthew. "Fellows Find: Photos, Playbills, News Clippings Document History of Blackface in Minstrel Shows." *Ransom Center Magazine*, July 13, 2011. Accessed Aug. 4, 2019. Available at https://sites.utexas.edu/ransomcentermagazine/2011/07/13/fellows-find-photos-playbills-news-clippings-document-history-of-blackface-in-minstrel-shows/.

Sweeney, James L. "Caribs, Maroons, Jacobins, Brigands, and Sugar Barons: The Last Stand of the Black Caribs on St. Vincent." *Newsletter of the African Diaspora Archeology Network* (Mar. 2007). Accessed Aug. 20, 2020. Available at https://scholarworks.umass.edu/adan/vol10/iss1/7/.

Swift, Mary Grace. *Belles and Beaux on Their Toes: Dancing Stars in Young America*. Washington, DC: University Press of America, 1980.

Szwed, John F., and Morton Marks. "The Afro-American Transformation of European Set Dances and Dance Suites." *Dance Research Journal* 20, no. 1 (Summer 1988): 29–36.

Taglioni, Filippo. *Jocko, O Sia La Scimia Brasiliana, Ballo in Tre Atti*. Naples: Tipografia Flautina, 1828.

Taylor, Diana. *The Archive and the Repertoire: Performing Cultural Memory in the Americas*. Durham, NC: Duke University Press, 2003.

Taylor, George R. "Gaslight Foster: A New York 'Journeyman Journalist' at Mid-Century." *New York History* 58, no. 3 (July 1977): 297–312.

Taylor, George R., and George G. Foster. "'Philadelphia in Slices' by George G. Foster." *Pennsylvania Magazine of History and Biography* 93, no. 1 (Jan. 1969): 23–72.

Theriot, Nancy M. *Mothers and Daughters in Nineteenth-Century America: The Biosocial Construction of Femininity*. Lexington: University Press of Kentucky, 1996.

Thompson, George Jr. *A Documentary History of the African Theatre*. Evanston, IL: Northwestern University Press, 1998.

Thompson, Katrina. *Ring Shout, Wheel About: The Racial Politics of Music and Dance in North American Slavery*. Champaign: University of Illinois Press, 2014.

Tocqueville, Alexis de. *Democracy in America*. 2 vols. Translated by Henry Reeve. New York: George Adland, 1835.

"Trans-Atlantic Slave Trade—Estimates." SlaveVoyages. Accessed July 15, 2022. Available at https://www.slavevoyages.org/assessment/estimates.

Trollope, Frances Milton. *Domestic Manners of the Americans*. London and New York: Whittacker, Treacher, & Co., 1832.

Ulle, Robert F. "Popular Black Music in Nineteenth Century Philadelphia." *Pennsylvania Folklore* 25, no. 2 (Winter 1975–76): 20–28.
"Union, New Jersey, United States." *Encyclopedia Britannica*. Accessed Sept. 5, 2021. Available at https://www.britannica.com/place/Union-New-Jersey.
"United States Abolition and Anti-Slavery Timeline." *American Abolition and Anti-Slavery Activists: Conscience of the Nation*. Accessed July 25, 2022. Available at http://www.americanabolitionists.com/us-abolition-and-anti-slavery-timeline.html.
van Wyhe, John. "The History of Phrenology on the Web." Accessed July 26, 2019. Available at http://www.historyofphrenology.org.uk/overview.htm.
Varon, Elizabeth. *Armies of Deliverance: A New History of the Civil War*. New York: Oxford University Press, 2013.
Vivian, Cassandra. "George Gliddon in America: The Awakening of Egyptomania." *Academia*. Accessed Mar. 1, 2022. Available at https://www.academia.edu/17667211/George_Gliddon_in_America_The_Awakening_of_Egyptomania.
Vogeley, Nancy. *The Bookrunner: A History of Inter-American Relations—Print, Politics, and Commerce in the United States and Mexico, 1800–1830*. Philadelphia: American Philosophical Society, 2011.
Walker, David. *Appeal, in Four Articles; Together with a Preamble, to the Coloured Citizens of the World, but in Particular, and Very Expressly, to Those of the United States of America*. Boston: Revised and Published by David Walker, 1830. North Carolina Collection, University of North Carolina at Chapel Hill, VCC326.4 W17a. Accessed Sept. 1, 2020. Available at https://docsouth.unc.edu/nc/walker/walker.html.
Wallis, Brian. "Black Bodies, White Science: Louis Agassiz's Slave Daguerreotypes." *American Art* 9, no. 2 (Summer 1995): 38–61.
Walsh, Anthony A. "The 'New Science of the Mind' and the Philadelphia Physicians in the Early 1800s." *Transactions & Studies of the College of Physicians of Philadelphia* 43, no. 4 (Apr. 1976): 397–415.
Ward, David C. *Charles Willson Peale: Art and Selfhood in the Early Republic*. Berkeley: University of California Press, 2004.
Warner, Michael. *The Letters of the Republic: Publication and the Public Sphere in Eighteenth-Century America*. Cambridge, MA: Harvard University Press, 1990.
———. *Publics and Counterpublics*. New York: Zone Books, 2002.
Warner, Michael, Natasha Hurley, Luis Iglesias, Sonia Di Loreto, Jeffrey Scraba, and Sandra Young. "A Soliloquy 'Lately Spoken at the African Theatre': Race and the Public Sphere in New York City, 1821." *American Literature* 73, no. 1 (Mar. 2001): 1–46.
Washburn, Patrick Scott. *The African American Newspaper: Voice of Freedom*. Evanston, IL: Northeastern University Press, 2006.
Watkins, Harry. *The Pioneer Patriot; Or, the Maid of the War-Path*. New York: William B. Smith, 1854.
Watson, John Fanning. *Annals of Philadelphia and Pennsylvania in the Olden Time: Being a Collection of Memoirs, Anecdotes and Incidents of the City and Its Inhabitants, and of the Earliest Settlements of the Inland Part of Pennsylvania from the Days of the Founders*. 3 vols. Philadelphia: Carey & Hart, 1845.
———. *Methodist Error, or, Friendly Christian Advice: To Those Methodists Who Indulge in Extravagant Religious Emotions and Bodily Exercises*. Trenton, NJ: D. & E. Fenton, 1819.

Welsh Asanti, Kariamu. "Commonalities in African Dance: An Aesthetic Foundation." In *Moving History/Dancing Cultures: A Dance History Reader*, edited by Ann Dils and Ann Cooper Albright. Middletown, CT: Wesleyan University Press, 2001.

Wemyss, Francis. *Twenty-Six Years of the Life of An Actor and Manager*. 2 vols. New York: Burgess, Stringer and Co., 1847.

———. *Wemyss' Chronology of the American Stage, From 1752 to 1852*. New York: William Taylor & Co., 1852.

West, Cornel. "Race and Modernity." In *The Cornel West Reader*. New York: Basic Civitas Books, 1999.

Whale, Henry. *Hommage a Taglioni, A Fashionable Quadrille Preceptor and Ballroom Companion*. Philadelphia: Musical Fund Hall, 1836.

Whipper, William. "An Appeal to the Colored Citizens of Pennsylvania." In *Minutes of the State Convention of the Coloured Citizens of Pennsylvania, Convened at Harrisburg, Dec. 13th and 14th, 1848*. Philadelphia: Merrihew and Thompson, 1849.

White, Shane, and Graham White. *Stylin': African American Expressive Culture from Its Beginnings to the Zoot Suit*. Ithaca, NY: Cornell University Press, 1998.

Wiegman, Robyn. *American Anatomies: Theorizing Race and Gender*. Durham, NC: Duke University Press, 1995.

Wilentz, Sean. *The Rise of American Democracy: Jefferson to Lincoln*. New York: W. W. Horton and Company 2008.

Williams, David. *A People's History of the Civil War: Struggles for the Meaning of Freedom*. New York: New Press, 2006.

Willson, Joseph. *Sketches of the Higher Classes of Colored Society in Philadelphia*. Philadelphia: Merrihew and Thompson, 1841.

Wilson, Arthur H. *A History of the Philadelphia Theatre 1835–1855*. New York: Greenwood Press, 1968.

Winch, Julie. *The Elite of our People: Joseph Willson's Sketches of Black Upper-Class Life in Antebellum Philadelphia*. University Park: Pennsylvania State University Press, 2000.

———. "Free Men and 'Freemen: Black Voting Rights in Pennsylvania, 1790–1870." *Pennsylvania Legacies* 8, no. 2 (Nov. 2008): 14–19.

———. *A Gentleman of Color: The Life of James Forten*. New York: Oxford University Press, 2002.

Winter, Marian Hannah. "Augusta Maywood" and "Juba and American Minstrelsy." In *Chronicles of the American Dance*, edited by Paul Magriel. New York: Da Capo Press, 1978. Originally published in 1948 by Henry Holt.

Winter, William. *Life and Art of Joseph Jefferson*. London: McMillan & Co., 1893.

Wittmann, Matthew. "Kelly and Leon's Minstrels (Part I)." Matthew Wittmann (blog). Sept. 15, 2012. Accessed Mar. 15, 2018. Available at http://www.matthewwittmann.com/kelly-and-leons-minstrels-part-i/.

Wolfe, S. J. "Bringing Egypt to America: George Gliddon and The Panorama of the Nile." *Journal of Ancient Egyptian Interconnections* 8 (2016): 1–20.

———. "From Eternity to Here: The Egyptian Mummy in Nineteenth-Century America." *Academia*. Accessed Feb. 25, 2022. Available at https://www.academia.edu/35729159/Egyptian_mummy_in_nineteenth_century_America_doc.

Wood, Peter H. "'Gimme de Kneebone Bent.'" In *The Black Tradition in American Modern Dance*, edited by Gerald E. Myers. Durham, NC: The American Dance Festival, 1988.

Wood, William B. *Personal Recollections of the Stage*. Philadelphia: H.C. Baird, 1855.
Wright, Francis. *Views of Society and Manners in America; In a Series of Letters from That Country to a Friend in England, During the Years 1818, 1819, and 1820*. New York: Bliss & White, 1821.
Wynter, Sylvia. "Sambos and Minstrels." *Social Text* 1 (Winter 1979): 149–156.
Yee, Shirley J. *Black Women Abolitionists: A Study in Activism, 1828–1860*. Knoxville, TN: University of Tennessee Press, 1992.
The Young Lady's Book: A Manual of Elegant Recreations. Boston: A. Bowen, and Carter & Hendee, 1830.

Index

Abolitionism, 7–9, 13, 28, 61–62, 87, 128, 153–55, 158, 188, 205, 210n13. *See also* Emancipation; Douglass, Frederick; Quaker; Women
Académie Royale (of Paris), 170, 176, 180
"Academy for Dancing Exercises," 179
Academy of Music, 142, 153, 167–74, 171f, 176, 179, 181, 201
Academy of Natural Sciences (Philadelphia), 16, 128, 149; museum of, 43
Achille (Soulier), M., 34, 37–40, 186, 214n30
Acrobatics (dancing and performance), 2, 9, 23, 42, 70, 118, 120, 166, 185, 199
Adam (biblical figure), 15, 42
Adams County (Pennsylvania), 130
Adams, John Quincy, 8
Adelphi Theatre, 71, 75, 166
Aeneid, The, 114
Aeschylus, 153
Africa (continental), 65, 81, 83, 97–98, 123–24, 129–30, 134, 144–46, 180, 204; characterization of people from, 41, 51, 54, 81, 124, 133, 141, 189; colonization of, 61; (traditional) dances of, 194–96; descent from, 4, 11, 61, 63, 84, 129, 134, 147, 152, 178, 194, 204–205 enslavement of peoples from, 15, 42, 52, 123, 128, 148; racialization of, 14, 43, 50–55, 50f, 81,
144, 192; stylization of (in performance), 20, 22, 42, 49, 55, 95, 133, 135, 193
African American(s). *See* Black communities and individuals
"African Fancy Ball, Pat Juba," 50–53, 50f, 57
African Grove Theatre (a.k.a. African Theatre), 19, 55–56, 212n81
Agassiz, Professor Louis, 142, 144, 149
Aiken, G.L., 153
"Akimbo" (stylization), 39, 48, 123, 198, 205, 244n63
Albert, Ferdinand, 187
Albright, William, 95
Aldridge, Ira, 55–56
Alexander's Messenger, 109
Alighieri, Dante, 173
Allen, Richard, 61
Alloggio Militare, 175
D'Aimée, or an Oriental Dream, 118
"An Amalgamation Polka," 53
"An Amalgamation Waltz," 53, 91
Amateur's Preceptor on Dancing Etiquette, 176
American Antiquarian Society, 213n4
American Anti-Slavery Society (AASS), 62
"American Medical College," 234n15
American Moral Reform Society, 62 131
American Philosophical Society, 16
American Phrenological Journal, 66

Amherst, Mr., 80
L'Amour, 100
(Anglo-)Saxon, 144, 146, 197
Anti-Slavery Convention of American Women, 62
Antonia, Mme., 179
Appeal in Four Articles, with a Preamble to the Colored Citizens of the World, 60
Apollo Belvedere, 64, 177
Arch Street Theatre, 104, 117–18, 150, 160, 169, 216n69, 224n118
Arnold, Lee, 213n7
Arraline, Mlle. (Brooks), 69, 101, 227n15
The Art of Dancing, Historically Illustrated, 178
Arthur, Timothy Shay, 111
Articles of Confederation, 60–61
Asama, 55
Aspasia, 165
Athens of America, 6
Atlantic, 83, 86, 88, 125, 158, 197; transatlantic, 19, 124, 194
Auber, Daniel, 69, 86, 115
August, B., 31, 95
Augustin, Peter, 28
Aumer, Jean-Pierre, 108, 122
Australia, 163
The Autobiography and Lectures of Lola Montez (Countess of Landsfeld), 164
Avenger of Sicily, The, 28

Babel (biblical), 79
Badger, Mr., 95
Bailey, John, 98, 226n162
Balilion, 55
Ball (formal social dance), 22, 30–32, 45, 52, 91, 93–95, 132–33, 135, 140–41, 197, 226n152; ballroom (culture and venue), 9, 21–22, 24, 27, 29, 32, 33–35, 45, 47, 53, 93–96, 177, 199–200, 207; masquerade variety of, 28–29, 33, 52–53, 174
Ballantyne, Tony, 11
Ballerina, beauty/allure of, 12, 18–19, 110, 115, 118, 200–201; (im)morality of, 19, 70–73, 105–107, 215n47; feminism of freedom of, 157–58, 184–85, 202; sexualization of, 19, 73, 81, 104–105, 107, 112, 115, 184. *See also* Ballet; Celeste, Mme or Mlle.; Elssler, Fanny
Ballet, 4, 18, 21, 23, 42, 100–101, 175, 182; Americanization of, 168, 171–72, 175–76; combined with opera, 151–52, 172–175; discourse and politics of, 5–6; exoticization or racialization of, 36, 58, 69, 73, 81, 104, 114, 118, 173, 186; fairy-like quality of, 20, 35–37, 114, 118, 175; technique of, 35, 39, 70, 76, 110, 114, 139, 185–87, 199–200, 221n52; rivalries within, 78. *See also* Ballerina; Blackface; Celeste, Mlle. or Mme.; Elssler, Fanny; French; Lee, Mary Ann; Maywood, Augusta; Ronzani Ballet (troupe)
Ballston Spa, 28, 140
Baltimore, 66, 71, 88, 90, 105
Baratti, Filippo, 172–74, 201
Barbary, 24, 36
Barber of Seville, The, 43
Barbiere (Barberre), Joseph, 34, 186
Barnett, Morris, 177
Barnum, P.T., 149; Museum of, 162
Barrooms, drinking, and taverns, 12, 47, 49, 57, 87, 97, 127, 134–35, 138, 155, 168, 180, 182 196, 205, 229n50, 240n151
Bartholomin, Victor, 118, 230n72
Bath (city), 10, 86
La Bayadere (choreographed by Marius Petipa), 69
La Bayadere (*or, Lah-Buy-it-Dear*), 151
La Bayadere; or, The Maid of Cashmere, 21, 67, 76f, 81, 86, 93, 104, 113, 115, 117, 168, 175, 187, 202, 220n44; association with Celeste, 60, 67–76, 68f, 73, 75–76f, 78, 166; association with Elssler, 108; Black version of, 139; burlesque versions of, 122, 151; exotic themes of, 73, 81
Beau Nash, 86
Beech, Mrs., 136, 179
Beggar's Opera, The, 86
Behn, Aphra, 54
'Bel of Prairie Eden: A Romance of Mexico, 112
The Belle of Madrid, 176
La Belle Peruvienne, 40
Bellini, (Vincenzo), 122, 151
Benoni, Bertrand, 44
Bernard, William Bayle, 75, 147
Bernardin, Estelle, 44
Bertin, Mlles. J., 166
Bethel African Methodist Episcopal Church, 7, 97, 196
Bible or biblical, 19, 65, 145, 149
Birch, Thomas, 12
Birch, William ("Billy"), 12, 123
Il Birrichino di Parigi, 174

Blache Frédéric-Auguste, 42
Blache, Jean-Baptiste, 70
Black Dancing Body, The. *See* Gottschild, Brenda Dixon
Black communities, cultures and individuals (in Philadelphia), activists, 61–62; free, 7–8; intellectuals, 15, 231n99; leadership of, 7–8, 61, 63, 65, 96, 125, 125–30, 145, 193; institutions of 7; performers, 19–20, 22, 28, 55, 96–98, 134–35, 139–41, 194–95; rhythmic structures of 52, 194–95, 198' rebellions of, 7–8, 123; workers, 3. *See also* Africa; Class; Religion and Spirituality
Black Masons, 25
"Black People's Prayer Meeting," 58, 96
Black up, 1, 56, 147, 150–51. *See also* Blackface; Blackface minstrelsy; Black up; Corked-up
Blackface, 4, 14–15, 20–22, 36, 49, 54, 60, 67, 82, 87, 92, 122, 127–28, 131, 143, 145, 147, 181, 194; association with ballet, 104–105, 113, 119–20, 122, 124, 188–89, 191–92, 203; and Irish performers, 199; association with opera, 151–53, 169, 177, 181; and T.D. Rice, 1, 8, 10, 15, 20, 54, 60, 82–96, 98, 120, 124; performed by, or appropriated from, Black artists, 126–27, 192–93; politics of, 5, 50, 122–23, 157, 182, 204–205; popularization of in Philadelphia, 8, 57–58, 119, 132, 197–98, 147, 155, 181; response from African Americans about, 33, 125–27, 130, 198, 206; (racist) themes in, 14–15, 36, 43, 65, 84, 86, 92, 132, 137, 140, 193; troupes in Philadelphia, 4, 10, 19–21, 88, 120–21, 147, 155, 167–68, 206; women performers or parodies of, 147, 150, 158, 165, 203. *See also* Blackface minstrelsy; Black up; Corked-up; "Ethiopian"
Blackface minstrelsy, alleged origins of, 120–21, 230n83; association with dance, 6–7, 84, 119, 122–23, 125–26, 192; critiques of, 128, 131, 157–59, 193; genre of, 1, 10–11, 104, 119–23, 139, 151; politics of, 6, 8, 20, 54, 57, 61, 123; popularization of in Philadelphia, 4, 120, 140, 142, 147–48, 150, 153, 168, 178; racial stereotypes within, 4, 8, 10–11, 49–50, 54, 56, 119–125, 145, 188; theories on African-derived influences on, 196–98; women performers of, 157. *See also* Blackface; Black up; Corked-up; "Ethiopian"

Blangy, Mme. Hermine, 94, 117, 185
Blasis, Carlo, 39, 43, 139, 177
Bleakly, William, 136
Blitz, Antonio, 150, 180
Blitz, Bobby, 172
Bloomer, Amelia, 158
Bloomerism, 157–58
Blue, Ginger, 86, 147–49, 203
Blumenbach, Johann Friedrich, 13, 130
Body or Bodies. *See* Ballerina; Ballet; Blackface minstrelsy; Delineation; Politics; Science
Bogle, Robert, 28
Bohemian Girl, The, 21, 189, 213n90
Boieldieu, François-Adrien, 43
Bonaffon, Anthony, 31, 95
"Bonaffon's Cotillion Parties, Valtz," 30–31, 31f
Bone Squash Diavolo, 15, 21, 60, 85–86, 88–92, 188, 203
Booth Jr., Mrs. Junius Brutus (Clementine De Bar), 159
Boston, 85, 108, 115, 149, 163, 174, 180
The Botanico-Medical Recorder, 137
Bouquet d'Amour, The, 70
Bourdeaux, 44
Bouxary, M., 117
Bowery Theatre, 119, 160
Boyd's Minstrels, 155
Breck, Samuel, 28
Breton, William W., 12
"A Brief Memoir of Fanny Elssler," 110
Brillant, Paul, 166, 175–76, 185, 202
British, 20, 26, 29, 34–35, 54, 83, 85, 159, 184, 194, 199, 203
British Isles, 49
Broad Street (Philadelphia), 171
Brothels and prostitution, 49, 71, 112, 134–135, 155, 221n56, 229n50
Brower, Frank, 10, 119–20, 150, 154, 158, 188, 191
Brown, Henry Box, 234n23
Brown, T. Allston, 192
Brown, William, 55
Browne, Peter A., 233n6
Brussels, 93
Bucks County, 62
Buckstone, William, 75
Buffalo (New York), 163
Bunker Hill, 108
Burns, Robert, 124
Burton, Antoinette, 11

Bushman, Richard, 170
Buy-I-Dare: Or, the Revolt of the Wool-Heads, 122
Byrne, James, 34
Byron, Lord, 173

"La Cachuchua" or *cachucha*, 40, 104, 117, 137, 139, 159, 176, 187, 191, 176, 227n13; association with Elssler, 100–101, 102f, 111–13, 122, 151–52, 167. *See also* Ballet; Exoticism; National dances
Cain (biblical figure), 70
Caldwell, Charles, 12, 32, 64–65, 69
Calhoun, Senator/Vice President John, 129, 143
California, 163
Caliph of Baghdad, The, 43, 216n69
Calladine, Mr., 168
Campbell, Mary, 179
Canada or Canadians, 164
Caribs, 64–65, 219n22
Caribbean, 42, 55, 83, 123, 197
Caricature, 8, 21–22, 56, 98, 203. *See also* Blackface; Blackface minstrelsy.
Carpenter, D.L., 95, 113, 136, 138, 176–77, 179
Carr, Benjamin, 139
Carrese, Guiseppe, 166–67
Cartwright, Samuel, 15, 178
Cartee's Lyceum, 150
Cartoons, 5, 8, 12, 66, 71, 86, 106f, 160, racism of, 12–13, 25, 90, 95, 121, 131. *See also* Clay, Edward W.; Visual arts,
Case Western Reserve University, 145
Cataract of the Ganges, The, 28, 140
Caucasian, 14, 55, 64–65, 74, 131, 144, 146, 189, 192
Cecchetti, Cesare, 172, 175
Cecchetti, Enrico, 172, 174
Cecchetti, Serafina, 172
Celeste, Mlle./Mme. (Céline Céleste-Elliott, Celeste Kepler), 40, 70, 72f, 74–75, 113, 157, 166, 186, 189, 213n90, 216n69, 221n52; in *La Bayadere*, 60, 67, 68f, 69; beauty and skill of, 67, 69, 71, 73, 191; financial success of, 18, 71, 184–85; influences on (or parodies by) other performers, 75, 78, 82, 85, 103, 122, 151, 163, 165, 189; gender-related transgressions of, 19, 64, 69, 71, 72f, 107, 111, 114. *See also* Ballerina; Ballet; *La Bayadere*
Celeste-al-Cabinet, 71
Celeste, La Petite (child performer), 187
Celtic, 46, 197, 199. *See also* Ireland; Irish
Cerrito, Fanny, 160, 174
Charles II, 164
Charleston Medical Journal, The, 15
Charlotte Corday; or, Jacobins and Girondists, 163
Checkini, Monsieur and Madame, 69, 220n40
Cherry and Fair Star, 3, 35–37, 184, 209n4, 213n90, 215n39
Chesapeake region, 196
Chestnut Street (Philadelphia), 150
"Chestnut St. Theatre, Pas de Deux" (print) 33f, 50–51
Chestnut Street Theatre 1, 9, 121, 127, 168–69; dance-related performances at, 37, 60, 75, 80–81, 94, 100, 103, 105, 108–109, 111–12, 168, 177, 186–87, 200–201; operatic productions at, 35, 92, 168, 187; racialized performances at, 56, 85, 153–54, 189; theatrical productions at, 28, 118, 153–54, 163, 168
chica, la (dance), 42
Chinese, 124, 147, 191. *See also* Exoticism
Christmas, 21, 154
Cibber, Colley, 40
Cinderella (of Sam Sanford), 151
Cinderella, or the Fairy and the Glass Slipper, 21, 213n90
Ciocca, Giovanna, 117, 160
Circus, 10, 20, 29–30, 41, 43, 83, 76, 79, 120, 137, 140, 155, 169, 180, 183, 193, 198, 206
Citizenship, 5, 6–7, 10, 60–61, 84, 140, 183, 203, 219n8
"City Assembly, Balancez," 26, 26f, 45, 50
City Dancing Assembly (a.k.a. Philadelphia Dancing Assembly), 25–26, 29–32, 95, 140, 179
City of Brotherly Love, 1, 8, 47, 63, 88, 155, 207
City Museum, 153
Civil War, 6, 15, 60, 147, 194, 203, 211n58
Claire, Elizabeth, 213n11
Class (in Philadelphia), 25, 46, 58, 84, 91, 98–99, 123, 142, 168, 176, 179, 207,

233n1, 235n30; artistic tastes of upper/elite, 20–21, 32, 119, 142, 152, 162, 167, 176; Black elite/upper residents and dancers, 52, 90, 95–96, 131–32, 180, 196; critiques of classism, 179; dancers of upper/elite, 10, 22, 27–28, 32–33, 45, 50, 94, 140, 178; lower class, 12, 21, 44–45, 49, 51–52, 168, 178; middle class, 22, 150, 177, 226n152, 235n30; upper/elite (general), 11, 21, 25–28, 30, 56, 83, 85, 90, 109, 135, 177, 204, 206, 213–19; upper/elite, White, 20, 28, 57, 59, 86, 122, 127, 181, 196–97; working class, Black or interracial, 47–48, 180; working class (general), 20, 22, 78, 82–84, 142, 150, 155, 162, 199; working class, White, 1, 20, 47, 88, 120, 124, 188, 231n105
Clay, Edward W., bodily understanding of, 25, 27, 31, 33, 46, 49; illustrations by, 2f, 26f, 29f, 31f, 33f, 45f, 46f, 48f, 50f, 76f, 87f, 116f; racism in, 12, 47, 50–53, 86–87, 92, 204–205; visual record of, 5, 31, 33, 38, 44–45, 57, 115. *See also Lesson in Dancing*; Visual culture
Clay, Henry, 92
Clemens, John, 57, 85
"Coal Black Rose," 82
Cobb, Sylvanus, 43
Cocombo; or, the Embassy to Smyrna, 70
College of Ohio, 137
Colonization, 11, 13–14, 32, 41, 61, 196
Colored American, 88, 96, 127
Columbia (Pennsylvania), 131
Commedia dell'arte, 21, 83, 199. *See also* Harlequinade
Comte de Buffon (a.k.a. Georges-Louis Leclerc), 13, 130
The Condition, Elevation, Emigration, and Destiny of the Colored People of the United States, 146
Congo, 84
Connecticut, 86, 130
Conner's Theatre, 159
Conway, Edmund, 35, 138
Conway, H.J., 163
Conway family, 34–35
"Coon" (stereotype), 91–92
Cooper, James Fenimore, 75
Coralli, Jean, 100, 222n80, 222n86

Corked-up 20, 55, 86; with burnt cork, 1, 10, 126–27, 168, 188–89, 191, 222n91. *See also* Blackface; Blackface minstrelsy
Corneille, Pierre, 107
Cornish, Samuel, 88, 96, 127–28, 193
"Correct Sketch of the Life of Mad'lle Fanny Elssler," 108
Cotillion, 25, 27–29, 31, 132, 136, 176; racialization of, 22, 139. *See also* Blackface; Blackface Minstrelsy
Cotton, Ben, 193
Covent Garden, 35, 67
Cowell, Joseph, 28
Coyne, J.S., 159
Cracovienne, 21, 100, 104, 108, 113, 139, 152, 176, 187, 191. *See also* Elssler, Fanny; National Dances
Crane, Susan, 11
Crania Aegyptiaca, 128–29, 145
Crania Americana, 14, 64–65, 75. *See also* Morton, Samuel George
Crow, Jim, 1, 2f, 3, 8, 20, 54, 82–86, 88, 93, 125, 203, 205, 245n82. *See also* "Jump Jim Crow"
Cruikshank, Isaac and George, 53
Cuba, 115, 214n24
Cubas, Isabel, 189
Currier, Nathaniel, 12
Curtis, Professor A., 137
Cuvier, Georges, 192

Daguerreotype, 12, 210n41
Daily Chronicle, 40
"Dancing for Eels, 1820, Catharine Market," 82, 196
Dancing master, 84, 160, 166; active in Philadelphia, 10, 31, 75, 93–96, 108, 113, 115, 135–36, 185; of elite society, 22, 28, 93, 140; European, 43–44, 67, 79, 100, 166, 184–85, 222n80, 222n133; invoking science, 176–80; of social dance, 25, 31–33; writings by/about, 27, 39, 138, 182, 200. *See also* Durang, Charles; Hazard, P.H.
Dandy 15, 86, 89; characterizations of, 1, 86, 121, 125, 129, 139–40, 183
Dandy Hall, 134, 135
Danes, 79
Darley, John, 36
Darley, Mrs., 36

Darwin, Charles, 15
Davison, Nancy, 51
Dauberbal, Jean, 44
Dawes, Gertrude, 168, 177
"A Dead Cut," 53, 86, 87f, 90, 204
Death of Abel, The, 70
M. Dechalameau ou la fete au village, 118
Declaration of Independence, 6, 67
"De Color'd Fancy Ball," 132
DeFrantz, Thomas, 11, 242n41
Delany, Martin, 15, 65, 146
Delattre-Destemberg, Emmanuelle, 239n133
Delaware River, 48
Deldevez, Édouard, 166
Delineation, in (still) imagery, 59; relation to blackface, 8, 15, 20, 57, 98, 147, 151–52, 182, 206; relation to minstrelsy, 4, 49, 124, 183, 191, 231n96; staging of, 1, 13, 43, 50, 55, 122, 145, 189, 203
Delineator, 155, 158, 192
Le Délire d'un Peintre (or *La Rêve d'un Peintre*), 119
La Déliverance des Grecs, 94, 201
Denham, Marie Anne, 168
Deshayes, André-Jean-Jacques, 43
Desjardins, Pauline, 101, 108, 227n15
Devil (theatrical representations of), 15, 86, 89–91, 107
The Devil's Violin, 187
Les Deux Roses, 118
Dewees, William P., 16–17, 63
Le Diable a Quatre, 119, 185
Le Diable boiteux, 79
Diamond, Master John (blackface dancer), 104, 113, 119, 121, 123
Diana and Her Nymphs, 161
Dickens, Charles, 49, 125–26, 133–34, 136
Dickson, Samuel Henry, 14
Le Dieu et la Bayadère, 69
Dimier, M'lle., 117
"Discourse on Woman," 114
Discoveries in the Moon, or Herschel out Herscheled, 85
Dixon, George Washington, 57, 82, 105
Democracy, 6, 8, 99, 179
Democracy in America, 8. *See also* de Tocqueville, Alexis
Democrat or Democratic (political party), 120, 225n125
Didelot, Charles, 43, 185
Dollé, Pierre-Françoise, 213n11

Dorney, D.J., 136
Douglass, Frederick, 15, 65, 126–27, 132, 134, 142, 146, 157, 203, 231n100
Douglass Jr., Robert, 12, 128
Douvernay/Duvernay, Pauline, 84, 223n110
Dover, Cedric, 74
Drama of King Shotaway, 55
"Dramatic Association" (of Philadelphia), 9
Dramatic Mirror, 85, 109
Dramatic Mirror and Literary Companion, 104
Drexel University College of Medicine, 234n15
Drury Lane, 67
DuBois, W.E.B., 95–96
Ducy-Barre, Louise, 167
Duff, William, 179
Dumont, Frank, 120–23, 193
Durang, Caroline, 179
Durang, Charles, 70–73, 108; as choreographer, 35–37, 152–53; commentary on racialized performances, 3, 41, 57, 85, 127; critiques of dancers, 35, 80, 100, 105, 108, 153, 161, 163; as dancer, 9, 34, 55, 117, 124; as dance teacher, 10, 101, 113, 136, 139, 179, manuals and publications of, 139, 177, 206; praise of ballerinas, 67, 69–71, 73, 78–79, 81, 109–10, 117–18, 166–68; praise of dancers, 40, 44, 70, 101, 113, 119, 185–86. *See also* Ballet; Dancing master
Durang's Terpsichore, or, Ball Room Guide, 139
Dutch, 124

Exoticism, 3, 64, 73; of ballet, 21, 40, 58, 67, 73, 173, 186; costuming, 12, 149; movement styles, 18, 20, 35; with racial overtones, 36, 42–43, 74, 81, 57, 148, 188. *See also* Ballet; *La Bayadere*; Elssler, Fanny; Muslim
Eastern Asian, 144
Easton, Hosea, 12, 15, 86–88, 194, 204
Eclectic Medical College, The (of Philadelphia), 234n15
Edwards, Robert, 121
Egypt, 128, 144–45, 147, 149, 192
Egyptology, 85, 143, 148–49, 157, 172
Elliott, Henry, 71
Elssler, Fanny, criticism of, 107–108, 111–12, 228n29; financial success of, 18,

105, 106f, 160, 184; influences on other dancers, 105, 175; national dances of, 101–102, 102f, 122, 152, 159, 167, 171–72; popularity of, 14, 101–103, 113, 117, 119–20, 166; praise of, 19, 101, 103–104, 109–11, 187, 200–201, 228n27; proto-feminism of, 17, 114–15; relation to phrenology and race, 110, 119, 122, 151, 165, 189, 228n45; United States debut, 100
Elsslermania, 103
Emancipation, 8, 51, 54, 124
Emerson, Ralph Waldo, 19, 105
Emmett, Dan, 119
Enfranchisement (voting rights), 7, 60–62, 87
England or English, 24, 34, 36, 43, 56, 59, 81, 86, 155, 159. *See also* British; Hornpipe; National Dances
Enslavement, 6–7, 9, 11, 14–15, 32, 57, 61, 120–21, 153–54, 195–96; debates and theories about, 128–30, 144, 147, 183, 203; laws regarding, 142, 152, 194
La Esmeralda, 118–19, 175, 185
Ernani, 188
Espinosa, Leon, 160
"Ethiopian," representations onstage, 57, 126, 153, 155, 192, 234n19; racialization of, 65, 124, 128, 151, 158, 169, 203; theories of, 129
"Ethiopian opera," 4, 20–21, 82, 86, 88, 119, 189, 231n101, 234n18
Ethiopian Serenaders, 126, 188–89
Ethnography (rankings of), 210n36
Ethnology, classification systems of, 13, 39, 41, 56, 142, 162; relation to race, 15, 51, 124, 129, 143, 145–46, 191–92, 232n114; research on or specialists in, 14, 43, 64, 128, 148, 178, 211n51
Europhile, 86, 189, 206
Eve, 15

Fall of British Tyranny, 54
Falls of Clyde, The, 21
Fanny Ellsler (balletic spoof), 151
"Fanny Elssler in the favourite dance La cachucha" (print), 102f
Fashionable Dancer's Casket, 177
Faust, 172–75
Fawcett, John, 41
Fawn's Leap, The, 104, 113
Females and Their Diseases, 17, 156–57. *See also* Meigs, Dr. Charles

Female Medical College (FMC) in Philadelphia 17, 66, 156–58
Feminism and women's rights movements, 9, 19, 67, 113, 115, 142, 156–58, 181, 205; suffrage of, 62
Ferrero, Edoardo and Adelaide, 178
Ferrero, Edward, 178
Feste, Irène, 213n11
La Fete Champetre, 70
La Fille du Danube, 187
La Fille mal gardée, 44, 94, 216n72
First Annual Convention of People of Colour, 61
Fisher, Sidney George, 15, 94–95, 109, 136, 144, 179
Fitzgerald's City Item, 175
Fitzjames, Nathalie, 166
Five Points, district of New York City, 49, 91, 95, 125, 133, 240n151; Philadelphia equivalent of, 127
"A Five-Points Exclusive," 95
Forten, James, 9, 54, 90, 96
Foster, George G., 99, 103, 117, 120, 127, 133–34, 141
Foster, Stephen, 85, 198
Fourth Street (Philadelphia), 55, 134
Fowler, Almira, 66
Fowler, Charlotte, 66
Fowler, Lorenzo, 66, 110–11, 137, 204
Fowler, Lydia, 66
Fowler, Orson S., 66, 157
Fowlers, 137
Fra Diavolo, 86, 111, 151
France, 20, 31, 59, 70, 109, 183, 214n24
Franck, Celestine, 185
Franck, Victorine, 166
Francis, William, 9, 34, 44, 168
Franklin House, 117
Frazier, C. Ignace, 31
Frederick Douglass' Paper, 132
Freedom's Journal, 52
Free state, 5, 7
Der Freischutz, 104
French (dance culture), ballet, 38, 40, 43, 107, 110; costuming, fashion, and theatrical forms, 21, 27, 35, 38, 88, 157, 193; dancers, 37–38, 43–44, 60, 67, 69–70, 94, 166; music 37, 43; style or training, 38–39, 78, 101, 113, 118, 136, 167, 184–87, 241n9. *See also* Ballerina; Ballet
The French Spy, 72f, 73–74, 114

The French Spy, The Wept of Wishton-wish, 166
Fries, Thomas and Tobias, 95
Fruitless Precaution, The, 44
Fry, William Henry, 141
Fuchs, Mme. Augusta, 71, 115, 222n80
Fugitive slave laws, 7 152. *See also* Enslavement
Fuller, Margaret, 18–19, 101, 105

Gaîeté, 37
Galen, Dr. (theatrical character), 148
Gall, Franz Joseph, 14, 130
Galletti, Annetta, 175
de Galaup, Jean-François, 41
Gardel, Pierre, 185
Garden of Eden (in Ethiopia), 129
Gardner, Dan, 151, 158
Gaskill Street (Philadelphia), 66
Gaszynski, 180
Gautier, Theophile, 79–81, 112
Gay, John, 86
Gender. *See* Ballerina; Feminism; Women; Women's health
Genoa, 175
Georgia Sea Islands, 83–84
German or Germany, 32, 79, 93, 104, 109, 136, 147
Gertrude, La Petite (young dancer), 22, 187
Gide, 100
Giselle, 19, 81, 94, 117–18, 166, 185, 187, 202
Gliddon, George, 142–44, 147, 149–50, 157–58
Godensky; or, The Skaters of Wilna, 70
Godey's Lady's Book, 95
Goethe, Johann Wolfgang van, 69, 173
Golden Horse, The, 175
Goodall, Jane, 42, 56
Gottschild, Brenda Dixon, 11, 49
Gourdoux-Daux, Henri, 27, 30
De Granville, Monsieur G., 176
Grecian, 67, 134
Great Britain, 130, 143
Greece or Greek, 40, 64, 70, 74, 164, 171, 178, 191, 234n22. *See also* Grecian; National dances
Green Bushes, The, 75
Grisi, Carlotta, 122, 166, 174, 189
Grosz, Elisabeth, 11
A Guide to the Stranger, or Pocket Companion for the Fancy, Containing a List of the Gay Houses and Ladies of Pleasure in the City of Brotherly Love and Sisterly Affection, 135
Guillou, Victor, 27, 30–31, 35, 95, 214n24
Gustavus 3rd, or, The Masked Ball, 21, 213n90

Haines, John Thomas, 74
Haiti, 31
Haitian Revolution, 7, 28, 196
Hamer, Lewis, 98
Hamilton, Thomas, 65
Hamilton, Mrs., 66
Hamlet, 55–56
Hammond, Governor James Henry, 129
"Happy Uncle Tom" (dance), 154–55, 158
Happy Uncle Tom (burlesque opera), 158
Harlan, Richard, 15
Harlequinade (or Harlequin), 9, 21, 34, 54, 199, 212n87
Harris, Michael, 24
Harris, S.E., 153
Harvard University, 144
Hathwell sisters (Matilda, Henrietta, and Louisa), 35, 36
Hawk and Buzzard, 90
Hazard, Mme., 94, 179
Hazard, P.H., 75, 78, 93–95, 104, 113, 115, 117, 135, 185, 187, 201 225n136
Hebrews (people), 27; Bible of, 15
Hemple, Samuel H., 168
Hennecart, Maria, 175
Herald, 100
Herbison, Matthew, 234n15
Hérold, Ferdinand, 108
Hewlett, James, 19, 55–56
Hill, Constance Valis, 123
Historical Society of Pennsylvania, 213n7
History (by Charles Durang), 70, 206
History of Woman Suffrage, 17. *See also* Stanton, Elizabeth Cady
Hodge, Dr. Hugh Lenox, 63
Hoffland, Thomas, 136
Horn, Eph, 119, 191
Hornpipe, 9, 20, 49, 136, 139, 161, 184, 217n85
Hottentot (racial construct), 144
Howard, G.C., 153
Hugo, Victor, 118–19
Les Huguenots, 175
Hungary or Hungarian, 119, 136, 160

Hutin, Mme. Francisque, 12, 34–35, 37–40, 51, 58, 107, 186, 214n30, 215n46–47

Iliad, The, 114
L'Illusione d'un Pittore, 175
Ince, Emma, 94, 104–105, 113, 184, 187, 201
Independence Hall, 62. *See also* State House
The Independence of Hungary, 119
India, 69, 73, 101, 129, 159. *See also La Bayadere*; Exoticism
Indian Removal (Act), 191
The Indian Girl, or, The Wept of Wish-ton-Wish, 75
Inkle and Yariko (by Colman and Arnold), 54
Interludes (danced) 18, 20–21, 34–35, 40, 43, 67, 113, 152, 168, 182
Interracial, encounters or gatherings (in Philadelphia), 47, 50, 62, 123, 127, 132, 134, 181–82, 189, 196, 198, 217n80; representations of, 57, 82, 134–35
Ireland or Irish, 100, 151, 159, 84, 100, 159; dance traditions, 34, 47, 152, 194, 197–99; immigrants, 47, 82, 123, 195, 199; discrimination against, 8, 93, 124, 147–48, 231n105; racism toward African Americans, 82, 127, 199
Isabelle: Or, Woman's Life, 34
Israel, 147
Italy or Italian, 80; academies, 39, 118; dance/dancers, 43, 117, 160, 177–78, 184, 191; opera, 21, 86, 88, 119, 122, 169, 171, 193; theatrical forms, 21, 124, 188, 198

Jackson, Andrew, 30, 71
Jacksonian era, 47, 73, 83
James, Thomas C., 16
Jannet's Birthday, 35
Japanese, 147
Jefferson III, Joseph, 1, 22, 85, 168, 209n1–2
Jefferson Medical College, 17
Jefferson, Thomas, 13
Jefferson theatrical family, 1
Jerrold, Douglas, 86
Jig or Jigging, 22, 45–47, 46f, 118, 121–23, 155, 183, 194, 197–99, 206
Jiggers, 119, 123–24, 197
Jocko, the Brazilian Ape, 3–4, 21, 42–43, 151, 166–67, 175, 185; version called *Weffo, the*

Mischievous Monkey, 188. *See also* Science; Simian tropes
Johnson, Francis, 20, 27–28, 31, 52, 55, 139–40, 197, 140f, 230n83
Johnson, Oliver, 177
Johnston, David Claypoole, 25, 57, 66, 160–61, 161f
La Jolie Fille de Gand, 187
The Jolly Millers, 175
Jones, Alan, 238n94
Un Jour de Carneval a Seville, 161
Juba (William Henry Lane), 49, 125, 133
"Jump Jim Crow," 1, 4, 47, 82–83, 147, 188, 197, 234n21. *See also* Crow, Jim

Kansas Nebraska Act, 152
Kelly, William, 57, 188
Kennard, James W., 124–24, 130
Kennedy, David, 12
Kepler, Constance and Celeste, 40. *See also* Celeste, Mlle./Mme.
Kim-Ka, or the Adventures of an Aeronaut, 176
King Lear, 55
Kinloch sisters, 118
Kirby, James, 41
Koecker, Leonard, 180
De Korponay, Mons. and Mme. Gabriel, 136
Krimmel, John Lewis, 46, 57, 97

La Scala, 80, 117, 170, 172, 175
Labasse, M., 34, 40
Labbé, Francis C., 31, 95
Lady of the Lake, 139
Lafayette, General, 34
Lamoureux, Louise, 172–74
Lancaster, Pennsylvania, 56
Lancey, Philip, 43
Landis, John W., 158
Lane, Peter, 123
Lane, William Henry (Juba), 19
Leacock, John, 54
Leaflets of the Ball Room, 139
Leaming, J. Fisher, 38
LeBrun, Napoleon, 171
Lecompte, Mme. Eugenie, 107, 115–17, 116f, 201–202
Lee, Mary Ann, 75, 85, 94, 113, 160, 168; praise of, 78, 80–81, 93–94, 186, 201; roles of, 75, 77f, 78, 135, 166, 168, 179, 187; training of, 80–81, 105, 135, 222n89

Lee, Charles, 78
Lehman family, 166, 175
Leprosy, 14
Lessons in Dancing: Exemplified Sketches from Real Life in the City of Philadelphia, 25, 26f, 29f, 31f, 33, 33f, 38, 44, 45–46f, 48 48f, 50, 52, 50f, 56, 58–59, 89, 95. *See also* Clay, Edward W.; Visual culture
Le Maître de Danse, Or, The Art of Dancing Cotillions, 35
Léon, Arnaud, 43–44
Leon, Francis (Patrick Francis Glass), 189, 190f
Léon, Virginia Corby, 44
Lewis, Benjamin, 129
Lewis, Robert Benjamin, 15
Lewis, William David, 206
Lhamon, W.T., 82–83, 88, 91, 123, 127, 193, 231n104
Llorente, José Maria, 167
Liberia, 144–45
Liberator, 146
Life in London, 53
Life in Philadelphia, 53, 86, 87f, 96
Light and Truth, 129
Linneaus, Carl, 13, classification system of, 38
Lippard, George, 112, 134
Liszt, Franz, 159
Lithograph or lithography, 12, 115, 119, 190f, 206. *See also* Visual arts
Little Red Riding Hood (ballet), 35, 184
Locust Street (Philadelphia), 97, 171
Lola Montes, 159
Lola Montez in Bavaria, 159, 163
Lombard Street (Philadelphia), 133, 180, 240n151
London, 4, 10, 44, 69, 71, 75, 100, 113, 116f, 121, 137, 166–67. *See also* England; Great Britain
London Mathews, The, 56
Long Island, 58
Long, Lucy (or "Miss Fanny"), 22, 122, 139–40, 151, 191
Longshore, Joseph, 156
Lott, Eric, 192
Louis XIV, 164
Love Among Roses, 35, 184
Ludlow, Noah, 67, 69–70, 105
Ludwig I of Bavaria, King, 159

Mabille, Charles, 80, 160
Madrid, 167
La Madrillenne, 167
Maguire, Jos. E., 136
Mahar, William, 198
The Maiden, 111–12
The Maid of Saragossa, 163
Maine, 129, 149
Le Maître de Danse, Or, The Art of Dancing Cotillons: By which Every One May Learn to Dance Them, without a Master, 138
Mallet, F.D., 31, 95, 201
Mallet, Miss R., 136
Manhattan, 82, 91, 125, 133. *See also* New York
La Manola, 168, 175
Mapps, Sarah, 157
Maretzek, Max, 168, 171
La Mariage, or Love Protected by Folly, 44
Martin, Egerie, 101
Martin, Jules, 101, 113, 115, 136, 179, 189
Martinetti family, 166, 175
Martinique, 27, 213n13
Marshall, Mr., 173
Maryland, 130
Marzetti, Joseph, 166, 172, 188
Masaniello (*La Muette de Portici*), 115
Masaniello, the Neapolitan Fisherman, 166
Mason-Dixon Line, 7
Masonic Hall, 26, 191
Massachusetts, 8, 147, 158
Mathews, Charles, 56–57
Mathias, Yrca, 151, 165–67, 172, 238n96
Maywood, Augusta (a.k.a. La Petite Augusta), 18, 75–76, 76f, 160, 166, 171, 187; criticism of, 80–81, 107, 172, 186; popularity of, 93–94, 184, 201; praise of, 78–79; training of, 75, 93, 222n80
Maywood, Robert, 76, 78–79
Mazarin, M., and daughter(?) Miss., 179–80
Maze, Georges, 67
Mazilier, Joseph, 166, 185, 222n80
Mazurier, Charles, 42
McAllister, Marvin, 40, 52
McArran's Garden, 104
McCrummel, James, 63
McDowell, E.T., 62
Meglin, Joellen, 99
Meigs, Dr. Charles, 17, 114–15, 156, 212n71
Meisner, Nadine, 239n133

Melodeon (performance venue in Philadelphia), 155
Mendelssohn, Felix, 86
Meredith, William, 167
Metropolitan Museum of Art, 217n77
Meyerbeer, Giacomo, 115
Miami, or the Green Bushes, 73
The Miami, the Huntress of the Mississippi, 166
Milton, 114
Mirror, 90
Modern Honor, 57
Melodrama, 21, 69, 71, 74–75, 88, 112
Melodies, 151
Merrifield, Rose, 153
Mestayer, Louis, 57
Mexico, 112
Middle East, 36, 143, 191. *See also* Exoticism; Muslim
Milan, 80, 170
Milon, Louis, 43
Miscegenation, 53, 91, 96
Mississippi, 75
Missouri Compromise, 7, 24, 152
Mitchell, 100
Moncrieff, William Thomas, 55
Mongolian, 144
Monplaisir, Adèle, 118
Monplaisir, Hippolyte, 118
Monsieur Molinet; or, a Night's Adventures (a.k.a. *Vol-au-Vent*), 70
Montez, Lola (a.k.a. Marie Dolores Eliza Rosanna Gilbert or Countess of Landsfeld), 12, 151, 158–67, 161f, 177, 180, 201–202, 237n67–68
Moore, Miss E., 113
Morality of theatre, 9
Morning Herald, 160
Morra, Gaetano, 117
Morton, Samuel George, 14–15, 17, 64, 74–75, 128, 142–45, 149, 192, 204
Mother Bethel AME Church, 61
Motherhood, 16–17
Mott, Lucretia, 63, 114–15, 153, 205
Mount, William Sidney, 58
Mowbray, Fanny, 168
Muller, Joseph, 140
"Mummy" or "mummies, 147–50, 234n23. *See also* Egypt; Egyptology
Mummy, The, 147
Murdock, John, 54

Musical Fund Hall (Philadelphia), 156, 164, 179
Muslim (or Andalusian, Arab, Middle Eastern, or "Moorish" stylizations), 28, 41, 54, 72f, 74, 79, 113, 118, 191. *See also* Exoticism
Myers, Richard, 121

Naples, 167
Nash, Gary, 12, 25
Nathalie, ou la Laitiere Suisse, 108, 115, 117, 168
Nathan, Hans, 198
Nathanson, Y.S., 205–206
Native Americans or Indigenous peoples, 64–66, 75, 98, 129; dances of, 178; racialization of 40, 54–55, 75, 184, 191
National Advocate, 56
National Amphitheatre, 152–53
National dances, 20, 22, 40–41, 70, 100–101, 104, 108, 159, 186–87, 190, 216n60. *See also* "La cachucha;" *Cracovienne*
National Gazette, 29–30, 40, 79
Naylor, Francis, 179
New England, 12, 101, 108, 124
New Jersey, 146
New Orleans, 143, 195, 206
New Orleans Opera, 150
Nero, Gaetano, 160
"New World," 37, 160
New Year's (performances on), 154
New York, 49, 66, 85, 95, 99, 138, 195–96; artists from/in, 1, 12, 37, 58, 78, 82, 110, 115, 119, 159–60, 163, 165, 178; compared to Philadelphia, 6, 120, 135, 170; people traveling to, 28, 44, 140, 174; press in, 38, 84, 102, 105, 155, 173, 205; theatrical venues in, 9, 34, 55–56, 100, 119, 160, 206; touring performances in, 19, 78, 84–85, 100, 109, 149, 167
New York Polyanthos, 105, 106f
New York Tribune, 173
Nina, ou la folle par amour, 43, 216n69
Noah, Mordecai, 101
North or Northern (antebellum United States). *See* Abolitionism; Emancipation; Politics
North American, 99
North Carolina, 61, 81
North Star, 126
Notes on the State of Virginia. *See* Jefferson, Thomas

Notre Dame de Paris, 119
Nott, Dr. Josiah Clark, 15, 128–29, 142–47, 192, 233n5
Noverre, Jean Georges, 139

Obi, or the Three-Finger'd Jack, 55
Oh! Hush!, 85–86, 151
Old American Company (OAC), 9
"Old Drury" (of Philadelphia), 1, 168. *See also* Chestnut Street Theatre
"old world," 4, 19, 70
Olympic Theatre, 100
Origin of Species, The. See Darwin, Charles
"Original Jim Crow," 20. *See also* Crow, Jim; "Jump Jim Crow"
Oroonoko, 54
Oson, Jacob, 15
Otello (version by T.D. Rice), 21, 85
Othello, 54–55
Ottoman Empire, 74

Paganini, Nicolò, 89
Palmo's Ethiopian Opera Company, 21, 122, 189, 206. *See also*: "Ethiopian opera"
"Panorama of the Nile," 149–50
Pantomime, 35, 69, 85, 182, 200; ballets, 3–4, 9, 21, 41–42, 69, 73, 108, 118–19, 151, 163, 166, 168–69, 175, 188, 200, 216n69; English style of, 9, 21, 34, 184; plays, 55, 147
Paquita, 166–67
Paris, 35, 42, 69–70, 78–80, 100, 113, 116f, 130, 167, 185. *See also* Ballet; French; Paris Opera
Parisian, 4, 20, 43, 184, 214n30
Paris Opera 27, 43–44, 67, 78–81, 93, 100, 117, 166, 185, 220n251
Park Theatre, 34, 100–101
Parker family, 34, 36–37, 184
Parsloe, Charles, 101, 108, 115
Patriots, 29, 43, 85, 119
Peale, Charles Willson, 12, 58
Peale's Museum, 43, 58
Pelham, Dick, 119
Penn, William, 6
Pennington, James, 15, 129–30
Pennsylvania Abolition Society (PAS), 7
Pennsylvania Freemen, 128, 177
Pennsylvania legislature, 9
Perouse, La, 41
Perrot, Jules, 42, 101, 118–19, 172, 185

de Persius, Louis-Luc Loiseau, 43
Petit, Emily, 136
Petit-Stéphan, Joséphine, 115
Petipa, Jean-Antoine, 42, 185
Petipa, Lucien, 100, 166
Petipa, Marius, 69
Philadelphia Association of Disabled Firemen, 162
Philadelphia Female Anti-Slavery Society (PFASS), 8, 62–63, 114
"Philadelphia in Slices," 99, 120, 127, 133–34
Philadelphia Monthly Magazine, 204
Phrenology, 13, 39; relation to arts and entertainment, 14, 67, 87, 89, 93, 110, 136–38, 204; relation to gender, 16–17, 66, 157, 164; relation to race, 14, 17, 64–65, 145, 38, 64–67, 89, 93, 107, 110, 136–37, 157, 220n17
Phrenology Vindicated, 64. *See also* Caldwell, Charles
Pierce, President Franklin, 170
Pindar, Peter (pseudonym), 108, 111
Pine Street (Philadelphia), 97–98
The Pioneer Patriot; Or, the Maid of the War-Path, 43
Pittsburgh, 146
Placide, Alexander, 9
Pocketbook, 63
Pohlman, Frederick, 95
Pointework. *See* Ballet; Virtuosity
Polish, 21
The Politicians, or A State of Things, 54
Politics, 4–5, 32, 57, 67, 152; commentaries of and debates over, 11, 22, 93, 120; overlap with aesthetics and theatre, 60, 91. *See also* Class; Delineation; Emancipation.
Polk, James, 92
Polka, 53, 132, 136, 139, 166, 174, 177, 189, 191. *See also* National dances
Polygenism, 15, 65
Pratesi family, 172
Pratesi, Teresina, 174–75
Pratt, L.T. (Manager), 105
Presbyterian, 136, 138
Presbyterian Magazine, 15
Preston, Ann, 17
Press, The, 164, 172
Price, Stephen, 100
Principia of Ethnology, 146

Print culture and media, 4, 128; of Black community, 15, 125, 127; documenting dance, 5, 33, 39, 44, 69, 71, 99, 101, 111, 119, 136, 138, 202; puffs of, 35, 53, 100, 150, 172, 200, 215n36, 244n69; racialization of, 49–53, 86, 120, 125, 143, 205; social or political aspects of, 6, 55, 99. *See also* Clay, Edward W.; *Lessons in Dancing*; *Public Ledger*; Visual arts
Prometheus, 153
Prosser, Gabriel, 7
Prostitution. *See* Brothels
Public Ledger, 99, 141; critiques of dance/dancers, 73, 102, 107–108, 113, 115; praise of performers, 101, 103, 138, 162, 165, 201; reporting on racialized performances, 92–93, 96, 104, 164
Pugni, Cesare, 119
Puritan, 75
"Physiognotrace," 57

Quaker, 9, 14, 22, 26, 29, 44, 103, 114, 196; abolitionism or anti-racism of, 7–8, 63, 130; as colony, 5; representations of, 44, 46–47, 49, 45f, 216n73; stance on dance, 22, 177; supporting women's rights, 156
Quaker City, 22, 52, 99, 107, 112, 151, 165
The Quaker City; or, The Monks of Monk Hall: A Romance of Philadelphia Life, Mystery, and Crime, 134
Queen Lily of the Silver Stream, 80

Race, Racialization, or Racism. *See* Black communities; Blackface; Blackface minstrelsy; Enslavement; Science.
Ravel, François, 118
Ravel, Gabriel, 3, 70, 118, 176, 202
Ravel, Jerome, 175–76
Ravel theatrical family, 1, 3f, 172, 174–175, 185, 189, 238n96; repertoire of, 3, 70, 151, 166, 176, 185, 202; talents of, 103, 118, 166–67, 176, 202; tours of, 4, 18, 118
Reed, Clara, 168
Reed, Emily, 118
Reed, Master William, 113, 118
Rees, 101, 104, 115, 117–18
Riesse, Herr R. (dramatist), 104
Religion and spirituality, 6–7, 57, 74, 124, 130, 137–38, 153, 195, 233n136; of the Black Church and African ancestors, 7, 61, 97–98, 130, 194–95, 205, 210n18, 245n91; relation to dance, 19, 109, 115, 177; relationship with science, 143. *See also* Presbyterian; Quaker
Renaissance, 29
Republican (concepts or values), 30, 150, 162; motherhood of, 17, 211n68
Revolt of the Harem, The, 113–14, 202
Revolutionary War, 6, 29, 43, 67, 108
Rhodes, Mr., 98
Rhodomontade, 163
Rice, Dan, 154
Rice, Thomas Dartmouth, blackface performer, 10, 15, 21, 60, 85–86, 88–93, 119–21, 154; celebrity of, 4, 82–85, 124–25, 206; portrayal of Jim Crow, 1, 2f, 3–4, 8, 20, 22, 54, 82–83, 98, 188, 205. *See also* Blackface; Blackface minstrelsy; Class; "Jump Jim Crow"
Richard III, 55
Ring shout, 97, 196
Rivers, Frank, 150
Robert le Diable, 115, 167, 116f
Robinson Crusoe; or, the Genius of Columbia, 55
Robinson, Crusoe; or, Harlequin Friday, 55
Rock, John S., 146–47, 179, 234n15
Romantic (style of Romanticism), 3, 13, 21, 39, 100, 184, 186–187, 212n73, 241n11
Ronzani Ballet (troupe), 171–76, 171f, 184–85, 187, 201, 239n116, 244n74
Ronzani, Domenico, 171–74, 176
Rope-dancer, 24, 70
Rosenbach Museum and Library, 213n4
Rossini, Gioachino, 43, 189
Rowbatham, 35
Rusert, Britt, 66, 157
Rush, Benjamin, 14, 130
Rush family (including Mrs. James Rush), 28, 178
Russett, Cynthia, 16
Russia or Russian, 44, 58, 70, 74, 89

Sailors, 48–49, 72, 82, 98, 129
Saint Domingue, 214n24
Saint Léon, Arthur, 187
Saint Léon, Michel, 39
Sambo (racialized character), 57, 82, 128, 193
San Carlo Theatre, 167
Sánchez-Eppler, Karen, 10

San Juan de Alfa Rache, 167
Sanford, Jim (or James, a.k.a. Cool White), 113, 121, 123, 158
Sanford, Sam, 10, 150–51, 153–55, 165, 168, 191, 205; Opera House of, 142, 150–51, 158, 181, 242n24
Sappho, 165
Saratoga Springs, 28, 140
Sarony, Napoleon, 102f
Science, 4, 149, 233n3; classification systems of, 4–5, 8, 13, 42–43, 53, 65, 142–44; critiques of, 15, 15; determinism and hierarchies of, 13–15, 65, 86, 136, 148, 183, 186; exclusion of African Americans from, 15; racism of, 11–12, 15, 42, 65, 83–84, 130, 143, 219n25, relation to dance, 64, 164, 176, 184–85
Scottish, 40, 65
Scribe, Eugene, 69, 86, 100, 108, 122
The Seashore at Malaga, 167
The Serious Family, 177
Seneca Falls Women's Rights Convention (1848), 114–15
Seven Ages of Woman, 158
La Sicilienne, 168
Shakers, 147, 234n18
Shakespeare, William, 54, 107, 124, 157
Shin de-heel-a!!: The Virginian Fairy, or the Gum Elastic Slipper (Cinderella), 21, 122
Shippen Street (Bainbridge), 49
"Shippen Street, Double Shuffle," 48f, 89
Shuffle (dance step), 49, 83, 89, 195, 199, 243n62
The Siege of Saragossa, 167
Simian tropes, 3, 25, 41, 53, 61–62, 65, 96, 103, 130, 137, 204. *See also* Jocko, the Brazilian Ape; Science
Sixth Street (Philadelphia), 62, 96, 98
Sketches of the Higher Classes of Colored Society in Philadelphia, 131
Slave state, 6–8, 121
Sliter, Dick, 123
Smith, George Washington, 94, 101, 105, 113, 160–63, 167, 175, 187
Smith, James McCune, 15, 130, 134, 145–46, 203
Snowden, Mme., 179
Social dance, 16, 22, 34–35, 47, 58, 93, 95, 140, 155, 176, 199. *See also* Ball
Society of Friends, 177
Som-Am-Bull-Ole, 122

La Sonnambula (opera), 122, 139, 151
La Somnambula or "Somnambula," 108, 122
Sorisio, Carolyn, 67
Soto (Aranda), Josefa ("Pepita"), 167, 175
South or Southern (antebellum United States). *See* Enslavement; Politics
South America 42
South Carolina, 8, 15
South Street (Philadelphia), 97, 133–34, 240n151
Southerne, Thomas, 54
Southwark (area) 49
Southwark Theatre, 9. *See also* Old American Company
Spain or Spanish, 121; artists from, 32, 159, 167, 183, 189, 214n29, 237n69, 238n102; productions set in, 113; stylized dances, 20–22, 35, 40, 101, 139, 151, 161, 191, 242n27. *See also* "La cachucha;" Exoticism; Montez, Lola; National dances
"Spider Dance," 159–161. *See also* Montez, Lola
Spurzheim, Johann, 14
St. Petersburg, 116f, 166
St. Thomas Episcopal Church, 7, 196
Stanton, Elizabeth Cady, 17, 114
Star Hall, 155
State House (of Philadelphia), 6
Stauffer, John, 203
Stéphan, Joséphine, 94
Stone, Lucy, 158
Stout, James (sculptor), 110
Stowe, Harriet Beecher, 152, 154, 188, 205
Sullivan, James. *See* Sylvain, James
Sun, 88
Svinin, Pavel, 58, 97
Swiss Cottage, The, 139
La Sylphide (a.k.a. *Dew Drop*), 104, 108, 113, 117–18, 176, 185, 202
Sylvain, James (a.k.a. James Sullivan), 100–101, 104–105, 108, 113, 115, 122, 187, 201

Tableau vivant (still-life nude show), 155, 184
Tacon, Don Francisco, 32, 214n29
Taglioni, Amalie Gastler, 94
Taglioni, Filippo, 42, 69, 108, 113, 115, 185, 187
Taglioni, Marie, 69, 79, 84, 122, 174, 200, 223n110
Taglioni, Paul, 94
Taglioni, La Petite (child dancer), 22, 187

Taming a Tartar; or, Magic and Mazurkaphobia, 166
La Tarantule, 79, 100
Tatin, M., 40
"Taylor's Alley Jig," 46–47, 46f
Teatro Carlo Felice, 174
Terpsichore or terpsichorean, 118, 135, 151, 166, 173–74
Terpsichore, Fete of the Muses, 176
Texas, 112, 120
Text Book of the Origin and History, &c. &c. of the Colored People, 130
Thackara, William, 25, 57, 204
Théâtre Royale Italien 37
Theleur, T.A., 39
de Tocqueville, Alexis, 8
Tom and Jerry, or, Life in London, 55
Transcendentalism, 101
Travesty performers, 3, 71, 73, 89, 122, 147, 150, 174, 189, 221n59
La Traviata, 175
trickster figure, 83
Trip to America, 56
The Triumphs of Love; or, Happy Reconciliations, 54
Trollope, Frances, 55
Il Trovatore, 171
Turnball, Julia, 101 115, 159–60, 189, 200
Turner, Nat, 8, 61
Twelfth Street (Philadelphia) 135, 150
Types of Mankind (or *Types*), 15, 143–48, 150, 152, 192, 211n58

Uncle Tom at Home: or, Southern Life as it Really Is, 155
Uncle Tom's Cabin; or, Life Among the Lowly, 152–53, 188, 205; theatrical version of, 153, 205
Uncle Tom's Cabin, Or, Real Life in Old Kentuck! (a.k.a. *Happy Uncle Tom*), 154
Undine, 168
Union (of United States), 28, 121, 142, 152, 188
Union Hall, 44–45, 45f, 49
Union, New Jersey, 44
United States Constitution, 6–7; three-fifths clause of, 6–7
University of Edinburgh, 14
University of Glasgow, 130
University of Pennsylvania, 15–17, 156, 233n5

Vallee sisters (Elisa, Henriette, Julia, and Amelie), 94, 101, 115, 117, 158, 191, 227n13
Van Buren, Martin, 71
Van Rensselaer, Cortlandt, 15
Van Winkle, Rip, 209n2
Vauxhall, 57
Venus (goddess), 67, 101; de Medici, 156
Verdi, Giuseppe, 171, 188
Vesey, Denmark, 7–8
Vestris, Charles and Caroline Ronzi, 31, 39–40, 107, 216n69
Victoria (Queen), 81, 222n85
Victorian (era), 73
Vienna or Viennese, 14, 22, 117–19, 172
The Vintage of Xeres, 167
Virginia, 7–8
Virginia Minstrels, 119, 121, 192, 230n81
The Virginia Mummy (The Sarcophagus), 85–86, 147–51, 188
The Virginian Girl, 189
Virginia Serenaders, 121, 189, 191
Virtuosity, 24, 39, 42, 89, 121, 160, 183, 189, 195; of female performers, 19, 70–71, 73, 75, 117 200; of French dancers, 37, 166, 184
Visual arts and culture, 4–5, 12–13, 25–26, 53–54, 58–59, 120. *See also* Clay, Edward W.; *Lessons in Dancing*
von Kotzebue, August, 41

Walker, David, 60–61
Wallace, Colonel, 162
Wallack, Mrs., 35, 37
Walnut Street (Philadelphia), 41
Walnut Street Theatre, 112–13, 117, 167, 169; ballets at, 44, 80, 85, 115, 118, 152, 166, 168; Blackface performances at, 1, 57, 60, 119, 140, 150; pantomimes at, 3
Walters, Anna, 112–13, 118, 168
Waltz, 32, 53, 132, 136, 139, 166, 176, 214n26
War of 1812, 24
War of Independence. *See* Revolutionary War
Ware, C.P.T., 159
Warren, Ellen, 168
Warren, H., 37
Washington D.C., 102f, 209n1
Washington, George, 162
Washington Square, 195
Watson, John Fanning, 97, 101

Weaver, Mathias, 119
Weiss, Josephine, 117
Wells, Harriet and Henry (siblings), 40, 118
Wells, Lewis George, 66
Wells, Louise, 168
Wemyss, Francis, 37, 78, 80, 85
The Wept of Wish-ton-Wish, 73 version entitled, *Wept of Wish Ton Wish, or the Indian Girl*, 191
West, Cornel, 233n2
West Indies, 28, 196
West Point, 178
Western Asia, 144
Whale, Henry, 31, 95, 136, 179
Whewell, William, 211n46
Whig, 92
Whipper, William, 131
White or Whiteness. *See* Abolitionism; Blackface; Blackface minstrelsy; Class; Politics; Quaker; Science
Whitlock, Mr. Billy (banjo player), 104, 119, 192
Wikoff, Henry, 100, 110
Wilks, Henrietta, 168
Williams, Moses, 12, 58
Willig, George, 139
Winnemore, Anthony, 188
Winter, William, 209n1
Willow Copse, The, 21
Willson, Joseph, 96, 131–32

The Wizard Skiff; Or, the Tongueless Pirate Boy, 73–74
Women, abolitionism and activism of, 8, 62, 114, 202, 236n58; entertainers for men, 155; exclusion from higher education or medical school, 16–17, 156; effects of dancing or dance spectatorship on, 24, 32, 63, 70, 101, 103, 105, 111, 161, 178, 196; fans of Lola Montez, 165; morality of, 64, 101, 103, 105, 111–12, 156. *See also* Feminism; Women's Health
Women's health, 10, 16, 19, 32, 114, 186; midwifery, 16, 64; obstetrics, 15–17, 19, 63, 156–57; pathological conception of, 63; as physicians, 156–58, 181, 186, 202, 236n59. *See also* Female Medical College; Feminism; Women
Wood., Mr. and Mrs., 168
Wood, William, 4, 105, 221n55
Wright, Fanny, 27
Wynter, Silvia, 128

Xlanties; or Forty Thieves, 151, 165

Yale Divinity School, 130
Yankees, 56, 79, 86, 124–25
Young, Madame, 66

Zavistowski, George, 179
Zip Coon, 92, 125, 139, 245n82

Lynn Matluck Brooks is Arthur and Katherine Shadek Professor of Humanities, Emerita, at Franklin & Marshall College. She is the author of *John Durang: Man of the American Stage*, *The Art of Dancing in Seventeenth-Century Spain: Juan de Esquivel Navarro and His World*, and *The Dances of the Processions of Seville in Spain's Golden Age*; the coeditor of *Dance and Science in the Long Nineteenth Century: The Articulate Body*; and the editor of *Women's Work: Making Dance in Europe before 1800*. She was the editor of *Dance Research Journal*, *Dance Chronicle*, and thINKingDANCE.org.

www.ingramcontent.com/pod-product-compliance
Lightning Source LLC
Chambersburg PA
CBHW031707230426
43668CB00006B/137